MW01286835

PEACE CORPS FANTASIES

How Development Shaped the Global Sixties

Molly Geidel

CRITICAL AMERICAN STUDIES

UNIVERSITY OF MINNESOTA PRESS

MINNEAPOLIS | LONDON

An earlier version of chapter 1 was published as "At the Point of the Lance: Gender, Development, and the 1960s Peace Corps," in *New World Coming: The Sixties and the Shaping of Global Consciousness*, ed. Karen Dubinsky et al. (Toronto: Between the Lines, 2009), 320–29; reprinted with permission of the publisher. An earlier version of chapter 6 was published as "'Sowing Death in Our Women's Wombs': Modernization and Indigenous Nationalism in the 1960s Peace Corps and Jorge Sanjinés' *Yawar Mallku*," *American Quarterly* 62, no. 3 (2010): 763–86; copyright 2010 The American Studies Association; reprinted with permission of the Johns Hopkins University Press.

Song lyrics from Stephen Sondheim's "Don't Laugh" reproduced in chapter 3 are originally from the musical *Hot Spot*, 1963. Reprinted by permission of the Stephen Sondheim Society.

Published by the University of Minnesota Press
111 Third Avenue South, Suite 290
Minneapolis, MN 55401–2520
http://www.upress.umn.edu

Library of Congress Cataloging-in-Publication Data
Geidel, Molly.
    Peace Corps fantasies: how development shaped the global sixties /
Molly Geidel. (Critical American studies)
    Includes bibliographical references and index.
    ISBN 978-0-8166-9221-7 (hc)
    ISBN 978-0-8166-9222-4 (pb)
    1. Peace Corps (U.S.) I. Title.
    HC60.5.G45 2015
    361.6—dc2

                                                            2014047960

Printed in the United States of America on acid-free paper

The University of Minnesota is an equal-opportunity educator and employer.

21 20 19 18 17 16 15   10 9 8 7 6 5 4 3 2 1

PEACE CORPS FANTASIES

CRITICAL AMERICAN STUDIES SERIES

George Lipsitz
University of California–Santa Barbara, Series Editor

CONTENTS

INTRODUCTION
The Seductive Culture of Development   vii

1. Fantasies of Brotherhood: Modernization Theory   1
   and the Making of the Peace Corps

2. Integration and Its Limits: From Romantic Racism   33
   to Peace Corps Authenticity

3. Breaking the Bonds: Decolonization, Domesticity,   71
   and the Peace Corps Girl

4. Bringing the Peace Corps Home: Development in   111
   the Black Freedom Movement

5. Ambiguous Liberation: The Vietnam War and the   149
   Committee of Returned Volunteers

6. The Peace Corps, Population Control, and   187
   Cultural Nationalist Resistance in 1960s Bolivia

CONCLUSION   231
Heroic Development in an Age of Decline

ACKNOWLEDGMENTS   239

NOTES   243

BIBLIOGRAPHY   285

INDEX   303

Introduction

THE SEDUCTIVE CULTURE OF DEVELOPMENT

> Are we ever going to realize the deep wounds that the seductive culture of development leaves on us? If we ever do, what can we do to heal such wounds?
>
> —Nanda Shrestha, *In the Name of Development*

In 1962, Peace Corps volunteers arrived in sixth-grader Nanda Shrestha's village, bringing with them "fancy chairs, desks, and tables . . . flown in from overseas" to inaugurate the first U.S.-run vocational schools in Nepal and *bikas*, the ideology of development.[1] "*Bikas* looked glistening and sumptuous, at least on the outside and at school," Shrestha remembers in his 1997 memoir. "We were all bewitched, and our lives were changing very fast. It was almost like taking a giant leap from the bottom of a stairway to the top without climbing any of the steps." But this euphoric "giant leap" was limited to the space of the school filled with shiny furniture and tantalizing school supplies. Development guaranteed Shrestha and his classmates neither a reprieve from hunger nor a demonstrably different future. "Every morning we went to school excited," he recalls, "ready to enjoy our new chairs and work with fancy tools, but after school the hard reality of life would set in as many of us returned home to face the same prospect of haunting hunger. Our expectations had, nevertheless, been raised, and disappointments were becoming more frequent as the distance between what material goods could be available and what was actually available to us was widening . . . Poverty had rarely been so frightening, or so degrading, in the past."[2]

As Shrestha's recollections suggest, *bikas* not only created needs it could not satisfy, but also manufactured new subjectivities and new, terrible understandings of the conditions in which he and his community lived. Describing his boyhood in Nepal, Shrestha writes, "Poor and hungry I certainly was. But underdeveloped? It never occurred to me that being poor meant being 'underdeveloped.' True, there is no comfort and glamour in poverty, but such a Darwinian concept was alien to me."[3] Very quickly, however, "the howling wind of *bikas*" permeated Shrestha's world, causing both the rich and the poor to abandon the view that poverty was "a communal and collective problem" and frame it instead as a problem of insufficient individual ingenuity:

> But now development, as defined and measured in materialistic (capitalistic) terms using such indicators as per capita income, energy consumption, resource use, and literacy, individualized poverty, meaning that the poor were generally viewed as *abikasis*, as cases of personal deficiency or self-inflicted failures. Poverty was thus projected as an unfortunate creation of the poor, not as an inevitable outcome of growth-driven development and social inequality. This new, Malthusian outlook offered a very convenient outlet for the dominant class to believe that their wealth was a fruit of their own mental dexterity and forward-looking economic mentality (rationality) rather than a benefit of their social position and that they had no role in causing poverty.[4]

Here Shrestha tracks how development and its associated metrics encourage the poor to attribute their poverty not to social injustice or even bad luck but instead to personal failings, while allowing the rich to exploit them unapologetically and even proudly. Elsewhere in the memoir he explains that local elites are not the only beneficiaries of the development networks crisscrossing the globe. Writing of the development workers who continue to inundate Nepal, Shrestha notes what has become common sense among historians, if not practitioners, of international development: "The irony is that while the development enterprise itself continues to expand by leaps and bounds, the levels of inequality, unemployment, and poverty have witnessed little decrease."[5]

Shrestha's identification of Peace Corps development ventures as a source of profound anxiety and social fragmentation might seem difficult to reconcile with the agency's place in the U.S. popular imagination, where it exists as an unimpeachable symbol of selfless altruism and the most successful program initiated during John F. Kennedy's brief presidency. However, the 1960s Peace Corps embodied this contradiction, mobilizing the idealism of its volunteers in a global modernization project whose explicit aim was to destroy "traditional" habits, values, and communities.[6] This book takes as its subject these contradictory impulses, examining the ideological work performed by the 1960s Peace Corps along with its impact on the "millions of people in Asia, Africa, and Latin America" who were, in the words of Peace Corps founding staffer Harris Wofford, "taught, tended, organized, irritated, charmed, and otherwise stirred to claim their rightful place in the twentieth century."[7] In this book, I offer a genealogy of how the imperative Wofford articulates, to create and regulate individual subjectivity through heroic development work, became intelligible and desirable in the United States and around the world.

Crucial to my account of the Peace Corps is an analysis of the means by which its officials and volunteers attempted to "irritate, charm, and otherwise stir" Third World populations: an interpellative process Shrestha describes compellingly as "seduction." Introducing the story of his own seduction by the promise of the Peace Corps volunteers and their glistening furniture, he muses, "Seduction is an interesting process, however. It makes people euphoric, but only until they realize they have been duped into doing something shameful or even harmful. Yet seduction involves no physical conquest, only an irresistible bait."[8] My interest is in how development discourse crafted such "irresistible bait," deploying iconic Peace Corps volunteers who would charm people into reimagining themselves and their nations at the behest of the rich and powerful. By focusing on Peace Corps volunteers like the ones Shrestha encountered as a child in Nepal, those real and imagined harbingers of modernity, this book elaborates on what I claim was most irresistible about development fantasies: modernization's promise of homosocial intimacy through participation in capitalist relations.[9]

The figure of the heroic development worker, the embodiment of the promise of modernity that guided the thoughts and actions of so many in the 1960s, is oddly absent from accounts of the United States in this period. In its absence, organizational and intellectual histories of postwar modernization theory and development policy have remained disconnected from social and cultural histories of the movements that attempted to fight poverty, form liberatory communities, and construct international solidarity with Third World liberation struggles.[10] Writing development workers back into the history of the 1960s United States connects these two stories, allowing us to see how development came to function as a hegemonic discourse that shaped the way social change could be conceived by volunteers and "underdeveloped" communities, policy-makers and revolutionaries alike. Such an account of how development came to seduce popular and elite imaginations is particularly needed now, when influential critiques of economic inequality in the United States are accompanied by both nostalgia for the development era and continued reliance on economic growth as the primary measure of social welfare.[11] Remembering the economic and psychological violence of development might help us expand our political imaginations, so that the comparatively rich and powerful might one day cease inflicting its "deep wounds" on exploited and dispossessed communities.[12]

The Towering Task

In early February 1961, less than a month before John F. Kennedy officially established the Peace Corps, State Department official Warren Wiggins submitted to the agency's task force a policy memo titled "A Towering Task." The paper, which recommended a dramatic increase in the size of the proposed agency, would soon become the foundational document of the Peace Corps. As agency legend has it, energetic founding director R. Sargent Shriver read the thirty-page paper at 2:00 a.m. on February 6, sent Wiggins a telegram at 3:00 a.m. asking him to appear before the task force in the morning, and had copies waiting for every task force member by 10:00 a.m.[13] Wiggins took the paper's title from Kennedy's warning in his January 30 State of the Union address that "our role is essential and unavoidable in the construction of a sound and expanding economy for the entire non-communist world . . . the problems in achieving this goal are towering and unprecedented—the response must be towering and unprecedented as well," a claim that indicates the sense of urgency the Kennedy administration brought to its task of capitalist expansion.[14] The story of Shriver's late-night reading and hasty mimeographing of (or more plausibly, of his instructions to his secretaries to mimeograph) the paper echoes the 2:00 a.m. moment of Kennedy's University of Michigan campaign speech in which the presidential candidate first proposed that young people defend their own "free society" through service work abroad, demonstrating how the early Peace Corps was also shaped by this belief in a pressing, eleventh-hour imperative to penetrate "the entire non-communist world."[15]

In his blueprint for the Peace Corps, Wiggins draws on Kennedy's argument for the necessity and urgency of expanding U.S. influence, contending that starting with a "cautious" five-thousand-volunteer program, as others on the task force had suggested, "is believed to be an insufficient number to produce a psychological impact of great enough importance to be a major justification for the National Peace Corps."[16] To make the case for the effectiveness of this large-scale approach, Wiggins proposes a program that would send seventeen thousand American English instructors and teacher-trainers over the course of five years to the Philippines, where, as he euphemistically claims, "history has provided an ideal social and cultural climate to receive American youth."[17] Locating the high point of U.S. educational efforts in the Philippines in 1902, when one thousand English teachers accompanied U.S. troops attempting to quell the independence movement there, Wiggins complains that since the end of U.S. annexation, "English language instruction has deteriorated at an alarming rate. This is partially due to the disappearance of American teachers and school administrators, increased population, lack of materials and a wave of nationalism."[18] Although the latter factor suggests that Wiggins knows Filipinos had mobilized an anticolonial nationalism specifically in opposition to U.S. domination of the islands, he nonetheless argues in "A Towering Task" that English "is the principal medium in which Philippine culture—its ideologies, doctrines, values, literature, and knowledge—is expressed," although "there is some danger that unless intensive effort is made to improve the teaching of English in the schools, English will become just another vernacular."[19] Wiggins further asserts that the "continued *deterioration* of the [Filipinos'] ability to use the national language" (after the official end of U.S. colonialism in 1946), despite many U.S.-backed education projects, is the result of previous aid efforts attempting "to fill a reservoir with an eyedropper. Gargantuan efforts are required."[20]

By invoking 1902 as a utopian moment of adequate English instruction in the Philippines while making no mention of the concurrent military campaign that allowed English to become "the principal medium" for expressing Philippine culture, Wiggins links the Peace Corps' "towering task" to an earlier contest for control of the nonwhite world, one in which the United States also attempted to suppress the struggles for self-determination that its own rhetoric had encouraged and to rewrite that suppression as both liberatory and pedagogical. In the U.S. conquest of the Philippines, the United States had initially used the Filipino nationalist insurgents, led by Emilio Aguinaldo, to aid them in wresting control of the islands from a crumbling Spanish empire. Once the U.S. and Filipino forces had defeated the Spanish, the United States disregarded Aguinaldo's 1898 declaration of independence and crushed the insurgency. The U.S. military killed two hundred thousand Filipinos and systematically tortured the insurgents, most famously by pouring large quantities of water into rebels' mouths and repeatedly forcing them to vomit, a tactic Wiggins eerily evokes when he states that "gargantuan" efforts must be made to fill the Philippine "reservoir" with the English language.[21]

But even as its army tortured and massacred the Filipino nationalists, the United States claimed that the annexation was necessary for Filipinos' freedom and progress. The U.S.-controlled Philippines' first governor, Jacob Gould Schurman, imagined the conquest as the dramatic rebirth of a nation, claiming that "the destiny of the Philippine islands is not to be a state or territory in the United States of America, but a daughter republic of ours—a new birth of liberty on the other side of the Pacific, which shall animate and energize these lovely islands of the tropical sea, and rearing its head aloft, stand as a monument of progress and a beacon of hope to all the oppressed and benighted millions of the Asiatic continent."[22] Schurman's dense metaphor characterizes the Philippines as part of a chain reaction, a republic created by U.S. annexation so that it can "rear its head aloft" and animate the other "oppressed and benighted millions" in Asia, giving them new life as characters in the Western narrative of progress. The volunteer teachers in the early 1900s similarly bolstered these attempts to characterize conquest and counterinsurgency as catalysts for a kind of domino effect, spreading liberation and Westernization over the Pacific. Describing her moment of embarkation in language that echoes William Howard Taft's characterization of the Filipinos as "our little brown brothers," teacher Mary Fee writes, "To me the occasion was momentous. I was going to see the world, and I was one of an army of enthusiasts enlisted to instruct our little brown brother, and to pass the torch of Occidental knowledge several degrees east of the international date-line."[23]

American studies scholars such as Amy Kaplan, Laura Wexler, and Gail Bederman have understood this early moment of U.S. overseas imperialism as an epistemic shift, a moment when new conceptual frameworks for understanding gender, race, sexuality, and nation emerged. Following Michel Foucault's contention that modern Western sexuality—widely assumed to be scientific, corporeal truth—is in fact a historically specific formation that accompanied the rise to global dominance of industrial capitalist nation-states, these scholars have traced connections between new understandings of the self and the expansion of U.S. state power, detailing how this late nineteenth-century epistemic shift produced state and imperial power through new kinds of gendered, raced, and sexualized bodies.[24] They show how the conquest of the Philippines, framed as an adventurous yet properly pedagogical exercise in torch-passing, facilitated new gender identities at home, producing middle-class conceptions of white manhood that valued physical aggressiveness rather than self-restraint while allowing middle-class white women to exercise power in ways that bolstered U.S. empire and white supremacy.[25]

While these scholars have established an important framework for understanding hegemonic discourses of body, race, nation, and empire at the turn of the twentieth century, a similar body of work does not yet exist for the post–World War II development era.[26] This absence may be partly due to the apparent continuities between the imperialist moment that Wiggins recalls nostalgically in "A Towering Task" and the one he enthusiastically plans in the same document. In the Philippines, both moments witnessed U.S. campaigns for the betterment of the Filipino people following military intervention—Wiggins had served in the International Cooperation Administration in the Philippines in the 1950s, where advertising executive turned psychological warfare tactician Edward Lansdale engineered the rise of President Ramón Magsaysay and the suppression of the communist Hukbalahap insurgency—and in both moments, the United States characterized its bid to dominate the islands as born from pedagogical and liberatory impulses. Both also imagined the islands as a model, a test case as well as a vehicle for the spreading of U.S. influence.

But important differences persist between the two plans for U.S. expansion, differences of scale and strategy that I want to highlight in order to argue that this moment in the twentieth century requires a new formulation of the relationship between gender, sexuality, and imperialism. Most notable are the differences of scale: while Schurman grandly imagines spreading the gospel of progress to the "oppressed and benighted millions of the Asiatic continent," Wiggins, via Kennedy, thinks even bigger, planning to produce a tremendous "psychological impact" on "the entire non-communist world" with his "gargantuan" and "towering" development program. And while Schurman, in the midst of a conflict over the island's sovereignty, naturalizes the U.S. possession of— or at the very least, its continued dominance, feminization, and diminution of—the Philippines by calling the islands a "daughter republic of ours," Wiggins makes no such claims. He insists instead that the Philippines develop its own national "ideologies, doctrines, values, literature, and, knowledge," provided they are expressed in English. The Peace Corps, he argues, must send volunteers "in numbers large enough to do an important *national* job" for their host nation, and would ideally initiate "a better program of English-language instruction which will be sustained and perpetuated by the Filipinos themselves long after the five-year period of teaching by the Peace Corps has ended."[27] In other words, Wiggins allows for the possibility that the "enormous psychological impact" of the heroic Peace Corps volunteers will effect a rapid and dramatic change in the Filipinos' subjectivity, allowing the Philippines to take shape not as a diminutive "daughter republic" but as a fully mature and independent nation.

These differences suggest that the postwar period marks another moment of epistemic shift: the replacement of the old colonial order with a new regime of social control articulated through modernization theory, the body of work formulated by postwar U.S. policy elites and social scientists that facilitated the United States' rise to global domination in that period. As Arturo Escobar and others argue, development discourse promised recently independent nations that true sovereignty would come only after their integration into the global economy and the subsequent attainment of modernity, allowing the United States, along with global governance agencies like the IMF and the World Bank, to remake the world and manage decolonization struggles.[28] Despite the often-disastrous results of large-scale development projects, modernization soon became the only thinkable endpoint of anticolonial struggle.

One explanation for the international development order's particular facility at managing decolonial energies is offered by Maria Josefina Saldaña-Portillo, who argues that the modernization regime incorporated the liberatory desires of revolutionary struggles into its vision of ever-deferred liberation through appeals to Third World masculinity.[29] In her reading of modernization theory, Saldaña-Portillo establishes how modernization theorists attempted to induce Third World leaders to subject themselves and their people to dispossession and exploitation through a gendered logic of penetration and humiliation. Threatening to intervene in countries that refuse to modernize, leaders of "developed" countries and global governance organizations equated modernity with full masculinity and "the promise of equal citizenship in the fraternal order of nations," compelling the leaders of these "developing" countries to destroy the "traditional" forms of social organization that development discourse characterized as passive and feminine.[30]

My study of the Peace Corps elaborates on Saldaña-Portillo's insights about gendered inducements to modernize, suggesting that modernization theory's masculine vision shaped the Peace Corps' structure as well as the volunteers' day-to-day work.[31] But it also reveals that beyond (and often in tandem with) this logic of humiliation and masculine challenge, Cold War visions of development also operated through more positively valenced gendered logics of desire and intimacy. American social scientists, I argue, articulated and assuaged their own anxieties about the affluent, atomizing, repressive society of the 1950s by creating intimate yet hierarchical masculine fantasy spaces of development while also offering to cooperative "underdeveloped" nations and populations a homosocial vision of belonging. This vision was embodied by the iconic Peace Corps volunteer, who was expected to work and play with a local counterpart who would eventually become a leader in his community. Extending these homosocial fantasies to include Third World counterparts allowed men in the global South to imagine themselves as members of this U.S.-controlled global brotherhood, albeit members who would have to subject themselves and their communities to upheaval in the hopes of one day transforming their subordinate fraternal attachment into an equal partnership. The logic of modernization thus characterized the "construction of a sound and expanding economy for the entire non-communist world" as both an urgent moral imperative and a thoroughly masculine enterprise in which one could participate either directly or vicariously.

This focus on the fantasy and promise that accompanied Cold War modernization allows me to further distinguish the Cold War capitalist push toward modernity from European colonial development ventures of the 1930s and 1940s, in which historians often locate the origins of the Cold War international development regime.[32] Unlike those projects, undertaken in order to contain increasingly powerful anticolonial labor movements, the new international development establishment told stories of a "free world" which eschewed colonialism entirely, and thus one in which the desiring subject was the crucial motor and rationale for the entire capitalist modernization enterprise. Without disregarding the compensatory psychological and material rewards European colonialism at times bestowed on its loyal subjects, we might still locate a new emphasis in the Cold War era on the pleasures, freedoms, and hyperbolic promises of development. Dipesh Chakrabarty, drawing on Max Weber, has considered how Western colonial modernity sought the "disenchantment of the world," attempting to stamp out all that was irrational and magical in colonized peoples and societies. This may hold true for the European colonial project.[33] But one need only recall Shrestha's sense of being "bewitched" and "seduced" by the "glistening and sumptuous" Peace Corps interventions, or read Wofford's imperative to "charm or otherwise stir" millions of people to throw over their traditions, to see that the Cold War development regime deliberately crafted an exceptionally enchanting vision, imbuing its own ventures and goals with magic and vitality while attempting to convince the "underdeveloped" not just of their anachronism but of their dreary stagnation, and even their lack of imagination.[34] The vision of modernity presented by the Cold War modernizers was so enchanting, in fact, that leaders and even ordinary people agreed (and sometimes even demanded) to undergo all manner of upheaval, to subject themselves to ceaseless striving in exchange for the promise of a euphoric, intimate modernity that never quite arrived.

In its focus on modernization and development as an organizing logic of postwar U.S. popular fantasy, this book brings together scholarly insights into postwar liberalism that emphasize particular strands of liberal thought and policy. Recovering the important symbolic role of development ideas and work in this period allows us to more precisely reconcile three different facets of postwar American liberalism: the extreme postwar marginalization of labor liberalism; the "anti-maternal" and generally misogynist cast, according to many scholars, of Cold War liberalism; and the "postwar liberal racial formation" that, in Jodi Melamed's formulation, both attributed inequalities previously imagined to be biological to "culture" and "sutured an official antiracism to a U.S. nationalism that bore the agency for transnational capitalism."[35] The framework of development and modernization can help us make sense of these intertwined strands of hegemonic postwar liberalism: it illuminates the international trajectories of a logic that targeted poverty without inculpating wealth and harnessed anthropological conceptions of cultural difference in order to assert that inequality stemmed from backward and matriarchal family and community structures.[36] The heroic development worker, I argue here, made this liberal vision of the world seem coherent and exciting.

Yet in the United States, and to some extent around the world, those who were seduced by this vision of heroic inducement to personal transformation were not just liberals, but also participants in the increasingly radical movements that sought to remake national life. As Elizabeth Cobbs Hoffman writes in her vivid organizational history *All You Need Is Love*, "Looking closely at the Peace Corps raises the question anew of why the sixties happened."[37] While my view of development differs sharply from Hoffman's, my study retains her important insight that the Peace Corps' heroic imaginary shaped the philosophies and strategies of activists at home and abroad throughout the decade. Enlarging the arena of development's influence to include the movements of the 1960s United States—further pursuing Saldaña-Portillo's insights and expanding on her brief but tantalizing account of Malcolm X's developmental thought—allows me to reconceive of these struggles, their transnational reach, and how they fell short of their goals.

Key histories of the movements of the 1960s United States, even fascinating transnational studies of those movements, have considered the pull and limitations of U.S. exceptionalism without according development the centrality I believe it deserves.[38] Likewise, histories connecting the Cold War to the civil rights movement trace a relatively straightforward connection between the United States' desire to position itself as a global exemplar of freedom and its leaders' eventual capitulation to civil rights demands.[39] However, my research points to another connection between the Cold War and the movement: I show how the logic of Cold War modernization and heroic development work came home to decisively influence the black liberation struggle, particularly after 1965, as activists began to focus more closely on an economic and internationalist agenda.[40] Similarly, many scholars have attributed the weakening and splintering of the white new left to the hierarchical tendencies of its leadership, as well as gender oppression within the movement and white activists' problems acting in solidarity with organizers of color; I argue that the development discourse that pervaded the sixties connects these difficulties in the new left, shaping the way activists imagined self-realization, community, and solidarity.[41]

In its study of Peace Corps work and cultural nationalist responses in Bolivia, and its examination of the centrality of population control to the Peace Corps' expulsion from that country, this book also engages with ongoing debates over the relationship between feminism, cultural nationalism, and communitarian values, particularly in what Escobar calls "an emergent Latin American decolonial feminism." In Escobar's formulation, this feminism attempts both "to question and deconstruct the colonialist practices of modernizing Western discourses, including feminism, particularly their reliance on the liberal notions of autonomy, the individual, and a particular notion of rights; and to question the exclusions and oppressions embedded in particular constructions of subaltern identities found within ethnic movements, particularly when they rely on discourses of authenticity, territory, and community."[42] The Bolivian indigenous cultural nationalist response to the Peace Corps' iteration of 1960s population control imperatives, which resulted in the agency's expulsion from Bolivia, provides a case study for evaluating these claims about the relationship between modernization and indigenous nationalism. It also offers an opportunity to contemplate the possibility of a feminism that does not force indigenous women to choose between relinquishing their bodies to the cultural nationalist project or abandoning their communities in favor of Western rights-based individualism.

Encountering and Countering Development

This book unfolds in six chapters. The first three chapters explore how the 1960s Peace Corps embodied a racialized, gendered vision of modernity that linked economic integration to freedom, frontier masculinity, and global brotherhood. Chapter 1 examines Peace Corps architects' deployment of the gendered anxieties and fantasies of postwar social science in the conception, formation, staffing, and early volunteer recruitment efforts of the agency. Placing these discourses in the context of late-1950s best-selling novels, then tracing them through Peace Corps volunteer memoirs, the second chapter attempts to understand how the Peace Corps inaugurated and codified new models for relating to racial and cultural others, using modernization doctrines to revise the romantic–racist vision of rebel masculinity that captured the popular imagination in the 1950s. The third chapter turns to the women in the 1960s Peace Corps, analyzing fictional texts about "Peace Corps girls" alongside memoirs and other nonfiction accounts by and about women volunteers. Here I demonstrate how they were accommodated and constrained by the discourses of development, global brotherhood, and frontier heroism produced by the agency in its iconic decade.

Following the paths of development workers and discourses as they returned home, the fourth and fifth chapters argue that the Peace Corps and modernization theory guided the vision and strategy of 1960s U.S. social movements, particularly in the later sixties as those movements attempted to become more internationalist and explicitly ideological. Tracing the connections between the War on Poverty, of which Sargent Shriver was the founding director, and the black liberation movement as it transformed from civil rights to Black Power, chapter 4 investigates how the civil rights and Black Power movements were influenced by liberal modernization theory and the ideal of heroic development work. The fifth chapter continues to trace the migrations of the gendered modernization ethos beyond the Peace Corps, delineating the agency's relationship to both the Vietnam War and the new left through an analysis of interviews and position papers from the Committee of Returned Volunteers, a national organization of returned volunteers who formulated increasingly radical critiques of U.S. foreign policy in the late sixties.

Moving to a closer study of the 1960s Peace Corps' on-the-ground impact, the last chapter chronicles the agency's work in and expulsion from Bolivia. It surveys the network of military and civilian government agencies, religious missionaries, and other development workers that spread across Bolivia in the 1960s, and reveals how the Peace Corps came to symbolize in the Bolivian popular imagination all these modernization efforts.[43] My discussion of Bolivian responses to the Peace Corps culminates in an analysis of Jorge Sanjinés's 1969 neorealist film *Yawar Mallku* (*Blood of the Condor*), the film that directly incited the Peace Corps' 1971 exit and spurred a cultural nationalist movement in Bolivia. This indigenous cultural nationalism became directed toward development discourse's ideal of a masculine utopia whose construction would entail controlling women's bodies. I conclude the book by showing how indigenous feminists have attempted in subsequent decades to re-theorize their own subjectivities, embracing neither Western individualism nor submission to cultural nationalist futures.

This focus on the case of Bolivia, and particularly my study of cultural and activist responses to the Peace Corps and population control, allows me to consider the question of why and how, if development failed on its own terms, it succeeded at a discursive level; how, in other words, it reorganized the subjectivities of people around the world. Borrowing a phrase from Chakrabarty, I argue in this book that development is at once an "indispensable and inadequate" frame for explaining the thoughts and actions of governments and people during and after the Cold War: indispensable because modernization theorists and development workers set out to colonize all other ways of thinking about both economic relations and the possibilities for improving people's lives, and to a large degree succeeded; inadequate because development became dominant in a historical moment already marked by ongoing struggles against colonialism and attempted to manage diverse and dynamic societies with their own particular lived traditions and prior relationships to Western ideologies of progress.[44] Thus, while I remain convinced that after the aggressive disseminations of the postwar period there is no space outside of or untouched by development, I am equally convinced that people's lives are never fully determined by development discourse.

The question thus becomes how to understand the reach of development—how to get at the ways "underdeveloped" people and communities came to see their own lives within the space of development and under-development.[45] Shrestha's wonderful firsthand account is relatively unique in its attention to the mental and emotional impact of development discourse.[46] In addition to collecting Bolivian activist and cultural responses to development and its aftermath, I have also attempted to trace in volunteers' memoirs, letters, and stories both the way the development mission influenced its objects and the extent to which local knowledge and practices persisted in the face of attempts to eradicate them.[47] Alyosha Goldstein has argued that "rather than simply stigmatizing entire nations and naturalizing an apparently irrepressible process of economic growth, underdevelopment also introduced a new space for strategic negotiations."[48] While many of the spaces under consideration here are less liberatory than Goldstein's characterization suggests, it is still possible to glimpse the many ways the individuals meant to serve as the Peace Corps' objects of transformation insistently exceeded the identities imposed on them by the logic of development. The memoirs, letters, and other documents I analyze in this book demonstrate how the "under-developed" both unsettled development logics and maneuvered within development's terms, sometimes making life difficult for the volunteers who attempted to modernize them.

The book's focus on a group of largely young and minimally trained, if exceptionally iconic and well-intentioned, U.S. development workers might raise a question for some readers: what about the endogenous development projects that existed in the 1960s, and exist today, around the world? To put it another way, doesn't development actually help people? In response, I would say of course, sometimes. However, development's persistent grafting of economic growth—to paraphrase Rist's definition, the destruction of social relations and the commodification of everything—onto every possible definition of a better future merits interrogation, especially given the violence experienced by "underde-veloped" communities like Shrestha's, in which even the least physically disruptive attempts to modernize a population produced devastating psychological and economic effects.[49] I am guided here in particular by Latin American indigenous movements, which have attempted to resist development imperatives by positing alternative visions of the good life that challenge the assumption that economic growth will automatically lead to a better life for all. These and other efforts to reconceive of social good against modernization's dictates suggest that it is possible to find better ways to organize our lives

While I return to some of these contemporary debates about development in the final chapter and the conclusion, this book primarily tells a story of the 1960s United States and how development discourse decisively influenced social movements and shaped key debates within them. Examining the ideals and fantasies of Cold War development, I contend, can help us understand the nature of the protest movements that flourished in the 1960s United States: their preoccupations with poverty and fraternal affects, their constant emphasis on both heroic vanguardism and individual self-realization. This history attempts to get at some of the limitations of those movements, to contribute to a sense of how the noble dreams and sincere efforts of so many in the 1960s failed to produce a more just and humane world. At the moment of this writing, development and nonprofit careers (or brief stints in Teach for America) constitute the horizon of imaginable "good work" for those young people in the United States who can still afford to be idealistic, and the restoration of a paternalistic welfare state occupies the horizon of the leftist transformative imagination. My hope is that recognizing how these creative waves of radical protest were contained and redirected by development's seductions might help us to understand how we got here and imagine other futures.

1

FANTASIES OF BROTHERHOOD
Modernization Theory and the Making of the Peace Corps

IN LATE OCTOBER 1963, after a year of enforcing brutal anti-union and anticommunist modernization measures, Bolivian president Victor Paz Estenssoro made an official state visit to Washington, D.C.[1] In its account of the visit, the *New York Times* admired Paz, observing that the moderate Bolivian leader had a "strong jaw, an athletic physique, and an intensity of feeling that he can communicate to a crowd and in conversation."[2] *Time* described Paz as "short and swarthy, with gentle brown eyes and a friendly humor," while noting, "Yet in 1952, he led a social revolution that emancipated the population from virtual serfdom."[3] While the U.S. press seemed upbeat about the success of the two governments in pursuing Cold War objectives in Bolivia, the Bolivian press more directly celebrated the visit and the alliance it suggested. Centrist La Paz newspaper *El Diario* celebrated Paz's visit with a headline reading, "Kennedy Warmly Welcomes President Victor Paz Estenssoro," formally identifying their own country's president while showing greater familiarity with "Kennedy."[4]

A two-page photo spread inside further commemorates the visit, with three of the four photographs focused on the relationship between the two presidents. One photograph in particular stands out as the largest in the sequence and the only shot of the men in motion: Kennedy and Paz walk together, descending a staircase. Kennedy strides forward, at once towering over and leaning into Paz, his fluid, dynamic motions suggesting natural grace and leadership, while Paz stands like a schoolboy, feet close together, arms at his sides, shoulders squared, hat in hand. Kennedy's dynamism is emphasized by the prominence in the photograph of his finger, pointing into the distance—both men gaze in the direction where he is pointing. The caption reads, "President Kennedy indicates a point of interest while he accompanies President Paz from his office in the White House after the private meeting between the two leaders."

El Diario frames this encounter as a ritual of initiation into a not-quite-equal brotherhood, a brotherhood shaped and controlled by Kennedy. The photograph naturalizes this hierarchy by calling attention to Kennedy's physical grace and decisiveness, while focusing on their shared "point of interest." The point of interest seems to lie immediately in a Washington, D.C., building, monument, or other symbol of modernity; more generally in the counterinsurgency and austerity measures Paz has pursued in the service of modernization; and most evocatively in the future promised by modernization doctrines and practices, the euphoric future modernity that justifies the labor crackdowns and cultural eradication of the present.

The future promised by Kennedy through his convergence with Paz at their mutual "point of interest" beyond the frame is one not just of euphoric modernity, but also of closeness, of homosocial bonding through the project of Cold War modernization. Saldaña-Portillo has shown how Cold War modernization doctrines and projects, particularly in Walt Whitman Rostow's formulation, appealed to Third World leaders by equating underdevelopment with passive femininity and threatening "humiliation" through penetration, posing the threat of military intervention (figured as male rape) so that leaders would defensively reassert their masculinity by modernizing their populations.[5] But while the early founding documents of the Peace Corps reiterate and build on this formulation, this photograph of Paz and Kennedy's closeness demonstrates how U.S. development policies and practices in the 1960s brought Third World leaders into the orbit of capitalist modernity not only with the threat of imperialist penetration and humiliation, but also with the promise that always implicitly accompanied it, of initiation into a modern world of correct masculinity and fraternal closeness. If theorists contended that a dramatic change in the subjectivity of individuals must be effected before a society could undergo economic modernization, politicians and development workers in the 1960s visibly tried to effect and envision that change through personal contact and charisma.[6]

In characterizing the development imaginary as homosocial, I draw on Eve Sedgwick's exploration of the confluences between "men loving

Photograph appearing in Bolivian newspaper *El Diario*, October 23, 1963: "President Kennedy indicates a point of interest while he accompanies President Paz from his office in the White House after the private meeting between the two leaders."

men" and "men promoting the interests of men." Sedgwick argues that a homophobic "schism based on minimal difference" has frequently structured modern Western male relationships, meaning that acceptable male intimacy must be triangulated through mutual desire, often for the same woman.[7] As John Ibson, Robert Dean, and others have shown, this structuring homophobia was particularly forceful in the 1950s United States, as the isolated nuclear family became a sanctified ideal, popular media images of male closeness disappeared, and suspected homosexuals lost their jobs.[8] The development mission, I argue, gave elite men an acceptable way to restore the homosocial spaces that had disappeared in the repressive 1950s, placing between them not women but the territory of the Third World, described in the language of frontier nostalgia. As evidenced by Kennedy and Paz's mutual "point of interest," these opportunities for triangulated intimacy were conditionally extended to Third World leaders, as well as to development workers and their on-the-ground counterparts.

In his 1969 memoir *Living Poor*, Ecuador volunteer Moritz Thomsen makes explicit the Peace Corps' iconic centrality to the masculine development imaginary, writing in the introduction that "the Peace Corps exists as a vehicle for acting out your fantasies of brotherhood and, if you are strong enough, turning the dream into a reality."[9] This chapter explores how Kennedy and the Peace Corps created such fantasies, framing the Third World as an idealized frontier space where men bonded through physical tests while securing contested territory and promising cooperative Third World counterparts inclusion in these spaces in exchange for participation in the U.S.-guided path to correct development. Tracing the production of these seductive fantasies of strength and brotherhood illuminates the nature of the hegemonic liberalism of the 1960s, demonstrating how the shared anxieties of social scientists and policy-makers impelled them to create an officially sanctioned fantasy space for the U.S. liberal managerial class in the Kennedy era and after.

"An Expanding, Aggressive Force": *Managing Decolonization and Domesticity*

In the United States, the heroic development imaginary gained prominence in response to two perceived crises that accompanied the country's increased wealth and rise to global superpower status: the crisis of capitalism brought on by decolonization, and fears of masculine atrophy in the face of affluence, suburbanization, and allegedly increasing female power. Decolonization reached its apogee in the 1950s and 1960s, as struggles that had raged for decades finally triumphed. Beginning with India in 1947, Asian and African peoples won their independence in rapid succession, throwing off the weakening European powers with varying degrees of force. In 1954, Vietnamese peasant armies defeated the better-equipped, U.S.-backed French colonial army at Dien Bien Phu; highlighting the injustice of racial empires in a world that had so recently vanquished Nazism, the Vietnamese hid near the French encampments at night and sang French Resistance songs. In 1957, through mass strikes, boycotts, and demonstrations by students, urban workers, and market women, Ghana became the first sub-Saharan African nation to win its independence. In 1960, seventeen other African nations followed, driven by a vision of nonaligned Third World solidarity that many of their leaders had powerfully articulated at the 1955 Bandung African–Asian conference.[10]

In the era of decolonization, U.S. policy-makers attempted to reconcile the United States' tradition of anticolonial rhetoric with its drive to secure unfettered access to the world's resources. The rhetorical tradition, illustrated most clearly in the 1941 Atlantic Charter, inspired decolonizing peoples around the world to imagine that they had an ally in the U.S. government. In the celebrated but nonbinding document, Franklin Roosevelt and Winston Churchill pledged to "respect the right of all peoples to choose the form of government under which they will live"; expressed the "wish to see sovereign rights and self government restored to those who have been forcibly deprived of them"; and promised to "endeavor, with due respect for their existing obligations, to further the enjoyment by all States, great or small, victor or vanquished, of access, on equal terms, to the trade and to the raw materials of the world which are needed for their economic prosperity."[11] Similar language found its way into the "Purposes and Principles" section of the 1945 Charter of the United Nations, in which founding members pledged "to develop friendly relations among nations based on respect for the principle of equal rights and self-determination of peoples" and that "members shall refrain in their international relations from the threat or use of force against the territorial integrity or political independence of any state."[12]

The words of the Atlantic and UN charters initially indicated to anticolonial leaders from Gandhi to Nelson Mandela that the Western world's vision of territorial sovereignty and human rights would apply to them. Ho Chi Minh, who had been convinced at least since 1919 of U.S. potential to aid Vietnam in the struggle for self-determination, wrote to Harry Truman in 1946 that "the United Nations ought to keep their words. They ought to interfere to stop this unjust war."[13] Representatives of new nations at the 1955 Bandung conference cited the Atlantic and UN charters in their final communiqué, affirming ten principles, including "abstention from intervention or interference in the internal affairs of another country"; "respect for the right of each nation to defend itself, singly or collectively, in conformity with the Charter of the United Nations"; "abstention from the use of arrangements of collective defense to serve the particular interests of any of the big powers"; and "refraining from acts or threats of aggression or the use of force against the territorial integrity or political independence of any country."[14]

While Churchill quickly disavowed the implications of this rhetoric for colonial subjects, the U.S. government had a more complex relationship to the decolonizing world.[15] Although its leaders would continue to advocate freedom for all peoples, the United States in practice would be more concerned with the objectives famously stated by George Kennan in 1948, when he bluntly explained the nation's geopolitical imperatives while also signaling the dawn of an era in which pop-psychoanalytic discourse decisively influenced Cold War strategy: "We have about 50 percent of the world's wealth but only 6.3 percent of its population. This disparity is particularly great as between ourselves and the peoples of Asia. In this situation, we cannot fail to be the object of envy and resentment. Our real task in the coming period is to devise a pattern of relationships which will permit us to maintain this position of disparity without positive detriment to our national security."[16] In accordance with Kennan's psychological assessment, if not always his concrete recommendations (he argues in the same paper for "dispens[ing] with all sentimentality" and pretentions to "world-benefaction," but also for "the economic development and exploitation of the colonial and dependent areas of the African Continent"), the United States in the Cold

War era attempted to form a "pattern of relationships"—personal and global; psychological, political, and ideological—to consolidate their disproportionate wealth while assuaging or suppressing "resentment." This pattern was developed through the widespread use of military force in the Third World (what Kennan called "containment" or "counterforce") as well as an array of modernization projects that included the Peace Corps. These latter projects embodied and enacted the principles of modernization theory, particularly in the 1960s, which Kennedy, at Rostow's urging, termed "the development decade."[17]

The United States thus expressed support for decolonization, as a 1945 public Treasury Department document indicates, from a "standpoint of trade expansion," from which "the underdeveloped countries offer immense stores of raw materials" as well as "the prospect of a substantial market for manufactured goods."[18] As Escobar and Saldaña-Portillo emphasize, the United States explicitly framed development not primarily as a sentimental exercise in "world benefaction" but rather as an opportunity to manage decolonization in a way that would consolidate its access to the world's markets, solving the crisis of capitalism brought on by its own rapidly expanding economy.[19] The Cold War lent greater urgency to this task of managing the decolonization process, particularly after the Soviet Union seemingly began distributing development aid without strings attached, and the Bandung conference brought the specter of Third World nonalignment to the fore. The task facing the United States was not just to assist development in the newly colonized world, but to carefully manage the course of that development.[20]

If modernization theory was meant to resolve a perceived crisis of capitalism by increasing the United States' access to the resources and markets of the newly decolonized world, development programs took the form they did in response to a perceived crisis of domestic masculinity. Kennedy and his advisers promoted the Peace Corps in particular as a chance to redress the allegedly imperiled and enfeebled condition of the many white men in the postwar United States who had used their GI Bill benefits to climb into the middle class and secure white-collar jobs. Concerned with the "softening" that accompanied suburbanization and affluence, liberal economists and popular sociologists fueled a national backlash against the postwar ideology linking the suburban acquisitive nuclear family with Cold War patriotism, an ideology termed "domestic containment" by Elaine Tyler May. Domestic containment appeared most iconically in the 1959 "kitchen debate" when Richard Nixon, surrounded by new American appliances, told Nikita Khrushchev that "what we want is to make easier the life of our housewives" and boasted that the Cold War would be won not by rockets but by washing machines and color televisions.[21]

But even as Nixon boasted, Kennedy and the liberal intellectuals who surrounded him mobilized a critique of domesticity that accused acquisitive housewives of draining rather than augmenting the Cold War arsenal. JFK's economic adviser James Tobin demonstrated the link between Cold War anxiety and the backlash against domestic containment in a 1958 article, arguing that money that could have been spent on missiles had instead been wasted on the development and marketing of new products "to a people who already enjoy the highest and most frivolous standard of living in history."[22] In bemoaning the frivolity of middle-class suburban life, Tobin echoed many popular social science texts produced throughout the 1950s, which worried about "organization men" losing their rugged individuality at managerial jobs and in "status-seeking" suburban consumerism.[23] David Riesman's *The Lonely Crowd*, William Whyte's *The Organization Man*, and other best-selling popular social science books uneasily combined nostalgia for "inner-directed" frontier masculinity with an anxious desire to consolidate the insulating wealth and alienating social system that produced these "soft" men. As Wini Breines notes, 1950s liberal social scientists found consensus in their fears of "gender convergence," which they argued was a direct consequence of the growing importance of consumerism and the nuclear family.[24]

Talcott Parsons, the preeminent mid-century sociologist whose "structural-functionalist" view of human culture and institutions decisively influenced modernization theory, set the stage for the 1950s anxiety over gender convergence, writing works in the 1940s that established proper sexual differentiation as crucial to the survival of the modern capitalist state. Parsons located in the American family a "typically asymmetrical relation of the marriage pair to the occupational structure," outlining "the elements of segregation which in many respects are even more striking than in other societies, as for instance in the matter of the much greater attention given by women to style and refinement of taste in dress and personal appearance." He argued that the gendered division of labor, while often a source of strain on women, was "essential to our occupational system and to the institutional complex in such fields as property and exchange which more immediately surround this system." Stark gender segregation, according to Parsons, benefited the U.S. economic order because it "require[d] scope for the valuation of personal achievement, for equality of opportunity, for mobility in response to technical requirements, for devotion to occupational goals and interests relatively unhampered by 'personal' considerations."[25] Modern capitalist societies, according to Parsons, could only function due to a strict gendered division of labor according to which men did meaningful, rational work, while women labored at tasks that were at once frivolous and necessary. Any threat to this rigid division, even if it took the form of overvaluing domestic labor, was also a threat to capitalist modernity.

By the late 1950s, liberal intellectuals' fears of gender convergence, and by extension the collapse of capitalism and the free world, had reached a crescendo.[26] Kennedy adviser Arthur Schlesinger Jr. articulated these anxieties in a 1958 essay, warning of women's encroachment on traditionally male territory:

> By mid-century, the male role had plainly lost its rugged clarity of outline. Today men are more and more conscious of maleness not as a fact but as a problem . . . The American man is found as never before as a substitute for wife and mother—changing diapers, washing dishes, cooking meals, and performing a whole series of what once were considered female duties. The American woman meanwhile takes over more and more of the big decisions, controlling them indirectly when she cannot do so directly . . . Women seem an expanding, aggressive force, seizing new domains like a conquering army, while men, more and more on the defensive, are hardly able to hold their own and gratefully accept assignments from their new rulers.[27]

Schlesinger's characterization of women as "an expanding, aggressive force" and "a conquering army" oddly and paranoically imagines women's roles, even when limited to the narrow space of the home, as overpowering; in a departure from critics before the Depression who had limited their censure to women who dared to enter public life, Schlesinger argues that women can emasculate their husbands without leaving home. The militaristic framing here evokes both Cold War fears and decolonization struggles concurrently sweeping the globe; both women and communism (as well as potentially the "nonaligned" Third World) threatened to erase capitalism's fundamental principle of "differentiation," "seizing new domains" and creating a world where all might labor equally.

These diagnoses, even vitriolic iterations like Schlesinger's, grew out of managerial-class men's genuine feelings of isolation and constriction in the face of the domestic containment ideal and the repressive postwar state. McCarthyism, the lavender scare, and the attendant suppression (and self-suppression) of dissent curtailed not only political expression but also men's expressions of affection for one another, which had been widely tolerated in the exceptional circumstances of World War II.[28] However, the social scientists and political advisers largely turned their frustration on safer targets. In a psychological orientation David Savran terms "white male masochism," these men constructed themselves as victims less of the state or capitalism than of the women, African Americans, and decolonizing Third World populations from whom they feared they were no longer distinct.[29] Schlesinger's essay dramatizes the mainstream adoption of the claims to victimhood that Savran describes. Magnifying women's power, Schlesinger imagines them in control of a powerful state apparatus and argues that they menace the rugged masculine individualism responsible for America's greatness.

In the 1960 presidential election, Kennedy recognized this cultural shift by explicitly rejecting the postwar domestic containment imperative. He warned in 1959 that white-collar men, and the America they represented, were going "physically, mentally, spiritually soft," and offered his New Frontier campaign slogan, suggested by Rostow, as an alternative to the domestic containment logic that equated consumerism and domesticity with national security.[30] In his fourth debate with Nixon in 1960, in which he distinguished himself by advocating an aggressive military campaign against newly communist Cuba, Kennedy mocked the vice president's equation of homefront prosperity with national security. "You, yourself said to Khrushchev, 'You may be ahead of us in rocket thrust but we're ahead of you in color television' in your famous discussion in the kitchen," said Kennedy. "I think that color television is not as important as rocket thrust."[31] By ridiculing women's power and affirming the primacy of the "rocket thrust," Kennedy signaled the disdain for domesticity and the embrace of male spaces and networks that would characterize white liberal and leftist thought in the coming decade, infusing both Tom Hayden's 1962 *Port Huron Statement* and Daniel Patrick Moynihan's influential 1965 report *The Negro Family: The Case for National Action*.[32] The Peace Corps provided the very frontier spaces for male bonding that these pivotal documents imagined would assuage both alienation and poverty.

If Kennedy proposed the Peace Corps as proof of his rejection of "softness" and domesticity, Shriver entered public life after a more personal brush with insufficiently contained female sexuality. In his authorized biography, biographer Scott Stossel recounts the story of Shriver's breakup with his first serious girlfriend, Eleanor, whom he had intended to marry. Stossel writes that "although not sanctimonious in his conviction, Shriver had never wavered in his belief that sex outside of marriage was sinful; this was what he believed on the night of August, 17, 1937, in Florence."[33] After dinner, Eleanor "explained that being out of the convent in France and traveling around Europe with her brother had made her feel free and different somehow, more adventurous. She had met an American soldier, she told him, and had briefly fallen in love with him. Her relationship with the soldier was now ended—but before it had, she said, they had slept together." In Stossel's telling, Shriver's reaction to Eleanor's news was immediate, physical, and definitive:

> Sarge felt as though he had been punched in the stomach. Stoically, without (he hoped) betraying how miserable he felt, he thanked her for telling him, told her that he still cared for her a great deal, and that he would see her tomorrow. He said good night and then exited briskly, closing the door behind him. Once in the hallway he ran to the balustrade and vomited out into the street below, his convulsing gut a direct register of the emotional trauma he felt. His respect for Eleanor never wavered. Nor, in some sense, did his affection for her. But something in him changed that night and he knew that he would never marry her.[34]

Shriver's revulsion at Eleanor's revelation, which both he and Stossel attribute to his unwavering Catholic piety, led directly to his entrance into the Kennedy family: Shriver met Eunice Kennedy at a 1945 party at Eleanor's house and began working for the Kennedy family shortly thereafter; in 1946 Joseph Kennedy sent him to Washington, D.C., to "help out Eunice" with her job as executive secretary for the Committee on Juvenile Delinquency.[35] Shriver's courtship of Eunice brought him into close contact with John F. Kennedy, who in 1961 would ask him to run the Peace Corps. Shriver's familial and political ties with the Kennedys, and his storied role in crafting American liberalism, were thus made possible only by this dramatic incident of violent revulsion, leading to the expulsion of what he imagined as an impure, feminine presence from his life.

Shriver had near-complete autonomy in running the Peace Corps: in 1966, a *San Francisco Examiner* article reiterated conventional wisdom when it claimed that "no other agency in Washington is so much the extension of one man's personality as the Peace Corps is of Shriver's."[36] Shriver's behavior on the balcony thus reveals much about the Peace Corps: his revulsion at Eleanor's sexuality and exit (onto the balcony, then eventually to the Peace Corps) anticipated the way that disgust at the feminized "softness" of the 1950s United States would impel managerial class men's voyages out into the newly formed Third World.[37] More concretely, Shriver crafted the Peace Corps as an alternative to the more subversive adventures like Eleanor's that the instability of wartime had allowed, infusing the agency with a frontier-masculine nostalgic vision in which women existed primarily to cement ties between men.

From their earliest speeches about the Peace Corps, both Kennedy and Shriver imagined the agency as a space in which the nation could quell anxieties about Cold War complacency and enact fantasies of frontier manhood. Shriver argued in 1961 that the Peace Corps would surprise "people who think that America has gone soft, people who think that the pioneering spirit in America is dead."[38] In a commencement address that same year, Shriver began by quoting Theodore Roosevelt's warning against "ignoble ease" and told them that around the world "there is one big question: *Is America Qualified to Lead the Free World?*" Warning of the "evidence that Americans have gone soft and are no longer capable of sustained sacrifice for their country," Shriver went on to cite (unnamed) "experts" who, he claimed, had concluded that "we are beset by 'spiritual flabbiness'" and "we are producing a strange new kind of human being—'a guy with a full belly, an empty mind, and a hollow heart.'"[39] Using the threat of male atrophy and flaccidity to promote expansionist policies, Shriver reiterated the perennial rationale for U.S.

intervention, formulated in the late nineteenth century as the United States reached the limits of contiguous territorial expansion, that figured overseas empire-building as a crucial vehicle through which to toughen the male body.[40] But he augmented this already paranoid discourse with Cold War terrors, equating feminine-coded "softness" with susceptibility to communist penetration. In order to oppose this "softness," he needed a language that would imbue his attempts at managing decolonization and revolutionary struggles with a frontier-masculine toughness. This language was provided by postwar modernization theory.

Taking It Like a Man: Modernization Theory's Threats and Fantasies

Postwar modernization theory, formulated and propagated by Parsons, Riesman, Schlesinger, and others, allowed these liberal intellectuals at once to imagine solutions to the crisis of white masculinity they had diagnosed and help the United States renegotiate its relationship with the Third World. Directed at Latin America as well as decolonizing African and Asian nations, modernization theory elaborated and instantiated Enlightenment discourses of rational progress; it drew on U.S. and European history to sketch a universal trajectory of national economic growth and integration into the world economy while prescribing military and economic intervention by wealthy countries in order to assure the Third World's adherence to that trajectory. But while the geopolitical conditions of the 1950s spurred modernization theorists to imagine a far-reaching cultural and social transformation of the Third World, they could not fully put their theories into practice until the 1960s; as Michael Adamson argues, modernization theory's imperatives "implied levels of cultural manipulation and external control greater than the [Eisenhower] administration was willing to accept."[41] It took the liberal, social science–enamored Kennedy administration to realize fully the modernization theorists' dreams of social control. In the 1960s, modernization theorists offered the "underdeveloped" world a seductive vision of psychological and national transformation, drawing on and reconfiguring their own masculine anxieties and hopes to appeal to Third World leaders.

Although they drew on a long Western tradition of developmental thought and planning, modernization theorists diverged in important ways from previous teleological theories of progress: most located the origins of the transition from underdevelopment to development within individual subjects rather than political–economic conditions.[42] Arguing that global poverty would be conquered by the widespread adoption of capitalist habits and values rather than by the redistribution of resources, modernization theory made a case for the aggressive management of the development process in order to create these habits and values.[43] Before a nation would be able to integrate fully into the global economy, argued the modernization theorists, its rural population in particular would have to undergo a spiritual shift, transforming from passive, tradition-and-community-bound villagers into rootless, individuated laborers. Daniel Lerner, in his 1958 work *The Passing of Traditional Society*, argued that U.S. policy could contribute to the rise of the "mobile personality," which would lead each individual to make "a personal choice to seek elsewhere his own version of a better life."[44] This emphasis on the idea that development first required a transformation of "personality" and culture—an emphasis enabled by the new prominence of sociology and psychology in American life and foreign policy circles—allowed the United States to enact a vision of heroic action while justifying non-redistributive global economic policies. If only cultural and community development could ameliorate poverty, then the remaking of subjectivities into more economically viable ones, rather than the more equitable distribution of global resources, was the answer. This meant that person-to-person development work, rather than development aid, became the most iconic realization of the United States' modernization efforts.

This emphasis on the imperative to effect a shift in the interiority of underdeveloped subjects through development work was perhaps most fully articulated by Walt Whitman Rostow. In his modernization classic *Stages of Economic Growth: A Non-communist Manifesto*, self-described "economist–biologist" and Kennedy adviser Rostow outlined the personal transformation that modernity required, arguing that "in rural as in urban areas—the horizon of expectations must lift, and men must become prepared for a life of change and specialized function."[45] Rostow, who wielded tremendous influence in the early days of the New Frontier—he coined the term "New Frontier," as well as Kennedy's campaign slogan, "Let's get this country moving again"—and again during Johnson's escalation of the Vietnam War, formulated his theory of universal "stages" of history in an attempt to do battle intellectually with Marx. Inverting Marx's prediction that the globalization of industrial capitalism would create the conditions for widespread worker revolution, Rostow argued that all underdeveloped societies would undergo a "take-off period," a transitional phase during which they were especially vulnerable to the "disease of communism." Intervention from developed nations, Rostow claimed, was necessary to impel nations through this crucial period and out the other side.

Rostow had not always been such an interventionist: in his early career, his State Department colleagues mocked him for advocating negotiations with the Soviets. Biographer David Milne writes that Rostow developed a "reputation for softness" so great that officials made up a song to taunt him, "to the tune of 'My Gal Sal'":

> They call him wistful Walt
> Hardly worth his salt
> A sad sort of fellow
> He thinks the reds will mellow
> That's our guy, Walt[46]

In the next few decades, Rostow set about proving his detractors wrong by becoming a vociferous advocate of escalating the Vietnam War, unparalleled among high-level advisers in his enthusiasm for the "bombing for peace" strategy and the nuclear option. But in the years immediately following his humiliation at the State Department, Rostow banished rumors of "wistfulness" by writing anticommunist economic histories that emphasized the need to forcibly modernize Third World populations. As Nils Gilman argues, modernization theory "turned antiCommunism from the hysterical red-baiting populism of McCarthy into a social-scientifically respectable political position," lending Cold War zeal both scientific credibility and masculine cachet.[47]

Decades before Rostow published *Stages*, Parsons had begun to formulate modernization theory's tenets, bridging the gap between the Chicago-school anthropologists and the Cold War foreign policy establishment with his concept of "structural-functionalism."[48] In his 1937 book *The Structure of Social Action*, a text that greatly influenced subsequent modernization theorists, Parsons begins to formulate the transition from tradition to modernity in the language of gendered shifts in subjectivity.[49] Calling India "the proverbial home of otherworldliness in the everyday sense of the term," Parsons diagnoses the British colony's underdevelopment as a problem of personality.[50] Government bureaucracy, he writes, "did not penetrate in its administrative functions directly to the individual, but, rather, stopped at the caste, village and other groups, leaving them essentially intact with a large degree of self-government . . . at no time did this development approach the rational bourgeois capitalism of the West."[51] Parsons's only reference to the colonial order comes when he explains that "such capitalism of this character as it exists in India today is clearly a European importation," and he fails even to mention the anticolonial struggle sweeping India by 1937.[52] In Parsons's framework, colonialism fails to "penetrate" far enough into the Indian individual to effect a true erasure of "otherworldly" subjectivity and an adoption-by-introjection of capitalism that would allow it to cease being a "European importation."[53]

In *Stages*, Rostow elaborates Parsons's violently eroticized logic of modernity, even more explicitly framing phallic/imperial penetration as a necessary step toward capitalist integration. As Saldaña-Portillo has observed, *Stages* justifies U.S. intervention and frames violent modernization as both desirable and necessary by equating underdevelopment with imperiled masculinity and imperialism with eroticized homosexual rape: Rostow argues that "men holding effective authority or influence have been willing to uproot traditional societies not, primarily, to make more money but because the traditional society failed—or threatened to fail—to protect them from humiliation by foreigners."[54] By mobilizing this discourse of invasion-as-rape/humiliation (and, therefore, national sovereignty as intact masculinity), Rostow attempts to produce a defensive reaction, a violent uprooting of "traditional societies" so that leaders might reassert their masculinity and nationhood.

Rostow provided the Peace Corps with a framework and a rationale for its development interventions and worked closely with the agency as an adviser. Addressing a Peace Corps directors' staff meeting in 1966, he described development in more whimsical language than he had in *Stages*, telling the directors that "when development begins to take hold and begins to show its magic, it gives the people a basis for forming their lives on a progressive basis," and imaginatively claiming that "ever since Manchester began pulling people in from the country, people have been drawn by bright lights and modern facilities."[55] But even as he framed development as magical and inexorable, obscuring the enclosure system that forcibly created the British proletariat, Rostow argued that intervention was necessary to hasten the modernization process and suppress calls for the redistribution of resources. "I would assume by definition that in the traditional society you're surrounded by clashes in the class structure," he said. "History must bulldoze these problems—maybe we can help the bulldozer a bit."[56]

Rostow provides a clue to how "history," helped along by bright lights and seductive development workers, might "bulldoze" the class structure, in a 1960 speech titled "Some Lessons of History for Africa." There he opines, "While conflicts of economic and group interest are part of the modernization process, in its largest sense it is a communal and a human task. It calls, essentially, not for class conflict but for a sense of brotherhood within nations and cultures and between nations and cultures."[57] For all Rostow's "rational" economic training, here he again formulates a foreign policy imaginary whose central goal is emotional and psychological transformation. Development is not meant to create equality at the global or national level—in fact, it requires rigid hierarchies—but rather to create a "*sense* of brotherhood," a feeling of masculine belonging among leaders that might replace further-reaching social transformation.

The Peace Corps attempted to follow Rostow's prescription for inducement-through-intrusion, using similar language—of both penetration and brotherhood—to describe their attempts at leadership-cultivation. One development consultant advised that "community development programs aim at making material changes at the place resistance to change is strongest" and that "material change cannot be accomplished (even if it benefits the people) until the people themselves can be induced to want the change."[58] But even more central to the agency was Rostow's vision of development as brotherhood. The Peace Corps enacted the promise of brotherhood and male closeness in exchange for modernization, offering powerful images of male heroism and bonding that could reconcile domestic fears about modernity's "softening" influence with the drive to modernize the world. One of the archetypal articulations of this appealing development vision comes in Shriver's 1964 manifesto *The Point of the Lance*, which adopts modernization theory's violently homoerotic vocabulary while crafting a nostalgic vision of frontier brotherhood.[59]

In *The Point of the Lance*, Shriver presents the Peace Corps as a vehicle for the recuperation of the frontier energy and ingenuity that social scientists and Kennedy's advisers worried American men had lost, arguing that one of the agency's core principles is "man's optimism—the belief that all things are possible to men of determination and energy and a willingness to toil," and that "this confidence came naturally to those who threw off the bonds of colonial rule and succeeded, with their own efforts, in subduing a wild and rich continent."[60] Using modernization theory's temporal logic to equate the decolonizing world with the United States at its frontier beginnings, Shriver argues that in the 1950s "we were in danger of losing our way among the television sets, the supermarkets, and the material abundance of a rich society," and that thus "our debt of gratitude to the developing and emerging nations of the world is that they have reminded us of our own traditions, and given us a treasured opportunity to work once more for the principles which created our own nation."[61] At the same time, he cautions that the United States must guide decolonial struggles to ensure that new nations build themselves in the United States' image: "the American Revolution, now in strange forms and shapes and going by other names, is rolling along among the world's people," even as its "leadership . . . has fallen into other hands." Organizations like the Peace Corps, he argues, are necessary "to recapture that leadership and assure that the basic ideas of our revolution are neither misunderstood nor misused."[62]

Offering the Peace Corps as a remedy for Third World nations' misappropriation of revolutionary desire, Shriver claims that he borrowed his book's title from a "revolutionary-minded" Bolivian official. Shriver's choice to appropriate and elaborate the metaphor of the "point of the lance" to explain Peace Corps ideology and policy demonstrates how the agency made use of the gendered strategies of modernization theory to harness and redirect revolutionary impulses. Here he frames national self-determination as an intermediate step on the journey to modernity and masculinity. *Punta de lanza* translates as *vanguard* or *forefront*, and Alfonso Gumucio Reyes, the Bolivian official from whom Shriver borrowed the title, seems to have used the phrase this way in the conversation Shriver cites directly after returning from Bolivia in 1961.[63]

But by the time of the book's publication, Shriver had embellished Gumucio's metaphor considerably, making the phrase his central metaphor for Peace Corps philosophy and policy. Employing Kennedy-era Camelot symbolism and phallic, militaristic language, Shriver uses the lance to articulate the Peace Corps' strategies of eroticized foreign intrusion in the service of peace, freedom, and development:

> [Gumucio] saw the Peace Corps as the human, cutting edge of the *Alianza para el Progreso*, as the sharpest thrust of the United States policy of supporting democratic change in Latin America. Our Volunteers, he said, are penetrating through all the barriers of protocol, bureaucracy, language, culture, and national frontiers to the people themselves. "They are reaching the minds and hearts of the people."
>
> The point of the lance is lean, hard, focused. It reaches its target. In our complex world that is what our political programs must do. And the "lance" Señor Gumucio referred to was a political one, with more than a Latin American meaning. It represents the force of ideas and people in action. Since "there is no alternative to peace," this is the most effective power we have.[64]

Appropriating and elaborating Gumucio's formulation to imbue it with "more than a Latin American meaning," Shriver frames the "protocol, bureaucracy, language, and culture" of other nations as barriers to be penetrated in succession by the "lean, hard, focused" lance. Protocol and bureaucracy, more commonly understood as barriers to intercultural understanding, cede naturally to language, culture, and nation, instantiating the logic, made familiar by experts like Lerner and Rostow, that the Peace Corps must eviscerate everything around the people it serves in order to develop them anew. But Shriver's scenario supplements modernization theory's vision of penetration and humiliation by imagining authentic human connection and transnational affective ties as the euphoric endpoint of development work—the goal is not primarily the restructuring of economies, but rather the restructuring of subjectivities through unfettered contact with their "hearts and minds." Cultural destruction becomes not a threat to be countered, but rather a rite of passage on the road to development and a strategy to attain intimacy with "the people themselves."

Shriver's and the Peace Corps' vision, then, worked in tandem with the more explicitly disruptive and coercive development imaginary of theorists like Rostow. Using modernization theory to situate Third World nations in the American past allowed development planners and workers to advance visions of seduction, male closeness, and frontier bonding that supplemented the more explicitly violent language of prodding and humiliation. If modernization theory provided a language and an impetus for inducing Third World leaders to throw over "traditional" modes of social organization, the very visible work of Peace Corps staffers and volunteers made the development project seem both seductive and invigorating, conducive to a male bonding that would redirect the energies of decolonization and combat the ennui stemming from managerial affluence.

Stealing Away: Seduction and Theft on the New Frontier

While directing the Peace Corps, Shriver cultivated a competitive intimacy with his Peace Corps colleagues, becoming known as not only a strong leader but also a seductive one: Elizabeth Cobbs Hoffman perfectly captures the director's powerful mystique in her description of Shriver's strategy for staffing the Peace Corps, writing that "stories abounded of talented individuals he tracked down in remote vacation hideaways or stole from other government agencies or talked off planes heading west . . . He became known as the capitol's most ardent suitor."[65] Staffer Peter Grothe similarly recalls the consensus that, in shepherding the Peace Corps bill through Congress, "Shriver and Moyers carried on the greatest romance act with the Congress since Romeo and Juliet."[66] *New York Times* writer Peter Braestrup also comments on the "outlaw" ethos that characterized the early Peace Corps, remembering that "[Shriver's] relationship to the White House was essential to the start of the Peace Corps. You had to have a license to steal to get it going— not to steal unlimitedly, but to steal. Staff it up with your own kind of person."[67] Indeed, the Peace Corps' mystique seemed to depend on its ability to poach employees, despite the dismay that other government agencies and the Kaiser Foundation registered at losing workers in high positions.[68] This language of romance and theft suggests the extent to which the early Peace Corps relied, even in its staffing decisions, on the invocation of vigorous frontier (in this case frontier-outlaw) tropes in assembling its appealing yet exclusive brotherhood.

Peace Corps staffer and Johnson aide Bill Moyers attests to Shriver's seductive powers, recalling Johnson's prediction, after discussions among the three men about how to get the Peace Corps bill through Congress, that Shriver's personality would come to stand in for the tangle of fantasies that underwrote the agency. "After Sarge and I left our first lengthy tutorial at Johnson's knee," Moyers writes, "the vice-president called me and said that the way to sell the Peace Corps was to sell Shriver: 'They won't be able to resist him.'"[69] Moyers himself reveled in his closeness to Shriver, writing to him in 1963 that "there is no substitute, of course, for contact with you. You are still the adrenalin around here."[70] Shriver, in turn, recalls that he and Johnson competed for Moyers's attentions, recalling that "one of the reasons that Johnson had a lot of respect for me, even to the point of making me head of the War on Poverty, was because for some reason or other he couldn't understand, Moyers had been willing to leave him to go work with me . . . here was this young man who was the apple of Johnson's eye, quitting to go work for me."[71]

One of those pursued by the Peace Corps was Frank Mankiewicz, a lawyer from a prominent Hollywood family who had worked on Kennedy's campaign. After top officials consulted his friend Franklin Williams, who assured them that Mankiewicz "would fit in perfectly at the Peace Corps," the agency requested an immediate meeting.[72] Peace Corps staffer Coates Redmon's history *Come as You Are* dramatizes Mankiewicz's giddy 1961 encounter with Peace Corps staffers, emphasizing both the informal evaluations and nepotism that led staffers to become objects of pursuit and the excitement the men evinced at bestowing portions of the globe on one another:

> Mankiewicz met Derek Singer, acting director of the Latin America Regional Office and, only incidentally, Ted Sorenson's brother-in-law. Singer said, "I don't suppose you speak Spanish. But, ah, do you?"
>
> "Yeah, I do speak Spanish." So, to prove that he did, Mankiewicz conversed with Singer in Spanish for a few minutes.
>
> Singer looked very pleasantly surprised. He said, "Okay, Frank, pick a country in Latin America. Where would you like to go?" I said, "What do you mean, pick a country?" Singer said, "We'd like for you to direct a Peace Corps program in Peru, Ecuador, Costa Rica . . ."
>
> Mankiewicz claims he was not exactly sure of the location of these countries and had never been to Latin America. But he was caught up

> in the mad excitement that then existed at Peace Corps headquarters
> and he recalled that an old friend of his . . . had just been appointed
> ambassador to Peru. "So I said, okay, fine—I'll take Peru."
>
> Singer stood up, shook Mankiewicz's hand vigorously, and smiled
> the blinding smile of conquest, said, "Great! That's it!" Mankiewicz,
> suddenly weak in the knees from such a rapid bestowment, asked with
> uncharacteristic meekness, "But what happens now?"[73]

Mankiewicz's weak-kneed "taking" of Peru, followed by a vigorous hand-shake initiating him into the Peace Corps brotherhood, demonstrates the Peace Corps' explicit framing of the Third World as a necessary staging ground for masculinity and male bonding. Singer's "blinding smile of conquest," the "mad excitement," their giddiness at taking Peru—all suggest that their mission in the Third World is self-consciously a conquering one. At the same time, the object of the conquest seems double: both Peru and Mankiewicz have been conquered by Singer's vigor. This is one moment, among many in the early years of the Peace Corps, which can be understood through Sedgwick's formulation of homosocial triangulation; aside from the proliferation of brother-in-law relationships among top staffers, the nation of Peru functions here as a necessary, but also completely arbitrary (in fact, randomly chosen), mechanism for facilitating and legitimating ecstatic male closeness.

Although its staffers worked in office jobs like the rest of the managerial class, Shriver and other recruiters constantly emphasized "strength" as a precondition for employment at the Peace Corps. Comments in memos to and from Shriver about potential hires included "Is he strong enough?" and "He seems quite nice, but not sufficiently mature or penetrating."[74] Despite the agency's interest in peace, conscientious objectors were discounted, and one application was dismissed due to a staffer's recollection of the applicant as "a pacifist, rather fanatic and irritable."[75] Instead, the Peace Corps staff concentrated on recruiting college athletes, often emphasizing the desirability of physical strength and athletic prowess. "He's 43, 240 pounds, and impressive. Was All-American end at Cornell in 1940. I'm not at all sure we can get him, but lets [sic] make a good try at it," wrote staffer William Haddad about Jerome "Brud" Holland.[76] Shriver likewise described one potential staff recruit as a "redheaded, torpedo-shaped individual with lots of thrust," and recounted in the next line of the memo that he was "talking to a thin, angular, knife-like former executive of the NAACP in California."[77] This constant attention to the physical attributes of the Peace Corps staffers ensured that they would be objects of fantasy for managerial-class American men: managers with office jobs who were also Cold Warriors on the New Frontier.

This anxiety about seducing away rugged Cold Warriors sometimes cut both ways, as when Shriver wrote Kennedy a memo to "urgently recommend" that the president take Peace Corps Latin America director Jack Vaughn on his next trip to South America. Boasting that Vaughn "knows all the officials in both Venezuela and Colombia . . . and is considered very 'sympatico' by the Latinos," but, perhaps wary of Kennedy's persuasive powers, Shriver warned his brother-in-law that "NO ONE IS TO BE PERMITTED TO HIRE VAUGHN AWAY FROM THE PEACE CORPS." The letter closes with a postscript trumpeting that "Vaughn went 6 rounds against Sugar Ray Robinson 10 or 15 years ago and subsequently was coach of the University of Michigan boxing team."[78] Kennedy followed Shriver's advice, taking Vaughn on his next Latin America trip but returned him to Shriver as planned, where he served on several Latin America missions and became the second Peace Corps director in 1966; his desirability to Kennedy and Johnson, despite his lifelong Republicanism, here, too, seems to hinge on his physical prowess and coaching pedigree at least as much as his rapport with "the Latinos."

Much of the U.S. news media assisted staffers in characterizing the Peace Corps as a frontier fantasy space. The *New York Times* embraced the Peace Corps with particular enthusiasm, writing 209 items on the agency in its first year.[79] The *Times'* Braestrup, who wrote the majority of these Peace Corps stories, later explained that "the *Times* loved the Peace Corps . . . What Kennedy had done was to tap into the upper-middle-class and give them a role in government, in the New Frontier. It was elitist, and I know that wasn't the intention, but that's how it turned out that first year. And that's what the *Times* liked. And there is no doubt that the *Times* had a great influence on the public's acceptance of the Peace Corps."[80] In its many early articles and editorials, the *Times* linked the impulse to join the Peace Corps with a reinvigorated pioneer spirit, remarking repeatedly on the rugged quality of Peace Corps training and service. "A Challenge to Youth" explained that "the fun won't be the sort of fun that results when a young man is sent off to college with an automobile, a handsome allowance and the thought that he will be young only once. Yet we have the feeling that the promise of hard work and hard times may attract more youngsters than would the offer of an easy and well-paid job." The *Times* cites "the promise of hardship" as a motivating factor at key moments in this history of U.S. expansion:

> It has sent missionaries into the rugged parts of the world; it was the great urge that caused our predecessors on this continent to go into the woods with a little powder, a little salt and a great deal of determination. It has sent many a ship to sea. It created the great procession of covered wagons that rolled across our continent. It has led to adventure in the air and to the conquest of the North and South Poles. Some young people will continue to like to take it soft. They wouldn't be good anyhow for the kind of work Mr. Shriver describes.[81]

Linking the Peace Corps' ethos with ruggedness and an unwillingness to "take it soft," the *Times* frames the volunteers as the inheritors of a frontier tradition, working not so much for the world's people as to test themselves physically. Native peoples appear nowhere in this account, except perhaps as implicit victims of the "powder"; the editorial accords "rugged" North American terrain explored by the early missionaries and settlers the same status as the "North and South Poles."

The *Saturday Evening Post* also wrote regular pieces equating the Peace Corps with masculine fitness and Cold War imperatives. One, bearing the headline "People on the Way Up," accompanied a photo of Haddad in a football uniform. The article explained: "Hard-running William F. Haddad, 33, sprints toward the Free World's goal—Peace. . . . he cites increased Red propaganda as evidence that the Corps is gaining yardage. 'The Commies are going after the Peace Corps because they're scared as hell we're going to succeed.'"[82] The *Post* suggests here that the Peace Corps brings a long-needed athletic sensibility to the Cold War, infusing the staffers' managerial jobs with a rugged masculine energy.

A mid-1960s Peace Corps advertisement similarly presents athletic frontier masculinity as a Cold War weapon, but also outlines how development workers might effect the enormous change in subjectivity that the modernization mission required of the Third World. The ad depicts a young, blond man with his feet aggressively propped on a desk next to a thick, unopened book titled *Chapters in Western Civilization*.

He just said **NO** to being an organization man.

He turned down fat offers from six big corporations. And said yes to the Peace Corps. How come?

Because he has to find out a few things about himself. What he can do. How much he can give as well as how much he can take.

The Peace Corps will give him that chance. He'll be sent to any one of 46 countries in Asia, Africa or Latin America. He'll be pretty much on his own. Making his own decisions. Figuring out what has to be done—and doing it.

Those two years will take all his courage and stamina and patience. Sometimes, he'll work 16 hours a day, seven days a week, and

much of that in the hot sun. That shouldn't be too tough for a guy who's stayed up a whole weekend at a stretch, cramming for finals.

He's going to have to be a leader—the guy who gets people started doing things they never did before—sometimes things they resent. That won't be easy for the guy who organized a Sunday afternoon football game —when all anybody really wanted was sleep. And he's picked up a few other things along the way that'll come in handy.

He can fix a broken-down tractor. After all, he's kept his car going since high school. He can teach first aid and life saving from what

he learned as a camp counselor.

Give a guy like this Peace Corps training, and there's almost no limit to what he can do. He can give inoculations—and show other people how to do it right. He can teach children to read—and get a library started. He can get people to work together to build a road, so farmers can get their produce to market.

The big organizations can have him later. Right now he's got things to do—things he can't do anywhere else but in the Peace Corps.

It's hard to imagine a fatter offer. If you have two years to lend to history, write to The Peace Corps, Washington, D.C., 20525.

Peace Corps advertisement, circa 1964: "He just said NO to being an organization man." Courtesy of the Peace Corps.

The advertisement's tagline proclaims, "He just said NO to being an organization man," echoing William H. Whyte and other popular sociologists who claimed, like Kennedy and Shriver, that the United States' postwar affluence had eroded the rugged individualism of the growing middle class. The small print explains that the reclining young man "turned down fat offers from six corporations" and "said 'Yes' to the Peace Corps" because "he has to find out a few things about himself. What he can do. How much he can give as well as how much he can take," invoking both the "stealing away" of resources and the masochistic abjection that Savran claims defined the Cold War masculine ideal. The advertisement presents a nearly endless answer to these questions, relying on the exceptionalist logic that after successfully navigating middle-class adolescence and a liberal arts education in the United States, young graduates could automatically excel at virtually any job in any country:

> Sometimes he'll have to work 16 hours a day, seven days a week, and much of that in the hot sun. That shouldn't be too tough for a guy who's stayed up a whole weekend at a stretch, cramming for finals. He's going to have to be a leader—the guy who gets people started doing things they've never done before. That ought to be easy for the guy who organized a Sunday afternoon football game—when all anybody wanted was sleep . . . He can fix a broken-down tractor. After all, he's kept his car going since high-school. He can teach first aid and lifesaving from what he learned as a camp counselor . . . He can give inoculations—and show other people to do it right. He can teach children to read—and get a library started. He can get people to work together to build a road so farmers can get their produce to market. The big organizations can have him later. Right now he's got things to do—things he can't do anywhere else but in the Peace Corps.

Imagining the Peace Corps as an extension of all-male, nostalgia-infused spaces like summer camp and Sunday afternoon football games (for which the energetic protagonist will have to awaken his sleeping friends), the advertisement offers the entire Third World as both a playground for young men and a fairly manageable test of their masculinity. Although in the late 1960s Peace Corps advertisements began to emphasize the difficulty and sometimes even the futility of volunteer assignments, the agency continued to promote the developmentalist idea that the United States could claim a special inheritance of ingenuity and rugged individualism, traits that, if properly transmitted, would allow anyone in the world to throw off the shackles of poverty. By highlighting the handsome young man's ability to "get people started doing things they've never done before," to awaken passive, stagnant Third World populations as he has awakened his slumbering friends, the advertisement suggests that modernization imperatives will replace the more straightforward attempts at racial eradication that characterized earlier "chapters in Western civilization."

The other remarkable thing about this advertisement is how quickly the "NO" becomes a "later." Even as it emphasizes the permanent changes the volunteer will bring about in the society where he serves, the advertisement underscores the temporality of his Peace Corps term, which will neither make him question the value of "the big organizations" nor jeopardize his place in them. Rather, his two-year stint will help him cultivate an authentic masculinity in order to enrich and enliven his future as a managerial capitalist.[83] By promising the man to the corporate world "later," the advertisement imagines a symbiotic relationship between insulating wealth and the rugged development missions informed by modernization theory.

In advertisements like this one, the Peace Corps provided a fantasy space for the regeneration of American masculinity and the seduction of Third World leaders into an imaginary global brotherhood. Development work, the rugged attempt to uproot and redefine individuals and communities, became central to the construction and maintenance of the liberal order. By vividly imagining the relationship between wealthy Americans and the world's poor and disenfranchised as one of enthusiastic, muscular mentorship (rather than exploitation and dispossession), the Peace Corps helped cement development as a compelling fantasy that quelled anxieties at home about both decolonization and domesticity.

Riots and "Red Hot Interests"

Before Jack Vaughn became the second Peace Corps director, Lyndon Johnson briefly wooed him away from his post at the agency in order to quell the 1964 flag riots in Panama. The conflict began when students in the U.S.-controlled and inhabited Canal Zone raised American flags in front of their high schools, defying a 1963 bilateral agreement, and

Panamanian students retaliated by scaling the Zone fence and planting their own flag; Canal Zone police fired on them and the conflict escalated into nationwide strikes and riots, with tens of thousands of Panamanian students and workers demanding a greater share of the profits from the canal. Before the riots were over, U.S. troops had killed twenty-four Panamanian protestors, and President Roberto Chiari had broken formal ties with the United States. After three months of failed negotiations—Johnson repeatedly rejected the compromise brokered by the Organization of American States, striking the word "negotiate" wherever it appeared as a possibility in the agreement they had prepared[84]—the president called Vaughn to the White House and ordered him to "sneak in there and get things back in shape."[85]

Three days after his arrival, in the face of overt and organized hostility from his beloved "Latins"—more than six thousand United Fruit workers in Panama were on strike, and protesters in Chile and Venezuela as well as Ghana and China expressed solidarity with Panamanians[86]—Vaughn wrote Shriver. He began by lamenting his "basically untenable position" in Panama, but devoted most of the letter to praising his mentor and friend. "I wanted to try to tell you of my profound gratitude for all the guidance, support and kindness you gave me all the while I was part of your great organization," Vaughn wrote. "I have frequently puzzled over whether it was you or the idea of the Peace Corps which was the greater. Finally decided it was you." After pledging his loyalty to Shriver in similarly effusive terms, Vaughn confessed to the dashing administrator, "I would love to have a signed, glossy, unretouched photo of you one day." He then turned his attention to his diplomatic troubles, bemoaning the Panama Peace Corps volunteers' support for the Panamanian protestors: "I really thought I was leaving the Peace Corps until Saturday, the day after I arrived, a Volunteer said 'down with the Canal Zone Company.' How do you stop Volunteers from holding press conferences?" He closed with a homoerotically charged plea to "please accept, excellency, the assurance of my continuing and red hot interest in the Peace Corps."[87]

Shriver honored Vaughn's request, sending him an eight-by-ten photo inscribed "To my good friend, *El Rubio*, with many thanks for all he has done for the Peace Corps," and Vaughn succeeded in suppressing the dissent of both the Panamanians objecting to U.S. empire and the volunteers who stood with them, reestablishing normal diplomatic relations in only a few months.

Though his rapid triumph earned him a reputation in Johnson's government as the "*campesino* [peasant] ambassador," Vaughn later framed the reconciliation as an inevitable romantic reunion, recalling that he "didn't do anything brilliant. It was just like a lovers' quarrel in which you realize that the pouting and vituperation don't accomplish anything. I arrived in Panama just when they were ready to kiss and make up."[88] But despite his disavowal of his own role in the process, Vaughn had successfully suppressed the threat of worldwide revolutionary decolonization struggles, encapsulated in Panamanian resistance. As his request indicates, to effect this suppression he needed Shriver's "signed, glossy, unretouched photo," a fetish object that helped him summon Shriver's charm in order to redirect Panama's calls for self-determination into a narrative of romance and reconciliation. Only with this talisman of Shriver, the man he deemed even greater than "the idea of the Peace Corps," was Vaughn able to obscure the ideological debate

Signed photograph of Sargent Shriver, sent to Jack Vaughn during Panama flag riots: "To my good friend, *El Rubio*." Photograph by Rowland Scherman. Courtesy of the National Archives, John F. Kennedy Presidential Library and Museum.

over Panamanian sovereignty through the combined application of dip-lomatic coercion and seductive charisma.

This story of the signed Shriver photograph's role in quelling Pan-ama's insurgency should resonate with the 1960s Peace Corps' pro-grams and fantasies I have delineated above. Vaughn's desire for and "red-hot interest" in Shriver (and only secondarily, the Peace Corps), professed as he applied diplomatic pressure so that Panama might "kiss and make up" with the United States, takes the form of what Eve Sedg-wick identifies as a triangular formation: "male heterosexual desire, in the form of a desire to consolidate partnership with authoritative males in and through the bodies of females."[89] However, as with Mankiewicz and Singer's giddy bonding over Peru, this desire is expressed, and this partnership consolidated, through the conduit of a feminized nation. At the same time, Vaughn's attempt to get pouting, vituperative Panama to "kiss and make up" hints at a not-entirely-passive role for the country, suggesting the way development offered Third World leaders the oppor-tunity to assume more active, if not equal, roles in eroticized global power networks, through the acting-out and working-through of nationalist resistance (in this case flag-planting). Like Paz and Kennedy's mutual "point of interest" just beyond the frame of the photo, this moment of brotherhood for Third World nations always seemed to lie just out of reach.

In this story of Vaughn using Shriver's photograph and "the idea of the Peace Corps" to quell nationalist insurgency, as well as more generally in this chapter's account of the Peace Corps' founding, the volunteers—seemingly the most essential part of the agency's work—appear almost nowhere. Vaughn mentions the volunteers in Panama "holding press conferences" only to implore Shriver to help him stop them, but in his account they seem to threaten rather than bolster "the idea of the Peace Corps" he extols. This, of course, is not always the case; the rest of this book will consider in more detail the variety of posi-tions the Peace Corps' volunteers took in relation to the fantasies cir-culated by its founders. However, I want to return once more to the Panama volunteers of the flag riot moment, who reappear in a memoir by American Canal Zone residents Herbert and Mary Knapp when they describe a Peace Corps contingent they encountered at a church meeting in the aftermath of the riots. In their story of the gathering, the Knapps vividly if derisively depict an even more militantly anti-imperialist Peace Corps presence than Vaughn suggests:

> [The volunteers] spoke with the certainty and idealism of nineteenth-century missionaries, but they preached a vague universal brotherhood rather than any divisive, sectarian form of Christianity. They boasted about how primitive life was in their villages and told us how much the people loved them. "They protected us during the riots," one bragged. Another announced, "People are basically friendly." A chubby girl stood up and said she identified completely with "her people." Raising her fist, she declared that if we drove through her village and her people threw rocks at us, she would, too.[90]

In the Knapps' account, we can detect some resonances with the Peace Corps' founding imaginary: the preaching of brotherhood, the boasts of primitive living conditions and "how much the people loved them." At the same time, the volunteers seem to have reinterpreted the ideal of "vague universal brotherhood" that Vaughn and Shriver mobilized to suppress the riots, instead citing it to contemplate violence in solidarity with Panamanian villagers. In particular the "chubby girl" with her fist in the air threatening to throw rocks at American civilians, in so many ways the opposite of the svelte, grinning fantasy-volunteer of the advertisement who would write his own "chapters in Western civilization" and return to "the big organizations," points to the potential for more subversive repurposings of the Peace Corps' homosocial imaginary. It also begins to illuminate the U.S. popular imaginary of the 1960s, in which liberal development dictates and militant solidarity practice were mutually, if contentiously, constitutive. The rest of this book examines how these confluences appeared in the work and popular representations of 1960s Peace Corps volunteers. In the next chapter, I begin my discussion of volunteer affects and experiences by discussing how the Peace Corps drew on and channeled the interracial desire that characterized white youth culture in the 1950s United States.

2

INTEGRATION AND ITS LIMITS
From Romantic Racism to Peace Corps Authenticity

"WHAT EVER HAPPENED TO THE BEAT GENERATION?" wonders a 1962 *New York Times* headline. Announcing that "the Peace Corps idea is spreading fast," the ensuing article by James Reston describes one domestic imitator, a "spontaneous volunteer student movement" at Michigan State University. Reston reports that the students, working "in the poor districts" of Michigan cities, "reasoned that they might be able to deal with some of the worst of the kids who came from broken homes and had no incentive to get an education," and that "the main thing is not so much to help the young laggards with their work, but to make friends with them and thus provide good examples that are not available in many homes." Countering the conventional wisdom of "professors in the sociology departments" and other unspecified interlocutors, Reston announces the end of "the American student" of the past, who, "it was said, wasn't engaged in anything and didn't care about anything" and was "always dropping out of school and into some bed: uninterested, uncommitted to anything but money, booze, and sex."[1] If this promiscuity and nonchalance defined the beat generation, the "Peace Corps idea" represented commitment, engagement, and heroism.

Six years later, in a moment of domestic turmoil and widespread opposition to U.S. foreign policy, the Peace Corps could still stand in popular discourse for an authenticity that other youth subcultures lacked. Frank Zappa and the Mothers of Invention drew on the agency's image in their 1968 song "Who Needs the Peace Corps?" which, much like Reston's article, uses the Peace Corps as shorthand for authentic cultural connection and heroic action, contrasting it with the consumerist, disengaged hippie counterculture. In his parodic rant against the subculture that inherited the beat ethos, Zappa pits the hypocrisy and laziness of "phony hippies" who "drop out and go to Frisco" and buy "books of Indian lore" against the stoicism, heroism, and genuine intercultural understanding of America's young Peace Corps volunteers.[2]

In what follows I attempt to explain this faith in the Peace Corps by even cynical observers like Zappa, arguing that the agency's ability to sustain its claims to authentic heroism into the late 1960s, despite widespread popular disillusionment with the liberal foreign policy establishment that had created it, stemmed from its ability to incorporate and reroute the romantic racism that had defined 1950s white youth cultures. Through a consideration of the masochistic masculine beat and beatnik subcultures that posited the permeability of the self by women and racial others, I argue that modernization theorists and Peace Corps staffers attempted to both capitalize on the interracial desires that drove these rebel subcultures and mobilize (while repurposing) the idea of the permeable self for the modernization mission. Tracing discourses of permeability and identification through popular cultural texts, modernization theory tracts, policy directives, and Peace Corps volunteer memoirs reveals how the 1960s Peace Corps managed to stand in for heroism in its time; how its discourses of interracial brotherhood and cultural, technical, and community development influenced both the conduct of volunteers and the conclusions drawn in official and media narratives about them; and how its policies and practices inaugurated and codified new models to help U.S. whites relate correctly to racial and international others.

Exchanging Worlds: Beat Ideology, Deviant Desires, and the Peace Corps

Throughout the 1960s, the Peace Corps and the U.S. newspapers covering it expressed a persistent concern with screening "beats" and "beatniks" out of the agency. In 1961, the agency's assistant director of training, George Guthrie, contrasted the Peace Corps' frontier ideal with the seamy cosmopolitanism for which beatniks (and Ivy Leaguers, a group to which all the most prominent beat writers belonged) were known, reassuring *Times* readers that volunteers "aren't Ivy League, or Beatnik. They come mostly from small schools and small communities."[3] Other depictions that same year also explicitly marked the connection and contrast between Peace Corps and beat ideologies: Max Lerner wrote in *Life*'s Latin America edition that "the Peace Corps marks the demise of the so-called Beat generation, of the American 'Beatnik,'" and the *Washington Post* featured a cartoon with a line of fresh-faced young men holding jackets over a puddle so that the Peace Corps, personified by a pretty young woman, can pass; the caption features her saying, "Goodness, are you the beat and angry young men I've heard so much about?"[4]

In 1962 a *Times* editorial celebrating the Peace Corps' first year claimed that "some feared that young idealists with weak characters, unfounded illusions and beards might be attracted. But beatniks were not welcome," and in a *Saturday Review* article, Shriver castigated "critics who saw in the Peace Corps a haven for bearded beatniks, confused liberals, and impractical idealists in revolt against the world."[5] A 1964 *Times* article claimed that "Peace Corps applicants are tested with a thoroughness known only to generations of white mice: misfits, beats, soapbox rebels and introverted malcontents are spotted and rejected with surprising skill,"[6] and the *Times* followed up in 1966, reporting that "staff members feel that another problem is how to keep the Peace Corps young as the idea grows old, how to keep the enthusiasm at a high peak, how to attract the best and most mature of the young activists, while screening out the 'beatniks.'"[7]

These and other articles evince not only anxiety about beats and beatniks in the Peace Corps, but also the conviction that they would want to volunteer in the first place.[8] At first glance, Peace Corps service would seem to contradict the anti-work and anti-authority sentiments that defined these subcultures. But the overlapping sensibilities of these two youth movements suggest that Peace Corps officials recognized that their volunteers might be driven by the same interracial desires and identifications that united the beats, and later, the counterculture—namely, a romanticized desire for the freedom that allegedly accompanied non-white poverty. Identifying this romanticized interest in nonwhite poor societies, the Peace Corps drew on the same desires and identifications that were becoming dominant in white youth culture and attempted to reroute those desires and identifications into the their own narratives of masculinity and modernity. It was because the Peace Corps recognized their affinity with the beats and beatniks that these subcultures became a symbol of the Peace Corps' fears of "softness," standing in, according

"Goodness, Are You The Beat And Angry Young Men I've Heard So Much About?"

Herblock cartoon from 1961, demonstrating the Peace Corps' power to oppose and reform "beat and angry young men." Copyright the Herb Block Foundation.

to Savran's frame, for the feminized, racialized double that the organization needed to incorporate and expel in order to consolidate its image of authentic frontier masculinity.[9]

The beats' romantic racism, which shaped the 1960s counterculture and its similarly antimodern racial fantasies, imagined domestic and foreign racial others as mystical, spiritual, sexually uninhibited, and free from the constraints of white-collar capitalism. Savran, Susan Douglas, Wini Breines, W. T. Lhamon, Barbara Ehrenreich, and other scholars have illuminated and sometimes celebrated the structures of racial fantasy that defined youth rebellion in the 1950s United States, suggesting that, influenced by the beats, white young people identified with and fantasized about blackness in order to escape the narrow confines of the domestic containment ideal and the repressive social order of the 1950s.[10] These structures of white desire were reinforced by "The White Negro," Norman Mailer's 1957 ode to beat/hipster appropriations of blackness:

> And in this wedding of the white and the black it was the Negro who brought the cultural dowry. Any Negro who wishes to live must live with danger from his first day, and no experience can ever be casual to him, no Negro can saunter down a street with any real certainty that violence will not visit him on his walk. The cameos of security for the average white: mother and the home, job and the family, are not even a mockery to millions of Negroes; they are impossible. The Negro has the simplest of alternatives: live a life of constant humility or ever-threatening danger. In such a pass where paranoia is as vital to survival as blood, the Negro had stayed alive and begun to grow by following the need of his body where he could. Knowing in the cells of his existence that life was war, nothing but war, the Negro (all exceptions admitted) could rarely afford the sophisticated inhibitions of civilization, and so he kept for his survival the art of the primitive, he lived in the enormous present, he subsisted for his Saturday night kicks, relinquishing the pleasures of the mind for the more obligatory pleasures of the body, and in his music he gave voice to the character and quality of his existence, to his rage and the infinite variations of joy, lust, languor, growl, cramp, pinch, scream and despair of his orgasm.[11]

Mailer's vision of black and white men's marriage, with black men bringing as "cultural dowry" a primal masculinity derived from living with constant violence and freedom from the "cameos of security for the average white," reified popular conceptions of authentic blackness, equating them unequivocally with hypersexuality, violence, and spontaneity. In his attempt to escape the middle-class constraints of "mother and the home, job and the family," Mailer celebrated white appropriation of a romanticized black subjectivity, conditioned by white-supremacist terror but nonetheless enviable. Mailer's account, of course, is not a marriage proposal: he inhabits and ventriloquizes black men in order to stage their consent to the hipster project, but does not imagine asking them if they want to participate in the transaction. As Mailer's contemporaries James Baldwin and Michele Wallace vividly explain, these characterizations of hypermasculine, uninhibited black authenticity had damaging consequences for African American intellectuals and social movements.[12]

The most influential beat staging of racial fantasy was Jack Kerouac's *On the Road*, the novel that inspired many young white Americans, some of whom became central figures in the new left and the counterculture, to reject the stability of the suburbs in favor of itinerant, homosocial worlds and contact with exoticized racial others.[13] The novel's narrator, Sal Paradise, journeys back and forth across the United States and finally to Mexico, framing his rejection of the segregationist domestic containment ethos as a wistful yet insatiable desire for blackness as well as a more general racial otherness. In the novel's most famous moment of racial longing, Sal bemoans his "white ambitions" and "wish[es] [he] could exchange worlds with the happy, true-hearted, ecstatic Negroes of America."[14] In a journey that greatly resembles Kerouac's own 1947 adventures, Sal continues to crisscross the United States until the last pages of the novel, when he journeys to Mexico, with his companion, idol, and love object, Dean Moriarty.

Although Sal and Dean see Mexico as their goal, their rebellious ethos is hardly antithetical to American patriotism; rather, the characters reenact their country's founding myths with intensity, exuberantly exploring the homoeroticism and romantic (if also genocidal) racial identification that underlay earlier frontier fantasies. Sal obsessively watches Westerns and equates himself and especially Dean with Western heroes: in the first chapter he lovingly labels Dean "a sideburned hero of the snowy West" and "a western kinsman of the sun," and explains that Dean's "'criminality' was not something that sulked and sneered; it was a wild yea-saying overburst of American joy; it was Western, the west wind, an ode from the plains, something new, long-prophesied, long a-coming."[15] Celebrating Dean's "criminality" as an "overburst of American joy," Sal suggests that Dean's exuberant homosexual feelings and encounters (which Sal and Dean constantly dissociate from homosexuality by denigrating "fags" and "queers"); occasional thievery; mistreatment and abuse of women; and cross-racial identification spring not from a lack of patriotism but rather from an excess of Americanness and modernity, a forward-looking recuperation of frontier wildness which Kerouac explicitly contrasts with the "white ambitions" of the new managerial class.

Modernization imperatives and the rhetoric of underdevelopment, as well as ecstatic homosocial bonding over land and women, guide Sal and Dean's adventures and transactions in Mexico.[16] When they drive up a remote mountain road and encounter young girls selling crystals, Dean neatly equates integration into the global economy with historical agency, exclaiming, "They've only *recently* learned to sell these crystals, since the highway was built about ten years back—up until that time this entire nation must have been *silent!*" Dean proceeds to "dangle his wristwatch" at "a particularly soulful child." Sal recounts that "she whimpered with glee. Then Dean poked in the little girl's hand for 'the sweetest and smallest crystal she has personally picked from the mountain for me.' He found one no bigger than a berry. He handed her the wristwatch dangling."[17] This ecstatic, violent, and eroticized scene depicts Dean as both rapist and seducer, "poking the little girl's hand" for the crystal/berry "which she had picked just for him"; together, Sal and Dean imagine that Third World labor and resources exist solely for Western expropriation. In exchange for the crystal, Dean hands over the "dangling wristwatch" which, along with Dean's observations about the girls' precapitalist silence, reveals the confluences between beat and development discourses: both imagine noncapitalist cultures as mystical and outside historical time, but also work to make their eradication of those cultures seductive. Like modernization theorists and development workers, Dean offers the little girl a new "modern" sense of temporality, erasing her history by enthusiastically declaiming her previous silence. The confluence of the berries, crystals, and rape imagery indicates Kerouac's celebratory understanding that modernity entails bestowing the correct "long-prophesied," "Western" modalities on indigenous peoples, and depicts the attempt to control Third World production and reproduction (Dean's forcible exchange of the berry/crystal for the watch) as an ecstatic seduction/rape.

But the beats can sustain neither their vigilant homophobia nor their adherence to modernization imperatives. Even Sal's extreme disavowals of his erotic bond with Dean (by sharing women and also by mocking "fags" and "queers" on the road and menacing them in the restrooms of San Francisco bars)[18] cannot dispel the beats' association with femininity and deviant sexuality; the beats ultimately are too interested in exploration and racial and sexual others to achieve the "differentiation" that Talcott Parsons argued was the bulwark of the modern capitalist society.[19] The beat writers' difficulty in differentiating themselves from racial and sexual others is evident throughout *On the Road*: Sal not only wishes he were black and Mexican (instead of "a 'white man,' disillusioned," as he identifies himself in Denver) at various points in the novel, but also claims those identities for himself.[20] The relationship between the beats' gender ambivalence and racialized poverty is evident in the Mexican brothel scene, in which Sal and Dean stand ogling the poorest of the prostitutes; they construct her matriarchal power and "unimpeachable dignity" as the source of her poverty and their (foreign, capitalist, and sexual) penetration as her potential salvation, but are unable to enact the transaction that modernization imperatives would require. Lost in their reveries about her beautiful abjection, and by extension their own, they fail to approach her:

> Of all the girls in there she needed the money most; maybe her mother had come to get money from her for her little infant sisters and brothers. Mexicans are poor. It never, never occurred to me just to approach her and give her some money. I have a feeling she would've taken it with a degree of scorn, and scorn from the likes of her made me flinch. In my madness I was actually in love with her for the few hours it all lasted; it was the same unmistakable ache and stab across the mind, the same pain. Strange that Dean and Stan also failed to approach her; her unimpeachable dignity was the thing that made her poor in a wild old whorehouse, think of that. At one point I saw Dean leaning like a statue toward her, ready to fly, and befuddlement cross his face as she glanced coolly and imperiously his way and he stopped rubbing his belly and finally bowed his head. For she was the queen.[21]

As they did with the girls on the mountain road, Sal and Dean consolidate their relationship through the bodies of Third World women, but here they also imagine themselves to be both subordinates of "the queen" and penetrable by her—Sal feels "the familiar ache and stab," while Dean begins impenetrably statuesque, "ready to fly," then folds under her gaze—despite (and also because of) her poverty, femaleness, and racial otherness. Given these lapses into vulnerability, it makes sense that their ecstatic conquering mission to Mexico ends with Sal's bodily failure; he falls gravely ill and must leave, unable to maintain the position of beloved conqueror for more than a few heady days.

Thus despite the tendencies they shared—the rejection of "softness" and domesticity for homosocial itinerant adventure; the embrace of "spiritual movements" as opposed to "politics"; the attempts to take on the trappings of poverty and racial otherness; the ideal of rural frontier self-sufficiency—the Peace Corps focused its energy on dissociating from the beat generation and expelling beatniks because of the beats' sustained forays into homosexuality and risky racial fantasy. The agency's prohibition of idealistic beatniks with "weak characters" in part reflected the knowledge that the beats had crossed the line from intense fraternal bonds into homosexuality, as the 1960s Peace Corps vigilantly attempted to screen out homosexual volunteers: Lyndon Johnson memorably advised Shriver to screen out "cocksuckers";[22] Robert Dean notes that "in the first batch of trainees at Iowa State University a 'confessed' homosexual was rooted out by the FBI";[23] and several volunteers observe that the practice of deselecting homosexuals continued through the late 1960s.[24] But the Peace Corps' dissociation from beatniks also responds to the beats' rejection of the imperative to eradicate indigenous cultures, due to their melancholic obsession with racial others as well as their uncertainty as to the value and coherence of the managerial–capitalist hegemonic self.

While the Peace Corps did adopt aspects of the masochistic beat philosophy in order to teach Third World men to "take it like men," (to accept penetration by the "lean, hard, focused" lance of the volunteers, leading to capitalist development in the service of modernity and full masculinity), it attempted to disavow the implications of these masochistic structures of masculinity by rejecting the beats who practiced that philosophy, instead relocating authenticity and vitality in frontier masculinity and expanding global capitalism. In order to reattribute virility to the white men Kerouac had depicted as melancholic and disillusioned, social scientists and development workers imagined white men as adventurous penetrators whose homosocial bonding and seductive powers facilitated a one-way transmission of vitality and knowledge, a spreading of identificatory desire, to people around the world. To facilitate this penetration of Third World cultures and economies, the agency had to adopt the language of "the new poverty" shaped by modernization theorists and advanced by social scientists at home, imagining the volunteers as purveyors of vitality, culture, order, and history and nonwhite communities worldwide as disorganized, passive, and feminine, lacking the very virility which Mailer had so vividly attributed to black men. The exoticizing desire expressed by Mailer and the beats, though already inflected by modernization theory, had to be refigured and contained to be of use to the modernization mission.

Even before the Peace Corps, Cold War liberals attempted to remove the mantle of authenticity and vitality from racialized and otherwise oppressed people and reserve it for the new white managerial class. In Arthur Schlesinger's 1949 Cold War classic *The Vital Center*, Schlesinger derides "Doughface progressives," taunting these incorrectly soft liberals for fetishizing workers. He writes that "one myth, to which the Doughface has clung in the face of experience with the imperturbable ardor of an early Christian, is the mystique of the proletariat."[25] Reattributing masculinity to the middle-class "center," Schlesinger mocks "the intellectual's somewhat feminine fascination with the rude and muscular power of the proletariat" as well as his "desire to compensate for his own sense of alienation by immersing himself in the broad maternal expanse of the masses."[26] Schlesinger here feminizes not only leftist intellectuals, scornfully attributing to them a "fascination" with and desire for "immersion" in working-class life remarkably similar to the sentiments concurrently being shaped and explored by the beat writers, but also the masses themselves, who over the course of a half-sentence lose their masculine "rude and muscular power" and become a "broad maternal expanse."

The discursive shift Schlesinger signals, from New Deal images of working-class power to developmentalist constructions of poverty as feminized dysfunction, disorganization, and pathology, was effected on a large scale by social scientists during the 1960s. As Alice O'Connor documents, "the Cold War made the problem of traditional culture a direct political concern," leading to vastly increased institutional and financial support for social science research.[27] Sociologist and former psychological warrior Daniel Lerner was one of those who, along with his colleagues at MIT's Center for International Studies, brought the imprimatur of scientific, quantitative analysis to the equation of poverty with psychological, emotional, and cultural deficiency. In his 1958 book *The Passing of Traditional Society*, which Nils Gilman calls "the first full expression of modernization theory," Lerner characterized the global poor as psychologically deficient, countering beat-like desires to search for authentic human connection in poor communities by claiming that "traditional" subjects, not wealthy and modern ones, lacked capacity for adequate identification with others.[28]

Lerner formulates underdevelopment as a problem of incomplete subject formation, arguing that "the problem of stimulating productivity . . . is basically 'psychological.'" Thus, in order to remedy underdevelopment, "isolated and illiterate peasants and tribesmen" must be given "clues as to what the better things of life might be," clues that stimulate "a massive growth of *imaginativeness* about alternatives to their present lifeways."[29] So motivated by this "massive growth" of their imaginations, the "isolated and illiterate peasants" will develop "mobile personalities," gaining capacities for identification that will allow them to thrive in an urban capitalist economy—Lerner argues that "empathy endows a person with the capacity to imagine himself as a proprietor of a bigger grocery store in a city, to wear nice clothes and live in a nice house, to be interested in 'what is going on in the world' and to 'get out of his hole.'"[30] To elaborate on the particular kind of empathic "enlargement" of the personality required by capitalist modernization, Lerner adopts psychoanalytic terms:

> The mobile person is distinguished by a high capacity for identification with new aspects of his environment; he comes equipped with the mechanisms needed to incorporate new demands upon himself that arise outside of his habitual experience. These mechanisms for enlarging a man's identity operate in two ways. *Projection* facilitates identification by assigning to the object certain preferred attitudes of the self—others are "incorporated" because they are like me . . . *Introjection*

enlarges identity by attributing to the self certain desirable attributes of the object—others are "incorporated" because I am like them or want to be like them. We shall use the word *empathy* as shorthand for both these mechanisms . . . we are interested in empathy as the inner mechanism which enables newly mobile persons to *operate efficiently* in a changing world.[31]

Inverting Mailer and the beats' formulation of the incorporation and introjection of racialized and feminized others as a remedy for the alienation and constriction of bourgeois white existence, Lerner argues that these processes constitute the "enlargements" and adaptations necessary for those newly dislocated from subsistence societies by global capitalism; the ability to "introject" the system and the nation into oneself, and the ability to "incorporate" others into a dynamically expanding system, constitute the fundamental skills that allow one to survive as a newly integrated capitalist worker. Lerner thus imagines the modernization process as a kind of permanent Lacanian mirror stage: through the mass media and contact with development workers, the underdeveloped subject gains a sense of himself as fragmented and incomplete, and constantly "incorporates new demands" in an attempt to attain a psychological wholeness promised, but always deferred, by modernization ideology.[32] Constructing this constant deferral as central to the "developing" consciousness, Lerner acknowledges that a thwarted, "deviant" desire always accompanies the "transitional" subject, making it difficult for him to remain in his "traditional" community: "The true transitional is defined, dynamically, by what he wants to become. What differentiates him from his Traditional peers is a different *latent structure* of aptitudes and attitudes . . . The aptitude is *empathy*—he 'sees' things that others do not see, 'lives' in a world populated by imaginings alien to the constrictive world of others. The attitude is *desire*—he wants really to see the things he has hitherto seen only in his mind's eye, *really* to live in the world he has lived in only vicariously. These are the sources of his deviant ways."[33] Dissatisfaction with one's own community here becomes the sign of the "true," and truly empathic, "transitional."

Throughout his study, Lerner contrasts this anxiously forward-looking "transitional" to the often female "traditional," exemplified by the "illiterate peasant woman" in Lebanon who "had never attended the cinema, had no contact with other media, had never heard of Europe," and who "speaks for extreme rural isolation."[34] Although Lerner explains that this woman's daily routine consists of almost constant contact with other women in her community, it is precisely this regular human contact and integration into her community that constitutes improper empathy and insufficient desire. While Lerner shares with the beat writers a desire to incorporate and render masculine the capacity for empathy, he corrals the potentially unruly permeable selves the beats imagine into a narrow developmentalist trajectory. It is not for the privileged Westerner to cultivate his empathy with the "underdeveloped"; rather, it falls to the "transitional" person to both introject the system in the form of his modern future self and incorporate other "transitionals" into the system along with him.

Curtailing Identification: The Ugly American *and Peace Corps Counterparts*

The Peace Corps, then, responded to anxieties about penetration by communists and racial others, both internal and external, by rejecting the romantic racism evinced by the beats and instead adopting developmentalist constructions of white middle-class "vitality" and bereft local cultures. In a news commentary celebrating the one-year anniversary of the Peace Corps, ABC's Edward Morgan begins to illuminate how the Peace Corps successfully quelled some of these anxieties:

> Just one year old this month, the Peace Corps is by far the bounciest and most promising baby yet spawned on the New Frontier. . . . It is difficult not to become excited about its potential. A year ago it sounded to skeptics like an operation on Cloud Nine, highly impracticable and loaded with dangers of international incidents involving soft young Americans. But except for a mild misunderstanding over a wistfully sincere postcard from Nigeria the record is almost unblemished.[35] With what must be called a touch of genius and a truckload of determination, Shriver and his small staff have recruited a Corps with such a blend of tender idealism and tough practicality that it fairly quivers with esprit and ingenuity. In Ghana, while Washington and Nkrumah were arguing over money for the Volta River project, the all-Negro faculties of four secondary schools elected four white Peace Corpsmen as their headmasters[36] . . . Diplomats with Ivy League degrees are not

going to be displaced en masse by raw-boned striplings from the Peace Corps but there is something to be said for the ambassadorial qualifications of the latter when they include a knowledge of the language and a knowledge of the country based on a two-year hitch in the backlands grappling with primitive but basic problems on ground a chief of mission probably never trod.[37]

Reiterating Shriver and Kennedy's characterization of the Peace Corps as a test of the United States' penetrability, Morgan evokes the fear that the "soft young" volunteers would humiliate the United States in the eyes of the world. But Morgan uses the Peace Corps' own frontier-fantasy imagery to explain that that Peace Corps was able to combat this "softness" by recruiting "raw-boned striplings" who, by "grappling with primitive but basic problems," were able to inspire faith in Third World people to the extent that recently decolonized Ghanaians elected white Americans to leadership positions.

Kennedy and others anticipated and prevented characterizations of a "soft" Peace Corps by using the 1958 best-selling novel *The Ugly American* as a model for their programs. The novel, whose argument is woven through Morgan's speech as well as throughout Peace Corps philosophy and policy, distills into parables a wide variety of fears U.S. policymakers and intellectuals expressed about the status of the Third World during the Cold War. Refuting the vision of racial and gender instability advanced by *On the Road*, *The Ugly American* provides a series of examples of ambassadors at various levels of the State Department who perform racial masquerades in order to seduce gullible natives while remaining steadfastly impenetrable to communism and interracial desire alike. In accordance with the novel's solutions to both external anxiety about Cold War vulnerability and internal anxiety about the stability of racial and gender categories, the Peace Corps constructed this impenetrability as authentic heroism and interracial contact. While Christina Klein convincingly reads *The Ugly American* as one of a set of Cold War texts advocating an imperative of integration as opposed to one of containment, I want to emphasize here the degree to which the novel and admiring organizations like the Peace Corps attempt to limit the integration they recommend. In the novel, as in the Peace Corps, too much love of, or penetrability by, "traditional" cultures leads to dire consequences at the individual and national level.[38]

The Ugly American greatly influenced U.S. foreign policy in the 1960s: in the Cow Palace speech where he announced the formation of the Peace Corps, Kennedy observed that many Americans had "shuddered at the examples in *The Ugly American*."[39] Kennedy reacted not just viscerally to the book, but also at the level of policy: he distributed copies to every one of his fellow senators upon reading it;[40] the Peace Corps took much of its design from the recommendations in the "factual afterword"; and the book's authors, Eugene Burdick and William J. Lederer, later worked as program evaluators for the Peace Corps in the Philippines.[41] Most famously, *The Ugly American* warns that the United States is losing the Cold War in Asia due to a decadent and feminized foreign service, depicting diplomats who speak only English and live in "golden ghettos" rather than among the inhabitants of the fictional country of Sarkhan, where most of the novel takes place.[42] But the novel is equally concerned with rejecting the romantic, anti-technocratic vision advanced by *On the Road*, attempting to demonstrate to readers that Third World adventure, frontier nostalgia, and transnational brotherhood can be attained without the abjection and penetration that the beats experienced in their travels. Indeed, *The Ugly American* preaches against irrational and perverse attractions to Third World peoples, showcasing its most sympathetic protagonists putting on black- and Asian-face to entice docile natives (who are equally susceptible to the wiles of communism and the authentic appeal of U.S. altruism) and solving problems with a technical expertise that transcends politics.

Chief among these protagonists is Colonel Edwin Hillandale, a thinly veiled depiction of advertising executive turned CIA psychological warfare expert Edward Lansdale. In the early 1950s, Lansdale worked in the Philippines, where he was instrumental in crushing the communist Huk rebellion. Lansdale and Philippine general Ramón Magsaysay, whom the United States had handpicked and then pressured the Philippine government to appoint, worked and slept in the same room and called each other "brother" in private.[43] Lansdale advised Magsaysay in psychological warfare to defeat the insurgents and destroy their base of popular support. Magsaysay began offering soldiers cash for Huk bodies; paying media outlets to broadcast anticommunist slogans; exploiting ethnic differences among the insurgents; and murdering and mutilating the Huks in ways that played on local superstitions, as when they killed captured soldiers and drained their bodies of blood to exploit local beliefs in vampires. Magsaysay was rewarded with hundreds of thousands of dollars in campaign contributions from the United States, which helped him win the presidency in 1953.[44]

After Magsaysay became president, Secretary of State John Foster Dulles sent Lansdale to Vietnam, instructing him to "do what [he] did in the Philippines."[45] Lansdale obligingly launched the largest migration in human history, touching off an exodus of Catholics from North Vietnam to South Vietnam by spreading rumors of famine, flood, war, and religious catastrophe throughout the North.[46] Another Peace Corps inspiration, charismatic "jungle doctor " Tom Dooley, gained fame ministering to these "refugees" through his largely fabricated, best-selling anticommunist tract *Deliver Us from Evil*. While in Laos, he wrote of "continually explain[ing] to thousands of [Vietnamese] refugees . . . that only in a country which permits corporations to grow large could such fabulous charity be found."[47] The Peace Corps drew much from his example of charismatic service, capitalist evangelism, carefully tailored publicity, and rhetoric of international brotherhood. In Kennedy's Cow Palace speech he cited the jungle doctor alongside *The Ugly American* as the dual inspirations for the Peace Corps, reminding his audience that "many Americans have marveled at the selfless example of Dr. Tom Dooley in Laos." Dooley's rakish yet devout public persona inspired many Peace Corps volunteers, and the Catholic Cold War networks upon which he relied were instrumental to both the Peace Corps and the Vietnam War.[48]

Like Lansdale and Dooley, the fictional Hillandale possesses a remarkable ability for racial impersonation and intercultural seduction. *The Ugly American* describes Hillandale, nicknamed "the ragtime kid," as "one of those happy, uninhibited people who can dance and drink all night and then show up at eight fresh and rested . . . at two AM he joins the orchestra in a jam session, playing his harmonica close to the mike, improvising Satchmo himself."[49] The "uninhibited" Hillandale's ability to "improvise" Louis Armstrong would have impressed readers, as the book was published on the heels of Armstrong's wildly successful State Department jazz tours, but it also indicates the extent to which this influential novel endorses black- (and Asian-) face performance as a cultural strategy.[50] When he arrives in the Philippines, Hillandale meets with suspicion from the Filipinos, who think he is a "rich, bloated American" until he takes out his harmonica and plays a few bars of the Filipino folk song "Planting Rice Is Never Fun." At once the Filipinos realize their mistake and begin to compete for his attentions. Hillandale "saunters" down the street as the Filipinos "look . . . at each other shyly," and begin to follow him, issuing competing offers to cook lavish meals for him.[51] In a successful deployment of anti-conquest strategies of innocence, which here consist of racialized folk music performance, he has already convinced the Filipinos that he is not rich; after a moment of incredulity, they believe him that his salary is commensurate with their own.[52]

After seducing the Filipinos with his Ragtime Kid persona, Hillandale is sent to Sarkhan, where he accumulates another title: "the six-foot Swami from Savannah." Hillandale performs a minstrel routine upon meeting the Sarkhanese people, charming them "with gesticulations, appealing grimaces, and laughter." Later, he learns the Sarkhanese tradition of palm-reading and asks to read the prime minister's palm in private: "The Ragtime Kid and the Prime Minister closed the door of the study and stayed there for half an hour. What went on inside the study none of the other guests knew. But when the door opened, the two men came out arm in arm, and the Prime Minister was gazing up at The Ragtime Kid with obvious awe."[53] Although Hillandale later reveals that he fabricated a story about Chinese military advances in order to mobilize the Sarkhanese army, the sexual tension in the encounter and reconsolidation of power relations by the end, evident in the secrecy, linked arms, and "obvious awe," informs readers that some manner of seduction has taken place.

Although *The Ugly American* recommends living among Third World peoples and learning enough about their customs to impersonate and seduce them, several of its chapters instruct readers that the seduction must go only one way, cautioning against beat orientalist fantasies. Two of the novel's parables feature otherwise competent and patriotic Americans abroad whose romanticization of "the orient" and "orientals" are recognized and exploited by subversive elements. Providing a model for the Peace Corps, *The Ugly American* recognizes the racial fantasies of the 1950s counterculture and attempts to disavow them and replace them with fantasies of white American leadership and heroics. The first victim of interracial desire, the innovative and generous "chicken man"

Tom Knox, attempts to take a stand against the stagnant Cambodian and international development bureaucracy in favor of bringing chicken enterprises to Cambodia, vowing to go back home and testify before Congress. Unfortunately for Tom, he is driven by orientalist fantasies as well as altruism: "a dream . . . Because of this dream he had never married, and because of this dream he had come to Cambodia . . . certain words meant enchantment to him. Words like 'cinnamon,' or 'saffron,' or 'Malacca Straits,' or 'Hindu' or 'Zamboanga' had magic in them." Communist elements are quick to capitalize on Tom's deviant, orientalist desires: before he can get home to testify, he is bought off by a "French diplomat," who sends him on a trip around the world, replete with rich food and Balinese dancing girls, until he loses his drive to save Cambodia.[54]

An even clearer parable equating romantic racism with susceptibility to deviant sexuality and communism features weapons expert "Captain Boning, USN," who is competently addressing "Asian concerns" at a weapons conference until he meets the beguiling "Doctor Ruby Tsung . . . a professor at Hong Kong university." Boning's friend who introduces them "did not know that Doctor Tsung had also been educated at a special school located on the outskirts of Moscow." Burdick and Lederer further emphasize Tsung's gender deviance (and deviousness) in her physical description, emphasizing her ability to look both feminine and scholarly: "Doctor Tsung looked like an oriental miniature of an English country squire's wife . . . her thick, gold-framed glasses gave her the look of a scholar." The wily Doctor Tsung, in fact, is sent to distract Captain Boning, who begins spending "most of every night with her" until he "comes to know her small body well" and begins to dose off and lose his cool during the day. After Captain Boning flubs a crucial question about thermonuclear bombs, the Asian representatives leave the talks and return "utterly opposed to the installation of atomic weapons in their territory."[55] In this short parable, Burdick and Lederer equate communist subversion, military impotence, and dangerous female power, cautioning that uncontained desire for Eastern cultures and women leaves good men vulnerable to all three.

More suitable models for intercultural relations can be found in the title chapter, which stars Homer Atkins, an "ugly man" with liver-spotted, scarred hands who wears "a rough khaki shirt, khaki pants, and marine boots." He is introduced in a meeting of development planners, where he attempts unsuccessfully to explain Vietnam's development needs to a room full of American, Vietnamese, and French "princes of bureaucracy" wearing "freshly pressed clothes, [running] their clean hands over their smooth cheeks." Of course, Atkins with his calloused hands knows better than these effeminate men, even the Vietnamese ones, what is best for Vietnam. Later in Sarkhan, Atkins models the mirror-stage relationship described by Lerner with the Sarkhanese Jeepo, so called "because of his reputation as a famous mechanic in the maintenance and repair of jeeps." In the tradition of native counterparts beginning with Robinson Crusoe's Friday, Jeepo has only one name to his counterpart's two, a name he skillfully won the right to receive thanks to his participation in the imperial economy. The two men meet and Homer immediately recognizes Jeepo's comparable physical characteristics, and more significantly, Jeepo recognizes and appreciates Homer: "Jeepo was ugly. He was ugly in a rowdy, bruised, carefree way that pleased Atkins. The two men smiled at one another." Later in the scene, as they attempt to sell their design for a new water pump, Jeepo rebukes the narrow-minded "headmen," explaining, "Men that work with their hands and muscles understand one another. Regardless of what you say, I will enter into business with this man if he will have me."[56] Jeepo's ability to see his reflection in Homer separates him from the mistrustful headmen in just the way Lerner suggests that transitionals must separate from their communities. His bold pledge to "enter into business with this man if he will have me" demonstrates how Burdick and Lederer rewrite Mailer and the beats' fantasy of male interracial elopement, policing its homosexual possibilities by emphasizing the business arena and the men's physical unattractiveness while obsessively staging the desire and consent of the nonwhite man.

Homer and Jeepo's partnership depends not only on their mutually recognized ugliness and Jeepo's desire for modernity, but also on the eschewal of explicitly political language and their embrace of neutral, technical fixes to local, regional, and national problems (problems that always, conveniently, are framed and solved by U.S. development workers). When Jeepo is asked to improve on Homer's design for a bicycle-fueled water pump, and the headmen of the tribe mutter with suspicion and dismay, Homer watches Jeepo: "He was quite sure that Jeepo had an answer for these comments, and he was also sure that it was not a personal or political answer, but technical." Through its vision of apolitical brotherhood in which power imbalances disappear and neutral technical skills win the day, *The Ugly American* resolves the Cold War dilemma of reconciling the principles of freedom and equality Americans professed with the U.S. exceptionalism that justified their presence in the Third World. If all things in a global contest were equal, Americans simply possessed more ingenuity and technical skill, which they could transmit to eager natives. Emma Atkins, Homer's wife, teaches the villagers of Cheng Dong how to preserve food (Burdick and Lederer ignore millennia of pickling traditions in Southeast Asia) and singlehandedly cures "the bent backs" of Cheng Dong's elderly by locating longer broom handles so that they can stand upright while they sweep their porches.[57] Thus *The Ugly American*, shaped by modernization theory's universalizing discourses, advances the notion of utterly bereft local cultures while holding out hope for the transmission of technical skill to a few counterparts.

The counterpart ideal modeled in *The Ugly American* found its way into the Peace Corps' philosophy and policy and continues to constitute one of its core principles. As Ecuador volunteer Paul Cowan explains, it was volunteers' job to "find a few local people who were 'natural leaders' and encourage them to create organizations in their *barrios*";[58] in other words, to identify local leaders and model modern, "organized" behavior for them. The concept of the counterpart was drawn not only from frontier mythology, most clearly as it was adapted for the Cold War in *The Ugly American*, but also from the overlapping discourse of modernization theory. In Rostow's sketch of a new, modern class structure for which "men must be prepared," he emphasized the need to create a new capitalist class, suggesting that the endpoint of development work would be the training of a new bourgeoisie. In the Peace Corps' attempt to apply Rostow's top-down model of the transition to industrial capitalism, the goal is to transform these leaders into an elite minority of inventors (like Jeepo), owners, and investors who will prepare the rest of the population for its role of performing "specialized, narrow, recurrent tasks."[59] This training, as Cowan suggests, required Peace Corps volunteers to identify "natural leaders" but not to identify *with* them; the successful transformation of a counterpart hinged on the volunteer's lack of sympathy with local worldviews, and even the dismissal of the idea that other worldviews existed at all.

Returned volunteer and Peace Corps "regional agent" Peter Easton enforces this disavowal of local knowledge in his 1967 assessment of the counterpart system, writing in a *Peace Corps Volunteer* feature that "given some training, given some time, nationals can run this country best. They know it better than anyone else. But they know it, for the most part, in an immediate and unobjective way." Easton explains that "one of our most important jobs is to help make conscious what for our counterparts is mostly unconscious—to get them to objectivize what they know about their own society and put that knowledge to use in answering the question, 'How might we best educate the adults of this country?'"[60] His insistence that counterparts "objectivize" their "unconscious" knowledge brings to mind Frantz Fanon's observation that "for the colonized subject, objectivity is always directed against him."[61] Taking for granted modernization's standard framing of native populations as passive and ahistorical, Easton assumes both that the counterparts have not achieved this double consciousness already, despite the colonial and neocolonial conditions under which the vast majority of them live, and that this adoption of the hegemonic Western gaze is a necessary condition for historical inclusion and progress. Adopting Lerner's model of subaltern possession by the dominant culture and Rostow's imperative of preparing an elite group to prepare the masses to embrace (or at least endure) "modern" modes of production, Easton reiterates the imperative to convince members of the emerging elite to disavow local and indigenous knowledge in order to view their own societies in a detached and utilitarian sense, as human capital rather than fellow community-members.

Easton, like Rostow, frames his comparison of volunteers to counterparts around an assumption of inferior national initiative and masculinity, arguing that volunteers "are endowed, for better or for worse, with a work drive all out of scale with host national character." Despite his assertions of the volunteers' generally superior "national character" and "work drive," Easton claims that the Peace Corps' central task should be to inspire confidence in host communities, attributing African deference to "a residue of respect for the European" and arguing that "until the population, from villagers to high officials, believes in its capacity to administer and lead, it won't really believe in its capacity to follow and change." Easton then proposes step-by-step guidelines for getting counterparts to implement new ideas, arguing that "the tactic can be boiled down to: make suggestions gradually, attach them to live evidence, wherever possible let your counterpart give them final form."[62] Easton argues that volunteers must implement development slowly and subtly, allowing counterparts to "administer and lead" by giving "final form" to modernization projects. As in the palm-reading scene in *The Ugly American*, the counterpart/volunteer relationship requires both racial impersonation and homosocial seduction.

In practice, local counterparts did not turn out to be as gullible or easily awed as the president of Sarkhan. A 1969 *Volunteer* article bemoans the difficulty of guiding counterparts, arguing that "the counterpart idea has lost popularity," and that "at worst, the so-called 'counterpart' is either the *patron* who receives the salary and the credit for what is entirely the Volunteer's work, or the obsequious and incompetent *main d'oeuvre*, who like the old dog, refuses to learn even one new trick."[63] This assessment demonstrates the difficulty of the counterpart idea in practice: the volunteer must convince the counterpart to pretend he has imagined and initiated the "new trick" that modernization theorists and Peace Corps staffers will pressure him to perform in any event, but in the process the volunteer is robbed of credit and compensation for his own frontier ingenuity.

Some mildly countervailing assessments were aired in the *Volunteer*, suggesting that deficiencies in Peace Corps work might not be entirely caused by counterparts' stubbornness and deficient "work drive." In 1967 "Indian Official" B. P. R. Vithal warned volunteers not to "let any number of instances that you may come across create in you any feeling of inherent superiority." Attempting to think through the implications of this equality, Vithal writes himself into a corner, explaining that the roots of the perceived ineffectiveness of counterparts exist within a system:

> If you find your counterpart failing in many respects, remember first what I have already said, that he is not a volunteer like you but an average Indian doing a job to earn his keep. Even so you will find that in terms of moral and intellectual qualities the Indians you could be meeting would be equal to their counterparts in any other society. Every society has its bad and its good. What prevents them from making

their due contribution, however, is not any individual lack in each one of them but the fact that all of them are prisoners of a system. It is the system that prevents the Indian official from giving of his best or from obtaining results even when he does give his best. The system has to be fought, it has to be reformed, and sometimes it has to be broken; but this is the task of the Indian, this is not your task. It is not for you to try and change the system. Your only task is to understand it, and, if possible, to see how with this understanding you can beat it, but it is not for you to undermine it.[64]

Vithal's struggle to assimilate structural analysis of global inequalities into a discussion of volunteers and counterparts shows just how incompatible such analysis was with the Peace Corps' work. At the very heart of Peace Corps philosophy and policy is the attempt to model and enact individual transformation, based on the presumption that poverty and disenfranchisement stem from archaic cultural habits and insufficient "work drive" and "vitality" rather than systemic inequality or exploitation. Because volunteers were discouraged from recognizing the inequalities perpetuated by global capitalism and U.S. interventions, and prohibited from fighting or criticizing those inequalities even if they did recognize them, they could only attribute their counterparts' "ineffectiveness" to personal failings. Thus the idea of the volunteers' "all out of scale . . . work drives" prevailed in the Peace Corps, often reinforcing rather than disrupting their presumption of their own superiority over the rest of the world.

The Peace Corps maintained this presumption of superiority, as I have been suggesting, by limiting volunteers' identification with Third World peoples, sometimes explicitly. A 1965 *Life* article on "the re-entry crisis"—which notes that "somewhat to the surprise and dismay of Peace Corps officials, only a minute 8 percent of volunteers ultimately enter the business world when they get out"—features a profile of "attractive young Peace Corps volunteer Janet Hanneman," who had become "a legend" for her accomplishments in Pakistani hospitals and returned to work at Peace Corps headquarters, calling her "a classic case of the re-entry crisis." *Life* reports that when Hanneman returned, she continued to wear the Pakistani clothing she had become accustomed to during her service until she "received a confidential letter from a high-ranking Peace Corps administrator whom she greatly admired. He told her that she had been wonderful overseas but that her insistence on wearing the Pakistani clothes at home—and the disillusionment with America that this behavior implied—was damaging both her reputation and her value to the Peace Corps."[65] Just as they feared beatniks' overidentification with racialized others, the Peace Corps warned Hanneman that her continued corporeal identification with Pakistan not only represented "disillusionment with America" but would also damage "her reputation," invoking the sexual liaisons that bring down the misguided diplomats in *The Ugly American*. *Life* reports approvingly that the day after reading the letter, Hanneman "went to a smart dress shop on Connecticut Avenue and bought a gold raw-silk suit for $110," relearning the correct identifications and consumption patterns that impel her to buy Asian raw materials only after their modification and refinement by Western tastemakers and manufacturers.[66]

So far in this chapter I have attempted to demonstrate how the Peace Corps, drawing on *The Ugly American* for ideological guidance, attempted to capitalize on, but also to curtail and police, volunteers' identification with counterparts and others in their host countries. But as some of these media accounts suggest, this curtailed identification was not always so neat or easy on the ground. Turning to four volunteer memoirs, the final section explores how these volunteers attempted to carry out their role as trainers and "objectivizers"; how modernization doctrines shaped their perceptions of their counterparts and other local people as well as the work they did; how they attempted to contain their identification with the societies in which they lived and worked; and how different people responded to the volunteers' attempts to transform them.

"Proud Black Prince, How You Could Play Othello": Identification in Volunteer Memoirs

Although he perhaps best articulated and described the fantasies of brotherhood and the volunteer–counterpart relationship that defined the 1960s Peace Corps, Moritz Thomsen was an atypical Peace Corps participant. A volunteer who enlisted in middle age, brought farming experience to his assignment, and was able to amass considerable resources for his development projects due to his successful appeals to readers of his regular *San Francisco Chronicle* columns, Thomsen made a greater impact on the economic structure of his host village than did most volunteers in the 1960s.[67] In doing so, he demonstrated greater ability to enforce modernization objectives than did most volunteers, illustrating and circulating a vision of what Peace Corps success at community development might look like. Thomsen's memoir *Living Poor* demonstrates the confluence of discourses that this chapter has argued shaped the 1960s Peace Corps' claims to authentic masculine heroism: racial identification, frontier mythology, modernization theory, and the characterization of poverty as an existential, spiritual condition. In the tradition of Kerouac, Burdick and Lederer, and the postwar modernization theorists, Thomsen imagines the communities he encounters as a century behind him on the old frontier, and constructs the local men as decorative, exotic objects and mystical beings. He attempts to implement development aims, pushing a few Rio Verdean men to become "objective" outsiders and rational capitalists who then attempt to manipulate, and therefore become alienated from, their communities. The book also demonstrates how the Peace Corps' fraternal ideal of the counterpart silences Third World women, further disenfranchising them and rendering them "objectively" unintelligible.

From the beginning of his stay in Ecuador, Thomsen is guided by the texts of both Cold War anticommunism and frontier nostalgia. Recalling his days of dissatisfaction with his first placement, he writes, "I locked myself in my room for three days and read Ian Fleming novels . . . The next morning I stuffed some CARE seeds in one pocket and a copy of Carl Sandburg's *Abraham Lincoln, the Prairie Years* in the other and went down to the wharf." Framing his journey to the new village through adventure narratives of both the Cold War and the American frontier, Thomsen, sitting rapt by the river, forgets about his last town and his half-finished projects there: "The country of Lincoln, that hard, coarse, brutal America of the 1830's, began to mix in my mind with this river settlement, the floating rafts, the badly fed people in ragged clothing who were bringing in canoe loads of bananas and staggering up the muddy banks to the packing shed."[68] Thomsen's projection of his reading material onto Ecuador demonstrates how development discourse, Cold War imperatives, and frontier fantasies converge in the Peace Corps: if "developing" countries are traveling behind the United States on the path to modernity, and if a romanticized-yet-brutal history of conquest modernized the United States and Europe, Cold War and capitalist ventures to secure the resources of the Third World, whatever Bond-style subterfuge or coercion they required, were natural and justified.

Fantasies of transforming feminized and matriarchal communities shaped Thomsen's work in Rio Verde, the town in which he settled. Synthesizing the beats' romantic–racist rhapsodizing with social science characterizations of poverty as gender and familial dysfunction, Thomsen diagnoses Rio Verdeans as part of "a tormented race, still without an identity, still searching for the qualities which will describe its soul," and claims almost in the same breath that Rio Verde is "matriarchal by default, and secretly." While he acknowledges that the women have no political power or legal rights, he argues that they, "with a fierce but hidden dedication which must spring from a feeling for order and a maternal impulse to protect their children, somehow keep the society from falling apart." The men, he argues, are "not working models but something decorative . . . to beautify the beach, to hang indolently from the windows of houses, and to brighten up the shady places" with faces that are "fragile and delicate, vulnerable as the blooms of maimed flowers."[69]

Even as he eroticizes the "decorative," "delicate" men of Rio Verde, Thomsen fulfills the other side of Peace Corps modernization imperatives by arguing that the Rio Verdeans' gender and sexual deviance must be remedied. Constructing the men as tragically impotent and in need of Western influences, he argues that "great lovers are nourished on roast beef and mashed potatoes, cream sauces and soufflés, not rice and platano. And yet, inexplicably, this is contradicted by the large size of their families." Thomsen seems to resolve this "inexplicable" contradiction, to characterize the Rio Verdean men as feminine (underdeveloped, penetrable) while acknowledging their large families, by attributing the family size to the pathologically maternal women of Rio Verde. Imagining the men as lacking control of the unruly bodies of "their" women, Thomsen demonstrates the logic that underlay the modernization-fueled population control campaigns of the 1960s as well as the Moynihan report and other anti-maternal tracts that gained popularity in the era.

Diagnosing Rio Verde as deviantly matriarchal, Thomsen attempts to transform the village, motivating a few villagers, most notably his protégé, counterpart, and "new brother" Ramón, to embark on lives of capitalist production. When Ramón tells Thomsen, "You should have a little more respect for our customs," Thomsen replies, "But that's the only reason I'm here. To destroy your crazy customs." Thomsen consistently uses the vocabulary of destruction and eradication as he formulates his plans for transforming Rio Verde, as when he speaks to his "cooperative" about their new business venture: "It was going to be a new kind of store, I explained. I wanted to destroy the strictly noncompetitive Latin idea."[70] Thomsen persists, despite the Rio Verdeans' attempts to tell him they do not want to amass wealth, pouring resources into a farming "cooperative" which soon dwindles to three people.

Because he has the greatest share in the cooperative, Ramón becomes "the richest man in town"; Thomsen brags that "his income jumped from around eight dollars a month to more than thirty." Ramón immediately wants to use his earnings to buy nice clothes and luxury items for his family, but Thomsen encourages him to reinvest his surplus, suggesting "rather obstinately that he use this money instead to hire workers to clear more jungle land, to plant more corn, and to think about two hundred chickens instead of one hundred." Determined to transform at least one villager into a capitalist, Thomsen pushes Ramón to expand his chicken enterprise until Ramón becomes anxious and miserable. He tells Thomsen (whom the Rio Verdeans call Martín): "Listen, Martín, it is not all my fault; it is your fault, too, because I always had it in my mind that I could dominate about six chickens, and at most a dozen, but seventy-three? My God. Before you came, we were living in blindness, yes, in blindness, and now we can see, but the change is very hard, and the one thing I am learning is that perhaps the pain and suffering of not being poor are worse than that blind poverty we lived in before."[71] Ramón's adoption of the development worldview and practices, which he here equates with revelatory sight, has both alienated him from the other villagers and convinced him of the invalidity of their cultural reality. With his life now organized around "dominating" chickens rather than the communal coping strategies that the other Rio Verdeans use to deal with both scarcity and capitalist encroachment, Ramón both suffers and sees no way out. He has entirely abandoned the worldview of his community (the "pre-modern" condition Kerouac's Sal imagines as "silence"), and has fully adopted the development model, in which all indigenous knowledge must be disavowed and economic rationality must become the basis for human relations, no matter how painful the process might be.

Thomsen continues to coach Ramón in proper investments, "enlarging" Ramón's worldly desires precisely in the way Lerner prescribes. Although he chronicles the pain and conflict that accompany Ramón's comparatively astronomical wealth, Thomsen's investments in the development model leave him no alternative but to mourn the alienation his intervention has caused. Here, Thomsen attempts to ventriloquize both the townspeople and the "middle-class storekeepers":

> Ramón with his composition roof was *egoisto*, the maverick; roofing a house with Eternit that would collect rain water, in this town of thatched roofs, had separated Ramón from the people. Ramón wanted a million things—a refrigerator, a larger house, a store-bought bed for the son he expected, and, not least, the respect of the middle-class storekeepers in Esmeraldas with whom he had done business all his life as just an undifferentiated shadow in the doorway, another beach *zambo*. Ramón didn't want to be poor anymore, and he was riding for a fall. The people had a growing contempt for his ambition and his aggressiveness and he, a growing contempt for their lack of drive, their acceptance of the old ways. The time will come when he will have to find a middle-class environment where he can be at ease.[72]

Thomsen's idea that the storekeepers view Ramón as "just an undifferentiated shadow in the doorway" echoes his earlier characterization of Rio Verdean men as decorative objects, "hang[ing] indolently from the windows of houses." These passages together suggest again the "differentiation," gender and otherwise, that modernization theorists and development workers attempted to impose on their allegedly precapitalist subjects. Thomsen also adopts modernization logic in assuming the inevitability of Ramón's trajectory, an inevitability that allows him to absolve himself for coercing his counterpart into a life of painful alienation. Having fulfilled his role as the counterpart and moved "forward" in time and into the capitalist world, Ramón must continue to use his newfound "ambition and aggressiveness" to manipulate and exploit his fellow villagers.

Despite his culpability in pushing Ramón into a "differentiated," antagonized, and alienated place in the village, Thomsen serves his two years and leaves Rio Verde behind, as he is supposed to. Directly before the last scene in *Living Poor*, he digresses into an explanation of his relationship to the women in the town, explaining that "the women of Ecuador lived in the other room; they appeared when it was time to serve you; they were very much the property of the men. Even my relationship with Ramón's wife, Ester, had always been very correct and almost formal. Ecuadorian women were not trained to be companions nor did they know how to carry on a conversation, and Ester, very typical, had always been reticent and shy, always in the background." Thomsen's characterization of the women contradicts his earlier claims that they run a secret matriarchy, but both descriptions seem like caricatures at best. He can only see the Rio Verdean women as silent and frozen in time, preservers of matriarchy or always "in the other room," as the men advance into the twentieth century. The last paragraph of the memoir depicts both Ramón's transformation, the path from "blindness" to leadership aggressively prescribed by Thomsen and illuminated by the "light of America," and Ester's utter unintelligibility:

> [Ramón] wanted to make a sign to hang outside the house by the gate—"Luz de America"—the Light of America. Ah, Ramón, proud, black prince, how you could play Othello. So I drank the coffee . . . and then I said good-by to Ester, and everything was under control, everything like a dream. But as I stepped down off the porch to leave, Ester screamed, and I turned to see her, her face contorted, and the tears streaming down her cheeks. We hugged each other, and Ramón rushed from the house and stood on the brow of the hill looking down intently into the town.[73]

Although Thomsen never records a word Ester speaks, he uses his characteristic claims to clairvoyance—a clairvoyance Ramón seems to have inherited as he, overcoming his former blindness, "[looks] down intently into the town"—to frame her scream as one of grief and thwarted desire. Ester functions here to articulate Thomsen's desire for Ramón and grief at leaving him and to demonstrate the extent to which the "proud black prince" (correctly goaded into modernity and patriarchy, in contrast with Kerouac's anticapitalist Mexican "queen") has become his counterpart and successor. But Ester's actions remain entirely unexplained: does she recognize that Thomsen has, Iago-like, sowed paranoia, destroyed their relationship with the community and then abandoned them without finding them a "middle-class environment" in which they can feel comfortable? Does she recognize the new position in which Thomsen has placed Ramón? Does she fear being married to the hated *patrón* of Rio Verde who is already surveying his domain even before Thomsen is out of sight? Because Thomsen depicts Ester's body without recording her words or otherwise granting her subjectivity, any interpretation necessarily relies on the scant evidence of women's agency that *Living Poor*, shaped by the homosocial ideals that fueled the early Peace Corps, provides.

Although Thomsen's memoir reveals the ways in which Peace Corps volunteers were trained to view the poor communities they encountered around the world through the lens of development ideology, thus characterizing these communities in the language of social/familial disorganization and deprivation, other volunteer accounts from the 1960s reveal the limitations of this liberal developmental frame. Memoirs by Paul Cowan, Leonard Levitt, and Ed Smith indicate that many volunteers, with varying degrees of consciousness, sought out different ways of relating to and seeing the communities among whom they lived. At the very least, these volunteers are haunted by the possibility of seeing the students and communities they were attempting to develop as more than culturally bereft vessels waiting for modernity. In each case, however, the universal descriptive and prescriptive tenets of modernization theory prevent the volunteers from either connecting the poverty they see to imperialist and capitalist exploitation or seeing the Third World cultures they encounter as in any way functional or valuable.

Paul Cowan's memoir *The Making of an Un-American* provides one example of how the discourses of modernization theory and romantic racism informed volunteers' thinking about poverty, particularly black poverty, at home. An Ecuador Peace Corps volunteer, Freedom Summer participant, and SDS activist, Cowan writes retrospectively about his early adoption of both romantic racism and modernization theory and his later attempts to reject both ideologies. Cowan recalls his yearning for contact with nonwhite peoples, which resembles Kerouac's melancholic desire to "exchange worlds." But his orientation also differs from beat romanticism; following developmentalist analysis of the new, racialized poor as lacking "internal vitality," he imagines his ability to bestow that vitality through unsolicited physical contact with black boys: "There is a kind of Jesus Christ complex that many middle-class whites bring to their relations with people they consider oppressed. I'd be walking down a street in Chicago, for example, notice a black child who looked broke and unhappy, and reach out my arm to touch his head. I felt that the mere fact of my attention would change the poor lad's life—my generosity would flow through my arm and convert to good fortune once it entered his brain—what a spreading, luxurious sense of power that thought afforded!"[74] In Cowan's recollection of touching the children and the fantasy that accompanied these actions, the "cultural dowry" has changed hands; it is now the job of the white man to bestow virility and authenticity on racialized poor communities. Cowan's fantasy of penetrating the black child's mind, consolidating his power and masculine identity through violent and unsolicited benevolence, revises the beat adventure by removing the sense of vulnerability that the beats exposed and explored.

After a frustrating Freedom Summer during which black activists largely rejected his paternalism, Cowan joined the Peace Corps. He recalls that during his civil rights work, despite the fact that "in conversations with other integrationists [he] had used the Peace Corps as a symbol of the patronizing attitude toward poor people we were all trying to love," he "had always felt a special respect for [his] contemporaries who volunteered for the organization" and "thought secretly that they were more compassionate and dedicated than [he] was." In the volunteers' silent toil, Cowan found evidence that perhaps the volunteers were the most authentic activists of all, attaining "salvation by works" by staying two years in remote villages.[75] Cowan's invocation of "salvation by works," not entirely cynical even in retrospect, suggests that he has not quite rid himself of the "Jesus Christ complex," informed by the modernization theory that constructed "the poor" as culturally bereft and in need of penetration by "vital" white men.

Although he never quite shed his "Jesus Christ complex," Cowan did worry during his Peace Corps training in 1966 about the condescension evinced by both himself and his trainers as well as the technocratic approach the agency took in its community development work. He and his wife and fellow Ecuador volunteer, Rachel, identified the connections between modernization theory and domestic social science, indicating the pervasiveness in the 1960s of views that the nonwhite global poor were uniformly "disorganized" and that this disorganization in fact caused their poverty:

A returned volunteer had been describing the standard method of community development to us. His ideas were new to me—I hadn't realized that the Peace Corps took such a mechanistic view of its work in foreign communities—but Rachel said that she had heard dozens of similar lectures during her two years at the University of Chicago's School of Social Service Administration. His operating assumption was that the slum dwellers with whom [we would] work would be totally disorganized. Most of them would be recent immigrants from rural villages who had come to the city in search of work, but found themselves jobless and confused, even more disoriented than the people who had remained in the *campo*. To accomplish the project's objectives, then, we would have to act as "catalysts" and teach them to work together harmoniously.

The Peace Corps, then, attempted to embody and codify the transaction Cowan attempts to enact by touching the black child, the osmotic transmission of virility and vitality to underdeveloped and disorganized racial others. To some extent, Cowan is able to criticize the way the Peace Corps channeled his romantic desire to bestow his presence on a poor black child into the technocratic language of development. After futile attempts to "organize" Guayaquil's slums, Cowan writes that his project is "doomed to failure" because the Peace Corps officials in charge of the program "believed that Ecuadoreans were striving so hard to achieve the things that North Americans had already obtained that they would subordinate themselves to the tutelage of any representative of the United States," and that "their training and their careers prohibited them from seeing the problem of poverty as a class issue." But while he resists Peace Corps official doctrines and realizes that his own presence in the *barrios* is doing nothing to alleviate the poverty of Ecuadoreans or change the socioeconomic structure of the country, Cowan uses the language of modernization theory to describe Guayaquil:

> If an outsider continues to perceive the "*movimiento*" in Guayaquil's streets as an inexplicable sort of frenzy, he will certainly use the word "disorganized" when he describes the city's poor, as our instructors did in training. But the situation can be more accurately summarized by the observation that the *mestizos* who compose the bulk of Guayaquil's population have at least as much energy and ambition as did the immigrants from Europe to America in the nineteenth century, but not

nearly as much focus for their drives. They are not yet comfortable with the modern technology that originally attracted them to the city. They are trying to leap centuries in a single decade, and in a country where even slow upward mobility is still restricted.

If one does not judge Ecuadoreans by the exact standards one has learned in the United States, it is possible to say that a beggar who works a twelve-hour day in Guayaquil is displaying the same kind of energy and initiative as a hawker in Juarez or an advertising man [in New York]. A street vendor labors at least as hard as a steelworker in Gary. But their circumstances are entirely different from those of most Americans. As Ecuadorian society is structured at present, it is impossible for them to find genuinely productive labor.[76]

Even as he attempts to question his trainers' characterizations of "disorganization" as the root cause of poverty, Cowan reiterates the development logic that underlies these characterizations. Accepting the inevitable trajectory suggested by modernization theory, he compares the urban mestizo class, which has the "energy and ambition" of the assimilation-bound nineteenth-century white immigrants and is trying to "leap centuries in a single decade" with a stagnant indigenous class, incapable of "genuinely productive labor." The distinction Cowan draws between the authentic productivity of the American steelworker or "advertising man" and the ersatz productivity of the Ecuadorean street vendor or beggar reveals the extent to which the Peace Corps was able to advance a vision of authenticity opposing that which the beats presented, attributing "genuine" productivity to managerial workers while constructing the labors of racialized poor people, particularly those not fully integrated into the capitalist system, as inauthentic and unproductive.

The Peace Corps' assurances of the backwardness and cultural dysfunction of the objects of development, compared with the level of (Western) knowledge they actually possessed, was sometimes stark enough that volunteers were left amazed and unprepared. Jim King, a Nigeria volunteer who taught science at a teachers' college, was surprised to learn that despite its "bush bush bush bush BUSH" location, the school "didn't really need a science teacher but that I was forced down their throats by the Ministry of Education" (and that the village had pushed four teachers from their homes to accommodate him). King was further dismayed to learn that he did not find the low-level students for whom he was prepared; he wrote home in 1966, "I should have known that Peace Corps was feeding us a bunch of bull when it said that we would only have to teach at the primary level since these people had no background. My students seem to know almost as much as I do."[77] King illustrates, and somewhat undermines, modernization theory's assumption that "traditional" peoples have "no background," an assumption which discounts non-Western forms of knowledge but that also erases extensive histories of contact with Western knowledge throughout the postcolonial world.

Tanganyika volunteer Leonard Levitt, though less reflective than Cowan and King about his own privilege and power, also worked to reconcile Peace Corps developmentalist characterizations of Africans as passive, dormant, and disorganized with the complex, dynamic people and societies he encountered. His memoir *An African Season* documents his modernization-theory-tinged perceptions of the high school boys he taught; he writes that "in a word—these kids were bright. But more than bright, they were eager," and that "they weren't afraid to speak up, these kids, and they would ask good sensible questions about the lesson we had just had." Levitt then attempts to explain the boys' shortcomings as students, using the language of cultural and specifically "scientific" deprivation:

> But bright and eager as they were, these boys, they just didn't know anything. Not that they were stupid or dull or that they couldn't learn, no, nothing like that—just look how quickly they had picked up the math. And in fact their English was not so bad at all, certainly good enough to understand what I was saying most of the time, and remember that they had just begun to speak English in grade four, which was only three years ago. No, it was nothing like that, it was just—well, in math they were so slow . . .
>
> But more than that—it wasn't merely math—they didn't seem to have any conception of things. Take science, for example. I brought them to the house once to demonstrate that water has more than one form, showing them the fridge, taking out a tray of ice cubes. Warily, they stuck out their fingers . . . and jumped back with squeals. Standing there, licking their fingers, stupefied—how could anything be so cold?—with no idea at all what they'd touched . . .
>
> Or when I had happened to show them a picture one day, something I had cut out of some magazine, of two sailors standing on a bridge of a ship in the harbor, the sun shining on the water, the skyline

of New York in the background. They had no idea what it was all about. Not the skyline—of course, they couldn't be expected to know what skyscrapers look like—but they didn't even know these men were on a ship. They didn't know that it was a ship, they didn't notice that these were uniforms, they just stared blankly, shaking their heads.

The two examples Levitt uses to demonstrate the boys' lack of "science" knowledge—their inability to identify ice (oddly anticipating the first lines of Gabriel García Márquez's 1967 anticolonial masterwork, *One Hundred Years of Solitude*, which equate the discovery of ice with the arrival of violent imperialist modernity) and their unfamiliarity with sailors in New York Harbor—are remarkable for their cultural specificity: of course the Tanganyikan boys have not seen snow or the New York Harbor. However, Levitt uses these examples to demonstrate the boys' lack of training in scientific inquiry and their inability to recognize the trappings of a modern nation: that they do not recognize the all-male, militarized environment of the sailing ship or even "notice that these were uniforms" signals, for Levitt, just how culturally bereft they are. Levitt's depictions connect his students' lack of modern knowledge to their unmanaged and therefore primitive, animalistic bodies: they "squeal," "licking their fingers," "stupefied," "with no idea at all what they'd touched." In his subsequent musings, he attempts to reconcile the intelligence he sees in class with their lack of "scientific" knowledge: "And how easy it would be to say, Well, they just don't know anything, they must be stupid or dull. But no, that wasn't it at all. It was just that when you got hold of these boys—even here in Standard 700—you were practically dealing with a clean slate. A real *Tabula Rasa*. As if they knew literally nothing about anything."[78] For Levitt, as for the theorists of "cultural poverty" and Peace Corps architects alike, local knowledge amounts to "practically" nothing at all; practically in the sense that their knowledge is of little importance to anyone, but also in the sense that it is of minimal use to the modernization mission; in fact, local knowledge must be effaced if the modernization mission is to make sense. Levitt's description of the boys as blank slates, whose very personhood depends on the "enlargement" of their desires through exposure to "science" in the form of technology and capitalism, signals his attempts to turn the children into Lernerian "transitionals." At the same time, his use of the qualifiers "as if" and "literally" suggest that maybe he is not quite willing to construct the students he knows so well as entirely without history and knowledge; he struggles with attributing utter blankness to the boys, but in the end is content to do so.

African American Ghana volunteer Ed Smith, writing in his journal in the early 1960s, seems to struggle much harder than Levitt to move beyond the framework of cultural deprivation in assessing and understanding the Ghanaian children he teaches. When he listens to a volunteer couple disparaging their students, he rejects the racism they evince. However, influenced by his training in social science constructions of underdevelopment, Smith lacks alternative frameworks through which to approach his students and understand the knowledge they bring to the classroom:

> The girl mumbled something about the girls in her school being stupid, anyway. No doubt she thought they ought to go back to the trees too . . .
>
> What the hell could any teacher expect of girls who for generations have been taught that education is for men; that the woman's place is at the home, looking after her kids and obeying her husband? And how could this girl's fiancé expect Ghanaian male students to perform mechanical tasks with the adeptness of American kids when many of them had never seen a screwdriver before?
>
> But then they weren't so different from teachers I knew back in the states who worked with "culturally deprived" kids . . . Every now and then a rough contempt broke through to permanently scar that flawless surface. What really troubles me is the thought that all volunteers are having more than some difficulty accepting their children at _whatever_ level of achievement they find them, and—even sadder—seeing Ghana through the hopes and aspirations of Ghanaian eyes.[79]

Here Smith begins to recognize the cultural specificity of the "intelligence"—or lack thereof—that the other Peace Corps teachers attribute to their students, but stops with this insight: he neither connects the students' "deprivation" to the colonial governance structures that constricted and exploited Ghanaians until 1957 nor considers that different gauges of "level of achievement" might be possible in postcolonial societies. He does, however, reach for these ideas, lamenting that volunteers have so much trouble "seeing Ghana through the hopes and aspirations of Ghanaian eyes." And though he cannot quite explain it, Smith is painfully aware of the damage that the teachers' developmentalist perspective causes their students, in contrast to teachers like Sierra Leone volunteer Elizabeth R. Roseberry, who earnestly attempted to impart to their students a sense of their own deficiencies. Roseberry wrote in her journal that in her health science class, "since one student brought up the point that all had equal ability to do school work I spent a little time on the influence of heredity and environment on individuals."[80]

In contrast with Levitt's attempts to teach his "blank slates" to use their senses, or Kerouac's ecstatic depiction of the "silent" precapitalist Mexicans, then, Smith argues that a Ghanaian worldview exists, with its own "hopes and aspirations" that may or may not dovetail with the universalizing development mission. Smith also argues here that the Peace Corps volunteers construct Ghanaians as blind, unable to see without Western instruction. But even as he critiques other volunteers for their inability to imagine a Ghanaian worldview, Smith remains suspicious of his Ghanaian friends' analysis of their own situation. In particular, he rejects their Marxist analysis of colonialism, emphasizing the "philosophical and psychosocial" aspects of racism rather than exploitation and unequal power relations:

> Ghanaians were always more willing to talk about the oppression of Ghanaians at the hands of the European overseer, but I wasn't so sure they saw in the plight of the Negro in America that very same kind of oppression, nor even considered "racial injustice" at the core of both. I was right. It was "political" or "economic" expedience that moved the colonialist to behave the way he did: thus it must be the same with the Afro-American and *his* master in the States. That "racial injustice" had philosophical and psycho-social implications just didn't occur to them . . .[81]

Smith thus constructs his inability to connect with Ghanaians as a lack of empathy on their part alone, imagining their deficiency much as Lerner characterized the deficiency of the "underdeveloped," as a lack of "enlargement" of "imagination." That McCarthyism has curtailed his own capacity for economic analysis is not a possibility that occurs to him. Instead, imagining that the psychological and philosophical implications of racism "just didn't occur" to Ghanaians who have just emerged from British colonial rule, Smith asserts his own superiority even as he desperately seeks inclusion in a Pan-Africanist project.

Though I will return in chapter 4 to the question of international solidarity within the space of development, these attempts by Smith, Levitt, and Cowan suggest the many ways that volunteers both failed at and questioned the modernization mission. The next chapter takes up these questions of dissent and failure more systematically, considering the contradictory and difficult work female volunteers faced as they attempted to imagine and carry out development projects in the spaces that the political and popular imaginary had designated proving grounds for frontier masculinity.

3

BREAKING THE BONDS
Decolonization, Domesticity, and the Peace Corps Girl

"MILLIONS OF INDIANS STILL SIT in their mountains waiting for history to begin," intones Walter Cronkite during the opening shots of *So That Men Are Free*, a 1962 short film about Vicos, Peru, a community that just two years later would become the site of a much-discussed Peace Corps debacle. "At Vicos history has begun, prodded into life by ideas springing directly from the American Revolution."[1] Indeed, ten years after Cornell anthropologist Allan Holmberg bought the community of Vicos from a Peruvian *patrón* in an attempt to create a laboratory for the implementation of modernization theory, the community had become a potato-growing enterprise with an annual income of $20,000. Through a series of shots depicting a disorderly and downtrodden population gradually corralled into orderly classrooms and town meetings, the film emphasizes this economic transformation to the modern capitalist order—the anthropologists' "gringo magic" (seed, fertilizer, and insecticide) that initiated the "great leap for [the Vicosinos] into the twentieth century world of science, commerce, and cash"—as well as racial and cultural eradication, arguing that "the Indian in modern clothes, speaking Spanish, thinking like a modern Peruvian, becomes *mestizo*, as modern immigrants became American."[2] Adopting the anthropologists' developmental logic, the film casts indigenous communities as passive (ignoring Vicos's long history of labor struggles)[3] and anachronistic. They can attain timeliness, freedom, and wealth, it suggests, only if they follow the example of the "modern immigrants" to the United States and leave behind their communal cultural practices in favor of nationalist and capitalist subjection.

Despite the title's focus on men, Cronkite assures the audience that women also figured into the development agenda at Vicos. Although "equality for girls took longer," Holmberg has taught the women how to make and sell lace instead of working in the fields and weaving "rough cloth" as they had done before. Holmberg also urged the men of Vicos to serve in the army, so that they "return now, speaking Spanish, with new ideas of a wife, one who can sew modern clothes, things both to wear and to sell. One observer said it is strange but suddenly an industrial revolution has everything to do with the deepest desires of a woman." Though no indigenous women (nor any women or indigenous people at all) are interviewed in the film, Cronkite and Holmberg alike presume that the Vicosinas' deepest desires are for containment, to stay home and make lace while the men join the army and return to the town as economic and political leaders.[4] The film declares the Vicos experiment a success and explains that it is "now a model for the U.S. Peace Corps, Peruvian agencies, the United Nations." The last scene depicts the Vicosinos celebrating "their independence day . . . the greatest fiesta Vicos has ever seen," while Holmberg smiles from a balcony, presiding benevolently over the party.[5] Holmberg's own report uses similar, if slightly less hyperbolic, language to describe the change in the Vicosinos, arguing that "it has been possible . . . to design a modest program of technical assistance and education which has gained fairly wide acceptance and has helped to awaken most members of the community to new opportunities for improving their lot through their own efforts."[6]

When the Peace Corps arrived in 1962, Holmberg stayed on, "carefully measur[ing] every aspect of Volunteer life over a period of two years."[7] Even after the Vicosinos voted to expel their Peace Corps volunteers in March 1964, Holmberg and two other Cornell anthropologists prepared a 329-page report to uncover the reasons for the expulsion. The anthropologists conclude in the report that while "the Volunteers fulfilled one of the three missions [of the Peace Corps] by contributing to the development of a critical country in the South American region," they fell out of favor with the villagers by flaunting their wealth and engaging in other faux pas.[8] "Allan," a Harvard-educated volunteer, behaved particularly egregiously: he "tried to use a new method of castrating a friend's donkey, and the donkey died, angering the friend's father and causing the friend to run away from home"; "irritated his Peruvian counterparts by building a corral for two horses behind their dormitory";

then "knocked down a pedestrian with his vehicle in nearby Huaraz, and incurred the wrath of police when he tried to 'arrange' the consequences of the accident." The report attributes Allan's behavior to carelessness and cultural unawareness, but argues that the "psychological gulf" created by the inequality of wealth is most clearly to blame.[9]

The anthropologists are less forgiving of the female volunteers. They argue that the "physical narcissism of young females" precipitated the expulsion, claiming in the report that "physical behavior by a few young Peace Corps Volunteers that proved provocative to others created a certain number of inefficiencies among other Volunteers and in relationship with male Peruvians." The report finds one volunteer's behavior especially egregious, stating that "the physical message of sexual promise this Volunteer conveyed to another Volunteer was so great compared to the reality of fulfillment that this frustration, combined with cultural shock and other factors, rendered the male Volunteer completely unfit to work in Peru." The anthropologists found two female narcissists in their Vicos sample, both characterized by "excessive grooming" and reported that while the female narcissists taught sewing and home demonstration courses that "made 'distinct gains' for the women in Vicos," they nonetheless "ranked among the lowest of the volunteers" and "made no significant contribution toward strengthening any organizations in Peru."[10]

What can Holmberg and the Peace Corps' inculpation of women volunteers' bodies and utter dismissal of their work, following so closely on the heels of their proclamation of "equality for woman" in Vicos, tell us about development and American liberalism more generally? What is it about the 1960s development mission that renders women volunteers both irresistible fantasy objects and intolerable obstacles? If, as I argued in the previous chapter, the Peace Corps drew on and redirected the interracial homosocial desires that defined 1950s oppositional youth culture in order to construct an aura of vitality around male development workers, this chapter considers how the Peace Corps, as well as the American popular imaginary, invested women volunteers with a more complicated symbolic power. In different moments, the female volunteer symbolized a young, naïve America desired by the entire world; the aspirations for freedom of newly independent nations, to be contained by a development romance with responsible and tough American leaders; and a symbol of the persistent idea of American innocence, a location where the violence inherent in the development mission could be exposed and countered.

This chapter traces these fantasies through the 1960s, first discussing how the Kennedy administration and the Peace Corps attempted to fit female volunteers into its anti-domestic masculine vision, using frontier nostalgia to construct an iconography and vocabulary of separate spheres where women's work with "traditional" female counterparts was considered both marginal and necessary. After considering these official depictions of women, I trace a different popular image of the Peace Corps girl that circulated alongside the organization's ideal, frequently appearing in newspaper features and populating romance, action/adventure, and pornographic novels, books which use formulaic narrative strategies to articulate and contain her desire for independence and to connect that containment to the United States' attempts to contain and manage anticolonial liberation struggles. The next section returns to the various ways women volunteers were figured as problems, reading these volunteers' writings to consider how they understood both the violence of the Cold War development project and their marginality to that project. The final section of the chapter attends to the way women volunteers imagined their own fantasies and desires in connection with both development discourse and feminism, arguing that development made it difficult for them to imagine collective action as a response to injustice.

Pioneer Women on the New Frontier: Women Volunteers in the Peace Corps Vision

In October 1964, Peace Corps associate director Warren Wiggins, author of "A Towering Task," gave a recruiting speech at the all-female Douglass College titled "Who Are We," which he identified as "the first speech delivered by a senior staff officer just about *women* in the Peace Corps." Wiggins's text diverges considerably from the agency's standard recruiting speeches: he begins by confessing that "the opportunity to visit your campus stirred a ripple of excitement in our headquarters." Noting the "convocation of lovely ladies," Wiggins attempts to outline the status of women in the Peace Corps, interspersing an argument about equality-in-difference with expressions of titillation at the spectacle of women volunteers:

> But when a woman is outstanding in the Peace Corps, she is known as an outstanding volunteer—not as an outstanding woman volunteer. Right from the outset in Peace Corps service, Volunteers carry identical responsibilities. Selection for service is completely without regard to sex. No attempt is made to strike a balance between men and women. Those fit to serve, go. Overseas, duties and work sites are assigned according to capabilities or aptitudes. Volunteers go where they can handle the job to be done. Is it any wonder that we have to stop and think, now, about this curious notion of "women" in the Peace Corps? Well, what about these women?
>
> First of all, they are feminine. Successful women—executives, scientists, authors—often have to trade their great talents for some loss of femininity. Charm, no. Of that, there may be plenty. But in those special, indescribable qualities that men prize and women enjoy, just a little something is lacking, sometimes. What is wonderful about the average Peace Corps volunteer who happens to be a girl is that she manages to stay attractive and feminine under the most trying of circumstances. She cares about her appearance, even while carrying very heavy responsibility, often isolated from familiar friends, food, and surroundings. And if you meet them on the job—or off—at graduation from training or on return from a two year assignment abroad—you will know what I mean. They are as feminine a bunch as you are likely to find. I guess a lady is a female who just naturally makes a man want to act like a gentleman. Such is the way of our Volunteers.[11]

Throughout the speech, Wiggins vacillates between emphasizing the "femininity" of the volunteers—their ability to be "prized" by men—and asserting their equal status, arguing that "we've built what we believe to be—now that you've made us think about it—the only working institution in America where women share equally in every opportunity and every responsibility—indeed, where the very notion of 'equality for women' rings foreign and strange, so fundamental is it to our way of doing things."[12] The idea that the Peace Corps does not imagine its women volunteers as "women" seems at odds with Wiggins's emphasis on the women's valiant maintenance of their femininity "under the most trying of circumstances," and in fact contradicts the agency's hiring policies, reflected in both the lack of women in staff positions and the gender-specific nature of many of the volunteer positions they sought to fill.[13] But this contradiction seems to be the point: by refusing even to consider "women" as a discrete category of volunteers, the Peace Corps could both imagine itself as a rugged frontier meritocracy and relegate its thinking about "women" to a private, sexualized realm.

By trumpeting the unprecedented opportunity for "equal responsibility" and adventure the Peace Corps presents (while promising them they will not lose their ineffable feminine qualities), Wiggins also acknowledges the dissatisfaction of many middle-class, college-educated women with the options the domestic containment regime offered them. This strain of his argument echoes Betty Friedan's *The Feminine Mystique*, published a year earlier, in which Friedan constructed an ideal of side-by-side adventure within established patriarchal structures, arguing for equality by nostalgically claiming that "the women who went west with the wagon trains also shared the pioneering purpose," and invoking women who "moved beside their husbands on the old frontiers" and accompanied them in "conquering the land."[14] Here, as well as in her commitment to ending the "mother–son devotion which can produce latent or overt homosexuality," Friedan's diagnosis of domestic containment as damaging to masculinity and heterosexuality dovetailed perfectly with that of the white male social scientists. Her prescription likewise looked very much like the nostalgic frontier heroism imagined by the Kennedy administration, which constructed the Third World as a location of escape from stifling domesticity while imposing strict, often paradoxical guidelines for women's roles in those fantasies.[15]

These guidelines for the specific work for women on the nostalgia-infused frontiers of the Cold War era were clarified by the Kennedy administration deputy assistant secretary for public affairs Katie Louchheim in a November 1961 address to the National Council of Negro Women. In this speech, Louchheim asserts that the "freedom" the United States is obliged to spread beyond the Cold War's "new frontiers, dangerous frontiers" depends not only on "the courageous, forthright, and far-sighted men" in power but also on women's willing subordination and occupation of domestic space, as well as their willingness to impose that domestic space on other women. "The countries of the world," she explains, "need large numbers of trained women . . . to teach children and adults how to use spoons, how to sleep on beds, how to wear shoes and boil water."[16] Through this formulation, similar to that which Amy Kaplan and Laura Wexler have identified in texts by late nineteenth-century women, Louchheim resolves U.S. women's place on the less exciting side of the domestic–foreign opposition by imagining an empire-building process that involves extending American domestic space throughout the world.[17] By teaching women in the Third World "more modern methods" and "stimulating" them to desire new products, Louchheim argues, U.S. women can "press for progress" and "help to extend the frontiers of world peace" at their own lesser but still important level, remaining contained in domestic space (and helping to contain other women) while exploring the "limitless" frontiers of a Third World newly dominated by the United States.[18]

Such nostalgic appeals to ideals of rugged pioneer life and separate spheres shaped Peace Corps attempts to conceptualize and advertise their development work in the 1960s. These assertions of separate spheres were particularly important as the Peace Corps tried to incorporate women into the nostalgic, anti-domestic space the agency was attempting to create. Early Peace Corps chronicler Charles Wingenbach wrote in 1962 that "though early studies omitted women from consideration, the Peace Corps has found wide use for them as teachers, home economists and so on," indicating that women's inclusion was tied to their ability to perform distinct jobs (although the vast majority of the volunteers in the early years, both male and female, had the same liberal arts degrees and lack of technical skills).[19]

The *Peace Corps Volunteer* magazine visually represented the frontier's imaginary history of gender segregation by juxtaposing images of exclusively male and exclusively female space.[20] On the magazine's covers, men coached, welded, farmed, and joked with local men and boys while women taught, cooked, and administered to women, babies, and young children.

The August 1965 cover is particularly striking in its twinned photos of male and female volunteers in mirrored poses: the first set features a white male and a white female volunteer, each crouched down in the middle of two West Africans of the same gender, each doing or explaining an indiscernible task, while the other set features another white male and female volunteer each with an African counterpart of the same gender; in that set, the bare-armed muscular men coach two African boys in

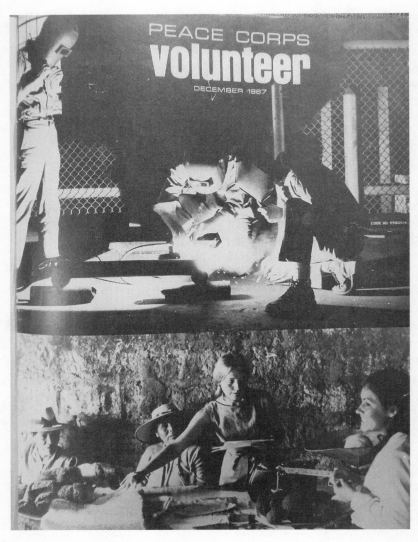

Men weld, women teach: December 1967 *Peace Corps Volunteer* magazine cover depicts the frontier-nostalgic ideal of separate spheres.

sit-ups while the women each tend to an African baby. The photo spread's careful mirroring of the men's and women's pedagogical poses in the strictly separated photos, in contrast with the indeterminate content of the actual lessons (except the sit-up coaching), reinforces the idea that the separate spheres are the point: the volunteers are modeling proper gender roles as much as, or more than, any particular skills.

Unlike the *Volunteer* magazine covers, the Peace Corps' advertisements in newspapers and magazines followed Wiggins in linking foreign adventure with romance and marriage, while simultaneously attending to Louchheim's invocation of women's supporting but still significant Cold War roles. A 1966 print advertisement hints at the way women volunteers' adventures might compare with serial romantic drama in their appeal to audiences at home: depicting a simple drawing of a radio, the advertisement reads "Can a young girl college graduate from the Middle West find happiness in the Peace Corps? Tune in here." A 1969 advertisement makes explicit the analogy to romance that the radio-drama tagline suggests, featuring a tall blonde woman walking in what seems to be an outdoor setting, surrounded and followed by Africans of various ages, mostly children, along with two adult women; no African men are visible. The white woman looks down and backward at one of the children, connecting with her and urging her on. The text reads, "Isn't it time you thought about raising a family?" Just as the "organization man" advertisement had ambivalently invoked the managerial masculine ideal, boldly eschewing it in the short term while promising it to the volunteer "later," the Peace Corps here attempts to attract women volunteers by promising to both free them from domestic space and transpose domesticity onto the Peace Corps spheres of frontier adventure. Seemingly incidentally, the advertisement infantilizes the African women, who follow happily behind the maternal volunteer.

The U.S. media paid more attention to women volunteers than the Peace Corps itself did: while the vast majority of the anecdotes Kennedy and Shriver told featured heroic male volunteers, *New York Times* coverage skewed the other way, devoting nearly all its considerable Peace Corps coverage to women. After its first national survey to glean college students' opinions about the Peace Corps, the *Times* reported incredulously that "often women students were more eager to join the corps than were men."[21] Stories from the early 1960s often assumed a cautionary

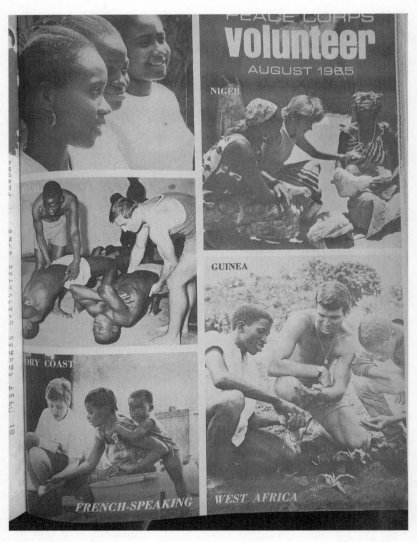

Peace Corps Volunteer cover from August 1965, portraying male and female volunteers in mirrored poses.

tone, such as 1962's "Peace Corps Woman Injured" about a volunteer from Chicago who suffered a "fractured hip, nose, and left wrist" in a traffic accident in Ghana,[22] but by the middle of the decade, the caution had changed to excitement. "Peace Corps Girls to Teach in Arabic," "Co-ed Volunteers for Peace Corps from Wheel Chair," and "5 Peace Corps Girls Tardy in Liberia after Sahara Trek" all headlined articles.[23] Marriage in particular interested the *Times*: although male volunteers married host-country citizens much more frequently, the paper's coverage again skewed much more toward women's experiences, including news articles titled "Nigerian Marries Peace Corps Girl," in which special correspondent Lloyd Garrison reports that "a tall, blonde former Peace Corps volunteer from Fort Worth, Texas has joined the small but growing number of American–Nigerian couples who have settled down to life in post-independence Africa."[24] In 1966, an article titled "Peace Corps Teacher Weds Sherpa in Nepal" claimed that "the marriage is reported in Katmandu to be the first between an American woman and a Sherpa."[25]

Life and Time also showed a fascination with the girls; in 1965, *Life* published "a rollicking diary of adventure" from Barbara, one of the five "tardy" Peace Corps girls who, on their vacation from teaching in Liberia, trekked across the Sahara to Algiers. The magazine reported that "the unlikely marathon turned into a success that was cheered around the world . . . the girls had enterprise and a charming ability to get along in what had been exclusively a man's world . . . They spent seven weeks traveling to and across the Sahara, leaving in their wake one oasis after another of goodwill—and a few aching hearts among lonely desert men."[26] The sensationalized story, seemingly crafted for readers like Wiggins who required the women to both be "enterprising" and charm (though not become involved with) the "lonely desert men," thrilled readers like R. M. Jali of Los Angeles, who wrote, "Wonderful, and yet again, wonderful—those girls who journeyed across the desert . . . somehow I can't worry about the future of the United States when there are eager, adventurous young Americans like these still around in the world."[27] Even in its 1961 account of the swearing-in ceremony for the first group of volunteers, *Time* focused on the "pretty girls" and reiterated the marriage comparisons being made by the agency: "'It's just like a wedding, isn't it?' giggled a pretty girl. And so it was: a long line of young men and women stood among the rosebushes in the White House garden, eventually meandered through the French doors leading to President Kennedy's office. The girls were bright in their flowered summer dresses, the men were turned out in their Sunday best, and everyone was smiling and chatting amiably—sometimes in Swahili and Twi."[28] *Time*'s construction of Peace Corps girls, like the proclamations by the agency itself and supporters like Louchheim, articulates an ambivalent relationship between the Peace Corps women and domesticity. If the ceremony is "like a wedding," is their service, paired with a host-country counterpart, like a marriage? Is it a substitute, or a rehearsal?

Many women who served in the 1960s Peace Corps wrestled with these questions, constructing their Peace Corps service as a temporary respite from the domestic containment ideal. A Colombia volunteer from the early 1960s remembers, "I broke an engagement in order to join the Peace Corps. I told the poor guy, who had been waiting for over four years, that I simply was not ready to get married, that I had to join the Peace Corps and explore the world first."[29] Others, like Ghana volunteer Laura Damon, conceive of their rejection of domestic ideals as perhaps more lasting. "I realized that year," she recalls, telling of her decision to join the Peace Corps, "that the little house in the country with the white picket fence and 4.3 children was not what was being cut out for me."[30] Turkey volunteer Susan Strane more enthusiastically rejected the domestic–suburban–managerial dream, recalling, "I wanted to do something that would be like jumping off a high diving board that I would never be the same after. I was so afraid that I would end up marrying a banker."[31] Both Damon and Strane, despite rejecting some aspects of the domestic lives they could so vividly imagine, retained the expectation that they would marry and have children after their Peace Corps service.

The above accounts demonstrate how, perhaps unsurprisingly, women volunteers formed ambivalent relationships to the domestic ideals that had shaped their mothers' lives. They were, of course, not the only relatively privileged young women to do so: as Wini Breines observes, "For young, white, middle-class women, the 1950s were a time when liberating possibilities were masked by restrictive norms." Breines identifies a "cultural lag" in which "despite greater educational opportunities and achievement, many 1950s daughters were encouraged neither to excel in school nor to prepare for careers."[32] A volunteer who served in Korea from 1968 to 1970 explains these contradictions, recalling, "I grew up with the expectation that I would marry and have children. I also expected to work in a fulfilling career. It was very unclear to me at the time of my Peace Corps service how I would manage to do both."[33] Many of the volunteers fit into this category, registering an ambivalence and uncertainty about their future as they prepared for careers they weren't expected to embark on and plotted to escape the domestic scenes of their childhood while still expecting to return to a life of marriage and children. The cultural representations around them articulated this ambivalence, not least the narratives that featured Peace Corps girls.

Postcolonial Seductions: Eroticizing and Containing the Peace Corps Girl in 1960s Culture

Paul Cowan introduces the Peace Corps section of his memoir with the recollection of telling an intermittent sex partner, "the English girl [he] had failed [sexually] in London," in a "tangled, boozy conversation" that he "would marry only the sort of woman who would willingly volunteer for the Peace Corps."[34] The girlfriend wants him to stay single, while he wants to marry his girlfriend, Rachel, who in fact does marry and join the Peace Corps with him, although she remembers in her own memoir that they "accepted the Peace Corps' offer mostly because we could think of no better way to avoid the draft."[35] In his recollection, Cowan contrasts the possibility of "secret, interwoven love affairs" with the Peace Corps ethos of "creation, not decay." His discussion both links the Peace Corps with these love affairs and disavows that link by contrasting the seaminess of his jaded English lover and the impotence he associates with her with the innocence, devotion, and optimism of Rachel, the "willing volunteer" he decides to marry. Cowan writes that his conversation with "the English girl" is "excellent material for a novel that has been written many times," and indeed, many novelists who wrote about the 1960s Peace Corps preoccupied themselves with just this contrast, pitting promiscuous and cynical British women against wide-eyed Americans as they tangle with the inhabitants of postcolonial spaces.[36]

Though male Peace Corps volunteers rarely appear as protagonists in 1960s novels, Peace Corps girls abound, appearing as protagonists in at least fourteen novels and two plays.[37] These narratives responded to middle-class women's dissatisfaction with the domestic containment ideal, fulfilling the desire articulated by Friedan in *The Feminine Mystique* for a return to the more adventurous female protagonists who populated magazine fiction before the domestic containment era. Recalling heroines who "were young in the same way that the American hero has always been young: they were New Women, creating with a gay determined spirit a new identity for women—a life of their own," Friedan assures us that the heroines succeeded as "career women—happily, proudly, adventurously, attractively career women—who loved and were loved by men."[38] The Peace Corps girl of the romance, action/adventure, and even the pornographic novels was young and heterosexual in just the way Friedan prescribed, both innocent victim and seductive adventurer. The anti-domestic ethos that characterized 1960s liberalism in this period shaped the paradoxical fantasies surrounding the Peace Corps girl; she wants to be independent and adventurous, yet her independence can only be conceived as a temporary stage along the path toward the goal of "loving and being loved by men." The formulaic Peace Corps fictional texts of the period use a variety of narrative strategies to contain Peace Corps girls' desire for independence, implicitly and explicitly connecting that containment to the postwar development regime and its attempts to contain anticolonial liberation struggles.

Most common were novels in the young adult and romance genres, nearly all of which begin with the protagonist breaking up with a dull or controlling boyfriend; typical in this respect is Kathy in *Kathy Martin, Peace Corps Nurse*, who, reflecting on her decision to reject Steve's marriage proposal, thinks "he was her rock, her deep-rooted tree—he was all the metaphors and similes in Roget's Thesaurus that stood for permanence and security—and yet here she was flying away once more."[39] The girl then sets her sights on the Peace Corps, usually encountering a dashing young volunteer with whom she reunites regularly enough during her Peace Corps service and whom she knows by the end of the novel she wants to marry; alternately, her love interest is a young doctor or businessman from the United States. In narrative strategies similar to those Kaplan and Melani McAlister have documented in 1890s and 1950s popular culture, these novels dramatize national fantasies about the trajectory of postcolonial nations—the liberation from old European powers and the eventual voluntary acceptance of U.S. hegemony—as hetero-sexual love stories, tracking the Peace Corps girls' liberation from their old, stuffy, controlling boyfriends and, after long and misunderstanding-ridden flirtations, their voluntary submission to new, exciting, and Peace Corps–affiliated ones.[40] Many of the books equate Peace Corps ser-vice and marriage, as when Kathy's friend Jenny Ramirez, filling out an application, says, "I feel like I'm planning to elope."[41]

Sharon Spencer's romance *Breaking the Bonds* makes especially explicit the analogy toward which all the books gesture, the correspondence between the liberation of Third World nations and the temporary free-dom that the Peace Corps allowed its female volunteers. Its epigraph excerpts and slightly adapts Kennedy's inaugural address, reading, "The Peace Corps is a pledge of our best efforts to those people in the huts and villages of half the globe struggling to break the bonds of mass misery . . . to help them help themselves . . . not because the Commu-nists may be doing it, not because we seek their votes, but because it is right."[42] While the reference to "bonds" suggests the context of decolo-nization, the speech also performs the rhetorical sleight-of-hand so char-acteristic of the development era: Kennedy's speech transforms the bonds of colonial domination, so recently broken for so many nations, into the bonds of a generalized "mass misery" in the world's "huts and villages"; implicitly, in the idiom of development, these are also bonds of "tradi-tional" culture and family.

Spencer's novel adds another rhetorical twist to the liberation narra-tive: although the novel periodically mentions the context of postcolo-nial development, the title more immediately refers to Anne's romantic life. In an early passage that articulates an ennui similar to the "problem that has no name" described in *The Feminine Mystique*, Anne contem-plates her dissatisfaction with her boyfriend: "Lately, their dates weren't fun at all. And it certainly wasn't Mike's fault. *He* hadn't changed, Anne admitted, wistfully shaking her head. No, Mike hadn't changed one lit-tle bit. He was the same serious, adoring Mike who wanted to marry her and waited and endlessly waited for her to say yes."[43] Instead, Anne feels a nagging discontent that she cannot quite explain.

Anne's unnamable problem leads her to break up with Mike and sign up for the Peace Corps. At the testing center she meets a handsome graduate student and would-be volunteer named Bob, who immediately asks her on a date. Thinking of her recent unsuccessful relationship, she refuses. Bob is devastated but changes strategies, deliberately ignoring her and then staring at her intensely during an assembly. "Maybe *that's* the way to handle her," he thinks, watching her react to his mixed signals. "Anne wasn't so indifferent to him after all. He had a clue now. Maybe there *was* a way to tame her."[44] Bob's framing of his courtship of Anne as an effort to "handle" and "tame" her invokes again the context of U.S. attempts to manage postcolonial nations, a project in which Bob will soon participate. Spencer, describing the volunteer group's first few weeks in Nigeria, writes that "during the course of training, Bob had emerged as the group's silently acknowledged leader. For one thing, he was a few years older than the other volunteers, and for another, his firmness of personality, the clear way in which he worked out problems, made him a natural leader."[45] The United States as well claimed "firmness" and "natural" leadership for itself and dispensed with formal mechanisms of colonial control in an attempt for "silently acknowledged" world leadership. As they begin their teacher training with Nigerians, Bob and his group initially encounter sullen fellow student teachers, who are angry that the Peace Corps volunteers are being served separate food in the dining halls. Using the same clever and evasive tactics with which he has "tamed" Anne, Bob proposes a hunger strike—that the volunteers threaten to deprive the other teachers of their presence if the staff continues to give them special treatment—and, with Anne standing adoringly alongside him, announces the strike to the Nigerians in the dining hall:

> "In the United States, there's an old labor custom which I'm sure you've heard of. It's called a 'strike.' When workers have a complaint or a grievance against their boss, then they go on strike. They just don't appear for work. In a way, that's just what we're doing. We came over here expecting to live just the way people live in Nigeria. We don't want there to be any doubt about that." As Bob spoke, he seemed to gather confidence. Strength was reflected in his deepening voice and the slow, deliberate way in which he made his point. Anne was bursting with pride. She'd known—it went without saying—that he'd handle the thing beautifully. Still, he was bringing it off even better than she'd thought. Already the faces of the students were softening,

resentment visibly giving way to understanding . . . Bob's talk was followed by a long dreadful silence before the first isolated claps. There was more clapping, then more—and still more. Soon everyone broke into wild applause. Weak smiles gave way to unreserved grins. Tense faces opened up and blossomed with friendship. Nodding and beaming, everyone smiled at Bob and Anne.[46]

Following the Peace Corps' own rugged fraternal ethos, Bob inverts the general premise of a strike, using it to protest the Nigerians' acknowledgment of the volunteers' relative privilege and status as enforcers of global hegemony. Furthermore, by allowing Bob's reference to the practice of striking as an "old labor custom" in the United States to go unchallenged, the novel both erases the recent history of militant general strikes that led to Nigerian independence and places class politics and labor struggles squarely in the American past, replacing them with a new politics of youth, volunteerism, and the "innocent vision" of "global authority" Mary Louise Pratt has deemed "anti-conquest."[47]

Bob and Anne's own reconciliation is not quite so easy: they must overcome various animosities and misunderstandings, most of them stemming from Anne's anxieties about Bob's superior teaching ability and the ease with which he has adapted to the country. After they are brought closer by a near-fatal traffic accident in which Bob saves the son of the local emir, Bob professes his love for Anne, and suddenly the "bonds" of marriage that Mike's steadiness had represented seem to her not only appealing but inevitable: "Anne could scarcely control her spinning, whirling dreams. Marriage! Those magical words of Bob's— 'I'm very much in love with you'—suddenly made marriage real for her. It was no longer the very special but vague thing she'd always known would happen to her—someday—now it was something warm and companionable and steady, something to be counted on and to build on. Could this be—? Would Bob be the—?"[48] The domestic life that Anne rejected in the beginning thus returns at the end as her freely chosen destiny; though they do not officially marry in the space of the book, Anne is clearly happy to submit to Bob's "silently acknowledged" leadership. This trajectory, in the context of decolonizing West African nations like Nigeria and the book's title and epigraph, clearly allegorizes the prescribed trajectory of newly independent nations: after an exhilarating yet frustrating attempt at "acting out," they will be tamed by organizations like the Peace Corps, happily acknowledging the "natural" leadership of the United States.

Many of the other Peace Corps girl stories feature African settings, seemingly because of the potential for emphasizing the parallels between decolonization and women's freedom, and all the Africa novels feature a bloody event toward the end that facilitates the central couple's closeness, reminding the protagonist of the heroic qualities of her love interest and his ability to bring order to a chaotic world. Even the pornographic novels depicting Peace Corps volunteers captured by sex-crazed African revolutionaries follow the formula fairly closely, emphasizing the parallel trajectories of decolonization/reconquest and white women's vulnerability and ultimate submission to white, authoritative men. In *Enslaved in Ebony*, a Columbia-educated revolutionary leader captures a straitlaced Peace Corps contingent in order to enact his (and, it turns out, their collective) interracial sex/rape fantasies. After the Portuguese drop napalm on the revolutionaries' compound, the Peace Corps girl escapes with the leader, saying, "I had begun to see him in a different light—a light that neutralized his color . . . He looked like a man, a marvelous artist and a dedicated patriot," and the other volunteers, through similarly transcendent sexual experiences, are converted to the revolutionary cause.[49] The bondage/torture novel *Peace Corps Bride*—according to the preface, "the story of a middle-class white girl who is thrown into the savage surroundings of the jungle, meeting for the first time Man in his most uncivilized form"[50]—is ultimately even more faithful to the trajectory of liberation-to-containment along the double axes of decolonization and gender, allowing its heroine to recover from innumerable forms of sexual torture by the caricatured Mau Mau revolutionaries and to fall in love with the white American doctor who rescues her by outwitting the Mau Maus, convincing them that Kenyan president Jomo Kenyatta's "perverted" teachings will cause them to "simper around like women."[51]

The sexual stereotypes dramatized explicitly in the pornographic novels found their way into popular culture, as when *Jet* picked up these snippets from a satirical Ghanaian newspaper column in 1969 in which columnist Malimoto offers "guidelines to the seduction of U.S. Peace Corps volunteers," advising African intellectuals to play to the Peace Corps girls' stereotypes of "raw, brute, savage Africa":

Malimoto recommends that to get on well with a white Peace Corps girl, an African should never intellectualize too much. "To meet a black intellectual kills their genius," he writes. "It disappoints them. They are in search of raw, brute, savage Africa. They want to visit the Masais and the Karamojongs in order to see their long, naked spheres [*sic*]. It is not equal humans they have come to see but lower humans they have volunteered to uplift. It is the real savage brute they search for to give them a real uninhibited experience untouched in silly niceties and sublimatory preliminaries."

Malimoto advocates that one sure-to-work approach is to mildly accuse a Peace Corps girl of white racism.

"She will turn red, then white, and protest her innocence. She will want to prove that even you can be her friend. What you do then is quote a very English proverb, "the proof of the pudding is in the eating" and proceed bedward . . .

Malimoto admonishes that the best time to approach a Peace Corps Girl is during the first week after her arrival in the locality. "During that week all rebellion against American racism, inhumanity, and all liberal schizophrenia is running high. The net result is that each girl would like to prove her individuality by offering her friendship to blacks," he prompts.[52]

Jet offers Malimoto's parodic reiteration of the racial stereotypes and desires that shaped the movement and popular cultures of the 1960s United States without contextualization or commentary; desires on both sides are understood as rebellious responses to confining social structures. The column bears out Breines's insight that white girls who grew up in the 1950s sought contact with exoticized black music and culture to escape the segregated domestic containment regime in which they grew up, but it also describes a historical moment in which guilt-ridden white women were vulnerable to this particular kind of manipulation and pressure. Malimoto's advice to use accusations of racism to seduce Peace Corps girls echoes the experiences of some of the white women who traveled south for Freedom Summer and discovered that, as Sara Evans observes, "the boundary between sexual freedom and exploitation was a thin one."[53]

The first published novel by a returned Peace Corps volunteer, Paul Theroux's *Girls at Play*, combines the racial and sexual stereotypes satirized and supported by Malimoto with the Peace Corps girl books' double emphasis on containing African decolonization and female sexuality. Theroux, whom *The Guardian's* Emma Brockes has called "the Indiana Jones of American Literature," became an established novelist and travel writer after writing various, mostly fictionalized accounts of his Peace Corps service.[54] His description of Guatemala City as "a city on its back," cited by Pratt to indicate Theroux's role as inheritor of the imperial gaze in travel writing, also suggests his conflation of, and interest in the subjugation of, women and Third World peoples.[55]

Despite the title and the setting at a Kenyan girls' school, Theroux does not attempt to differentiate the students at the school. The most extended scene with them is at the very beginning, when Theroux pans down to a hockey field where "the black, large-buttocked girls" are enjoying their game: "If the fat black girls had not been there and playing, the order of this playing field in the highlands of east Africa would terrify. The order seemed both remote and unreasonable. Explorers have come upon abandoned buildings deep in Africa and suddenly felt despair, confronted by roofless walls, broken lizard-cluttered stairs, solid doorways opening onto dense ferns and dark towering trees. A discernible order in a place where there are no people (the dry mosque in the dunes) is a cause for alarm; it means failure; the decaying deserted order is a gravemarker."[56] Theroux's immediate digression from the playing girls to the desolation "explorers" might find and the "despair" they might feel encountering the landscape, points to the book's central argument, that postcolonial Africa is in fact a place of "decaying deserted order": of animal violence, feminine corruption, and inevitable brutal death. The Kenyan girls flicker in and out of the novel, remaining barely human presences, as Theroux indicates by describing how "in their green bloomers and grey jerseys, which showed their swinging unsupported breasts, they ran heavily hunched and held their sticks low, yelping cheerfully."[57] This dehumanization and erasure of the girls, filtered through the colonial gaze of the imagined "explorers," encapsulates the novel's larger argument that without white men running things, social order deteriorates into savage play and, eventually, desolation.

The form of play most evident throughout the novel is the extended skirmish between the promiscuous British émigré Heather, and the reclusive headmistress Miss Poole, whose family was dispossessed after decolonization. They are joined by a naïve Peace Corps volunteer named B.J., whose innocent stupidity and kindness to Kenyans precipitate the book's multiple deaths, including her own. B.J. is described as appealingly naïve, craving tactile experience in a way that Theroux argues is uniquely American and feminine. Heather, the most astute presence in the novel, observes of B.J. that "the girl was young, she knew absolutely nothing," and that she had "a typical American face: empty, without a trace of sin in it."[58] Theroux's limited-omniscient glimpse into B.J.'s consciousness tells a similar story: "B.J. was pretty, she gave off perfumes, but she was dense. Her nerves lived deep in her sweet pink flesh. She had to be touched to be awakened, physically touched. Slapped, she got angry; caressed, she felt desire, and swallowed."[59] Eroticizing and parodying the Peace Corps' focus on physical existential experience, Theroux argues that the Peace Corps girls' experiential desire, exemplified by Kathy Martin in her favorite quotation, Millay's "O world, I cannot hold thee close enough!" has a seamy underside, particularly when applied to dangerous Third World men.[60]

B.J. espouses both an exoticizing desire and the idea, depicted by Theroux as childish, that Africans are people; she is eventually punished for both these sentiments. When she discovers the other women's fear and disgust at Africans, B.J.'s initial response looks much like that of the white Peace Corps girl Malimoto imagines. She tells Heather, "'Africans are people, too. I know the memsab [Miss Poole] hates them, being born here like she was, but gee whiz,' she said, pained, 'they're *people*, you know.'" In the same conversation, she argues that "Africa is the sexiest place in the world . . . the sun, the grass, all the naked people. It's smelly. It's really wild." We later learn that B.J., in response to her father's racism, once "resolved . . . to date, in private, as many Negroes as she could . . . there was a certain something she liked about them, she never knew what, maybe their tremendous vim." Likewise in Africa she dates a Kenyan, Wangi, who, when pressed, explains to her that he participated in the Mau Mau rebellions:

> "The British are terrible. They hate you and they don't say it, but you know they hate you. It's terrible. You never know if they hate you, but you know if they're British they have to. That's the way the British are. So we killed them."
>
> "Were you in those gangs?"
>
> "Oh, yes."

"Wow," said B.J. softly.

"No," said Wangi, "two of them: Mau-Mau."

"You don't mean you actually . . ." B.J. swallowed, wondering whether to ask. "You actually . . . ah . . . killed—"

"Oh, yes," Wangi said, brightening. "Everyone had to. That's how you get free. It's not easy. They used to call us natives and what-not."

"Sure, but a native just means someone who lives in a particular—"

"That's what I used to hate, when they said 'You bloody natives.' So I didn't mind joining up, and one night," Wangi continued, interspersing his story with little bursts of laughter, "we went to a farm in Nyeri District. My uncle said that now we ha-ha just have to do this. These buggers have been treating us too badly. I took my knife ha-ha and was creeping slowly ha-ha-"

"Please, Wangi. Tell me about your village."[61]

Constructing the Mau Mau rebellion as both unthinkably brutal and unmistakably childish, Theroux argues that the anticolonial struggle was motivated by a combination of visceral hatred for the British temperament and juvenile reaction to being called "bloody natives"; B.J.'s feeble protestation emphasizes both her naïveté and the senselessness of the decolonial violence Wangi describes.

Refusing to face Wangi's subhuman brutality, B.J. continues to date him for "many reasons, a little bit of politics, maybe some guilt, and even if there was no love there would be sympathy and curiosity. He wasn't a bad guy. And even if he was (but he wasn't) life at the school was dull and why else had she gone all the way into Los Angeles to take the Peace Corps exam and put up with the Mickey Mouse of three months training if not to get to know Africans?" B.J.'s naïve quest "to get to know Africans" leads Wangi to rape her, after which she drowns herself, haunted by the eroticized memory of "the black man" who was "close, like an insect in a hairy suit, bulbous eyed, with long flicking arms and sticky gripping fingers." Theroux stages B.J. replaying the rape over and over in her mind in the hours before her suicide, paying particular attention to her mix of disgust and desire: "As the black man stroked the girl and slobbered at her neck, disgust rose in B.J.'s throat and weakened her. It was not rancid hatred; it was the wet reality of animal desire mixing with the knowledge of the weakness, for while her mind was made up, her body was not."[62]

It is because of this relentless corporeal desire for "the black man," dramatized repetitively by Theroux, that B.J. must die. She runs toward the sound of running water: "As each thing touched her—the deep grass, the bamboo stalks, the reeds, the hairy tufts of papyrus—it was as if those black arms pursuing her had reached out to embrace her and, as she pulled away, clawed her." She ends up killing herself by sinking into a bog, trapped in her desire for primordial blackness and violence: "B.J. looked up one last time before the mud gave way; she was in the churning blackness, being sucked breathlessly down from the black air to the black swamp. The incubus had pursued her, embraced her, engulfed her in sensational black folds. In her ears a riot of liquid voices started, an annoying roar of bubbles that increased in volume as she gulped at the poisoned blackness; she swallowed again, and again her mouth was filled with a demon's sour fingers. Her body became stupid with heaviness, like the water around it."[63] The combination of "the black incubus" and B.J.'s "stupid body" incarnates Theroux's derisive characterization of anticolonial struggle as both childish and demonic; engulfed by primeval blackness, B.J. seems childish and naïve at best for having believed that "Africans are people." In Theroux's eyes the Peace Corps, embodied by B.J., is stupid and masochistic, motivated by romantic interracial desire that ignores the uncivilized nature of its objects.

Girls at Play received favorable reviews: writing for the *New York Times*, Laurence Lafore compared the book to *Hamlet* and *King Lear* before calling it "very convincing," writing that Theroux "knows his milieu thoroughly from the teaching level." Lafore goes on to praise the book's macabre atmospherics, arguing that readers can learn much about Africa from its characterizations and "stunning logic," and that "the punctilious realism of the details, the strange, haunting ubiquity of the African landscape, the plausibility of characters divested of the straitjackets of their own conventional worlds, are lessons in a course in the high cost of sudden social change."[64] Evident from Lafore's review is that Theroux's Peace Corps experience lent him credibility, allowing him the authority to caution readers against "sudden social change," which seems to encompass both decolonization itself and the loosing of innocent white women upon the world. The Peace Corps' own stance dictated Theroux's alarm about both projects: decolonization and women's autonomy alike were depicted as ugly and in need of containment by daring white men like the "explorer" of the first few pages, without whom horror would ensue.

In all these novels, Peace Corps girls symbolize American naïveté as well as a potential alliance and identification with postcolonial nations that must be managed by white male leadership. In these texts, Peace Corps girls' work is either characterized as inferior to that of male volunteers (as in *Breaking the Bonds*) or is barely mentioned (as in *Girls at Play*). However, almost universally for women volunteers serving in the 1960s, in both letters home and later recollections, work was the central focus of their Peace Corps experience. The next section explores women's attempts to do meaningful development work within an organization that maintained an iconographic imaginary of separate spheres, opposed and trivialized domesticity, and equated underdevelopment with femininity. These attempts were often challenging; sometimes, as in Vicos, women volunteers, somewhat paradoxically given their ancillary roles, accepted the consequences for the failure of the entire development mission.

Work, Frustration, and Sacrifice: Women Volunteers in Action

For a few months in spring 1963, forty-one-year-old Judy Holliday, beloved for her comic performances of inarticulate, naïve heroines in 1950s films, starred as a Peace Corps girl in *Hot Spot*, a Broadway musical that would be the last role of her career and a monumental flop. *Billboard's* headline, "They Didn't Do Right by Judy," represented the critical consensus, and its assertion that "the theme of a little lady who joins the Peace Corps and gets U.S. foreign aid for a destitute country by discovering 'make-believe' communist elements is about as original as the cold war," reflected the ubiquity of Peace Corps girl stories (as well as a certain Cold War weariness).[65] *Time* chimed in, offering a derisive synopsis under the headline "Poor Judy," mocking the setting as "a semi-Tibetan, semitropical country populated in its whimsical, multi-altitudinal way mostly by yaks and native girls in hula skirts," and scoffing that "when Judy isn't scaring up a bogus Red-underground menace to get her man, the handsome Ugly American consul (Joseph Campanella), she drones through some tuneless tunes decomposed by Richard

Rodgers' daughter Mary . . . As the corn-pone Congressman says, 'You fellahs should have known what was going to happen when you sent overdeveloped girls into underdeveloped countries.'"[66]

The media's attack on the premise of the musical, coming the same year as the critical acclaim for the film version of the jingoistic best seller *The Ugly American*,[67] seems to have more to do with its utter irreverence toward U.S. foreign policy than its lack of realism or originality; after all, *Hot Spot* was the only cultural production about the Peace Corps to mock not the volunteers but the entire development enterprise. After a few weeks of bad reviews, Stephen Sondheim attempted to rescue the play by collaborating with Rodgers and Martin Charnin on a song for Holliday titled "Don't Laugh." Despite the critics' ongoing complaints, the song's particular articulation of adventurism, double-binds, and guilt-ridden development efforts captures much about the way women volunteers' work was understood by the Peace Corps, media texts, and even the volunteers themselves. The majority of the song is a catalog of clumsiness and failure; although it culminates in a more confident stance, apologetic striving remains the dominant mood:

> Show me a glass of water,
> I'll show you a soggy dress.
> Show me a tube of toothpaste,
> I'll show you a mess . . .
>
> Maybe it's my name
> Maybe it's my face
> Maybe it's my—both . . .
>
> If I can convince—
> Don't laugh—
> Me.
> Why can't I convince—
> Don't leave—
> You?
> Give me half a chance,
> Just half,
> And then—
> Don't laugh—
> Maybe I could be
> Proud of me too.

Show me a barren hillside
I'll show you a field of grass
Show me an empty schoolroom
I'll show you a class
Show me an epidemic
I'll show you a board of health
Show me a starving people
Show me an insurrection!
Show me the way to get there!
Show me what's on your clipboard![68]

Vacillating between summoning the independence and fortitude to confront "a starving people" and pleading with the interlocutor to take her seriously, "Don't Laugh" captures the anxiety expressed by and about young women of the Peace Corps, interpellated by the contradictory domestic containment regime and sent on adventures in which many of them were assigned tasks considered both necessary and frivolous. The plaintive "Don't laugh" mixed with the ambiguous "Show me an insurrection! Show me the way to get there!"—does she want to put down the insurrection, or join in?—also anticipates second-wave feminists' early, tentative attempts to articulate their experience of gender oppression, beginning a year or so later in the new left and civil rights movements, attempts which were often met with ridicule.[69] Like the early feminists and the women volunteers, Holliday's character pessimistically pleaded for "half a chance" to "do good" and "do well," timidly attempting to be a public actor in a postwar world that demanded her relegation to private space.

Questions about appropriate work for women, though not a preoccupation of Peace Corps staffers, were repeatedly raised by volunteers, particularly in Latin America, where the most common assignments were "community development" ones.[70] Six women volunteers in Panama described their struggle to do meaningful work in a detailed 1968 report about their relationship to the Peace Corps and local institutions, arguing that "a reorientation in Peace Corps thinking on women's programming" was necessary. They wrote that although their training had been in community development, "according to prevailing attitudes towards female volunteers, we were to consider our work with women as something quite apart from our essential assignments as rural community development workers . . . we were expected to work with women as a matter of course, but were not encouraged to consider our opportunities for work with women as community development—after all, with the women, we just cook, sew and demonstrate . . . no one thought community development had any application in women's groups."[71] In their work with housewives' clubs, the volunteers found that they spent hours "looking through the Sears catalog" with the women, performing tasks that were unnecessary for the women and ridiculed by both the Peace Corps and the local community:

> The [volunteer's] disillusionment became stronger when she finally realized that the whole thing was pretty much a laughing matter. A snicker and a sigh of futility was the standard reaction to the mention of *Amas de Casa*. We were beginning to understand that no one was really interested in the program—neither the members, the Agent, the Peace Corps, nor even [the Panamanian 4-H organization] which had created it. Programming of projects in the real sense was impossible and emphasis was placed on foolish handi-crafts (i.e., pillow making for nonexistent furniture). This practice only served to intensify the club's bad image in the communities, most importantly among the husbands of the members who rightly considered such activities a waste of time in view of more pressing needs in the household.[72]

Although the volunteers resent that their work has become "a laughing matter," they cannot quite question the system that relegates women to housework and "foolish handi-crafts" and then ridicules those jobs, realizing perhaps that handicraft-making and catalog-browsing fulfill the Cold War dictates, articulated by Louchheim and others, of instilling capitalist desires in Third World women. Thus, instead of questioning either the idea of development or its inherently masculine character, the authors recommend training volunteers so that "both male and female trainees consider each other's complementary but distinct roles in depth" while arguing that "women's groups can become a real force in promoting community development, in that they act as pressure groups in the community in the promotion of betterments which directly effect their home." The women recognize that even their limited demands would require "a reorientation in Peace Corps thinking on women's programming" in order to allow the agency to see women as a category in development work at all.[73]

This sense that the Peace Corps saw women volunteers' work as incidental, unimportant, and even silly pervades many women's accounts, particularly accounts produced during or shortly after their service. Brazil volunteer Rafaela Castro, teaching first aid classes in the favelas of Recife, echoes the Panama volunteers' sentiments that her work is considered unimportant by both the surrounding community and the Peace Corps: "At times I feel like I am working so alone. I work because I push myself. Nobody really cares if I work or not, except myself."[74] In general, women "found the frustrating work experience more of a problem than men did," according to a survey of 4,260 volunteers who completed their service in 1966; men were more frustrated with dating and administrative concerns, but more satisfied in their jobs. The survey found that women made up three-fourths of Peace Corps health workers and that "the health worker was the least likely among all types of volunteers to say that he or she made a contribution to the country's economic or social development," whereas the vast majority of the mostly male agriculture volunteers and cooperative development workers reported satisfaction with their contribution to the development of their host country.[75] This gap demonstrates again the tautological definitions with which the Peace Corps and its volunteers were working: community development was simply something men did.

The volunteer teachers, most of whom were deployed to newly independent African nations, were the only surveyed group with a significant proportion of women in which most said they had contributed significantly to national development. Although volunteers felt satisfied with their teaching, they also felt pressure from the Peace Corps staff to do more community development projects after school, when both they and their fellow teachers felt that they should be planning their lessons. Sierra Leone volunteer Gwynne Douglas indicates these expectations by beginning a 1965 *Volunteer* article defensively: "No, I didn't build any bridges. I don't know anything about culverts or soil conditions, I didn't organize any clubs and I haven't started any libraries. I never did much of that sort of thing before I came here and I probably won't start now. I just go to school every day and do my job. I have 100 students that I try to teach every day, and for me, that's a full-time occupation."[76] Other volunteers shared Washington's feeling that "the teaching was secondary" to "winning friends" and more physically taxing projects like digging latrines.[77]

Even in the few 1960s programs in which the Peace Corps was involved that did conceive of women as the primary objects of the development mission, such as the Applied Nutrition Program in India, volunteers struggled to establish connections with them. The ANP's Master Plan explained that "the special targets of the program are village women who are expectant or nursing mothers, and pre-school children" who "are not appealed to by the old standards of family and caste. A new social identity, a new way of seeing oneself, is essential." With the Peace Corps' help, along with "new institutions, new buildings, new social organizations," the Master Plan dictated that "women must accept themselves as members of a voluntary association, of a mahila mandel. This is neither a natural, nor an easy identity for them, but it is the basis of the program."[78] But in practice, volunteers had trouble showing the women, even those trained as social workers, the value of these organizations. One woman attempting to organize social workers confessed that "as I look back on my year . . . it's a complete failure," explaining the social workers' lack of enthusiasm as well as the expectations on both sides that women will "perform":

> Do you know when we go to mahila mandel meetings I ask my Indian co-workers, "What are you going to present to the ladies?" She says, "Oh, you give a demonstration. It's like performing in a show." I'm a performer. It's frustrating to go to a different village everyday and put on a performance five days a week. Frustrating because I want them to interact. I want them to assume some part of it . . . The days that I didn't play anything, that I wanted them to take over, it was like—blah. There was no interaction. The only thing that came between us was: "You do something." "No, you do." "We're all ladies here. Why all this confusion. Sing!" Oh, you shame them into it eventually, by fussing with them. But it should be that automatically they would . . . I mean, well it's their own community with no men around. Still, they won't perform.[79]

Expected not only to impose a new identity and social structure on the Indian women but also to make the women "assume some part" in this imposition, this volunteer, along with many others in the India group, became frustrated. Both the volunteer and the women with whom she works push against their roles as display objects, searching for alternative ways to interact in these all-female spaces. But they can only imagine making meaningful connections by commanding the other women to "perform" for them, a move which spurs further resentment and mis-understanding on both sides.

This tension between women volunteers' dual roles as passive dis-play objects and active disseminators of development ideology also per-vades "Don't Laugh": Sally insists on her independence and competence; frets over her appearance—"Maybe it's my name / Maybe it's my face / Maybe it's my—both"; and pleads with her love interest "Don't leave." The *Hot Spot* senator's warning against sending "overdeveloped girls into underdeveloped countries" works the same way as Wiggins's "Who Are We" speech, leaving women unsure whether they are supposed to conceal their sexuality in an attempt to approximate the masculine de-velopment ideal or deploy it in the service of the development mission. Jack Vaughn, touring Peace Corps sites in 1966, crowed that "volun-teers are so attractive. Everywhere I've gone I have been impressed by this, I don't know what it is about them—their behavior, their attitude, their dress."[80] The Peace Corps expressed particular interest in recruit-ing attractive women volunteers; frequent editorials featured in the *Vol-unteer* worried that the Peace Corps was either sapping the femininity from female volunteers or recruiting women with insufficient reserves in the first place.[81] Peace Corps psychiatrist E. Lowell Kelly cautioned that choosing strong women would force the agency to accommodate their weaker husbands, noting that "married couples are usually selected on the basis of one. This often works out satisfactorily when the solid member is the man, but the type of woman that we want usually has a passive spouse who does not make an adequate PCV [Peace Corps vol-unteer]."[82] A *Time* article from 1967, stating that "today's plain Janes have the opportunities their spinster aunts never did—trips to Europe, a Peace Corps assignment in Asia, interesting jobs in research or govern-ment," touched a nerve among Peace Corps men.[83] India volunteer Larry Hayes used the *Time* quotation to begin his meditation on femininity, in which he complains of finding Peace Corps women "unladylike, too bold, too competing, too demanding, too-everything."[84] The skills Hayes pointed to as being "unladylike" and "bold" included language competency and geographical knowledge, suggesting that the very ability to navigate their sites and perform any kind of work there rendered women volunteers unfeminine.

Host country counterparts also expected, and found ways to capitalize on, the femininity of Peace Corps women. Margot Jones, a volunteer in Ecuador from 1965 to 1967, recalls the "sweet little women" in her town bringing her to ask a local general to send the village a shipment of much-needed soil. As she talked to the general, she remembers, "They would mouth messages to me like 'smile' and come over to me and fix my hair." Although Jones says she did not mind, she was aware that "those women knew what they were doing; they knew they had a patsy on their hands. The captain sent the dirt, and of course I had to be there when it was delivered . . . No one had explained to me exactly what my role was going to be in Ecuador—which was basically window dressing."[85] Kay Dixon describes her counterpart in Colombia using similar terms, recalling that "she knew how to use us. I was tall and blonde, so if she wanted to get things done, she'd say, 'Send Kay in there.'"[86] Peace Corps staffers generally looked approvingly on these seductions, reporting that "three girls in Valparaiso [Chile]" had solved the problem of "middle-class apathy" there by "asking their numerous upperclass boyfriends to look at the poblaciones where they work."[87] But the seduction-for-development framework could turn bothersome and dangerous: Nigeria volunteer Frieda Fairburn recalls an African American woman, briefly her roommate, who rode around on her motorcycle "waving at everybody, which was great" until men mistook the affinity she had constructed for sexual aggressiveness and started following her home every day. Overwhelmed by the constant visits, she left her post.[88]

Sometimes the consequences of the volunteers' role as seductive emissaries of the modernization mission were even more violent, as with Peru volunteer Grace Schubert, who was raped during her term of service. In her account of her experience, Schubert recalls that after getting to know the community, "it was apparent to me that the advance of Western civilization was inevitable. Nevertheless, how that advance took place involved options. Change could take many forms. Some forms were less painful than others for the people experiencing the change."[89] Recalling that she attempted to assuage the effects of "the change" her culture was imposing on the Peruvians although she had "no tools, not even seeds, to distribute," she writes, "I truly had nothing more to give than myself."[90] The juxtaposition of her rape story with the "painful advance" narrative frames the rape as a kind of sacrifice, a giving of herself in exchange for Western civilization's rape and plunder of Peru.[91] The Peace Corps staff reacted to her story by alternately blaming her and keeping silent; they resisted even acknowledging the rape, much less viewing it the way she did, as a violent reaction to the unwelcome yet "inevitable" advances of Western civilization:

> The reaction of people in the central Peace Corps office and host country supervisors who needed to be informed was most surprising to me. These folks had been friendly and supportive, but when they found out about the rape, it seemed that cold distancing set in, as if they were afraid of me, as if I had done something wrong. Secretaries and one fellow volunteer who happened to be in the office at the time muttered *Pobrecita* (poor little thing) under their breath as I went by. The report showed that the rape was not my fault. I had never seen the rapist before, and I never saw him again. He was a boat loader passing through town, according to the people who had stood in the doorway witnessing the rape scene. I quickly learned that facts and details make little difference in people's emotional reactions when it comes to a matter like this.
>
> In retrospect, it is clear to me that people were doing their best to deal with me; however, the effect of the utterances like *Pobrecita* on me at the time was to make me want to get away from there as soon as possible. Another person said in passing, "I heard what happened. Couldn't you fight him off?" "I did the best I could," was my response. Nevertheless, the person did not seem to understand. I simply wanted to get away from that office as soon as possible and go home—back to the people I had come to love, in the tropical Peruvian communities that I had become a part of.
>
> When I got back, people were anxious to learn more about what had happened. My in-country supervisor suggested that I not say anything about the rape and simply direct attention to the work I was doing. I was strongly tempted to share my feelings with my Peruvian friends. In a sense, it probably would have made me feel better. But I followed orders and kept quiet.[92]

The Peace Corps' attempt to shame Schubert into silence and blame her for her inability to "fight him off" prolonged her suffering and eventually led her to characterize herself as the problem—to retrospectively imagine that "people were doing their best to deal with [her]." But the agency's silence and blame also allowed the Peace Corps to disavow the connection she was making, the connection the Peace Corps novels also make, between the narratives of seduction and rape that characterized modernization discourse and the sexual violence that those narratives engendered. But despite her plaintive protest that the rape was "not her fault," Schubert, in her subsequent essay, embraces her role as sacrifice, concluding that her "own expectations, gains, and losses don't really matter."[93] As the agency did with the women at Vicos,[94] the Peace Corps characterized Schubert as deficient in order to reject a systemic explanation for antidevelopment violence. Cold War development, to echo Lyndon Johnson's characterization of the Vietnam War, could still be framed as "seduction, not rape."[95]

The first two high-profile Peace Corps murder cases, both of which saw male volunteers accused of killing female volunteers, reveal even more clearly the positioning of women's bodies as necessary sacrifices, diverting and concentrating the violence of the development mission. In both cases, the first in Tanzania and the second in Tonga, the Peace Corps mobilized massive resources for the defense of the accused male volunteer to counter eyewitness testimony from the local community, overwhelming juries by flying in more expert witnesses than the country could afford to produce. Bill Kinsey, acquitted in 1966 of murdering his wife, Peverley, after Lyndon Johnson intervened on his behalf and the Peace Corps supplied an international team of lawyers to defend him, returned to Washington to become an editor of the *Peace Corps Volunteer* magazine. In Dennis Priven's Tonga murder trial, witnesses confirmed that he had stalked Deborah Gardner for months in Tonga and stabbed her twenty-two times, but he was found not guilty in the first insanity defense the country had ever seen. The Peace Corps again whisked Priven to Washington, where he was declared sane by a psychiatrist and given an ordinary completion of service discharge. In each case, fellow volunteers (and in the Kinsey case, even the victim's parents) closed ranks around the accused volunteer, and only the Tanzanian and Tongan prosecutors and observers retained a sense of outrage at the murders.[96]

These brutal outbursts of violence, and particularly the degree to which the Peace Corps worked to conceal them, suggests that some early Peace Corps women functioned as what Elizabeth Povinelli (via Ursula

Le Guin) calls "the child in the broom closet," sacrifices that obscured and concentrated the otherwise-overwhelming violence of the liberal modernization project.[97] The women at Vicos, Schubert, and these murder victims all seem to have functioned similarly as sacrifices, standing in for the breathtaking violence of modernization that the Peace Corps' heroic image partially obscured. The violence these women suffered, along with the more routine slights and difficulties experienced by many Peace Corps women, also reveals just how much development in its heyday was imagined as a masculine undertaking. This meant not just that development work was planned and undertaken by men, but also that its central goals were to reinvigorate American managerial-class manhood and transform subjects around the world into enthusiastic participants in an international brotherhood. This masculine orientation is evident in the Peace Corps' early publicity materials, in the surveys and reports evaluating volunteers' work, and the frustrated testimony of the women volunteers. But the fictional texts, with their variation on the Peace Corps' romantic imaginary, perhaps even more starkly reveal the power dynamics of the new development regime, in which "breaking the bonds" was inevitably followed by acquiescence to freely chosen new ones.

Carrying a Sign: Women Volunteers and Movement Politics

Women in the 1960s Peace Corps, in their attempts to do meaningful work within the modernization regime, occupied a vexed position: they served as symbolic objects representing American innocence and seductiveness, but also decolonial energies and the backwardness that impeded development. As the national popular imaginary gravitated toward images of young, adventurous Peace Corps women, they became a site for working out the contradictions in both unassailable dreams of development and domesticity—both of which promised freedom and happiness while requiring submission.

Given these contradictory conditions that women volunteers encountered and visibly embodied, it is perhaps surprising that more of them did not embrace movement politics, and that they particularly rejected feminism. The vast majority of women Peace Corps volunteers fit Breines's description of "white, middle-class girls who were taught in the 1950s that their main goals in life were to become wives and mothers and only ambivalently internalized these values and sometimes rejected them outright, embracing instead a wider world."[98] Breines suggests that these women found their way to feminism in a roundabout way, first seeking out exoticized racial otherness in an attempt to rebel against the safety and homogeneity surrounding them, finding those spaces of otherness in beat and musical subcultures as well as the civil rights movement, and finally developing a critique of the way dominant patriarchal structures were rearticulated within these subcultures and movements that became the basis of the second-wave feminist movement. Most of the young women in the 1960s Peace Corps started out on the trajectory Breines sketches, seeking out dangerous adventure and racial and cultural otherness as a respite from stifling domestic suburban life. But after their Peace Corps service, many disassociated themselves from the movements, embracing "a wider world" without challenging the power structures that made it difficult for them to do so.[99]

Peace Corps volunteers' skepticism of movements and movement politics often rested uneasily beside their commitments to justice and equality. Alice O'Grady, a teacher from the first Ghana group who developed close and lasting connections with her former students, remembers that she "related to [feminism] but never became active in it. I was not active in the civil rights movement, you know I followed it, but I never took any action. I write letters to my congressmen but that's about as far as it goes. I've never marched in any kind of march." But she continued to long for a visible marker of her allegiance to black people, eloquently lamenting her inability to show her solidarity upon her return:

> [The Peace Corps] also changed my attitude toward black people, whereas before . . . I never thought about my relationship with another race, but when I came back, I wished and other volunteers have agreed that it's this funny situation, you want to carry a sign that says I'm your friend, you know I'm not a white enemy or something like that, and again, at that time that was more pertinent than it is now. And so it was difficult to realize that my skin said that I was maybe an enemy, I know enemy is too strong a word but a member of the opposition, and yet I didn't feel that way anymore, and so that was hard, too.[100]

O'Grady's desire "to carry a sign" seems strange in light of her assertion that she "never marched in any kind of march," a space in which sign-carrying would have been welcomed. But I want to conclude this chapter by arguing that the contradictions between her longing for visible affirmations of solidarity and her decision to avoid marching in the mid-to-late 1960s perfectly encapsulate the Peace Corps' ethos, which, because of its emphasis on self-help and cooperation with authority, made protesting difficult to imagine. The sign O'Grady (and, as she suggests, many other volunteers) wished for, with its plaintive declaration of friendship, also echoes the Peace Corps ethos, effacing power and oppression in order to imagine intimate connections with oppressed people.

While some early volunteers did participate in civil rights work upon returning from their service, often working in War on Poverty programs, returned female Peace Corps volunteers rarely joined or associated themselves with the feminist movement, bearing out O'Grady's statement that "I don't connect feminism with the Peace Corps."[101] Going even further than O'Grady in rejecting a movement ethos, and connecting this rejection explicitly with the Peace Corps' development mission, another volunteer acknowledges power differences between men and women but rejects the help of "any movement" or even the idea that it should be changed:

> My mother shaped my ideas about women's rights and responsibilities— she simply told me I could do anything I wanted, as she had done. Our culture is structured in a way that gives men power at birth. Women, by and large, have to "earn" it. This is a social construct, however, not the "truth" of who we are. I have always felt it was my job to earn that power and freedom on my own, not through any movement. I support civil rights movements around the world, but do not support women's rights, gay rights, etc. I believe the focus needs to be on freedom for all in a civil society—encouraging other countries to establish structures as we have in the U.S. Peace Corps left me with a profound understanding of my "place" in the world and my responsibility to my fellow man, especially those less fortunate. The modern "movements" of our country have never moved me very much, as I believe we each and all have the rights necessary to make a life and a life worth living. I am moved by those people in other countries who do not have those basic rights.[102]

While this volunteer's statement that "the modern 'movements' of our country have never moved me very much" evinces a more oppositional stance toward the movements than most 1960s volunteers took, her rejection of movement tactics and emphasis on "earn[ing] that power and freedom on my own" echoes the ideas expressed by many of her Peace Corps contemporaries. Anticipating the alliance traced by Alice Echols between liberal and cultural feminists, groups "united by their common distaste for confrontational politics" and collective struggle, the volunteers who do identify as feminists mostly do not connect their stated allegiances with movement politics.[103] Characteristic is Fairburn's assertion that she is a feminist "in practice. I'm not an advocate, necessarily" and another volunteer's answer that she is "not directly [a feminist]. I am the mother of 4 girls, who I raised to be independent, and to think they can do anything they want to do."[104] A Colombia volunteer who thought the "Peace Corps changed [her] life and outlook fundamentally" writes, "I am a feminist because I have seen how powerful women all over the world are and yet how little recognition they give themselves and each other and how little recognition they are given by men. As women, we give away our power and our talent and by doing so we help to keep ourselves in powerless positions."[105] Thus these volunteers who came of age during the high point of radical feminism eschew systemic analysis, arguing that women "can do anything they want to do" and that they should not "give away [their] power." Judging themselves and other women through the developmentalist frameworks into which they were uncomfortably interpellated by their years in the Peace Corps, they fault women for keeping themselves "in powerless positions," framing women's oppression as a problem of self-esteem and willpower rather than structural injustice and material inequality.[106]

This rejection of collective, political solutions to women's shared problems made the feminist movement seem either irrelevant or superfluous to many returned female volunteers. Having internalized the Peace Corps' liberal view of the world as a meritocracy where self-help rather than structural change would lead to better lives for all, the volunteers could only imagine the binds in which they themselves were trapped as obstacles they could have and should have been able to overcome. An India health volunteer who reflected, "My major accomplishments, the ones I previously thought were the only countable ones, are for the present nil," nevertheless echoes many of the other volunteers' hopeful confusion as she explains how she has grown while serving in the Peace Corps: "I've grown here, gotten more than I could ever give. I'm eager to get home, yet I don't know how I'll ever leave here. I'll never be able to do the same old job again. I have to have more education, and do interesting things in my life. I've gotten a sense of family . . . These women don't feel fulfilled, or like women, until they've had children. I guess it's catching, because I don't want to wait much longer."[107] "Eager to get home" while uncertain how she will bring herself to leave India, caught between her desire to "have more education, and do interesting things in my life" and the certainty that those things will not make her a "real woman," this volunteer has internalized perfectly the paradoxical identity that Wiggins and the rest of the Peace Corps imagined for her. She yearns to "feel fulfilled" in her work and personal life and knows this option will not be open to her in the world that exists, but is still unable to convert that yearning into participation. Speaking fifty years later, the women volunteers still do not imagine their "failures" at perfect domesticity and personal success as political, as when O'Grady attempts to explain why she did not marry and have children:

> I don't think I ever said I didn't want to be a housewife, but I didn't want to be just a housewife. Yeah I definitely wanted a career, and people said then, I don't know if they say it to you now, it's something to fall back on. If you can't find a husband, or God forbid something should happen to your marriage, you can fall back on this career. And I don't think there were any examples in my family of single women, there weren't any single women in my family. But it wasn't a decision to stay single, it was a decision to have a career, and I can't tell you why.[108]

Behind O'Grady's puzzled reflection on her inability to realize the dream of being "a housewife" but "not just a housewife" lurks the impossible model, articulated by Wiggins, Friedan, and the Peace Corps romances, of glamorous women who found career success and adventure while remaining charming display objects and submitting to men's "natural" leadership. Similarly resistant to making political meaning of her experience, Connie Jaquith reflects that "compromising my life goals, like graduate school, for the current goals of my new husband, that's where the greatest compromise was for me, putting him before myself. I'm that kind of person anyway, I do that in relationships, so I think it makes sense."[109] Characterizing her choice to abandon her career for her husband's "current goals" as stemming from her personality—rather than tracing it back to the culture of domestic containment, as Friedan had in *The Feminine Mystique*, or a more comprehensive structure of patriarchal oppression, as the radicals did later—Jaquith, like so many other volunteers, accepts her sacrifice as necessary for the men of the Peace Corps and the modernization goals they served.

If the heroic development ethos that characterized the Peace Corps made feminism difficult to imagine for non-movement-affiliated women, it also curtailed and preempted other social movements' experiments with feminism. In the next chapter, I explore in more depth this relationship between movement politics and the Peace Corps, examining the effects on the African American liberation struggle of the dominant liberal-developmentalist vision of overcoming poverty through a reassertion of patriarchy. I trace these diagnoses of cultural poverty, as well as the attendant program of personal masculine transformation and patriarchal reassertion, through their international iterations in development policy and back home, where they guided the War on Poverty and infiltrated the black liberation movement.

4

BRINGING THE
PEACE CORPS HOME
Development in the Black Freedom Movement

IN THE MID-1960s, as domestic social protest spread from the South to the rest of the United States, the Peace Corps changed its recruiting strategy, focusing on returned volunteers' ability to be useful at home. Advertisements emphasized volunteers' potential to connect with poor African Americans (and secondarily, other poor communities), arguing that because of their development work abroad, returned volunteers were in a better position to understand and assist similarly underdeveloped communities at home. One tagline of a 1968 advertisement exhorts volunteers to "Make America a better place. Leave the country," while the small print equates the Third World, framed as sleepy and stagnant, with U.S. regions being torn apart by riots, promising volunteers, "You could be the outsider who helps bring a Jamaican fishing village to life for the first time in 300 years. And you could wonder if your country has outsiders enough. In Watts. In Detroit. In Appalachia. On its Indian reservations."[1] The enumeration of these particular locations indicates the connection between the Peace Corps' vision of usefulness—its ability to create "outsiders" who could "bring a village to life"—and participation in the War on Poverty service programs overseen by Sargent Shriver.

Another advertisement from 1968 explicitly connects this ideal of service in poor communities with the civil rights movement, featuring Annmary Dalton, a young white volunteer, holding tightly to a naked black baby and gazing into the camera with a mixture of maternal solicitude—even as the outdoor location clearly delineates nondomestic space—and self-satisfaction. The advertisement sketches Dalton's adherence to the typical Peace Corps girl trajectory, tracing her rejection of the imperative to "marry a split-level house" in favor of "[doing] something

[she] wasn't supposed to do. Go far away. See things. Expand [her] mind. That stuff," and her initial experience of the Peace Corps as "so wild and new and, you know, definitely scary." The advertisement chronicles Dalton's disjointed musings about birth control (for other women), "American lipstick" (for her), and civil rights struggles (to be considered from afar), culminating with her return, where she finds romance and fulfilling work in Harlem:

> And then something different starts. I taught kids. I taught teachers. Me. I went home with them. I'd sit and we'd all worry about something. A pickup truck with a busted fuel pump. Could I get some American lipstick. Maybe mention that a woman wouldn't have to have a million kids if she didn't want to. Malaria.
>   . . . And you'd get a magazine. And you'd think about America. Martin Luther King. I never seriously thought I would change the world. Does anyone believe it anymore?
>   Then I came back. And I'm a teacher. And I've been seeing this guy, Ronnie. He's a teacher. We teach at P.S. 201. It's in Harlem.[2]

Beginning with Dalton's transgressive desires to do forbidden things and "expand [her] mind," the advertisement demonstrates how the Peace Corps channeled such proto-feminist and interracial desire into development projects, heterosexual romance, and antipoverty service (rather than movement activism) at home. By equating spaces like Harlem with a Third World in need of masculinization and development and their own modernization efforts with the work of Martin Luther King Jr., the Peace Corps sought to both channel would-be civil rights activists into development work and solidify development as the dominant framework for thinking about poverty at home and abroad.

Liberal development became the organizing framework for movement approaches to poverty within the United States in part because the repressive climate of the Cold War made it difficult to articulate systemic critiques of economic injustice. In her influential history *Cold War Civil Rights* Mary Dudziak argues that even as increased international scrutiny helped pressure the U.S. government to implement civil rights reforms, the Cold War dictated the kinds of claims civil rights activists could successfully make, "limit[ing] the field of vision to formal equality, to opening the doors of opportunity, and away from a broader critique of the American economic and political system."[3] While Dudziak's insights about the Cold War as both spurring and limiting civil rights goals are important, bringing development back into the story suggests another connection between Cold War imperatives and civil rights strategies and visions: activists did not ignore economic issues so much as adopt the capitalist development imperatives that the Peace Corps was so iconically enacting abroad, imagining that poverty could be remedied through personal and communal transformation, spurred by charismatic leaders into risk-taking, surplus-generating societies.

This chapter traces these adoptions of development discourse to diagnose domestic poverty, not only by Shriver and others in the War on Poverty he directed, but also by activists in the civil rights and Black Power movements. Fantasies of rescuing young men weakened by centuries-old "cultures of poverty," embodied by Peace Corps volunteers bringing initiative and ingenuity to passive traditional societies, extended beyond Johnson and Shriver's War on Poverty to shape civil rights and Black Power visions. As the black liberation movement changed its focus in the mid-1960s, moving beyond the fight for legal rights to the broader pursuit of economic power and international black solidarity, militant and moderate leaders alike adopted gendered modernization discourses to understand and address economic disparities. Development discourse and its "indelible antipopulism"—its emphasis on charismatic male leadership and technical knowledge—decisively influenced the Black Power movement, guiding Black Power leaders' relationships to their movements, their constructions of international solidarity, and their equation of economic and social advancement with men's control over women's bodies and their communities' reproductive power.[4] This meant that even as they adopted more radical structural analyses of U.S. foreign and domestic policy, movement leaders formulated their demands for economic change in terms of development discourse's imperative of personal transformation to masculine subjectivity, as well its promise of inclusion in fraternal spaces of power.[5]

Leapfrogging the Movement: Liberal Diagnoses of Black Poverty in the Civil Rights Era

On May 25, 1961, the day the first group of freedom riders were unfairly tried (the judge turned his back while the defendants' lawyers tried to argue their cases) and sentenced to sixty days apiece in the Mississippi State Penitentiary, John F. Kennedy delivered a "Special Message to the Congress on Urgent National Needs."[6] Though he had spent the previous few days hurriedly brokering a compromise between civil rights leaders and white southern officials, he referred neither to the freedom riders languishing in the jails of the U.S. South nor to any part of the civil rights movement. Instead, he argued that "urgent national needs" lay elsewhere. Proclaiming that "the great battleground for the defense and expansion of freedom is the whole southern half of the globe," he asked Congress to establish a new Act for International Development; increase military aid for "the crisis in Vietnam" to $1.9 billion; and, most famously, set a national goal of "before the decade is out, landing a man on the moon and returning him safely to earth."[7]

Kennedy's shifting of "the great battleground" from the U.S. South to the global South constituted an early attempt to reconcile an aggressively interventionist foreign policy on behalf of the "free world" with a domestic policy that often attempted to slow or suppress movements for civil rights at home. Upon hearing of the freedom riders, he ordered his friend and adviser Harris Wofford, "Get your friends off those buses!"[8] However, when Wofford's friends did not heed his warning, Kennedy's administration and Johnson's subsequent one developed more sophisticated tactics to redirect the transformative demands made by the civil rights and Black Power movements. Their central strategy for this redirection of militant energies was a sustained focus on diagnosing endemic black (and to a lesser degree, Latino, Native, and rural white) poverty, a task to which they applied the modernization frameworks they had pioneered abroad.[9] Pathologizing "the poor" as culturally deficient and their communities as improperly matriarchal, Johnson, Shriver, and the economists, social scientists, and antipoverty workers who advised and served them designed and implemented policies they imagined would end poverty by transforming poor undisciplined boys into men fit for supporting families. In doing so, they disseminated powerful discourses of cultural pathology and the masculine imperatives to overcome it that reached beyond the liberal establishment and into the most radical struggles for black equality.

The Peace Corps and the War on Poverty constituted pivotal sites for disseminating this development framework and thus for containing domestic social movements. Both the Peace Corps and the antipoverty programs enticed would-be civil rights activists into development work and instantiated development as the dominant framework for thinking about racialized poverty, locating its cause in cultural and familial "disorganization" and its solution in transforming young men of color into rational economic actors, proper patriarchs, and nationalistic citizens. Although Shriver's desire for the War on Poverty "to proceed with the same sense of urgency, to gather the same kind of momentum, to tap the same volunteer spirit, as the Peace Corps has done overseas" was not entirely fulfilled, his Office of Economic Opportunity programs did succeed in framing the problem of racialized poverty at home as a problem of cultural deficiency.[10]

From the beginning, the Peace Corps siphoned off people and resources that might have gone to civil rights. In his study of African American volunteers in the 1960s, Jonathan Zimmerman writes, "It seems clear that a small, liberal contingent in the White House was dissatisfied with the pace and direction of Kennedy's approach to civil rights. Almost to a man, the Peace Corps' early leadership derived from this dissident camp."[11] Wofford writes in his 1980 memoir that he wanted the job of Assistant Attorney General for Civil Rights, but that Attorney General Robert Kennedy considered him "too committed to civil rights" for the job and appointed Burke Marshall, who had no movement ties; he also recalls that Kennedy's southern campaign coordinator, Robert Troutman, told Shriver after the inauguration, "I hope all you bomb-throwers will now be corralled in one place, like the Peace Corps . . . so all your energies can be directed overseas instead of toward Georgia."[12] Indeed, Wofford remembers that he accepted the job directing the Peace Corps in Ethiopia because of "the affirmative pull of the Peace Corps," but also because he became frustrated with his role as "a buffer between [Kennedy] and the civil rights forces pressing for presidential action."[13]

Volunteers as well as staffers were diverted from civil rights work. Brazil community development volunteer Nancy Scheper-Hughes recalls "two very different recruiters" who "arrived on the unremittingly urban campus of Queens College in Flushing, New York," in spring 1964. Scheper-Hughes contrasts the "smooth, energetic, and charismatic" Shriver recruiting for the Peace Corps "under the catchy slogan 'How much can you give? How much can you take?'" with the "nervous young man in overalls representing the 'Mississippi Freedom Summer.'" She applied for Freedom Summer, along with her classmate Andrew Goodman, but, unlike Goodman, was rejected: "Male recruits were wanted first. By the time the summer project had reversed that sexist mandate and invited me to join, I had already accepted the Peace Corps' invitation."[14] Scheper-Hughes's account documents how the Peace Corps' early confidence and gender-blind incorporation of women enabled the organization to draw her away from civil rights organizations. A few years later Rachel Cowan, spurred by her husband's desire to avoid military service, tore herself away from her work with a New York tenants' organization—she writes that she was "sad to leave [her] friends in the middle of their fight"—to work on less confrontational community development projects in Guayaquil, Ecuador.[15]

The trajectory of these Peace Corps staffers and volunteers indicates a larger transformation of the civil rights ethos as would-be activists became volunteers and staffers who then returned to serve in the War on Poverty. The War on Poverty affiliated itself with the civil rights movement at a moment when organizers had begun to look beyond voting and the integration of public space and were beginning to formulate a broader struggle for economic justice; the poverty program offered the movement an understanding of poverty as underdevelopment and deficiency that could be solved through self-help and assimilation. Shriver and his returned volunteers carried the development discourses they had honed in the Peace Corps with them to the War on Poverty, using them to help shape Johnson's domestic agenda for addressing racialized poverty and managing the demands of civil rights activists.

The War on Poverty, which grew out of the Kennedy administration's attempts to solve the problem of juvenile delinquency, had relied from its inception on prominent social scientists' claims that urban communities of color suffered not from exploitation and injustice but rather from self-inflicted "cultures of poverty." Theories of cultural poverty and disorganization attained national prominence in the postwar years, as social scientists elaborated their ideas about racialized poverty in "underdeveloped" populations around the world. Alice O'Connor argues that as "the Cold War made the problem of traditional culture a direct political concern," these social scientists obtained immense institutional and financial support for their global poverty research.[16] Anthropologist Oscar Lewis, who coined the term "culture of poverty" in 1959, used his fieldwork collecting life histories and psychological studies in Mexico and Puerto Rico to adapt and revise sociologist E. Franklin Frazier's characterizations of family "disorganization," emphasizing female power as the root cause of—rather than, as Frazier suggested, a coping strategy for dealing with—nonwhite poverty.[17] O'Connor argues that although Lewis's family studies provided little evidence for the pervasiveness or uniformity of the culture of poverty he described, his definition—in which he identified "matrifocal families," "maternal deprivation," and "high tolerance of psychological pathology" as some of the "traits" endemic to the culturally poor—was immediately accepted, adapted, and disseminated by the social science establishment.[18]

Lewis's idea of domestic cultural poverty reached popular consciousness via the 1960 documentary *Harvest of Shame* and Michael Harrington's 1962 book *The Other America*, both of which constructed "the poor" very differently than had the class-conscious vocabulary that pervaded the 1930s and 1940s. Eschewing his long-professed socialism, Harrington adopted modernization theory's gendered, frontier-nostalgic language, arguing that the poor in the 1960s were different from "the adventurous seeking a new life and land" who had colonized the American frontier.[19] This new poor, the book contends, lack the "internal vitality" that characterized these adventurers, and many even "view progress upside-down, as a menace and a threat to their lives."[20] By eschewing class analysis and embracing modernization theory's rhetoric about men lacking "vitality" who have not yet learned to embrace "progress," Harrington succeeded in drawing national attention to the problem of domestic poverty.

If Harrington borrowed the vocabulary of liberal development to call attention to domestic poverty, the Peace Corps helped middle-class Americans visualize solutions to racialized poverty and dislocation. By holding volunteer trainings throughout the 1960s in urban "slums," as well as on Indian reservations, the Peace Corps equated racialized poverty at home with the underdevelopment they were fighting in Third World communities. The media made much of this equation between domestic and foreign "cultural" poverty: the *New York Times* reported in 1962 that "eighty members of the Peace Corps ventured into the slums of New York yesterday" to "observe some problems that occur when migrants from rural lands move into large cities," filling the front page with photos of new volunteers.[21] The Peace Corps' highly publicized presence in "underdeveloped" areas at home visibly enacted modernization doctrines that "cultural poverty" and "disorganization" were universal and globally uniform problems, and that they could be solved through the inculcation of modern habits and values. This meant that, rather than fueling outrage at the extreme poverty that existed within the "developed" United States, the Kennedy administration's consideration of a "domestic peace corps" was lauded: in 1962 the *Wall Street Journal* reported in a front-page headline, "Kennedy Aides Ponder a Peace Corps to Toil within United States: Volunteers Would Minister to Slum Dwellers, Migrants, Indians, Mental Patients." The article explained that volunteers would "combat slum-bred juvenile delinquency, truancy, school drop-outs, malnutrition, family friction," as well as "ease some burdens of catch-as-catch-can living for migratory workers" by "stimulating community interest in providing better shelter."[22]

By 1964, this public dissemination of Peace Corps volunteers' attempts to manage racialized poverty abroad and at home had popularized and elaborated liberal social science constructions of pathological racialized poverty, and the idea of a culture of poverty had become the dominant framework for thinking about both Third World poverty and black, Latino, and Native American (and to some degree, rural white) poverty at home.[23] Aware of the iconic status of the Peace Corps, Johnson attempted to replicate its ideological work domestically by insisting that Shriver run the War on Poverty. Shriver's leadership meant that the Peace Corps' ideas, iconography, and volunteers were visibly applied to domestic nonwhite poverty; like the volunteers abroad, antipoverty workers at home attempted to eliminate "cultures of poverty" and make modern men. In the February 1964 conversation in which he persuaded Shriver to serve as the first director of the War on Poverty's Office of Economic Opportunity, which supervised the vast majority of its programs, Johnson reiterated the gendered developmentalist objectives that the Peace Corps so iconically illustrated. When Shriver expressed caution about how Johnson's announcement of his new role would affect Peace Corps staffers, Johnson responded by impugning Shriver's manhood and imagining "women" as the cause of his reluctance:

"I am going to make it clear that you're Mr. Poverty, at home and abroad, if you want to be. And I don't care who you have running the Peace Corps. You can run it? Wonderful. If you can't, get Oshgosh from Chicago and I'll name him . . . You can write your ticket on anything you want to do there. I want to get rid of poverty, though. . . . The Sunday papers are going to say that you're Mr. Poverty, unless you've got real compelling reasons which I haven't heard . . ."

Shriver: "This ought to be a bombshell."

LBJ: "No, hell, it'll be a promotion! . . . I don't know why they would object to that. Unless you've got some women that think you won't have enough time to spend with them.

"You've got the responsibility, you've got the authority, you've got the power, you've got the money. Now you may not have the glands."

Shriver: "*The glands?*"

LBJ: "Yeah."

Shriver [with mild annoyance]: "I got plenty of glands."

LBJ: "Well, all right . . ."[24]

This conversation, in which Johnson secured Shriver's leadership in War on Poverty, typified the president's vulgar bravado but also set the terms for the poverty programs themselves. Johnson suggests that spending time with "some women" would keep Shriver from putting his "glands" to work making modern men.

The poverty programs enacted this gendered developmentalist vision. Using the logic of "cultural poverty" to argue that black men needed liberation from the maternal power that retarded their progress, Shriver encouraged the removal of these young men from their supposedly pathological families and communities to remote camps for Job Corps programs, his pet War on Poverty project. He originally formulated the program as a collaboration with Secretary of Defense Robert McNamara: together Shriver and McNamara imagined creating Job Corps centers in abandoned army facilities, with the Department of Defense housing and feeding the young people while government-contracted corporations educated and trained them. However, congressional opposition to such strong military control (with veterans in Congress citing their own horrific basic training experiences) prevailed, and LBJ forced Shriver to cut McNamara's direct ties to the program.[25] Still, Shriver maintained the partnerships with contractors and continued to push for militarized job training above all else, arguing that young men of color needed guidance by [presumably white] "men of unquestioned authority." He recalled in a 1980 interview:

> What we were trying to do is exactly what they do in the army. In the army you try to make a soldier out of a civilian. You take him and put him in an environment which is totally different from what he's been in, and you try to control that environment so you can make him into a different kind of person. We were trying to do the same thing in the Job Corps: teach or train people to participate as job holders in an industrialized society. I believed then, and I still believe, that a great deal of unemployment, particularly what they call structural unemployment, that is people who *can't* hold a job, comes from the fact they've been in an environment, in a culture—they used to call it the culture of poverty. You cannot cure that malady by leaving the victim in the middle of the area of contagion, to use a phrase out of medicine. So what you do is you take the person out of that environment, put them in a different environment, and you try to mold them into a different kind of person. Therefore, taking somebody from Georgia and putting them in Idaho is not harmful; it's helpful. It's helpful for them as an individual.[26]

Framing "structural unemployment" as the principal cause of poverty and locating its roots not in mismatches between available training and jobs, but rather in persistent, pathological problems in personality and culture, Shriver echoes the language of pathology popularized in the 1960s to reframe black communities as "areas of contagion" from which young men needed to be freed. Guided by the powerful pervasive theories of development that imagined modernization as personal transformation to manhood, Shriver was able to construct "poverty programs" that looked more like the Peace Corps' community development projects than the New Deal redistributive policies that had successfully alleviated widespread white poverty during the 1930s.[27]

Moynihan's August 1965 report on the black family, *The Negro Family: The Case for National Action*, most notoriously elucidates the developmentalist ideas undergirding War on Poverty diagnoses of black poverty and the policy prescriptions that would shape the attempts to fight it. Broadly sketching a narrative of African American history in which black men were deprived of control over women's bodies,

Moynihan claims in the report that "in essence, the Negro community has been forced into a matriarchal structure which, because it is so out of line with the rest of the American society, seriously retards the progress of the group as a whole, and imposes a crushing burden on the Negro male and, in consequence, on a great many Negro women as well."[28] Attributing black poverty to "retarded" progress, whose root cause was excessive female power, Moynihan focused and codified dominant misogynist and anti-maternal sentiments and prescribed the "utterly masculine world" of the armed forces as a "dramatic and desperately needed change: a world away from women, a world run by strong men of unquestioned authority."[29] The discourse of development enabled Moynihan and the many policy-makers who adopted the language of pathological matriarchy in the 1960s to explain the problem of economic oppression as one of imperiled masculinity; men of color, in his, Rostow's, and crucially Shriver's formulation, had been held back from their potential as human capital by their over-powerful women, and thus it fell to powerful, authoritarian white men to remedy this disparity by rebuilding black men's dominance in their families and communities.

Although Moynihan's sensationalistic language generated anger among social scientists and activists alike, the report only made explicit the gendered diagnoses that others had been advancing for decades: O'Connor is among the historians who substantiate Moynihan's own claim that his report "reflected what [he and others at the Office of Policy Planning] saw as a consensus among social scientists."[30] Likewise, although Johnson publicly distanced himself from the report after its release, the pathologizing discourse articulated by his adviser and speechwriter reflected and intensified the diagnoses and strategies already deployed in the War on Poverty. Though *The Negro Family* itself did not offer solutions to the "tangle of pathology" allegedly constituting black "matriarchal" families, beyond the "world away from women" provided by the military, Moynihan wrote in a 1965 memo to Johnson summarizing the report that "more can be done about redesigning jobs that are thought to be women's jobs and turning them into men's jobs: his type of job is declining, while the jobs open to the Negro female are expanding."[31] He explained in a subsequent interview that "a series of recommendations was at first included, then left out. It would have got in the way of the attention-arousing argument that a crisis was coming and that family stability was the best measure of success or failure in dealing with it." The recommendations he left out included "guaranteed full employment, birth control, adoption services, etc. *But first of all a family allowance.*"[32] These recommendations make explicit the sexism in the "family wage" ideal that guided much liberal thinking in the twentieth century: the "full" in "guaranteed full employment" completely erases women, since Moynihan recommends eliminating job opportunities for them.[33] But the fact that Moynihan excluded these recommendations from the final report, leaving only his exhortation that young black men learn proper discipline in a highly structured "world away from women," is also telling; the Office of Economic Opportunity programs guided by the report concerned themselves not with reforming the economy to make a "family allowance" more possible (as the New Deal had done for many white families), but rather with transforming individual men of color into properly disciplined laboring subjects who would dominate their families while correctly submitting to their bosses.

Johnson demonstrated that he shared Moynihan's preoccupation with black family dysfunction, as well as the accompanying developmentalist prescription of individual transformation to proper masculinity, in his June 1965 Howard University commencement speech, co-written by Moynihan and delivered to much fanfare and multiple standing ovations. Moynihan wrote the legendary speech specifically to allow Johnson to "leap-frog the movement," as one of the president's aides put it, anticipating and managing civil rights organizers' growing concern with economic justice by attributing inequality to underdevelopment, cultural deprivation, and insufficient male authority.[34] In the speech, Johnson touted his legislative accomplishments and then famously proclaimed that "freedom is not enough," rearticulating the shift that the movement was undergoing as activists realized that integrated public facilities did nothing to remedy poverty and exploitation. By way of diagnosis Johnson warned that "Negro poverty is not white poverty," and spoke ominously of "differences—deep, corrosive, obstinate differences—radiating painful roots into the community, and into the family, and the nature of the individual." To explain these corrosive differences, Johnson evocatively claimed, "Much of the Negro community is buried under a blanket of history and circumstance. It is not a lasting solution to lift just one corner of that blanket. We must stand on all sides and we must raise the entire cover if we are to liberate our fellow citizens." Locating the root cause of black poverty not in the structure of the economy but rather in the homes, and specifically the bedrooms, of African Americans, Johnson argued that the larger society could liberate black Americans only by lifting the "blanket" of cultural, familial, and gender pathology, the goal of which would be bringing black families into line with white patriarchal norms. Johnson made the goal of this blanket-lifting clear when he claimed that "perhaps most important—its influence radiating to every part of life—is the breakdown of the Negro family structure," which "flows from centuries of oppression and persecution of the Negro man. It flows from the long years of degradation and discrimination, which have attacked his dignity and assaulted his ability to produce for his family."[35]

The Howard speech demonstrates just how strongly Johnson and Moynihan's ideas about black poverty echoed the Peace Corps' equation of underdevelopment with diminished masculinity and insufficient patriarchy. The exhortation in the speech to "raise the entire cover" blanketing black family life, in order to coach black men into full manhood and economic incorporation, evokes Rostow's call for "intrusion" and "the threat of humiliation" that would incite allegedly passive populations of men to "reactive nationalism." Moynihan and Johnson also echo Talcott Parsons, who had identified the United States' relatively extreme and rigid gender "differentiation" as the key element of its Cold War capitalist modernity.[36] Johnson's speech identifies the black family's attainment of this "differentiation" (in which the black man would "produce for his family" and the black woman would stay home and do domestic tasks) as the crucial step toward ameliorating black poverty. Reiterating the development discourse being instantiated around the world, Johnson's speech substituted the attainment of full masculinity, articulated through men's complete incorporation into the capitalist system (an incorporation framed explicitly as a reclamation of patriarchal power from black "matriarchs"), for a more equal distribution of power and property as the endpoint of liberation struggles.

This argument attributing nonwhite poverty to family dysfunction, which had circulated nationally and internationally for years, finally found its policy expression in 1960s Office of Economic Opportunity programs.

But this pathologizing logic reverberated even beyond the realm of policy-making: Johnson's Howard University audience applauded enthusiastically as he explained the importance of invading African American homes and bedrooms to remedy "the breakdown of the Negro family structure," and Martin Luther King Jr. told the president that the speech was "the best one you have ever made and the best statement and analysis of the problem" he had ever heard.[37] These glowing responses indicate that by 1965 such modernization-theory influenced arguments made sense not just among white liberal administrators and development workers, but also in many African American communities and even in the movement for black liberation. The next section of this chapter explores how development influenced movement leaders in the transition from civil rights to Black Power, guiding them as they attempted to define themselves in relation to antipoverty programs, narrate their own personal transformations into revolutionaries, and understand their relationship to activists on the ground.

Sciencing Out the Revolution: Development in the Transition to Black Power

Martin Luther King Jr.'s 1965 visit to Watts occurred shortly after the neighborhood went up in flames, exploding in an outbreak of mass violence in which thirty-five thousand people, accompanied by over sixty thousand sympathetic onlookers, damaged $200 million worth of property; sixteen thousand troops eventually suppressed the rioters.[38] When King addressed crowds, calling for nonviolence, audiences booed and demanded more uprisings. Their reactions reflected the majority of the rioters' assertions in subsequent weeks that the riots King called "blind and misguided" had been a coordinated effort and a political tactic. These claims have since been echoed by historians, who have pointed out both that rioters were on average better educated and more likely to have jobs than nonrioters, and that the vast majority of the property damaged in the Watts uprisings was owned by wealthy and middle-class white people.[39] Nonetheless, though he encountered community groups unified in their militancy and their demands for better housing and services, King remarked to Bayard Rustin that the visit had shown him the "material and spiritual desolation" of urban African Americans.[40]

In a November *Saturday Review* article, King reflected on the Watts uprisings, proclaiming himself "increasingly disillusioned with the power structures" of the urban North. However, despite this gesture toward systemic critique, the article prominently employs the familiar rhetoric of passivity and gendered pathology, arguing that during the past decade, "the civil rights revolution appeared to be draining energy from the North, energy that flowed south to transform life there, while stagnation blanketed northern Negro communities. It was a decade of role reversal. The North, heretofore vital, atrophied, and the traditionally passive South burst with dynamic vibrancy." He goes on to explain the black family structure in language remarkably like Moynihan's, taking for granted both the "matriarchal" nature of black families and the threat to black male integrity that this alleged matriarchy poses: "Not only are the Negroes in general the first to be cast into the jobless army, but the Negro male precedes his wife in unemployment. As a consequence, he lives in a matriarchal society within the larger culture, which is patriarchal. The cruelest blow to his integrity as a man are laws which deprive a family of Aid to Dependent Children support if a male resides in the home . . . He is coerced into irresponsibility by his responsible love for his family."[41] King's approach to understanding Watts demonstrates the extent to which the discourses of cultural poverty and dysfunctional matriarchy had indeed leapfrogged the movement, pervading leaders' rhetoric as they became more focused on economic concerns. The rest of this section considers the way development imperatives shaped movement leaders' stories and organizing strategies: I focus on Black Power leaders' memoirs in order to explore how development shaped their ideas about revolutionary consciousness, the liberal power structure, and the masses they dreamed of mobilizing.

Had Cold War pressures to articulate their liberatory demands in civic and capitalist terms not been so great, nonviolent civil rights activists might have turned to Gandhian thought to formulate strategies for reconsidering and remedying the economic situation of poor black southerners. Gilbert Rist identifies Gandhi as the last decolonial leader to propose a substantive economic alternative to development, arguing that Gandhian thought was centrally structured around an ideal of "village self-sufficiency on the basis of the principles of *swadeshi* (interiority or endogenousness) and *sarvodaya* (improving everyone's living conditions)."[42] These ideas of local self-sufficiency and noncompetitive interdependence directly contradicted the principles of development being worked out by colonial powers in the 1930s and 1940s and by modernization theorists in the 1950s, and might have constituted a discursive challenge to both communist and capitalist development. But as Rist points out, this philosophy never became policy, as independent India very quickly committed itself to industrialization. In the translation of Gandhian thought to the U.S. civil rights movement, these ideals of local self-sufficiency were almost entirely ignored; Nico Slate has found that increasingly after 1960s, the principle of nonviolence stood in for the breadth of Gandhian thought in the activist and popular imaginations.[43] This synecdochic association of Gandhian thought and practice with civil disobedience in the American imagination meant that the movement took up his tactics but did not engage his economic vision, as indicated by the sit-in movement, in which activists struggled for the right to buy goods and services from white-owned businesses. This equation of freedom with proximity to whites and the right to participate in capitalist relations represented a moderate strain of the nonviolent movement, one that shaped the *Brown v. Board of Education* case, in which the NAACP transformed student demands for equal facilities into a bid for integration, and found its apotheosis in Martin Luther King Jr.'s oft-quoted dream that "one day on the red hills of Georgia the sons of former slaves and the sons of former slaveowners will be able to sit down together at the table of brotherhood."[44]

Despite the movement's (often strategic) decisions to privilege proximity and civic and consumer subjection over equality, glimmers of an alternative to development logic emerge in the organizational structure and transformative visions of more radical civil rights organizations like CORE and SNCC. They appear in SNCC's emphasis on local people's (particularly disenfranchised black sharecroppers') knowledge and agency—the insistence of movement mentors like Ella Baker that oppressed people themselves, in dialogue with their communities, could figure out the best way to fight their oppression; in its emphasis on contingency and context rather than grand doctrine, in James Lawson's words "the Gandhian idea of being engaged in an experiment where you have to keep figuring out what happened, and why, and what didn't happen";[45] and even in its religious vision of beloved community that sought to change American society not through individual striving but rather through communal interdependence, support, and spirituality. In the posters and other photographs it created and circulated, SNCC also made a point to avoid images of heroic assistance, relying instead on images of activists and sharecroppers that emphasized anonymity, community, and dignity.[46]

Despite SNCC's deeply egalitarian practice, and its faith that oppressed people knew what liberation looked like, the group was less sure of its approach to poverty. Wesley Hogan observes that in SNCC, "the experiences of sit-ins, Freedom Rides, and voter registration drives did not routinely or automatically equip anyone to figure out what to do about poverty in the African American community . . . despite the fact that it was relatively easy to demonstrate that black poverty was a direct legacy of America's racist heritage."[47] This difficulty in thinking about poverty led SNCC to draw on the expertise, and thus the discourses, available in the culture around them: in late 1963 they requested a speaker from SDS to discuss "the integrated nature of problems of unemployment, the vote, and cultural poverty" in black communities, indicating that they, too, were vulnerable to the sense that poverty in particular was the purview of white experts, as well as to the rhetoric of familial dysfunction that "cultural poverty" implied.[48]

These movement alternatives to development logic disappeared after the mid-sixties, when civil rights groups succeeded in dismantling the Jim Crow system of legal segregation in the South. Witnessing the distance between formal and substantive equality, black liberation groups turned increasingly to visions of anticapitalism, internationalism, and separatism. But even as they expanded the black liberation agenda beyond inclusion and citizenship, leaders began to imagine gender and sexuality more narrowly and movement structure more hierarchically. Erica Edwards writes that after 1965, "the three-way contest between the black elected officials, protest leaders, and cultural figures ushered in the post–civil rights era as a series of manly contests for political sway" and that "with blacks' entry into formal American politics, nonheteronormative difference posed a threat to a new, official political blackness."[49] In 1967, King signaled his broadened and radicalized agenda by enumerating economic inequalities and institutional racism and then arguing that "to upset this cultural homicide, the Negro must rise up with an affirmation of his own Olympian manhood."[50] By 1968, when Eldridge Cleaver wrote, "We shall have our manhood. We shall have it or the earth shall be levelled by our attempts to gain it," those two goals seemed compatible: Cleaver refers to revolution, which has become in movement discourse indistinguishable from the seizure by black men of white men's violent patriarchal power over women and children, but his phrasing also indicates the extent to which this revolutionary "gain" requires a Newtonian (Isaac, via Rostow) "leveling" of nature.[51]

The obsession with attaining full manhood and its equation with world-remaking, revolutionary power, as Michele Wallace explained in 1978, was the predictable outcome of a psychosexual racial order in which white America—Mailer and the beats as much as white supremacist southerners—was obsessed with black male genitalia. But we might also consider the particular form this reclaiming takes—the yoking of manhood-affirming, culture-preserving, and earth-leveling—as a developmentalist one, stemming both from Black Power intellectuals' political education as well as their participation in Shriver and Johnson's antipoverty programs.[52] Through their participation in these programs, Black Power leaders adopted the liberal establishment's developmentalist framework for thinking about social change, accepting that black poverty and subjugation would be overcome through black men's individual transformation to full modernity and masculinity.[53] Even as they became disillusioned with the antipoverty programs, Black Power leaders retained the cultural poverty frameworks that those programs had emphasized, continuing to frame black empowerment as a shift to full male employment and increased power over black women and to imagine poor black communities as disorganized and underdeveloped in their radicalism even when nationwide urban uprisings indicated otherwise.

In his 1970 autobiography *Seize the Time*, Black Panther Party cofounder Bobby Seale recounts his success in "using the poverty program" for radical ends and his frustration with its liberal leadership. Seale, Huey Newton, Bobby Hutton, and other early Panther recruits met in a North Oakland antipoverty program; Seale led a "summer work program [that] provided jobs for about 100—twenty-five girls and seventy-five boys. They worked in the community cutting lawns, digging up grounds, etc. They were supposed to do repairs on fences and steps and things like that, but the equipment wasn't available." Seale recalls that "through working in the poverty programs I was able to meet a lot of the young cats who would later become lumpen proletarians."[54] Seale and Newton wrote their party platform, "What We Want, What We Believe," in the North Oakland antipoverty center, sneaking in at night to print more than a thousand copies of their manifesto. They also collaborated with the center's advisory committee on petitions, one for a community police review board, another to establish a traffic light at a dangerous intersection in the face of a sluggish city council: Seale contends that the advisory committee was able to pressure the council in part because of Newton's threat that armed Panthers would take over the intersection if the light was not installed.[55] The Panthers drew national attention to their affiliation with the government program in the summer of 1967 when Seale, a year after taking the antipoverty program job, recommended in a speech to one hundred young people at a Community Action Program (CAP) in Oakland that "if we organize and use gun power in a strategic fashion against a racist power structure, the power structure becomes aware of the facts that we are correctly educated on the true understanding of politics," and proclaimed that it was time to "forget the sit-ins, and shoot it out." Shriver responded by ordering his Inspection Division to purge the Bay Area CAPs of militant activists and "publicize the facts" in San Francisco.[56]

Antipoverty money also funded East Coast programs like Amiri Baraka's (then Leroi Jones's) Black Arts Repertory Theater/School (BARTS) program, which used $44,000 in antipoverty funds in the summer of 1965 to teach four hundred students drama and black studies. "Bringing art to the people, black art to black people, and getting paid for doing it was sweet," Baraka recalls in his autobiography, but Shriver pulled the funding after he came to New York to visit the program and Baraka refused to let him in the door.[57] Baraka recalls telling his friend to relay the message "fuck Shriver" to the director and his entourage and then looking out the window, seeing "the white faces turning red and the Negro faces turning Negroier." Writing in 1984, he regretfully muses that "in retrospect, that obviously wasn't cool . . . But we were too honest and too naïve for our own good. We talked about revolution because we meant it; we hooked up programs of revolutionary and progressive black art because we knew our people needed them, but we had not scienced out how these activities were to be sustained on an economic side."[58] Shriver retaliated by cutting the program funding for BARTS, telling the media that the antipoverty money had been mistakenly channeled to support "vile racist plays in vile gutter language unfit for the youngsters in the audience."[59]

Baraka's retrospective regret that he had not "scienced out" his revolutionary dreams both contextualizes his later entry into electoral politics and indicates the extent to which the poverty programs, with their reverence for the social sciences, shaped black radical leaders' work and ideas about poverty and development. A "scientific" (Marxist) sense of correct political action also suffused the Black Panthers, shaping their hierarchical organizational structure. The influence of the War on Poverty's ideologies became clear in the Panthers' demand for "full employment" for black men, which perfectly echoed Parsons, Moynihan, and Johnson's patriarchal dream of fully incorporated black workers earning a "family wage" that would enable their wives to serve as correctly "differentiated" housewives at home.

The centrality of developmentalist thought to Black Power leaders' ideas about economics suggests that while the antipoverty programs offered resources for activists to appropriate for their own ends, they simultaneously curtailed movement leaders' ideological radicalism, reframing their relationship to the increasingly militant poor communities they attempted to organize.[60] The extent to which developmentalist discourses of deprivation and cultural poverty pervaded the rhetoric of movement leaders as they became more radical and focused on economic concerns was evident in Black Power leaders' responses to the urban uprisings of the late sixties. Even as groups like the Panthers theorized black America as an internal colony, they borrowed language from social scientists to label rioters a "disorganized" and "culturally poor" surplus population rather than seeing them as they saw themselves, as potential revolutionaries who might take back some of the wealth that the people in their communities had worked so hard for so long to produce. Black power leaders were hesitant to ascribe revolutionary agency to rioters; their absorption of modernization ideology left them disconnected from the urban masses of African Americans they attempted to organize and discipline.

This sense that the masses were not "ready" for revolution, that they had to undergo (and perhaps also narrate) a personal transformation to become fully functioning revolutionary subjects, pervades Black Power thought to a surprising degree. In their memoirs, Seale and Baraka dramatize particularly stark revolutionary awakenings, both catalyzed by Malcolm X's death, as well as subsequent attempts to fit mass action into a development framework. Saldaña-Portillo argues that developmental narratives contain a pivotal moment of choice when "the underdeveloped subject must make the ethical choice to enter development and thereby history, to leave behind a prodigal life in favor of a productive one, with this prodigal life most often thematized negatively as ethnos—as clan, caste, tribe, or extended family."[61] Reading Malcolm X's characterization of the "huddled" black hustlers he hung around with in his early life "who could have probed space, or cured cancer or built industries," Saldaña-Portillo demonstrates that Malcolm understood the black underclass as prerevolutionary subjects whose "unhoned resistive knowledge operates as a preconsciousness that holds the potential for transformation into revolutionary collectivity under Islam and Malcolm X's guidance."[62] Just as he had disciplined and transformed himself, Malcolm aspired to recruit and discipline the masses to pursue science and technology careers and capitalist accumulation in a new, modern black nation.

After Malcolm's assassination, a new generation of Black Power leaders like Seale and Baraka attempted to carry on his legacy, taking a similarly developmentalist approach in narrating their attainment of revolutionary consciousness. Saldaña-Portillo remarks that the *Autobiography* "begins with a scene of chaos and violence—his earliest memory—that serves as the birth of the revolutionary," then narrates Malcolm's father's death and Malcolm's "reestablish[ment] of the mythic patronymic relationship in the narrative through the reconstruction of his father's life in the epic terms of black nationalism."[63] Seale and Baraka, in turn, both stage their "births" as revolutionaries at the moment of Malcolm's death, births which allow them to decisively reposition their family relationships. Seale recounts his reaction to Malcolm's death in the opening lines of *Seize the Time*, in a chapter titled "Who I Am": "When Malcolm X was killed in 1965, I ran down the street. I went to my mother's house, and I got six loose red bricks from the garden. I got to the corner, and broke the motherfuckers in half. I wanted to have the most shots that I could have, this very same day Malcolm was killed.

Every time I saw a paddy roll by in a car, I picked up one of the half-bricks, and threw it at the motherfuckers. I threw about half the bricks, and then I cried like a baby."[64] Beginning his story with the moment of his transformation into a new man and Malcolm's disciple, Seale pinpoints the violence of breaking his mother's bricks and throwing them as the moment of his birth, the "crying like a baby" marking him as newly born. Seale's moment of rebirth fits the Black Power moment particularly well: while he attributes his revolutionary masculine genealogy to Malcolm, he enacts this ritual by using his mother's resources, deliberately reconfiguring "labor" by rewriting women's labor (in both senses) to narrate male rebirth into a masculine world of theft, violence, and eventual revolutionary discipline. Similarly reading the above scene as "a paradigm of the terms on which the New Man gives birth to himself," Robert Carr argues that the "imperviousness of the police" in the scene "already predicts the military superiority of the state's forces" and their brutal suppression of the Panthers.[65] But if Seale's rebirth already foreshadows defeat, he directly follows the scene with a more triumphant moment, skipping in a seeming non sequitur to the moment of his son's birth:

> When my wife Artie had a baby boy, I said, "The nigger's name is Malik Nkrumah Stagolee Seale."
>
> "I don't want him named that!" Artie said.
>
> I had read all that book history about Stagolee, that black folkloric history, because I was hung up on that stuff at the time, so I said, "Malik Nkrumah Stagolee Seale!"
>
> "Why Stagolee?" Artie asked. "Because Stagolee was a bad nigger off the block and didn't take shit from nobody. All you had to do was organize him, like Malcolm X, make him politically conscious. All we have to do is organize a state, like Nkrumah attempted to do."[66]

In contrast to the disorderly, tragic rebirth he narrates directly before, this birth allows for Seale's reassertion of control over his world. The name he gives his son, over his wife's objections, allows for both the assimilation of divergent radical black traditions and the establishment of an organized black nationalism, rehearsed metonymically in the realm of the family. Seale's rapid restoration of his own authority, over women and children if not the larger power structure, means he is on his way to becoming a disciplined masculine leader who must reject the "disorganized" tactics of the masses in favor of orderly self-defense and dialogue with power.

Baraka also narrates his conversion at the moment of Malcolm's death as both a rebirth and a reassertion of control in the familial realm, which in his case takes the form of a break with the women on which he (like Seale) had relied for material support. Directly before the incident, he recalls feeling himself drifting away from his wife and feeling a "fury, which had no scientific framework," that caused him to "thrash out at any white man." He writes, "During this period, I got the reputation of being a snarling, white-hating madman. There was some truth to it, because I was struggling to be reborn, to break out from the shell I could instinctively sense surrounded my own dash for freedom."[67] He is able to break out of "the shell" when he hears of Malcolm's death in the middle of a book party in the West Village; accompanied by his wife and two young daughters, he is "being personable and knowledgeable" when his friend Leroy McLucas bursts in:

> He was weeping. "Malcolm is dead! Malcolm is dead! Malcolm has been killed!" He wept, repeating it over and over. I was stunned. I felt stupid, ugly, useless. Downtown in my mix-matched family and my maximum leader/teacher shot dead while we bullshitted and pretended. The black core of us huddled there, my wife and family outside that circle. We were feverish and stupefied. McLucas wept uncontrollably. I called a couple fellows in the corner over, but they were dazed and couldn't hear immediately. Joel Oppenheimer said, "That's the trouble with the black revolution. Roi's giving directions and nobody listens!"
>
> But who and what was I to give anything, or he to make such a statement. "It's all bullshit!" went through me. "All!"
>
> In a few days I had gotten my stuff out and gone uptown . . . My little girl, the older one, Kellie, picked up instinctively on my departure. She said to me, "You can't go anywhere. You're one of the funny things."
>
> But in a minute or so I was gone. A bunch of us, really, had gone, up to Harlem. Seeking revolution![68]

Narrating his rebirth, Baraka echoes Seale in dramatizing the ritual of "feverish," "stupefied" weeping, this time in a "black core" group that excludes his "mix-matched" daughters as well as his wife but includes white male poets like Oppenheimer, this last detail indicating the extent to which blackness and maleness were casually conflated in the terms of the freedom struggle. The huddle prefigures the collective revolution-seeking exodus and eventual adoption of a "scientific" revolutionary leadership stance, the scene for which Baraka must leave not only his white wife but also his biracial daughters. Kellie's remark, which casts him as "one of the funny things" necessary to her world as well as the downtown racially mixed art world, marks his break with his queer-identified, bohemian, prerevolutionary self.

All three Black Power leaders, then, narrate the disciplining of their unruly prerevolutionary pasts in order to explain their work disciplining potential revolutionaries. Seale writes of cautioning crowds against "spontaneous rioting" in the wake of the assassinations of both King and Hutton, "because that's not the correct method," despite his desire to "tell all those people at the rally to turn Oakland upside down."[69] His designation of the potential uprising as "spontaneous," even while speaking to a crowd willing to take orders from him but also ready to take over the city of Oakland, indicates his understanding of would-be rioters as an underdeveloped, potential lumpenproletariat he must prepare for revolutionary transformation, rather than a class of people who have been radicalized by their everyday experiences of oppression and who were, in fact, ready to revolt in a non-"spontaneous" way. Directly after the story of defusing the uprising, Seale models a properly disciplined, fully masculine performance of revolutionary subjectivity, recounting his work on Newton's subsequent U.S. congressional campaign and his success at getting Newton on the ballot.[70]

Baraka similarly narrates his experience interacting with popular insurgencies as one of both desire and discipline. In his Kerouacian narration of his experience joyriding with friends through the 1967 Newark uprisings—"all that was pent up and tied is wild and loose, seen in sudden flames and red smoke, and always people running, running, away and toward"—he focuses once again on the lack of "science" informing the uprisings, recalling that "the police were simply devils to us. Beasts. We did not understand then the scientific exegesis on the state—though we needed to." Brutally beaten and arrested by Newark police despite his role as a spectator, Baraka recognizes the uprising as "a rebellion"—though, as he makes clear, not a potential or failed revolution—and imagines it as a personally, spiritually transformative force, writing of his realization that "one had to organize, one had to arm, one had to mobilize and educate the people. For me, the rebellion was a cleansing fire." He further explains, "I had been through the fire and had not been consumed. Instead, I reasoned, what must be consumed is all of my contradictions to revolution. My individualism and randomness, my Western, white addictions, my Negro intellectualism." His self-discipline leads him to become Sunni Muslim and, by the aftermath of King's assassination the following summer, to suppress rather than revel in the uprisings, "[telling] people to cool it" and negotiating with Newark police. Soon afterward he starts the Committee for United Newark, whose goal is to bring young black artists and nationalists into contact with "middle-class blacks interested in electoral politics" and to run candidates for city council and other local offices.[71]

Seale and Baraka's narratives of their revolutionary awakenings demonstrate how development discourse, to the extent that the leaders of the 1960s radical movements adhered to its aspirations of full masculinity and incorporation into the global economy, severed them from the mass base of their movement at crucial moments of potential transformation, preventing them from being able to view the urban uprisings as anything but disorganized, spontaneous, and, in Baraka's case, aesthetically interesting. The kind of dialogical movement-building characteristic of early SNCC activists seems very distant from these top-down efforts at suppression and redirection. The final section of this chapter delineates the broader effects of the civil rights and Black Power movements' absorption of modernization theory, exploring how its hierarchical vision impeded international as well as cross-gender alliances.

The Peace Corps and Movement Attempts at Third World Solidarity

In her memoir *Coming of Age in Mississippi*, a book whose title suggests its critique of anthropological discourses that would label its black southern setting uncivilized, exotic, or otherworldly, civil rights organizer Anne Moody indicts the United States government for using the Peace Corps to divert resources away from the task of allaying the desperate poverty and racist violence in the U.S. South. She recalls thinking, after learning that white supremacists have murdered her uncle and three other men, that "beyond focusing attention on the area, we, the civil rights organizations, were powerless when it came to doing something about the murders. Yet the United States could afford to maintain the Peace Corps to protect and assist the underprivileged citizens of other countries while native-born American citizens were murdered and brutalized daily and nothing was done."[72] Moody's musings demonstrate the extent to which the Peace Corps had become meaningful to civil rights workers as a symbol of U.S. potential for benevolence, as well as the difficulty activists had imagining transnational black solidarity: though Moody has experienced unremitting abuse from white employers, police, and other authorities, she still pits herself against "underprivileged citizens of other countries" vying for the Peace Corps workers' "protection" and "assistance," rather than imagining herself in solidarity with Third World peoples in an interrelated struggle against racism and imperialism.

By 1966, civil rights activist turned Black Power leader Stokely Carmichael could articulate a more militant position of transnational black solidarity, publicly characterizing African Americans and Africans as collective victims of imperialist resource extraction and development discourse. Speaking to predominantly white students at Berkeley, Carmichael equated the philosophy and work of the Peace Corps with that of the War on Poverty, confronting both the coercive nature of modernization theory and the false promise of equality it offered:

> Now we have modern-day missionaries, and they come into our ghettos—they Head Start, Upward Lift, Bootstrap, and Upward Bound us into white society. They don't want to face the real problem. A man is poor for one reason and one reason only—he does not have money. If you want to get rid of poverty, you give people money. We're not talking about a policy of aid or sending Peace Corps people in to teach people how to read and write and build houses while we steal their raw materials from them . . . America keeps selling goods back to them for a profit and keeps sending our modern day missionaries there, calling them the sons of Kennedy.[73]

Pointing to the absurdity of attributing poverty to personal "backwardness" and sending in young volunteers to model "white society" behavior while the same white society continues to profit from the labor and resources of the domestic and foreign poor, Carmichael argues that the development ideology advanced by U.S. policy-makers has allowed them to both manage and maintain poverty, at home and abroad. Yet, despite his critique of development discourse and his insight that it shapes racist transnational conceptions of "cultural poverty," Carmichael accepts the universal imperative of rapid industrialization and incorporation into global capitalism, arguing that "what underdeveloped countries need is information about how to become industrialized, so they can keep their raw materials where they have them, produce goods, sell them to this country for the price it's supposed to pay."[74] Although Carmichael's attempt at solidarity goes further than most, he still does not question the inevitability and desirability of industrialization and incorporation into global capitalism as the endpoints of Third World revolutionary struggle, indicating how powerful and pervasive modernization theory's tenets had become. This section considers the accounts of black Peace Corps volunteers and others who attempted to make transnational connections, further demonstrating how the racialized, gendered rhetoric of modernization theory prevented broader struggles for justice that would include meaningful expressions of international, much less cross-gender, solidarity.

In her study of the African American press, Penny Von Eschen finds that the Cold War precluded the "claims of political reciprocity between Africans and African Americans," founded on an articulation of shared exploitation by the white capitalist power structure, on which the prewar black movement in the United States had relied. According to Von Eschen, the postwar black freedom movement forgot its prewar articulations of diasporic solidarity and organized within a discursive framework that accepted the United States' role as global hegemonic power, a framework bolstered by the black presses' use of "metaphors from developmental psychology" to characterize Africa as passive, primitive, exotic, and monolithic. Von Eschen argues that the return to exoticizing views of Africa constituted an "especially pernicious reinscription of the primitive" because these racist ideas were "now cloaked—and legitimized—by emerging modernization and development theory."[75] This infusion of developmentalist language into black American characterizations of Africa happened on the verge of widespread African decolonization, preventing many black Americans from aligning their fate with that of the Ghanaians, Congolese, Tanzanians, and others who were throwing over their white oppressors. When the Black Power movement did turn to Africa for inspiration in the later 1960s, they often embraced an exoticized historical fantasy, "the colonial paradigm of anachronistic space" revived for the development moment.[76] Inverting the valences of the developmental narrative but adhering to its characterization of Africa as a monolithic place outside time and history, they imagined an ancient land of (properly dominant) kings and (properly ornamental) queens rather than a diverse continent in which trade unionists, market-women, and guerrilla fighters had toppled seventeen colonial governments by the end of 1960.

This masculine developmental language, as well as its imperatives, shaped the Peace Corps' attempts to recruit African Americans, whom they desperately wanted to serve in recently independent sub-Saharan Africa but who largely stayed away from the Peace Corps, often due to economic and movement obligations. Zimmerman writes that "rather than 'discriminating' in favor of people of particular races, then, Peace Corps officials devised measures to choose 'culturally deprived' candidates of all races, adjusting their entrance exam criteria for students from Southern colleges," a tactic which backfired when almost all the "deprived" volunteers turned out to be white.[77] Imposing a "cultural deprivation" label on would-be volunteers who would then be required to both advertise the U.S. system and transmit initiative and "democratic values" that would allow Third World communities to overcome their own "deprivation" seems ironic at first glance, but makes sense when read through the framework of a new global developmentalism, which demanded the inclusion of African Americans while divorcing that inclusion from any acknowledgment of structural racial injustice. The new framework required both the language of "cultural deprivation" and the separation of African Americans from the even more "culturally deprived" Africans, Asians, and Latin Americans they would teach and modernize. The Peace Corps, then, encouraged black volunteers to understand their problems (and the problems of people they might have been in solidarity with overseas) as problems of deprivation that could be solved by modernization, and in so doing helped to drive a wedge between the volunteers and their Third World counterparts, imagining them always at irrevocably distinct points on the development trajectory.

But as the attempt at recruiting "culturally deprived" students indicates, African Americans volunteered at considerably lower rates than did whites. A 1968 Peace Corps–sponsored survey found that African American college seniors viewed the Peace Corps "positively, though remotely," but most agreed with the statement that "there are enough problems facing Negroes in the U.S. and someone who is really concerned about others should be working against those problems here rather than going abroad with the Peace Corps."[78] When African Americans did volunteer, the task of representing both the "free world" in charge of modernizing "deprived" societies and the black freedom struggle at home, in which most black college students had participated by the mid-sixties, proved confusing and complicated. Juanita Ann Covington reflects in *The Crisis* in 1964 that "being a negro in Ethiopia, I find myself in a novel position. A position where my color enhances, rather than hinders," and goes on to articulate the contradictory job she must do in her quest for both good publicity for the United States and solidarity with the civil rights struggle:

> My time in the Peace Corps has been one of the most rewarding periods of my life. Rewarding in the sense that I felt I was helping America, Africa, and myself. As a Negro I feel that my mere presence in Africa does a great deal to counteract many misconceptions Africans have of the American Negro and of the United States. Some were surprised to see Negroes because they thought we were not permitted to attend school. The Africans, from my experiences in Sudan, Kenya, Tanganyika, as well as Ethiopia, would like to be of some help to us in our fight for complete first-class citizenship. We can be of great help to them in their struggle for educational, scientific, agricultural, and technological advancement. And most of all, they want us![79]

In her attempt to explain the rewarding nature of her Peace Corps service, Covington accepts that Ethiopia and other African nations need all kinds of "advancement," despite acknowledging that the United States does not grant "first class citizenship" to everyone and that she is actually treated better in the allegedly "backward" nations than in her own country. The plaintive "most of all, they want us!" seems to refer both to the Africans' desires for U.S. technicians of all races and to the welcome they have extended specifically to African Americans, who have yet to receive such enthusiastic acceptance at home.

Ghana volunteer Ed Smith, despite his considerable attentiveness to decolonization struggles—he writes that he joined the Peace Corps to serve in "an independent country of black people striving to demonstrate to the world their ability to conduct their own affairs and determine their own future"—experienced similar confusion throughout his stay.[80] He complains throughout his memoir that Ghanaians' analysis of colonial and racial oppression neglects the particular pain of emasculation from which he suffers:

> It was "political" or "economic" expedience that moved the colonialist to behave the way he did: thus it must be the same with the Afro-American and *his* master in the States. That "racial injustice" had philosophical and psycho-social implications just didn't occur to them—mainly because they saw discrimination in purely personal terms . . . Yes, it was horrible about the Negro in the States, they had no idea *how* bad until I told them, but what did it have to do with them? The Afro-American would some day liberate himself the way they had, and everything would be alright, wouldn't it? No it wouldn't, I said, because for the black man to be really free, he must have the world's respect for his identity *as a black man*—an identity that can be forcefully stated only when black men everywhere take on each other's struggle for their own.[81]

Bringing to mind Michele Wallace's recollection that it took her "three years to learn that the speeches that all began 'the black man . . .' did not include me,"[82] Smith attempts here to convince his Ghanaian friends that in order for true black nationalism to exist, the Ghanaians would have to understand not the common experiences of economic exploitation and political exclusion that black people around the world shared, but rather the shared "psychosocial" experience of emasculation that denigrated one's identity "*as a black man*." Smith further outlines his commitment to black liberation as a purely masculine endeavor when he recounts the story of commiserating with other black volunteers over another black expatriate friend caught assaulting his Ghanaian wife and mother-in-law:

> Late into the evening Afro-American Volunteer Sims rushed into the hostel hollering for War, and, not finding him, poured out his grief to me. It seems that Fred, an Afro exile in the Worker's Brigade, beat his wife, a Ghanaian, then his mother-in-law when she tried to protect her

daughter. Poor Fred, trying so hard to be African and not making it, never making it, for American Negroes are caught in just as much of a dilemma here as they are in America. "Oh, what has this white man done to us?" Sims says, his face crumpled in despair, and I sympathize with him, because I too am ashamed. Later, cringing on the roof until dawn, I find myself thinking about Odel, one of two Negro female volunteers here, who married an Indian and is already suing for divorce. And it is said she had even bleached her light brown skin to appear European . . .[83]

Again Smith frames the black struggle as a quest for an authentic masculine subjectivity (framed here as unattainable Africanness) that would entail total control over women's bodies, only able to claim solidarity with African men through the shared experiences of emasculation by "this white man." Smith and his friend Sims feel immediate sympathy with Fred, rather than with the Ghanaian women he has beaten, on the grounds that African and African American men share "the dilemma" of being unable to "be African." His association of the domination of women with true Africanness signals Smith's subscription to Black Power's cultural nationalist fantasies of ancient, authentic, properly patriarchal African cultures in which women knew their places, fantasies conjured in reaction to the conventional developmentalist wisdom that African and African American men were dominated and stifled by slavery-induced matriarchies. Thus interpellated by the reactionary currents of black nationalism, Smith turns his thoughts to Odel as the embodiment of self-hate, racial betrayal, and the psychological ravages of internalized white supremacy. Whether he is equating Odel's marrying "an Indian" and skin-bleaching with Fred's wife-beating and attributing both to internalized racism, or imagining Odel conspiring with white and Indian men and Ghanaian women to emasculate black men, Smith is unable to imagine her, much less the victims of Fred's beating, as his partners in struggle; African and African American women alike appear as the source and sign of failed black masculinity.

A Peace Corps roundtable about black volunteers in the summer of 1968 occasioned a sustained discussion of the issues Smith raises about gender and freedom. The roundtable discussion addressed the question of why African Americans were underrepresented in the Peace Corps, the challenges they faced upon their return to the United States, and their relationship to movement struggles. The conversation featured three participants: returned volunteer and urban development graduate student Earl Brown; secretary of the ambassador to Niger Omarou Youssefou; and Willie J. Hardy, a civil rights activist and director of the Washington, D.C., Community Action Project. In the transcription of the roundtable published under the title "Needed: Abroad or at Home?" Brown characterizes his Peace Corps experience as one of self-discovery, explaining, "You might say I took a leave of absence from America to step away and really find out where I stand and what I am. As a result . . . you're no longer an American, you're Earl Brown, a human being. When you find yourself, then you're ready to really do some work on domestic problems."[84] Brown maintains that the Peace Corps allowed him to both criticize and serve his country, arguing that "I did not join the Peace Corps for America; I joined for Earl Brown . . . I think Volunteers are very critical of America, as a matter of fact. It's like looking at a painting sometimes. When you step away from it, the light shines just a bit differently and you get a greater perspective on it."[85]

Hardy attempts to remind Brown of both the collective nature of the fight for social change and the irony of representatives of a racist America attempting to instruct already-decolonized African nations in their affairs, replying that "any African nation that really knows how its black brothers are treated here would have some real hang-ups if we went over and started telling them how they could best do things. These developing countries are talking about freedom. They're talking about sustaining themselves. They're talking about being their own masters. We black people in America cannot talk about that." Here Hardy uses Black Power's internationalist perspective to highlight the contradiction between U.S. expertise in "democracy" and the lack of even basic civil rights, much less economic justice, for many black Americans. She goes on to discount the Peace Corps' modernizing narrative, arguing, "I don't know what we could possibly give a country that's talking about that kind of thing."[86]

However, the constraints of Black Power's vision of women's roles mean that Hardy can draw only implicitly on her work as an activist in arguing for the irrelevance of the Peace Corps to the freedom struggle. Her repeated rejoinder to Brown's celebration of self-actualization— "What I'm trying to do is get beyond you. I'm trying to get to how you do this for my six children. How can you translate this?"—suggests the challenge of Black Power's collectivist vision, its difference from the Peace Corps' liberal individualism. But it also suggests that she must downplay her organizing experience and appeal instead to her identity as a mother. Even as she invokes both a collective vision and an anti-imperialist panorama of "developing countries" that are "talking about sustaining themselves," Hardy is only able to conceptualize racial equality in terms of manhood, as a developmentalist process of "black brothers" becoming their own masters. At the same time, her constant invocation of her children reveals Black Power's insistence on a vision of masculine liberation and reproductive futurism, her slightly muffled sense, echoing Wallace, that she herself is decisively not included in the community of "black brothers" and future children who will be liberated by the struggle.[87]

The devastating impact for black women like Hardy of the black movement's absorption of Moynihan's equation of poverty with insufficient masculinity provides a focus for Michele Wallace's *Black Macho and the Myth of the Superwoman*. Arguing that the Black Power movement failed to restructure U.S. society because the male would-be revolutionaries adopted Moynihan-influenced misogyny and prevented women from joining them as equal partners in the struggle, Wallace mourns the failures of the movement: "Perhaps the single most important reason the Black Movement did not work was that black men did not realize they could not wage struggle without the full involvement of the women. . . . Look at how important women have been to the liberation struggles in Africa. By negating the importance of their role, the efficiency of the black movement was obliterated. It was just a lot of black men strutting around with afros."[88] Alluding to the Moynihan report's famous contention that "the very essence of the male animal, from the bantam rooster to the four-star general, is to strut,"[89] Wallace argues, as Ed Smith's Peace Corps scenes above also indicate, that the men in the Black Power movement were too busy strutting (i.e., performing their claim to the patriarchal power white supremacy had long denied them, but was now conditionally offering them) to pursue substantive revolutionary solidarity.

In mourning the black movement's lost opportunities to draw on the example of women's participation in African liberation, Wallace traces the Black Power movement's misogyny not only to the direct influence of Moynihan's arguments, but also to black cultural nationalism's attempt to oppose development through their antimodern mobilization of a mythologized African history. Though she does not use the language of development, Wallace pinpoints the nexus between the black movement's failures at cross-gender and Pan-African solidarity: as the Black Power movement reclaimed Africa in the terms of a developmentalist imaginary that placed African culture in an ancient and exotic past (albeit attempting to change the valences to revalue premodern African kingdoms), women's participation in recent continent-wide liberation struggles was erased in favor of an exoticizing mythology that painted black women as passive, venerated African queens whose job was to be revolutionary symbols and vessels rather than fighters.

Cultural nationalist leaders, at least in retrospect, corroborate Wallace's critique of the movement's gendered exoticizing of African cultural practices. Amiri Baraka reflects in his autobiography on how male chauvinism became both the rationale and the guiding principle of the cultural nationalist communities he joined. His involvement with a Yoruba temple run by his friend, Serj Oserjeman, provided him with a way to counter "cultural poverty" diagnoses through his recovery of an idealized past of black male supremacy:

> Some of us were influenced by the Yorubas because we could understand a connection we had with Africa and wanted to celebrate it. We liked the African garb that Serj and his people wore. The lovely long dresses, the bubbas and lappas and geles of the women. After so much exposure to white women, the graceful dress of the sisters in their African look, with their hair natural, turned us on. Plus, Oserjeman and the rest talked about and practiced polygamy, and certainly for some of us who were used to ripping and roaring out of one bed and into another, this "ancient custom of our people" provided a perfect outlet for male chauvinism, now disguised as "an ancient custom of our people."[90]

Baraka's recollection illustrates the way the essentialized invented past of black nationalism gave some male activists a framework that allowed them to celebrate and naturalize the sexism they were already practicing; in Baraka's case, his invocation of ancient Africa legitimized and made revolutionary the same male dominance and promiscuity (albeit within a more strictly heterosexual framework) that characterized the apolitical, largely white beat subculture to which he had previously belonged. A mythologized ancient Africa, oppositional to the extent that it coded an exoticized African past as masculine rather than feminine and passive, became the means by which black male leaders could fix black women's roles as objects of beauty and vessels for the nation while still defining themselves in opposition to the equally patriarchal white mainstream.

Discussions of genocide and sterilization in the Black Power movement became particularly suffused by this gendered struggle between development and cultural nationalism for masculine control over women's bodies. The 1960s saw an escalation of population control programs as well as ongoing forced sterilizations of black women in the U.S. South.[91] In response, Black Power leaders pressured women to eschew birth control entirely and fulfill "nation-building" obligations. In her 1970 essay "The Pill: Genocide or Liberation?" Toni Cade Bambara describes this dynamic, recounting a meeting about Vietnam War resistance in which "one tall, lean dude went into deep knee bends as he castigated the Sisters to throw away the pill and hop to the mattresses and breed revolutionaries and mess up the man's genocidal program." Bambara writes that this speech echoed "the national call to the Sisters to abandon birth controls, to not cooperate with the enemy all too determined to solve his problem with the bomb, the gun, the pill." In the essay Bambara eloquently decries this response to the specter and fact of population control, locating the imperative to "hop to the mattresses" within "the male–female division chumpbait we've eaten up of late via a distortion of our African heritage."[92] Bambara's account resonates with other women's stories in *The Black Woman*, the 1970 collection in which "The Pill" appears; faced with a developmentalist platform meant to eradicate black culture and control the population, black men drew on an exoticized patriarchal vision of the African past and attempted to regain control of "their" women in just the way Moynihan recommended.

In her essay, Bambara uses the language of development to conclude that birth control serves the revolution, contending that the revolutionary imperative should not be to reproduce in large numbers but rather to "raise super-people," to "focus on preparation of the self" in order to "create an army for today and tomorrow."[93] Here Bambara ingeniously negotiates the debate between the liberal establishment that would control the black population and the cultural nationalists who would take away the pill from women, using the language of development to argue that the technology-aided "preparation of the self" that would result from women's control of their own bodies would also allow those women to create and raise "super-people" who could bring down the white establishment. Reclaiming the language of both social engineering and revolutionary nationalism, her formulation reaffirms core principles of both discourses while pointing to the absurdity of the hypermasculinity that accompanies and shapes them.

Although in "The Pill" she effectively and creatively uses the language of development to question the cultural nationalist project and advocate for women's bodily autonomy, elsewhere in the collection Bambara begins to question development's all-encompassing frame. For instance, she muses on the difficulty of understanding gender roles in non-Western societies:

> I don't know if there are any viable models in pre-capitalist, non-white societies. I don't know that I can trust the anthropological studies that attempt to illuminate and interpret how the sexes operated in so-called primitive societies, or just how the self was viewed. For much of the work I read is either written by white males steeped in the misogynistic and capitalist tradition, which means that the material is always slanted to reinforce the myth of male superiority, female inferiority, and separation and antagonism between the sexes; or written by women with axes to grind so that the material is always slanted to "prove" that women in the so-called primitive societies were dominant and warlike. When I am left to my own devices—and I am neither a man nor a woman who wishes to be a man—I tend to find no particularly rigid work assignments based on sex. The pre-capitalist, non-white lifestyle seems to be worth checking out.[94]

Bambara's meditation here reveals her dissatisfaction with the epistemological options available to her, as she attempts to reject both development discourse and the primitivist exoticism that might oppose it. Her cautious conclusion that "so-called primitive societies" are "worth checking out," along with her skepticism of the trustworthiness of anthropological accounts that would mediate any such "checking out," constitutes an inchoate meditation on the possibility of an "outside" of the development imaginary: the possibility of the gendered division of labor not as an evolutionary adaptation in all societies but rather as a historically contingent phenomenon that need not connect to gendered bodies at all. But her formulation also suggests the difficulty of reaching that outside. Bambara's use of "pre-capitalist" and "so-called primitive" indicates the impossibility of escaping developmentalist vocabularies of natural progression, even as she and others attempted to piece together a new, more egalitarian and humane world.

Vietnam Solidarity and the Developmental Lens

In the preceding pages I have traced the influence of international development discourse on 1960s black liberation movement rhetoric and practice. Modernization theory, I have argued, disseminated popularly through iconic scenes of heroic development work in global slums and rural areas, exercised a particularly strong influence on the civil rights movement as it transitioned to Black Power, when the attainment of formal black equality in the South left activists looking for new ways to diagnose and fight continuing economic inequality and institutional racism. The influence of modernization discourse, and particularly its emphasis on charismatic, technocratic leadership and masculine subjection, widened the gulf between leaders and militant activists on the ground while making international solidarity difficult to enact and gender equality impossible to imagine; this was as true in the Black Power organizations that emphasized capitalist modernization as in the ones that mobilized Marxist–developmentalist visions or antimodern cultural nationalist reactions.

Development discourse limited black radicals in their attempts to enact international solidarity not just with decolonizing Africans, but also with the Vietnamese and others in the noncapitalist world, often leading them to imagine those societies along a schematic development trajectory. Judy Tzu-Chun Wu has recently documented this hyper-attentiveness to developmental stages in the radical solidarity movement, recounting how after a solidarity trip to China, North Korea, and Vietnam, Black Panther leader Elaine Brown paid China and North Korea the highest compliment of the development age, arguing that in those countries "one gets the feeling of being catapulted ahead in time and visiting some sort of future society."[95] Brown also said in a radio interview about North Korea, "You don't have the feeling that this is some underdeveloped country. This is a highly developed industrial, agricultural state."[96] Furthermore, Brown wrote in *The Black Panther*, "The main thing you see is the fact that the Vietnamese people have been stifled in their growth. They achieved liberation, but yet they have not been able to move within, in terms of socialist construction . . . they cannot put their full emphasis and full concentration on developing the society in terms of agriculture and industry."[97] Despite the delegation's attempt at expressing and enacting solidarity with the Vietnamese, Brown still argues that "the main thing" about the Vietnamese is their *lack* of development, evaluating them largely according to their ability to progress along schematic industrialization trajectories (in this case, toward socialism).

These schematic evaluations of Vietnamese development and under-development suffused 1960s radical as well as liberal thought, occupying as much space in activist writings as the romantic characterizations of peasants that have been much better remembered. The next chapter examines these liberal and radical evaluations of Vietnam and the U.S. war there, as well as the attempts by development workers and others to oppose the war. In particular, I consider how fantasies and experiences of development work influenced the solidarity practices of the largely white new left, focusing on returned volunteers turned activists in order to explore how development ideology impeded their understanding of the very struggles they yearned to assist.

5

AMBIGUOUS LIBERATION

The Vietnam War and the Committee of Returned Volunteers

In an October 1965 speech at Stanford University titled "From Applied Altruism to Nation Building," Peace Corps staffer Warren Wiggins attempted to win back a student population increasingly disillusioned with the U.S. government and its escalating war in Southeast Asia. "You and I, I think, see the same kind of world," he assured the students. "We both see people being trampled—their opportunities for self-expression being denied. For the militant, however, it is important to look not only at the situation in Viet Nam, but also at the rest of the world. People are pushed down not only by *bullets* and *brutality*, but by malnutrition, poverty, and the inability to read. They are not necessarily helped simply by stopping a war or giving tons of food. They need to have hope."[1]

Having established common ground with militant students based on the desire for self-expression, Wiggins proceeded to explain that the Peace Corps had learned a surprising lesson from the student movements: that this very self-expression, at least by privileged Americans, could catalyze (and even constitute) revolutionary change. He argued that while the Peace Corps had begun as a struggle "just to prove that Americans could live abroad without supermarkets, without drycleaners, without housemothers," the agency had "turned a corner and seen ourselves in a mirror and we have been surprised to find that we are more than we thought. We might not have looked and we might not have noticed the difference except for what has been called 'The Student Movement.'"[2] The central lesson of the movement, Wiggins thus contended, was not about fighting racism or imperialism but, on the contrary, that students from the United States can (and should) undertake "nation-building" projects around the world:

In the same way that the Student Movement has changed and blossomed, the Peace Corps has. Anybody who characterizes the Peace Corps as applied altruism misunderstands what it is, what it represents, and most important, what it can become. It is as inaccurate as the idea that the civil rights movement is nothing more than a chance for "college kids" to blow off steam. And here is where we think we are. We believe that it is fair to begin talking about the Peace Corps in terms of nation building. That's a big concept—more ambitious than talking about helping a village or teaching children. Another way to put it is that we believe Americans, particularly college students, can be a critical element in the evolution of a society. That in fact the change is so important and so great that we might as well talk about revolution.[3]

His mirror metaphor is apt: in his telling, the student movement, rather than serving as a critical interlocutor, provided the Peace Corps with an opportunity for self-reflection and, ultimately, self-aggrandizement. The metaphor is also apt in that a certain reversal has taken place: the main insight the Peace Corps seems to have gained from the student movement is that "we [Americans] are more than we thought." For Wiggins, even a movement whose goal was to oppose American violence could provide yet another rationale for the projection of U.S. power internationally.

Wiggins's attempt at mirroring (both imitating and reversing) the ideas and energy of the student movements culminated at the end of his speech, when he returned explicitly to the subject of Vietnam, affirming that "many of us believe it may be necessary for the United States to be involved in a massive military operation in Southeast Asia." In a final rhetorical twist, Wiggins warned potential volunteers against expressing opposition to U.S. interventions abroad, designating as "colonialist" and "imperialism" not the extension of U.S. military might, but rather any expression of opposition to those ventures. "It is irrelevant whether I or anyone else in the agency agrees or disagrees with you about the U.S. position in the Dominican Republic or Viet Nam," he argued. "Exporting political opinions of any sort is imperialism. It involves a colonialist mentality which is inept, out of date, and offensive to those who think."[4] In place of the forbidden expression of "political opinions" overseas, Wiggins recommended sentimental self-expression, arguing that "the Peace Corps may be one of the best ways in the world for you to express your feelings—and to apply them in a direct and specific way that will in actuality make a difference in the world."

The combination of admiration and admonition in Wiggins's speech, his attempt to connect with "the militant's" energy and sympathy for Third World peoples while dismissing the movement's central aim of "stopping a war," characterized the Peace Corps' approach to the escalating conflict in Vietnam. As the movement's protests against the war—a liberal Cold War intervention, one of whose central goals was the modernization of the South Vietnamese people—threatened to expose the violence of the United States' entire Cold War modernization project, Wiggins and other Peace Corps officials attempted to redirect the movement's energy. Specifically, they argued that undertaking development projects and engaging in and facilitating "self-expression" in the Third World would be a better use of the movement's time than attempting to explain and oppose the violence carried out by their own government.

While Wiggins's adoption of the decolonization and student-movement rhetoric of nation-building, revolution, and self-expression in order to advocate for a greater U.S. role abroad constituted a fairly common liberal strategy for incorporating the rhetoric of dissent into a military–interventionist project, perhaps more remarkable is the degree to which his ideas resonated with antiwar activists. About a week after the "nation-building" speech, SDS president Carl Oglesby and national secretary Paul Booth gave a press conference announcing their "Build, Not Burn" platform, in which they expressed their desire to "put the money being spent on the Vietnam War into programs for helping Third World people get a grip on life."[5] Leftist journalist Andrew Kopkind approvingly reported this conflation of new left and Peace Corps energies, writing in the *New Republic* that "it would delight SDS to know that as their own paper was being written, the Peace Corps' Warren Wiggins was delivering a speech called 'From Applied Altruism to Nation Building.' It amounted to the same thing." But Kopkind went even further, designating returned Peace Corps volunteers rather than activists the true, and more evolved, "post-radical" contingent: "Most of the returnees will be post-radical. They do not have to buy credentials by joining. They have gone, to borrow the title of a current SDS monograph, 'from protest to radical politics.'"[6] Kopkind's attribution of highly evolved "radical politics" to an agency in which volunteers were forbidden even to criticize U.S. foreign policy suggests that the Peace Corps' rhetorical strategy was succeeding: they were able to at once deploy volunteers in projects that served the interventionist state and convince leftists at home that their work put "revolutionary forces" in motion.

Kopkind found more evidence of the Peace Corps' "post-radicalism" in volunteers' expulsion from the Peruvian village of Vicos (detailed in chapter 3). Taking at face value Peace Corps staffers' public reframing of the debacle in Vicos as a success, Kopkind wrote, "So effective was the organization, and so determined were the volunteers to get the Indians to think and act for themselves, that one of the villagers' first acts was to kick the Peace Corps out of town. Officials in Washington couldn't have been more pleased." Kopkind, despite his general skepticism of U.S. government claims, credulously inferred from the official account that the Peace Corps had adopted a "daring new look"; the agency, he wrote, was learning from social movements at home how to "promote social revolution abroad," which entailed getting the eternally passive "Indians" to "think and act for themselves."[7] Kopkind's attribution of revolutionary vanguard status to the Vicos delegation indicates the Peace Corps' facility at appropriating the language and the look of revolution, convincing even radical observers at home of their commitment to Third World people's self-determination.[8]

This adoption by a prominent leftist journalist of the Peace Corps' vocabulary to describe global social change indicates the extent to which development, and the ideal of the heroic development worker, pervaded the new left. Indeed, Wiggins's suggestion that volunteers use the Third World as a staging ground for "self-expression," and his accompanying argument that self-expression by young Americans would lead to "evolutionary" nation-building overseas, both drew on and guided the new left's attempts to transform the United States and its role in the world. This chapter traces these overlaps between the Peace Corps, the liberal militaristic establishment, and the new left, considering the Peace Corps' official stance and ideological importance in bolstering the developmental logic of the Vietnam War; its treatment of draft resisters and early volunteer protest; and the recollections and writings by those who took part in the antiwar, anti-imperialist Committee of Returned Volunteers (CRV). In the first part of the chapter, I examine the heroic modernization discourses that defined liberal establishment policies and Peace

Corps stances toward the Vietnam War, and show how State Department and Peace Corps officials attempted to carve out an image of Peace Corps volunteers as politically neutral, humanitarian "quiet activists." They did this by refusing to lend Peace Corps volunteers to the war effort in Vietnam while emphasizing volunteers' and soldiers' affinity and shared mission, and by first punishing volunteer dissent, and then eventually incorporating it into their vision of modernization. The second part of the chapter argues that the CRV's continued valorization of the Peace Corps ideal of apolitical heroism, along with their inability to imagine an alternative to the developmental trajectory their service and the postwar mood had instilled in them, impeded their attempts at substantive solidarity with Vietnamese nationalists and other Third World peoples, and left them vulnerable to incorporation and erasure by the very agency they were attempting to abolish. Finally, I connect the CRV's radicalization and fragmentation with that of the larger new left, exploring how development discourse embodied by heroic Peace Corps volunteers both shaped new left ideology and led to the movement's co-optation by the very structures it hoped to overturn.

"Quiet Activists": Wartime Development Visions and the Beginnings of Dissent

In the same speech where he threatened protesting volunteers while valorizing "self-expression," Wiggins also cited the most iconic example of the heroic, humanistic neutrality that volunteers were required to embody. "You know the story of the Peace Corps in Dominican Republic," he told the students. "The volunteers continued with their work without interference—working on both sides of the military line and crossing more or less at will."[9] While Wiggins was correct that Peace Corps work in Santo Domingo during the 1965 U.S. invasion quickly became legendary, the agency's role was more complicated than he suggested. In that invasion, twenty-three thousand U.S. marines and thousands more U.S. paratroopers brutally suppressed a popular insurgency that was attempting to restore liberal anticommunist president Juan Bosch, who had been elected in 1962 after thirty-one years of repressive dictatorial rule and deposed in a coup after seven months in office. The day before the first marines landed, Sargent Shriver wrote in a memo to

Lyndon Johnson, "No problems are foreseen for the Peace Corps if former President Bosch returns to power."[10] But once officials saw that Johnson was determined to keep Bosch from the presidency, they quickly fell into line, silencing the volunteers who voiced their objections to U.S. attacks on behalf of the junta. The volunteers closely observed the United States' suppression of the popular insurrection: thirty-three of them stayed in Santo Domingo for most of the fighting, many of them health workers who treated both the constitutionalist insurgents and the right-wing military loyalists (seventy-five other volunteers remained in the countryside, away from the U.S. rocket attacks and heavy fighting).[11] Observing the near-universal Dominican support for Bosch's restoration, volunteers sent a letter to Shriver and Johnson objecting to the intervention that read, "We are firmly convinced that for both the United States and the Dominican Republic, U.S. commitment to the Dominican Constitutionalists fulfills long-range mutual self-interest."[12] But Johnson's White House suppressed even this measured criticism: Johnson aide Bill Moyers told Frank Mankiewicz, "You better go down there and shut those guys up, or the President's going to pull them all out."[13] Mankiewicz relayed the message, and the volunteers agreed not to release the letter to the press. Volunteer Kirby Jones said in a 1991 interview, "Maybe we were chickenshit, but I felt very satisfied after the meeting. I shook Mankiewicz's hand at the door."[14]

Despite the volunteers' thwarted attempts to side with the Dominican people, Wiggins's account demonstrates how quickly their work in the Santo Domingo hospitals was mythologized as the embodiment of a humanistic sensibility imagined to be free of ideological content. *New York Times* writer Tad Szulc echoed this mythic portrait, dedicating his book-length account of the invasion "to the Peace Corps volunteers in Santo Domingo," specifically the "Peace Corps girls" who "were the real heroines of the civil war."[15] And it was not just the mainstream media and the liberal militaristic establishment that celebrated the Peace Corps' neutrality as symbolized by the volunteers' dutifully indiscriminate ministrations: new left and antiwar activists were, if anything, more celebratory of these volunteers, writing romantically of their transcendent bravery in the midst of crisis.[16] The example of the volunteers in the Dominican Republic became a model for neutral humanitarian heroism, privileging person-to-person contact in the face of death-dealing machines and institutions over a program that might dismantle those machines and institutions. As Wiggins's speech demonstrates, the idea of volunteers' neutral heroism became a rhetorical strategy that distanced the Peace Corps from the increasingly violent U.S. presence in Vietnam without explicitly opposing that presence.

This rhetorical separation was difficult to effect in the case of Vietnam, since the Peace Corps' philosophy and policy had from the beginning been entangled with U.S. objectives in Southeast Asia. Democratic congressman Henry Reuss proposed the Peace Corps precursor Point Four Youth Corps in 1957 after visiting Indochina and Cambodia; it was his proposal that first brought the idea of the Peace Corps to Kennedy's attention. In proposing the Peace Corps, Kennedy explicitly drew inspiration from "jungle doctor" Tom Dooley's ministrations to Vietnamese Catholics, as well as from *The Ugly American*, which featured development workers in the fictional Southeast Asian ex-French colony Sarkhan.[17] Conversely, the modernization theory embodied and disseminated by the Peace Corps served as a central strategy and rationale for the United States' escalation of its war in Vietnam.

Kennedy vividly outlined the United States' developmental mission in Vietnam (and admitted that the South Vietnamese state had been a U.S. creation) in a 1956 speech warning against the free elections that the French and the Vietnamese had agreed to hold that year, memorably stating, "If we are not the parents of little Vietnam, then surely we are the godparents. We presided at its birth, we gave assistance to its life, we have helped to shape its future. As French influence in the political, economic and military spheres has declined in Vietnam, American influence has steadily grown. This is our offspring—we cannot abandon it, we cannot ignore its needs."[18] Indeed, Kennedy, Rostow, Robert McNamara, and other Vietnam war architects aggressively attempted to raise "little Vietnam," enthusiastically following Edward Lansdale's blueprint for "Civic Action" military modernization programs and initiating the strategic hamlet program, in which U.S. and South Vietnamese troops forced villagers out of their homes, burned down their villages, and supervised them as they constructed barbed-wire-enclosed concentration camps ("hamlets") with "modern" amenities in which they were then forced to live under the surveillance of U.S. troops and USAID workers. Michael Latham details how the Kennedy administration, imagining the camps as part of an overarching modernization project, "encouraged the formation of hamlet organizations, supported 'self-help' plans, and called on South Vietnamese province chiefs to increase their contact with local settlements" in an effort to force peasants to "look beyond their isolated communities and develop an allegiance to Diem's regime."[19] This effort failed miserably, leading many South Vietnamese men and boys to escape and join the nationalist struggle.[20]

While following his predecessor in imagining Vietnam as a passive, pliable body, Johnson revised Kennedy's familial metaphor by repeatedly characterizing the country as a semi-willing sexual partner. He told *Times* columnists Rowland Evans and Robert Novak in 1965 that "the slow escalation of the air war in the North and the increasing pressure on Ho Chi Minh was seduction, not rape," and assured Senator George McGovern that he was anticipating China's possible intervention on North Vietnam's behalf by telling him, "I'm going up her leg an inch at a time . . . I'll get to the snatch before they know what's happening."[21] Sometimes he directed his rape fantasies at Ho Chi Minh, as when he said of his decision to bomb Vietnamese harbors after the Gulf of Tonkin incident, "I didn't just screw Ho Chi Minh. I cut his pecker off."[22] Johnson, unlike Rostow and Shriver, did not coherently frame these seduction/rape/castration schemes as rituals of initiation into modernity; his metaphors, instead, forecasted just the kind of chaotic, sexualized violence that many of the troops committed on the ground in Vietnam, exactly what the Peace Corps hoped to avoid with its more palatable forms of penetration and domination.[23]

As the U.S. campaign in Vietnam became more and more destructive, Johnson's visions of development became ever more grandiose. In a 1965 speech to students at Johns Hopkins University, Johnson explained that he was forced to continue on the "painful road" of escalation in order to fulfill a promise the United States had made in 1954 (when France officially surrendered its former colony) to protect and modernize South Vietnam. He outlined his plans to undertake "a greatly expanded cooperative effort for development" in Southeast Asia, proclaiming that "the vast Mekong River can provide food and water and power on a scale to dwarf even our own TVA," and announcing plans to assemble "a special team of outstanding, patriotic, distinguished Americans" headed by former World Bank president Eugene Black. He warned that "in areas that are still ripped by conflict, of course development will not be easy. Peace will be necessary for final success. But we cannot and must not wait for peace to begin this job . . . we can do all these things on a scale never dreamed of before."[24] As he had pledged, Johnson sharply increased the number of USAID workers in Vietnam: by 1968, 2,300 were working in the country.[25] In an April 1965 meeting, a staffer's notes record Johnson musing, "If we can first get our feet on their neck. Rural Electrification—Brotherhood Operation." The notes then indicate that Johnson continues "full of determination," proclaiming, "We have set our hand to wheel. Get plenty more targets—damn many planes trying to find 'em. Hold out promised land."[26] As these notes and speeches indicate, Johnson pursued development in Vietnam haphazardly, on a large scale and with messianic zeal, characterizing the "feet on their neck" and the bombing of ever "more targets" as a necessary middle step toward electrification, brotherhood, and the "promised land."

Recognizing the power of the Peace Corps' vision of brotherhood in his attempt to pacify and modernize Vietnam, Johnson requested in the spring of 1964 that USAID recruit former Peace Corps volunteers for its "Vietnam Rural Affairs Program."[27] USAID, the more resource-rich, aid-focused development agency created by the Kennedy administration in 1961, described its rural affairs program in terms that followed Rostow's "non-communist manifesto," calling it "a massive program of rural development, guaranteed to strengthen quickly the will of the Vietnamese peasants to resist Communist subversion, propaganda and terror." They further explained that they were "playing an unprecedent [*sic*] operational, advisory and supporting role" in the "political, economic, and social, as well as military defense of South Vietnam."[28] USAID ultimately backed away from Johnson's idea, arguing that a "heavy preponderance" of ex-volunteers in Vietnam and Laos would be damaging to both agencies' reputations. Instead, USAID borrowed the Peace Corps' image, circulating a news story calling themselves a "heavy-duty Peace Corps" and claiming in brochures that they were "working side by side with the Vietnamese" in order to emphasize the agency's brotherly mission over its military and bureaucratic one.[29]

As the fighting escalated, the Peace Corps considered sending volunteers to Vietnam. In a November 1965 regional directors meeting, most participants seemed enthusiastic: William Josephson suggested that sending in volunteers to "work with the Red Cross or refugees" might allay international criticism of the United States and help recruiters answer potential volunteers who "want to talk about Viet Nam." Other directors concurred that Peace Corps volunteers could support a health program in South Vietnam, and Wiggins even suggested, perhaps remembering the legendary Dominican volunteers of the previous spring, that some "could also work in North Viet Nam in a non-political job such as nursing."[30] However, when Wiggins and Regional Director Ross Pritchard visited Vietnam in early 1966 "to discuss where the Peace Corps could be of assistance, perhaps in relation to the refugee problem,"[31] International Voluntary Service (IVS) head Don Luce recalls that the men did not reveal their names; they arrived "apparently without the knowledge of the Vietnamese government," and claimed that "their trip had been instigated by pressure from VIPs returning to Washington from a tour of Southeast Asia." Luce remembers that Wiggins was cautious, worried that sending volunteers to Vietnam would "cause the Peace Corps to be seen as a directly political tool of American policy." Regional Director Pritchard, in contrast, "bristled with aggressive designs" and "did not seem at all embarrassed over the fact that the Vietnamese government had made no requests and did not even know of their visit." Luce recollects that Pritchard's bluster was supported at the highest levels of the Johnson administration, but that Wiggins's more cautious faction triumphed:

> [Pritchard] shocked his American dinner companions one night with brash plans to "move in." "We could have a thousand volunteers here within six months," he bragged. "Besides that, our volunteers could perhaps serve as intermediaries between the Viet Cong and the Americans out in the villages." McGeorge Bundy of the White House staff, who visited Vietnam with Vice-President Humphrey, seemed to reinforce this kind of thinking. "If IVS can't do the job and raise its numbers of volunteers," he said, "perhaps the Peace Corps can." Our conception of "the job," however, was not to escalate to a thousand volunteers. Two hundred, we felt, was the largest number that could be accommodated, given security conditions and Vietnamese feelings against increased numbers of Americans taking over the country. We did not, especially at that point, share the feeling of the U.S. government that Americans could do the job if the Vietnamese wouldn't. In the end, reason won out

in Washington, and the Peace Corps has maintained its integrity through not being pushed headlong into the Viet Nam morass.[32]

While IVS, a smaller development organization and Peace Corps predecessor begun in 1953, shared much with the Peace Corps, Luce reacted with horror at Pritchard's suggestion to deluge the Vietnamese with volunteers for whom they had not asked; the IVS director, who had worked in Vietnam since 1958, seemed equally disturbed at the official's claim that volunteers could serve as "intermediaries" (his words again recalling the heroic neutralist ideal of the Dominican Republic volunteers) between the North Vietnamese and U.S. development workers. Luce's conclusion that staying out of the "Vietnam morass" preserved the Peace Corps' integrity suggests that the movement's politicization of the war had made it impossible for the Peace Corps to enter Vietnam as a neutral heroic presence, stoically ministering to "all sides" as they had in Santo Domingo. The only way to remain neutral on Vietnam, it seemed, was to avoid the country altogether.

Even without the Peace Corps, development remained central to the U.S. mission in Vietnam, as evidenced by soldiers' testimony as well as these high-level directives. Emmanuel Holloman, an African American army translator who did the wrenching work of offering monetary compensation to South Vietnamese families when U.S. troops accidentally killed their family members, exemplifies this ambivalence toward the Vietnamese people and their development. He argues that he and other black soldiers "seemed to get along better with the Vietnamese . . . a black would try to learn some of their words. And try to learn a few of their customs so they wouldn't hurt them," while also acknowledging that "a lot of times [American soldiers] raped the women in the villages they were supposed to be protecting" and committed other atrocities.[33] Despite the senseless violence he continually witnessed and apologized for, Holloman remains convinced of the good of the developmental mission, and imagines himself returning "as a missionary" in order to continue the work he started:

I know we hurt a lot of people over there. But we done good, you know. Look what they got out of it. They got, oh my gosh, everything. Roads, factories, machinery. They got everything. They never really had advanced this far, you know.

I'd go back the first chance I got. I would go right now, regardless of the situation, because I feel like I belong there. I would like to work as a missionary. Back in the same areas where I worked before. I know right now it is impossible, but I will always be hoping. I liked to work with the Vietnamese people. That can't change.[34]

Here Holloman tragically lays bare the contradictions inherent in the development mission. While he understands the tremendous destruction wrought by U.S. forces, he continues to believe that before the war the Vietnamese people "had never really advanced this far" and that because of the war they "got everything." He acknowledges his connection to Vietnamese people and culture, but can only dream of going back as a missionary, with the goal of changing or even eradicating that culture. If the Peace Corps wisely remained neutral in Vietnam, the development project it symbolized continued to justify the U.S. presence there.

While Peace Corps officials remained reluctant to associate themselves with U.S. policy in Vietnam, they were even more vigilant in their attempts to distance the Peace Corps from draft dodging and resistance. The draft had presented a problem for the Peace Corps from its inception: the agency wanted to claim that its brand of service was as important and physically demanding as military service, but officials worried that officially exempting male volunteers would attract "draft-dodgers" fit for neither rugged service nor promoting their country and its values. The Peace Corps attempted to resolve this dilemma by crafting a compromise policy, deferring but not exempting their male volunteers. The *New York Times* reported this policy by paraphrasing Representative Henry Reuss in February 1961: "Many men, after service in the program from aiding underdeveloped nations, would have passed the age limit for the draft or would have too many dependents. Further, he said, local draft boards would be asked to give 'discretionary consideration' to Peace Corps service as a factor favoring draft exemption."[35] The Peace Corps refused to grant exemptions throughout the 1960s, over the complaints of many young activists like SDS's Oglesby and Booth, who after their "Build, Not Burn" press conference sent Johnson and Attorney General Nicholas Katzenbach telegrams in October 1965 proposing draft exemptions for Peace Corps volunteers and participants in domestic service programs.[36] The Peace Corps ignored these calls for exemption and continued to emphasize that their ethos was not compatible with draft avoidance, claiming in November 1966 that "the Peace Corps today is no more a haven for draft dodgers than it was in 1961" and that "it is possible to identify those [applicants] whose prime motivation is draft avoidance."[37] Echoing the press release's anxiety that pathological "draft dodgers" might taint the Peace Corps image, Jack Vaughn told the *New York Times* in December 1966, "The Peace Corps is no haven for draft dodgers. Our psychologists are primed to spot them."[38]

Volunteers remember the story differently, recalling that through-out the decade young men joined to avoid the draft, even though they were not allowed to say so. Paul Theroux claims that even in 1963 he "joined the Peace Corps to avoid being drafted," and Nancy Scheper-Hughes similarly remembers that the draft preoccupied her 1964 train-ing group, which "included hawks and doves, nonviolent resisters, and conscientious objectors. There were pacifist Quakers, along with a large number of ordinary guys who, without too much depth of insight or reflection, simply wanted to postpone having to kill for their country. Many hoped the war might be over before we returned to the states."[39] As the war escalated, men joined the Peace Corps almost solely to avoid the draft. Liberia volunteer Faith Fogle remembers encountering many "classic draft-dodger types" in her 1968 training group,[40] while 1968–70 Bolivia volunteer Connie Jaquith recalls that although she herself sup-ported the war in Vietnam, her husband and the other twenty-one men in her group had all joined the Peace Corps to avoid being drafted:

> So, all of the war, all of that was very tied up in all of this, I think it was for all twenty-two couples. When we finally got to Utah State University, almost every man, every husband, said they were there as alternative service to the war. Every one. Now you didn't talk much about that to Peace Corps, because again, if you had demonstrated against the war, if you were vocal about the war, that would get you eliminated. So there was a psychological thread, sort of you know, the elephant in the living room, underneath our training experience. Nobody talked about the war, nobody admitted they were doing it to avoid Vietnam, every husband . . . So I mean it was truly a part of everybody's decision to go into that program and to go into Peace Corps.[41]

Jaquith's recollection indicates the war's constant if tacit presence in the Peace Corps by 1968; virtually all volunteers were understood to be avoiding the draft, but those who had expressed antiwar sentiments or attended antiwar protests were in danger of dismissal. Keeping the presence of draft dodgers in their ranks an open secret allowed the Peace Corps to privately use the threat of the draft to keep volunteers in line— Susan Strane remembers that many men in her 1965–67 Turkey community development group quit out of frustration with their badly run program and widespread anti-U.S. sentiment, until "finally [Peace Corps officials] came in and they said OK, the next guy that quits is 1-A to go to Vietnam"—while publicly framing them as neutral warriors for peace, sharing equally with the soldiers in Vietnam the task of bringing modernity to the Third World.[42] Vaughn reiterated this equation in the December 9, 1966, *Times* article, titled "Peace Corps Volunteer Deemed as Vital to U.S. as Servicemen," arguing that volunteers were "second to no other Americans" in the importance of their national service.

Johnson also sought to connect the volunteers' work with soldiering, publicly praising their efforts as symbolic of the same commitment to modernization that underlay his escalation of the war in Vietnam while differentiating the necessary work of the soldier from that of the volunteer. Seizing the occasion of Vaughn's swearing-in as the second Peace Corps director to link the Vietnam War to U.S. development work at home and abroad, the president imagined a day when the Peace Corps would spread their spirit of "quiet courage" and "private dedication" to "the hamlets of Vietnam":

> In a world of violence, these volunteers have shown that there is really another way—the way of private dedication and quiet courage working unheralded for ends that each has accepted as valuable and as vital. In this way those of you in the Peace Corps have carried forward the real revolution of this day and time, the revolution of peaceful change. In this way you are really waging the only war that we in America want to wage—the war against the inhumanity of man to his neighbor and the injustice of nature to her children.
>
> In Vietnam there is another war. It is fueled by those who believe that they somehow might be able to accomplish their ends by means of terror and violence. America's purpose there is to give peaceful change a real chance to succeed. In that struggle, soldiers are necessary not only to prevent but to halt aggression, and to provide security for those who are determined to protect themselves and to raise their families. So, too, are the other workers of peace necessary who

must lay the foundation for economic and social progress in that land . . .

The day, I hope, will soon come when the Peace Corps will be there too. It must somehow find the day and the time that it can go and make its contribution when Peace is assured. The same spirit that the Peace Corps volunteers brought to thousands of villages and cities in 46 countries should be carried to the hamlets of Vietnam.[43]

Johnson's contrasting of the "quiet" and "private" Peace Corps with both the bombs and soldiers he was deploying to suppress the Vietnamese nationalists accords the Peace Corps volunteers the status of "real" peace advocates, displacing the antiwar protesters who were considerably less quiet. Peace Corps advertisements from the late sixties echo this message of making peace without protesting war: one, headlined, "Make Your Own Peace," reads, "The Peace Corps doesn't shout, 'Come Make Peace.' Peace doesn't come that easily. It's more of a separate peace. Maybe yours. No banners. No bands. No medals."[44] Likewise a 1966 *Time* article quoted Wiggins saying that the Peace Corps sought "quiet activists" who "don't carry placards."[45] This paradoxical fantasy of the quiet activist was key to the Peace Corps' vision; it aimed to appropriate the humanist ethos of the civil rights and antiwar movements while leaving behind their oppositional stances and voices, particularly the antiimperialist ones. The repeated classification of Peace Corps volunteers' and staffers' work as "quiet" recalls Graham Greene's 1955 protagonist, "quiet American" Alden Pyle, a naïve anticommunist zealot who plants bombs in crowded cities while seducing the British protagonist's Vietnamese girlfriend.[46] Like Pyle, volunteers were supposed to pose a stoic and seductive alternative to the old colonial order.

The Peace Corps' emphasis on "quiet" intensified with Vaughn's ascent to the position of Peace Corps director. Though Vaughn lacked Shriver's flashy charm, Peter Grothe wrote that "the consensus of Peace Corps staffers who have worked with Vaughn is that he has a kind of quiet charisma. He never raises his voice; he never blusters. Yet, in his quiet way, he is tremendously disarming." Grothe goes on to describe Vaughn's literal disarming of Panama, writing that as ambassador he "attacked the ugly situation with such skill that President Marcos Robles said, 'Ambassador Vaughn has given Panamanians a new image of the United States.'"[47] Vaughn, whom Kopkind describes as having "the air of a failed preacher," often discussed peace in apocalyptic tones, arguing in a 1965 speech, "I mean in Peace the hard, gritty job of grappling once and for all with complex issues affecting our very salvation."[48]

Vaughn expanded on his definition of peace in a 1968 speech, arguing that "peace is a silent passion. It is a one on one relationship, a quiet persuasion. Totally, it is self-discipline and self-control. In the pursuit of peace you bite your tongue 100 times for every time you speak a word. Peace is a process of bitter encounters with reality. It is fit work for rare people." Having defined peace (perhaps via William James) as a kind of masculine training regimen, Vaughn argued that the war, in fact, mattered little to the Peace Corps' success: "Some have suggested that the war is undercutting the work the Peace Corps is doing. But this is not so. A volunteer who has worked hard in Brazil for two years need not feel that his work there has been undone by what is going on in Vietnam, and I suspect that Brazilians feel there is virtually no relationship between what the volunteer has accomplished in Brazil and what is happening in Vietnam. The friendship and relationship between the Brazilians and the volunteers are established through the work the volunteer does, not through American tactics elsewhere."[49] Imagining politically neutral work, self-discipline, and friendship as sufficient counters to "American tactics elsewhere," and ignoring the Brazilian students who were explicitly connecting their own dissent against their own U.S.-backed military dictatorship with the Vietnamese fight for sovereignty, Vaughn remained confident, at least publicly, in the power of U.S. development work.[50] If done correctly and stoically enough, he argued, the Peace Corps' work could remain completely separate from other, more destructive, forms of foreign intervention.

Volunteers' experiences on the ground did not always bear out this separation. In 1966 letters home, Nigeria teacher Jim King repeatedly connected cuts in Peace Corps salary and hostel-closings to escalating war budgets while also reflecting on the war's damage to America's image. "Newspapers are full of the bombing of Hanoi here," he explained to his family. "People are openly hostile to us, call us barbarians and war seekers now."[51] In another letter considering police brutality in his hometown of Los Angeles, King writes that the rest of the world sees Americans as "money grubbing, war pushing, color hating, science mad, and communist fearing people all clamoring and screaming." While not an antiwar activist—though he did launch an unsuccessful letter-writing campaign to Vaughn to restore volunteer services the Peace Corps had cut—King sympathizes with Nigerians' critiques of the United States, and muses that "to offset such an image is far more than a few dollars and a few scrubby PCVs will ever be able to do. Keep it up USA and the day will come when you will stand alone without a buyer for your dreams, tanks, and detergents."[52]

While these critiques occasionally appear in letters home, many volunteers shared Vaughn's values, framing their attempts to stay neutral in the face of both war and antiwar protest as the ultimate test of courage. Paul Theroux in his 1967 essay "Cowardice" writes, "I intend to give in neither to the army nor to the peace movement," explaining that he refuses to go to war himself while insisting that pacifism and antiwar protest stem from men's inability to admit their fear of the physical tests war provides.[53] A male India volunteer, speaking at the end of his service, made similar connections, painstakingly distinguishing between the "objective" sensitivity he learned in the Peace Corps and the "mushiness" he associated with movement affiliation:

> It's made me extremely interested in myself, and I don't know whether it's selfishness or self-centeredness. I don't think it's that . . .
>
> The combination of being alone and in a foreign situation where I'm thrown back on myself brought all this out. Now I feel alive. I see these things, and my perception is heightened a little bit more. I've become a little more sensitive, and when I say sensitive I don't mean mushy. Yet, I don't automatically become affiliated with civil rights or ideas like that. I don't automatically accept something. I haven't become sensitive to things like demonstrations and being against the war in Viet Nam. But I have become very sensitive to myself and my reactions to things. In a way, I've become objective about things.[54]

Internalizing exhortations like Wiggins's to imagine the Third World as a space of self-discovery and expression, this volunteer has discovered much about his "own reactions to things," a process he connects to the disavowal of political stances. Characterizing his solipsistic gaze as "objective," he aspires to the neutrality that Wiggins and Vaughn encouraged.[55]

Public dissent from development workers began relatively early in the war: Weather Underground activist David Gilbert remembers "sitting there gasping" in 1965 after hearing a former USAID worker tell stories of "prison, torture, and assassination" by the South Vietnamese; Gilbert identifies that moment as "the center point of [his] transitions" to radicalism and the beginning of his support for the National Liberation Front.[56] As the U.S. military presence grew, groups of development workers spoke out more strongly, emphasizing the futility and absurdity of the development mission in Vietnam in the face of the mass destruction inflicted by the U.S. military. In 1967, four IVS volunteer leaders resigned over U.S. policy in Vietnam, and fifty more volunteers signed a statement in support of the resignations but stayed on, continuing to believe that their work was ameliorating South Vietnamese living conditions. Upon his resignation, IVS director Luce testified in front of the Senate Judiciary Committee, "I have made suggestions on our refugee policies, our destruction of villages, our use of defoliants. People in USAID listen and suggest we write a report and then nothing happens. It's become a land of report writing . . . As individuals, we cannot become part of the destruction of a people we love."[57] The IVS workers received acknowledgment from neither U.S. ambassador Ellsworth Bunker nor the president, but the *Times* covered the protest extensively and wrote an editorial supporting them, quoting Henry Cabot Lodge two years earlier when he called the IVS volunteers "one of the success stories of American assistance in Vietnam" and "indispensable to military success," and arguing that "their warning must be heeded that the United States is losing that 'other war' which Mr. Lodge and other officials have said is vital for 'victory.'"[58]

These dissenting development workers, mostly from IVS, became some of the first early, universally credible eyewitnesses to the United States' failure and destructiveness in Vietnam. In contrast, Peace Corps volunteers who attempted to speak out did not find support among their leaders. The Peace Corps' strict policy on punishing overseas critics of the Vietnam War was tested when Chile volunteer Bruce Murray, a music teacher from Rhode Island with no history of political activism, wrote a letter criticizing the war as well as the Peace Corps' policy of silencing antiwar protest and published it in the Chilean newspaper *El Sur*. The Peace Corps quickly summoned him home, and Murray found a draft notice waiting in his mailbox even before he was officially notified of his dismissal from the Peace Corps. Murray sued the Peace Corps, accusing them of illegally colluding with the draft board to reclassify him in punishment for speaking out, and won the case in December 1969; Rhode Island federal judge Raymond Pettine ruled that although Murray lacked evidence to prove conspiracy, "the sins of Rhode Island selective service" were "many and varied." Judge Pettine concluded that the Peace Corps was wrong in secretly dismissing Murray, falsely filling out the checklist on termination documents, and not giving Murray a chance to defend himself.[59]

In the wake of the Murray case, facing increasingly widespread antiwar sentiment, the Peace Corps relaxed their standards: it quietly kept dissenting volunteers on instead of dismissing them, and adopted less direct strategies to contain their protests. In 1970 Morris Chalick, a "Peace Corps doctor who has studied Volunteer activism for several months," explained in the *Peace Corps Volunteer* that volunteers' antiwar dissent stemmed from "post-adolescent emotional problems," explaining that "I get the feeling sometimes that there is some sort of child–parent game being played by Volunteers and staff in some of these instances."[60] Chalick's metaphor keeps volunteers' dissent "in the family," characterizing it as an immature act of rebellion—an "acting out" mirroring the kind of rebellions in which "developing" nations were engaged—while allowing the Peace Corps' public stance against protest to remain firm. This strategy, of placing "immature" volunteers and "immature" countries on parallel timelines of personal and national progress, allowed the Peace Corps and the State Department to acknowledge and even capitalize on dissent without seeing it as a disruption of their overarching vision of liberal–capitalist economic integration. As the next section of the chapter explores in more detail, even the Committee of Returned Volunteers, the returned development-worker dissenters who joined the antiwar movement, eventually found their protests against the war and the agency transformed into an advertisement for the Peace Corps.

"Abolish the Peace Corps": The CRV and the Limits of Developmentalist Radicalism

The first national Returned Peace Corps Volunteers' conference, held in Washington, D.C., March 5–7, 1965, barely registered the initiation, three days earlier, of the Operation Rolling Thunder bombing campaign over North Vietnam. Of the one thousand volunteers who attended, almost none expressed an interest in politics, although most had some sympathy for both the civil rights movement and the War on Poverty. Harris Wofford remembers in his 1992 memoir that the "first session ended in an overflowing State Department auditorium with Harry Belafonte linking arms with Chief Justice Warren, Secretary of State Rusk, Secretary of Defense McNamara, Shriver, and the Vice-President, and leading everyone in singing 'We Shall Overcome.'"[61] In small group discussions, volunteers focused on re-entry (some worried about the hypocrisy of using Washington connections to help them find jobs after they had preached self-help overseas) and addressing domestic problems, agreeing that "applying the human-relations skills that they acquired overseas is a matter of learning how to deal with particular American conditions and recognizing the universal culture of poverty."[62] Secretary of State Dean Rusk cast himself as a humanist and a humanitarian in his speech to the volunteers, telling them, "Those who are committed to peace must be prepared to protect it," and proclaiming, "I am convinced that power has not corrupted the American people. Their purposes have remained simple and decent—to organize a tolerable world community, with its members living at peace with their neighbors, settling their disputes by peaceful means; getting on with the great humane purpose of the human race, human rights, and economic and social developments."[63]

Briefly interrupting these celebratory discussions, a few returned volunteers circulated an antiwar petition and attempted to picket while in Washington; according to Wofford, "The issue was whether a group of protesting Volunteers should use the Peace Corps name on their signs at the White House. Shriver made one point to them: Most of the Volunteers at the conference had opposed any organization of ex-Volunteers speaking in their name. Did they feel they had a right to use a name earned by such a large group with so many different views?"[64] Shriver's argument convinced Tanganyika volunteer George Johnson, the organizer of the protest, and the protesting volunteers removed Peace Corps references from their signs and even sent the petition from Yale Law School the following week to avoid any association with the Peace Corps. Wofford laments that "this was the last time in the sixties, in my experience, when young people would show that spirit of compromise."[65] Though George Johnson was taken off the docket of keynote speakers after warning Shriver he would speak against the war, he did address the conference. In his speech, the antiwar activist took the position that "not all the obstacles to a peaceful world lie in the Communist bloc"; attacking calls from the right for increased bombing and leftist demands for immediate withdrawal as overly simplistic and not reflective of "our proper goal," he argued for a political solution that would allow the United States to "rightly resist totalitarianism—but do it with methods that build, rather than destroy, the values we seek to defend."[66] Johnson's measured critique of U.S. foreign policy was also well within the "spirit of compromise" Wofford observed and the dictates of neutrality the Peace Corps imposed. Even as he criticized Rusk's policies, Johnson accepted the secretary of state's ethical dictates, affirming the United States' right and responsibility to defend its "human" values, "protect peace," and promote development the world over.

If many volunteers opposed the war cautiously and quietly, some volunteer dissenters in the mid-sixties moved away from this "spirit of compromise" and attempted to challenge the U.S. foreign policy establishment for which they had worked. In the four years that the Committee of Returned Volunteers comprised an active faction of the U.S. antiwar movement, the organization changed considerably, becoming more radical along with the rest of the new left in both their analysis and the tactics they endorsed. However, the CRV's positions continued to be shaped by their Peace Corps training, often echoing the Peace Corps ethos of heroic–masculine development and American exceptionalism. The CRV's continued reliance on this ethos, as well as their construction of their expertise from the very experiences they condemned as manifestations of U.S. imperialism, made it more difficult for them to act in solidarity with insurgent Third World peoples as well as with increasingly radical Black Power and cultural nationalist groups at home. Examining the CRV's radicalization and the group's internal conflicts over its role in an escalating global anti-imperialist struggle illuminates the similar disputes that pervaded and ultimately fractured the larger new left.

The group that would become the CRV called their first official meeting in late 1966, when, after some unsuccessful attempts at uniting his liberal crowd of returned volunteers doing graduate work at Columbia with a more radical faction of Tanganyika volunteers around NYU, co-founder Aubrey Brown decided to extend his organizational vision beyond ex–Peace Corps members. He recalls that late one night after running into some ex-volunteer friends at a party "it just dawned on me that one could narrow the focus to policy questions and broaden the constituency, so it wouldn't be a matter of using the Peace Corps name; it would simply be a voluntary organization of people who shared the same questions on social/political issues."[67] Even with the CRV's formation, however, pressure from the radical Tanganyika faction continued. Brown further recalls how they thwarted the organization's early decision not to focus on Vietnam:

> At our first returned volunteer meeting, our little group . . . was not particularly militant, was not movement-oriented, we saw ourselves as a policy organization, you know to work on issues of policy, toward more sensible policies toward the Third World, and we told ourselves that other people were working on Vietnam and so we weren't going to tackle that. Well, the Tanzania people around NYU showed up at our first organizational meeting. And they said, we have to talk about Vietnam. And we struggled all day long about that . . . Finally we agreed to set up four committees: an Asia Committee, a Latin America Committee, and Africa Committee, and a Vietnam Committee. Within a few days we had a statement against the war, and people fired it off to their friends around the country . . . Within no time flat there was a Berkeley chapter, we didn't even have a name for the organization but it was up and running and we had hundreds of signatures. And so we kind of hit the road running on the war issue which we had not even thought we were gonna get into.[68]

The statement against the war, which they expanded at the urging of journalist I. F. Stone and published as a position paper in *Ramparts* in September 1967, illustrates how the early CRV relied on and strategically deployed the development rhetoric they'd absorbed during their Peace Corps service. Imagining themselves as the intellectual wing of the antiwar movement, the former volunteers traded on their experiences of service overseas, framing them as a source of both information on Third World liberation struggles and respectability for the movement. In their attempts to convince the mainstream media and intellectual establishment of the wisdom of an antiwar stance, co-founder Joe Stork recalls, "we very self-consciously wanted to exploit what then was still the very wholesome image of the Peace Corps."[69] Co-founder Alice Hageman remembers similar strategies and goals, writing that "in retrospect, our assumptions were very naïve: if we made enough information available to government officials and the public, U.S. policy would change."[70] This tactic is much in evidence in their *Ramparts* position paper, which employs developmentalist and patriotic frameworks to criticize the war:

> We oppose the war in Vietnam because it destroys in one developing country what we have worked to build in so many other developing countries. The increasing destruction wrought by United States forces in Vietnam reveals a basic contradiction in our nation's policies overseas, a contradiction between that which builds up and that which destroys. For those of us who worked to build a school or dispensary, for those of us who saw dysentery decrease because we helped the people dig a well, for those of us who helped a village realize its ambition to have a bridge to get its goods to market; for those of us who helped a child discover the meaning of electricity, each bomb in Vietnam that destroys a school, a well, a bridge, or a child destroys the very kinds of things which we considered most important in our service as volunteers.[71]

The volunteers' insistence on the value of their role in pushing villagers to desire capitalist modernization—to help the underdeveloped world "realize its ambition"—suggests that they remain convinced of, or at least are willing to strategically mobilize, their power as heroic development workers. They continue to align themselves entirely with U.S. national interests and to employ the heroic–masculine framework advanced by both Peace Corps staffers and Vietnam War architects, arguing that "to admit that we have made a tragic mistake [in Vietnam] will require great courage." "Nevertheless," they proclaim, "we believe that U.S. withdrawal at this point, rather than undermining the honor of this nation, on the contrary will be a sign of its strength and health." In a set of internal talking points from their September 1967 newsletter they also place themselves firmly in the "loyal opposition" camp, arguing that "even the most extreme opponents of the war are deeply concerned with the moral and physical interests of the United States," and citing Abraham Lincoln, William James, Mark Twain, and Andrew Carnegie as examples of "perfectly loyal Americans [who] were outspoken critics of other military adventures."[72]

The moderate platforms and clean-cut image the CRV worked to cultivate were prominently on display in August 1968 when legendary pacifist Dave Dellinger asked CRV activists to lead the protest marches at the Chicago Democratic National Convention. In Chicago, Wofford joined the returned volunteer delegation after a Nigeria volunteer he knew urged him to "come along!" He recalls, "Some of my friends had heard demonstrators chanting 'Fuck you LBJ!' and the Black Panther–coined cry of 'Pig!' was used by some as a sure way of enraging the police. I wanted no part of that, so I listened to everything the Peace Corps Volunteers said on their bullhorns." Wofford describes the volunteers' role in policing the march, remembering that "the Peace Corpsmen kept the several hundred marchers on the sidewalks, obeying traffic lights, until the police blocked the way and started preparing to use tear gas . . . Once or twice someone shouted 'Pig' at policemen wearing gas masks (which made them look pig-like) but others told them to shut up . . . After unsuccessful negotiation with the police and National Guard, the Peace Corpsmen led the march back toward the Hilton. Each time we passed a large group of police, the Volunteers started the chant 'More pay for cops!'"[73]

The CRV's display of respect and advocacy in Chicago did not protect them from the police brutality that erupted there. CRV members Rita and Joe Sklar suggest that this experience had a radicalizing effect on the ex-volunteers, writing in a January 1970 article for SNCC's newspaper *Movement* that "the police riot in Chicago brutally educated our CRV contingent. Fearful and very angry they learned about the powers that be and what they will do to protect themselves."[74] A full-page graphic panel in CRV's short-lived, beautifully designed magazine *2 . . . 3 . . . Many* (named for Che Guevara's famous 1967 call for "two, three, many Vietnams") illustrates the radicalization process the Sklars describe.[75] The graphic depicts the transformation of a young, white American woman from naïve cultural tourist to antiwar protester to militant radical, rising like a phoenix from the flame of her own political and intellectual awakening after being struck on the head by the baton of state repression. The question mark blanketing the last panel of the graphic signals her ambivalence, shared by the CRV and the new left, as to whether her newfound political militancy could or should extend to bearing arms on behalf of the revolution.

In addition to these personal experiences of persecution and resistance, the Sklars identify two other factors that pushed the CRV from liberalism to radicalism: first that "the imperial nature of the US became increasingly apparent—especially in Vietnam but in Thailand, Laos, North Korea, Greece, Angola, Mozambique, South Africa, Bolivia, Brazil, Mexico, and Cuba, etc."; and second, "our attempts to change US foreign policy and domestic policy as well, and the resulting frustration of our efforts to change things, changed us."[76] Brown similarly recalls protests leading to a radicalization of tactics, remembering that after the 1967 beating of demonstrators at the Pentagon, "the slogan began to circulate of, from protest to resistance, and the next step that I recall, I think, were the days of rage in Oakland, with people shutting down the military recruitment centers, turning over cars. There was some effort to have the same kind of militancy."[77]

The final pivotal radicalizing experience the Sklars identify is the CRV's summer 1969 Venceremos Brigade trip to Cuba, which, they write, "blew people's minds. Cuba was doing all the things the Peace Corps and

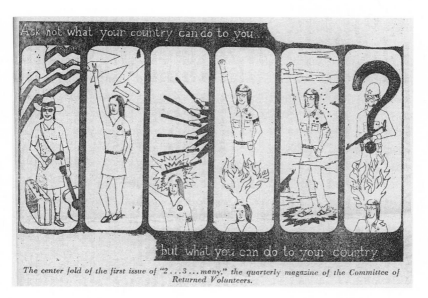

The center fold of the first issue of "2 . . . 3 . . . many," the quarterly magazine of the Committee of Returned Volunteers.

"Ask Not What Your Country Can Do to You" cartoon from the Committee of Returned Volunteers' short-lived magazine *2 . . . 3 . . . Many*, depicting the trajectory from overseas volunteer to revolutionary.

other organizations claimed they would do in underdeveloped countries. It exposed the Alliance for Progress and other US 'development' schemes in general, as shams and mere palliatives to further US penetration and control."[78] The Sklars' reflections here show both how much development was on the former volunteers' minds as they radicalized, and also how much development paradigms influenced their analysis: while they critique development schemes that allowed the United States to extract raw materials more efficiently, they are heartened by Cuba's "authentic" aspirations to fulfill different, but related, Marxist modernization ideals (e.g., increasing monocultural sugar production for global markets rather than developing diverse sustainable food production at home). On the Cuba trip, the CRV members were reminded of their relative lack of militancy through constant conversations they had with the newly formed Weather Underground, who made up the other half of the Cuba delegation. Hageman recalls the two groups working together to clean fishmeal out of a boat that would transport them back to Canada, and then staging "some heavy shouting matches on that boat about what's the best way to effect change, do you blow it up or do you do nonviolent passive resistance."[79]

Even as their stances became more radical, the CRV often continued to advance a discourse of American exceptionalism, bringing to its movement work a faith in themselves as educators and models for the world that looked much like the faith placed in them as volunteer–exemplars of modernity. Senator J. William Fulbright in a 1967 editorial was already citing "letters to the president from student leaders and former Peace Corps volunteers" as examples of dissenters who "believe their country was cut out for something more ennobling than imperial destiny."[80] Andy Berman, writing for the CRV newsletter in October 1970 in an article titled "Smash the Politics of Guilt!" exuberantly proclaimed his exceptionalism, writing, "What is so great about America is that our revolution is going to be the most liberating the world has ever seen!!!! Our nationalism ought to come from our love for the history of our people's resistance, and the uninhibited nature of our present-day struggle. Our revolution is going to be the greatest because we are not going to be hung up on questions of personality cults, political dogmatism, bureaucracy, drugs, sex, as are many of our revolutionary comrades in the socialist countries."[81]

Thus, even as they began to reject the Peace Corps, which had encouraged them to privilege individual friendship and small-scale development assistance over global redistributive policies, many ex-volunteers continued to imagine themselves as models for Third World people, and particularly for the "uninhibited" and dogma-free self-expression the Peace Corps also emphasized. A 1970 CRV newsletter piece about the multi-group-sponsored People's Peace Treaty articulates this continued exceptionalist stance, advancing the anachronistic claim that the Vietnamese Buddhists' occupation of a pagoda borrowed its rhetoric from the U.S. antiwar movement. The article celebrates "the symbolism of the militant Buddhists who staged a take-over of the National Pagoda (pro-Thieu) with the US-inspired slogan 'The pagoda belongs to the people'" and "the appeal of the Saigon Student Union for immediate action by US students and intellectuals to protest their repression."[82] In this rewriting of Vietnamese history, which erases the fact that Vietnamese nationalists had been appropriating land "for the people" since the 1950s and talking about it since at least the 1920s, the CRV indicates that many of its developmentalist assumptions remained even as its critique of U.S. hegemony became more radical.[83]

Perhaps the moment of the CRV's furthest-reaching, most radical critique of U.S. foreign policy occurred during its call for the abolition of the Peace Corps itself. In May 1970 the organization took over a Peace Corps headquarters for two days, writing in its manifesto, "We went abroad to help Asians, Africans, and Latin Americans develop their resources and become free people. Once abroad, we discovered that we were part of the U.S. worldwide pacification program. We found that U.S. projects in these countries are designed to achieve political control and economic exploitation; to build an empire for the United States. As volunteers we were part of that strategy; we were Marines in velvet gloves . . . we urge volunteers around the world to terminate their employment in the U.S. strategy of domination and to return home where they can struggle most effectively to defeat imperialism."[84] Volunteers occupied the Peace Corps headquarters for two days, unfurling a banner reading, "Liberation Not Pacification," before voluntarily leaving the building.

Yet at the moment when the organization's radicalism reached its height, CRV members began to question their strategies of critique,

"Liberation Not Pacification": CRV members occupy the Peace Corps offices, 1970. Photograph courtesy of the Peace Corps.

exposure, and even protest. Stork, who now works at Human Rights Watch, echoes Hageman's earlier insight, saying in a 2010 interview, "I guess I thought at the time, and for a long time after, that by uncovering the truth and exposing, that that was how you change things. And obviously, I mean that has to be a part of it, and I'd like to think I've participated in that process. But social change is something else much bigger. And I'm not sure anymore how relevant that kind of work is anymore [*sic*] to a social movement, building a social movement. I think it's relevant, I don't want to suggest otherwise. But it's clearly not the straight line I once thought it was."[85] Writing in 1969 about the demonstrations at Nixon's inauguration, CRV member James Herod eloquently articulated a similar disillusionment with the tactics of denunciation and peaceful protest: "Perhaps it was so peaceful that it was a 'non-event.' Who cares if 6000 people walk through a deserted city on a sleepy Sunday afternoon in the middle of winter? . . . Can students, dropouts, yippies, middle-aged ph.d. candidates, and scattered and powerless professionals *ever* achieve a democratization of the power structure and an equalization of income? Or can these crucial changes be wrought only by *organized workers who are in a position to paralyze vital processes of the society?*"[86] Herod makes clear the tensions between the model of a loose coalition that might protest a war on the grounds that it is unjust and the increasingly popular goal of violent resistance in the service of social transformation; his invocation of the power of "organized workers" also reflects the personal transformations many in the CRV and new left had undergone from liberal antiwar activists to radical anticapitalists with a much broader agenda. Herod's gloss of the protest and its goals reflects one of the major contradictions of this radicalizing movement of white college graduates.[87] The CRV had begun by trading on their privilege and power as elite and educated experts who had lived abroad, which made sense as they tried to educate the liberal policy establishment and ask it to modify its policies. But if their goals were "the democratization of the power structure and an equalization of income," their expertise, and even the extent to which they were needed at all, became less clear. The 1970 cartoon with the question mark over the returned-volunteer-turned-protester-turned-armed-insurgent voiced the doubts sweeping the organization about what returned volunteers could, in fact, "do to their country," raising questions not only about the ethics of taking up arms but also about what role, if any, they could play in a truly revolutionary movement.

While many in the CRV began to rely on more overtly radical and Marxist rhetoric like Herod's, schisms also began to develop—Aubrey Brown claims that "as the movement developed, [the CRV] largely moved with it," recalling that the CRV, like the larger new left, split bitterly over tactics, with many opposing violent resistance tactics at home even as they began to stand in solidarity with revolutionary movements abroad.[88] Brown explains that the CRV split into two factions, divided over questions of procedural democracy as well as whether to embrace radical and revolutionary tactics or remain in their role as movement intellectuals.[89] The tensions dividing the CRV came to a head in August 1970 when a group of CRV women "liberated the national office from elitist leadership," citing the CRV president's "counter-collective decision making" and international travel without consulting the group.[90] The women attempted to restore collective decision-making, but the restoration proved short-lived, and the CRV dissolved a few months later. Many members went on to form research groups on Africa, Latin America, and the Middle East, while others became writers and professors, attempting to produce knowledge even though they worried that it would not bring social transformation.

If speaking truth to power did not effect the kind of social change the CRV and the larger new left wished to see, it did get at least one CRV member killed. A few days after the U.S.-backed coup in Chile overthrew Salvador Allende, Frank Teruggi, a former volunteer and journalist living in Santiago, was taken from his apartment, tortured in the national stadium, and assassinated. The U.S. government turned a blind eye to Teruggi's torture and murder, and FBI documents released in 2000 suggest that State Department intelligence given to the government of Chile alerted them to Teruggi's antiwar activism and led them to single out him and American journalist Paul Horman while releasing the twenty to thirty other U.S. citizens they detained. December 1972 FBI documents call Teruggi a "subversive" for his CRV involvement, explaining that "CRV is a national group composed of mainly former Peace Corps volunteers who espouse support of Cuba and all Third World revolutionaries and oppose United States 'imperialism and oppression' abroad."[91] Lubna Qureshi, along with many journalists and Chilean witnesses, argues that "the Chilean military classified Teruggi as a special case" because the U.S. government informed them of his "possible antiwar activism."[92]

Teruggi's case was unique among CRV members. Compared to other organizations with an anti-imperialist orientation, particularly black nationalist groups, the CRV faced very little scrutiny or government persecution, much less outright violence. A more representative strategy for containing returned volunteers' dissent was the effort by the Peace Corps itself to incorporate CRV protest into the agency's liberal developmental vision. By the beginning of 1970 the Peace Corps featured an advertisement proclaiming, "Help Us Get Rid of the Peace Corps, Join CRV." The text of the advertisement reimagines the CRV's demands as utterly compatible with the Peace Corps' own vision:

> We've done a lot of good for a lot of emerging nations. So much, in fact, that we can start thinking about finishing the most successful projects and coming home. If this were a perfect world, we could do it. Everywhere. But, right now, the world needs all the help it can get. There are farm programs to be gotten off the ground. Trade schools

Peace Corps advertisement circa 1970, "Help Us Get Rid of the Peace Corps, Join CRV." Courtesy of the Peace Corps.

to be set up. Hospitals to be built. All of which takes people. Everyone from recent high school and college graduates to professionals and skilled craftsmen. Almost anyone who's had experience working with his head and his hands. Our ultimate goal is simple. To help these countries get to point where they no longer need our help.

Signaling both the notoriety the CRV had achieved and its own ability to incorporate opposition back into its heroic–developmental narrative, the Peace Corps reframes the CRV's call to "abolish the Peace Corps," transforming it from a militant reimagining of U.S. power and policies into evidence that the Peace Corps has been so successful it will soon outlive its usefulness. Folding the CRV back into the Peace Corps community, the advertisement frames the CRV's demand to abolish the Peace Corps as simply a premature articulation of an inevitable phase in the growth of both the young volunteers and the young nations, promising that after more patience and ideologically neutral hard work "we can start thinking about coming home." Framing the returned volunteers' dissent as an intermediate stage of development, a necessary part of the overarching capitalist imperialist system rather than a threat to it, the Peace Corps advertisement demonstrates the developmental narrative that eventually framed new left radical protest as simply a phase of adolescent acting-out in a larger narrative of national–hegemonic progress. Here the Peace Corps exemplifies the way, in the words of Mimi Thi Nguyen, "liberalism's empire claims to desire an end to itself," while ceaselessly deferring that end.[93]

The Development Imaginary in the Rise and Fall of the New Left

The CRV's trajectory, from self-discovery and pursuit of authenticity to confident attempts to speak truth to power to despair (for some) and radicalization (for others) when those attempts went unheeded, looked very much like that of the larger new left, particularly the largely white students who populated it in its early years.[94] The defining texts of the new left, too, share much with the sociological works that shaped the Peace Corps, bemoaning the comfort and conformity of managerial-class men and their "beat and angry" sons and searching for more authentic community and fulfillment.[95] Paul Goodman's 1960 book *Growing Up Absurd* provides perhaps the clearest example of this confluence, linking juvenile delinquency to "the organized society" and arguing that "the structure of society that has become increasingly dominant in our country is disastrous to the growth of excellence and manliness."[96] Proudly excluding women from his account because "a girl does not *have to*, she is not expected to, 'make something of herself,'" Goodman explicitly reframes problems of class and labor as problems of isolation and insufficient "man's work," arguing that "because of their historical theory of the 'alienation of labor' . . . the Marxist parties never fought for the man-worthy job itself."[97] Enormously influential in the early days of the new left, Goodman's book conveys a sense of how thoroughly the attempt to regain authentic masculinity and fraternal community came to substitute in the new left imaginary for old left struggles for less, better-compensated, and safer work.[98]

The 1962 *Port Huron Statement*, the early movement-defining manifesto for SDS, elaborates many of the same themes as Goodman and the liberal social scientists, articulating the predicament of young middle-class white activists in similar language but with more ambition: "We began to sense that what we had originally seen as the American Golden Age was actually the decline of an era. The worldwide outbreak of revolution against colonialism and imperialism, the entrenchment of totalitarian states, the menace of war, overpopulation, international disorder, supertechnology—these trends were testing the tenacity of our own commitment to democracy and freedom and our abilities to visualize their application to a world in upheaval."[99] This list of threats to their "commitment to democracy" indicates the apprehension of SDS at decolonization and class struggle alike, echoing the Peace Corps' developmental vision in framing anticolonial revolution, sheltered affluence, and "overpopulation" as challenging their ability to live authentically and freely. Thus the Peace Corps and the new left diagnosed the problem of postwar period in the same way, and offered similar solutions: the Peace Corps' vision of person-to-person modernization appealed to the anti-"supertechnology" new left, allowing it to adopt the Peace Corps' heroic developmentalism in its struggle against the liberal establishment.

The "values" section of *The Port Huron Statement* demonstrates the American-exceptionalist, romantic vision of brotherhood that allowed new left activists to connect with the Peace Corps' vision and imagine it as a transformative "post-radical" one: they claim, for example, that "unlike youth in other countries we are used to moral leadership being exercised and moral dimensions being clarified by our elders," leaving ambiguous the question of whether moral leadership is exercised by the young in these "other countries" or whether it simply does not exist at all.[100] A few paragraphs later, the declaration explicitly rejects leftist movement predecessors, dismissing "all the old [anticapitalist] slogans" along with the liberal anticommunist ones, adopting instead a vision of reinvigorated masculinity and brotherhood. "We regard *men* as infinitely precious and possessed of unfulfilled capacities for reason, freedom, and love," wrote the activists, in perhaps the most famous sentence in the document. The solution to the confusion and alienation brought on by modernization and decolonization alike, they argued, was to form "personal links between man and man," links that would "go beyond the partial and fragmentary bonds of function that bind men only as worker to worker, employer to employee, teacher to student, American to Russian. Loneliness, estrangement, isolation describe the vast distance between man and man today."[101] In response to the alienating aspects of modernity, the new left thus affirmed its commitment to fully realized manhood and brotherhood.

The early new left's feelings of alienation from modernity did not impede their enthusiasm for the modernization mission, particularly as it was embodied by the Peace Corps. In his 1988 memoir, Tom Hayden recalls Frank Mankiewicz offering him a regional directorship in 1964. "The Andes could be mine, he said laughing," Hayden remembers, writing that he rejected the offer of Peru but responded that the SDS national committee could run VISTA (Volunteers in Service to America) trainings.[102] Likewise, after Booth and Oglesby gave their 1965 "Build, Not Burn" speech, the Peace Corps contacted them the next day and invited them to speak to volunteer trainees in Puerto Rico, and Wiggins himself nearly convinced SDS to take over the entire Peace Corps training program, telling Oglesby, "I think the Peace Corps needs the kind of juice that SDS people could bring to it."[103] Although the national committee ultimately decided against running the training program, Oglesby recalls that "several dozen SDSers actually did go to the camp in Puerto Rico on their own."[104]

As indicated by their emphasis on masculinity and brotherhood as the endpoints of social transformation, the new left, like the Peace Corps, sometimes had difficulty accommodating women, much less seeing them as equals. Doug Rossinow explains that the new left "imagined a society alive with participatory democracy. Yet the young radicals still equated this invigorated citizenship with masculinity, viewing it as a triumph over effeminacy. The role that women might play in such a democratic revival was unclear, yet they certainly would have difficulty qualifying for citizenship in such a regime of manliness."[105] Accounts by Sara Evans and Jennifer Frost enumerate the particular difficulties faced by women organizers attempting to imagine roles for themselves in the masculine vision of the new left, and the ways that this inhospitable climate weakened the

movement while laying the groundwork for feminist analysis and organizing. Jean Tepperman, an organizer from SDS's Economic Research
and Action Project (ERAP), remembers being banished from a mid-
sixties meeting: "[A male organizer] ordered all the women to leave.
'Because,' he said, 'we got serious things to talk about here and we can't
have women with all their legs all hanging out all over the place.' The
concept was . . . having all these sex objects around here was so distract-
ing that they couldn't have their serious discussion. And so we left. We
all left."[106] Tepperman's account not only indicates how SDS women's
organizing experiences served as catalysts for their feminism, but also
suggests continuities with the Peace Corps' heroic development work.
In ERAP's organizing as well as in key Peace Corps locales like Vicos,
women were framed as obstacles to the serious work of reactivating
masculine capacities and forming connections "between man and man."

Though Hayden, Oglesby, and Booth's Peace Corps–influenced developmentalist masculine ethos continued to define the white new left for
most of the decade, the end of the 1960s saw that sensibility challenged
by more militant visions. Oglesby recalls then-national secretary (and
future Weather Underground leader) Bernardine Dohrn telling him in
1969, "Some of us think you want something a little too much like the
Peace Corps." Oglesby, who had proposed sending what would eventually become the Venceremos Brigade to help with the sugarcane harvest
in Cuba, acknowledged the agency's influence on his vision, asking
Dohrn, "Wouldn't setting up an illegal Peace Corps in revolutionary
Cuba be terrific?" and telling her, "The basic aim of this proposal—you're
right about this—is *not* to make the revolution. I admit it. It's to make the
revolution *less necessary*." In Oglesby's recollection, Dohrn emphasized
the fundamental incompatibility of her vision of the destruction of racism
and capitalism with his liberal developmentalist vision of averting revolution through mutual understanding: "Keep trying to remember, Carl,
that our side favors the revolution, okay? And we don't expect it to be
nonviolent."[107] When SDS expelled Oglesby, they read off charges against
him that included his "relationship with one Warren Wiggins" and his
"flirtation with the Peace Corps" as well as his meetings with corporate
executives. Thus, as was the case with CRV, it was the question of what
progress meant—"blowing it up" as opposed to development projects
that make revolution "less necessary"—that ultimately broke SDS apart.

These debates—skirmishes waged over liberal SDS activists' prox-imity to the Peace Corps as well as the viability of various teleological narratives of progress (peaceful development that would make violent revolution "less necessary")—signal the central role played by develop-ment discourses and projects in the new left's philosophical debates and ultimate dissolution. As the new left's leadership fractured, every faction remained invested in a developmental trajectory that denied power to masses of people: Oglesby's "Build, Not Burn" ethos imagined peaceful, mature collaborations "between man and man," with government and business leaders supporting self-help programs in Cuba; the Progressive Labor Party's orthodox Marxism refused to recognize the nationalist struggle in Vietnam as authentically revolutionary; and Weather Under-ground activists attempted to construct authentic solidarity with (and often, to match or outdo the macho posturing of) cultural nationalists and international revolutionaries who increasingly framed their own revolutionary struggles as attempts to reclaim their manhood.[108] The counterculture, for its part, indicated its despair with the development imperative, choosing subjective experience and fantasies of Third World otherness over pretentions to objectivity and rational progress.[109] This critique mostly remained implicit, forging imaginary rather than sub-stantive alliances. But even if the counterculture's rejection of develop-ment had been more explicit and grounded in solidarity practice, there was little room for it to reimagine global social change, partly because the heroic development worker already occupied the realms of authen-tic experience, self-expression, and intercultural connection.[110] Nonethe-less, the counterculture's antimodern, communal orientation, even as expressed in cultural consumption, must be seen in the context of a growing activist despair at the tremendous violence of both communist and capitalist modernizing regimes.[111]

The difficulty of mounting a revolutionary challenge to the mod-ernization teleologies that would anticipate and contain radical ener-gies, already evidenced by the experience of the various U.S. radical movements I have traced in this chapter and the prior one, is dramatized most fully in my next and final chapter, in which I consider how the Bolivian revolutionary indigenous nationalism that emerged at the close of the 1960s became hopelessly entangled with the Peace Corps devel-opment discourses it sought to challenge. In Bolivia, where indigeneity

was inextricable from national narratives of progress, cultural nationalist movements and cultural workers produced particularly trenchant
critiques of the international development enterprise. However, those
movements and cultural works still took shape under pressure from the
development regime, and adopted development narratives, structures,
and imperatives despite themselves. This was particularly true in the case
of Bolivian indigenous cultural nationalism's response to the development establishment's population control discourse and practices. These
discourses and practices, and the cultural nationalist response they incited, led to an ongoing popular equation of liberation from imperialism
with the reassertion of communal control over women's bodies.

6

THE PEACE CORPS, POPULATION CONTROL, AND CULTURAL NATIONALIST RESISTANCE IN 1960S BOLIVIA

Yawar Mallku (*Blood of the Condor*), filmed by Jorge Sanjinés and the Ukamau collective in the rural Bolivian community of Kaata, was scheduled for release in La Paz in July 1969, but Bolivian government officials locked the doors of the theater on the first night it was to be shown, saying they were acting on "higher orders." The source of the orders seemed obvious to many: *Yawar Mallku* depicts a naïve yet ruthless group of young Americans called the Progress Corps who secretly sterilize indigenous women in their shining new health clinic, and ends with a shot of rifles raised in the air in an anti-imperialist call to arms. Upon hearing of the film's suppression, crowds of would-be filmgoers protested in the streets for twenty-four hours until the government relented and released the film, which was then seen by more Bolivians than any other movie, domestic or foreign, in the country's history.[1] *Yawar Mallku* encapsulated and focused concerns about the international development establishment's persistent linkage of development aid to population control, and its impact on Bolivian politics and culture was rapid and dramatic: the March 1970 front page of the leftist *La Prensa* newspaper echoed its equation with a headline reading, "Birth Control: Peace Corps = Genocide."[2] By 1970, indigenous groups as well as leftist students and other activists were carrying out protests and attacks on Peace Corps offices, and in April 1971, faced with evidence of the agency's participation in IUD-insertion projects in indigenous communities and pressured by an increasingly radical anti-imperialist movement, General Juan José Torres's short-lived leftist government expelled the Peace Corps.[3]

This widespread animosity toward the Peace Corps, the most visible symbol of the U.S. development enterprise, had arrived relatively recently to Bolivia, a country deemed a development success story by modernization theorists just a few years earlier. One of the world's largest recipients of per capita U.S. aid in the 1960s, Bolivia became an important Cold War outpost in those years: its government's U.S.-guided shift from the radical redistributionist aims of its 1952 national revolution to a staunchly anticommunist modernization program became an important model for the United States as it searched for ways to contain and co-opt other Third World revolutions. By 1966 the *New York Times* contended that Bolivia was "virtually run by U.S. technicians and administrators."[4]

Of all the development workers and planners attempting to run Bolivia and showcase its population for anticommunist Cold War ends, Peace Corps volunteers were the most iconic and densely concentrated. Even though they generally did not succeed in transforming the communities they encountered, volunteers represented the benign face of a process Bolivians increasingly came to understand as population control and cultural eradication. After providing some background for 1960s modernization efforts in Bolivia, this chapter demonstrates how volunteers there attempted to convert indigenous men into correctly masculine national subjects, model heterosexual marriage and housekeeping, and assist with population transfer projects in the service of modernization; how, in other words, development workers in Bolivia tried to control populations and eradicate indigenous ways of life. Next I examine the centrality of population control (construed more narrowly as mass birth control or "family planning") to the 1960s vision of capitalist development, discussing the Peace Corps' population control programs and examining the popular opposition to those programs that grew in Bolivia until the agency's 1971 expulsion. I then analyze *Yawar Mallku* as a powerful indictment of Peace Corps developmentalism, arguing that the film, as well as the cultural nationalist movement it incited and prefigured, understands Peace Corps population control programs as symbolic of the cultural eradication that constituted the horizon of development discourse. At the same time, I argue that both the film and the movement it depicted and catalyzed adopt development's gendered vision of individual transformation to full masculinity, centrally understood as the power to control women's bodies and therefore the future of their communities. Finally, I consider how Bolivian indigenous feminists (and nonfeminist women) have responded to the bind created by development and cultural nationalism and attempted to negotiate a balance between community and bodily autonomy.

Latin Lovers and Model Campesinos: The Peace Corps and Bolivian Development

In April 1952, after just days of fighting, the Bolivian people seized the government from the military and toppled the tin- and land-baron oligarchy that controlled the country's resources. The revolution was led by a coalition that had formed after a radical indigenous movement in the countryside challenged the established neo-feudal order in the 1940s, demanding that the government abolish slave labor and regulate landowner–tenant farmer relationships. The state responded with violent repression, imprisoning many movement participants, but the indigenous communities persevered, forming alliances in prison and elsewhere with miners, urban students, and other dissidents.[5] The MNR (Movimiento Nacionalista Revolucionario, or Revolutionary Nationalist Movement), a group of liberal and leftist intellectuals, assumed leadership of this coalition; they encouraged workers to organize and won a 1951 election, which the military then annulled. MNR leaders initiated the revolution on April 8, 1952: armed civilians fought side by side with the La Paz police, and a battalion of miners overpowered the army in the capital. Though the military initially fought back, on April 11 the government formally surrendered.[6]

In the year or so immediately following the revolution, indigenous groups in the countryside began seizing property, forcing landowners off their haciendas. The new MNR government initially seemed to follow their lead, implementing land reform, instituting universal suffrage and education, and nationalizing the mines. But the MNR government's rural program primarily took the hierarchical form of a pedagogical modernization project rather than a collaborative radical one, encouraging (and often forcing) indigenous Bolivians to eschew their local, communal identities and adopt individualist, nationalist, capitalist ones. The MNR attempted to banish the word *indio* from the Bolivian vocabulary, designating indigenous people *campesinos* (peasants) instead; erased from the historical record the indigenous radicalism that had driven the rebellions leading up to the 1952 revolution; and generally characterized indigenous culture as anachronistic and ornamental.[7]

The MNR government not only disavowed the radicalism of its indigenous rural constituency, but also soon abandoned even the labor–left vision of its remaining radical wing, working closely in the mid-to-late 1950s with the U.S. government and the IMF to implement austerity measures for public workers.[8] Bolivia's dependence on the United States for markets for its tin exports and monetary aid meant that the MNR had little choice but to comply with U.S. dictates, and by the mid-1950s the MNR had largely agreed to follow the national modernization plan that U.S. ambassador Merwin Bohan had proposed in 1942. The Bohan plan urged Bolivia to export more raw materials and effect a massive population transfer of the politicized highland communities to the fertile but sparsely populated eastern lowlands. Economic pressure, mainly from the United States, ensured that an agenda of economic growth, population transfer, and labor austerity replaced the more egalitarian vision for which miners and rural communities alike had fought.[9]

If Eisenhower's government had pressured Bolivia to implement capitalist development and cut social welfare programs in the wake of the national revolution, the Kennedy administration took an even more interventionist approach. The Alliance for Progress poured hundreds of millions of dollars into military modernization and anticommunist projects: not only did Kennedy make Bolivia's receipt of Alliance money dependent upon the jailing and expulsion of leftists and the suppression of striking workers, he also increased military aid to Bolivia by 800 percent, inaugurating a program called Civic Action that gave the Bolivian military new functions building roads and airstrips, conducting literacy campaigns, clearing land, and providing medical services.[10] By involving the military, the U.S.-backed MNR government blurred the line between military and civic life, militarizing development work while softening the image of the re-empowered military. The MNR also cultivated an enmity between indigenous peasants and organized labor, officially codified in President Rene Barrientos's 1966 Military–Peasant Pact, which guaranteed peasants the continued implementation of the revolution's 1953 land reforms in exchange for their promise to fight on the side of the military against the organized left.

The Bolivian government's efforts to militarize indigenous communities and employ the military for development projects led to its fame in U.S. development circles; in October 1963 USAID acting director Samuel Eaton told newly appointed U.S. ambassador Douglas Henderson, "I am sure that my favorite country could not be in better hands."[11] Civic Action strengthened the military to the point where it seized power in a 1964 coup d'état, and emboldened it to massacre at least eighty-seven miners during a June 1967 conference at which they had gathered to declare their support for Che Guevara.[12] When Bolivian soldiers killed Guevara that October, Walt Rostow trumpeted the success of the military modernization strategy in a letter to Lyndon Johnson, writing that the revolutionary's capture and assassination "shows the soundness of our 'preventive medicine' assistance to countries facing incipient insurgency."[13]

Of all the technicians and administrators converging on Bolivia in the 1960s, Peace Corps volunteers were the most visible. The *New York Times* reported in December 1962 that at Kennedy's behest "the Peace Corps is shifting its primary emphasis from Africa to Latin America," and that Bolivia was a particularly important target; in 1968 a Peace Corps report claimed that "with a PCV/population ratio of one to 12,500, the program is one of the heftiest on the continent. Peace Corps/Bolivia's program memorandum proposes to increase the intensity of the contact to one PCV to every 7,500 Bolivians by 1970."[14] These volunteers were not evenly distributed throughout the country; ratios were much higher in lowland areas already thick with missionaries and other development workers. Peace Corps volunteers attempted to work within (and sometimes against) these existing development networks until Bolivians began to reject them, treating their population control programs as symbolic of the cultural eradication that constituted the horizon of development discourse.

Jack Vaughn, who worked for the U.S. Information Agency in Bolivia in the 1950s before going to work for the Peace Corps, often touted Peace Corps success in modernizing Bolivian Altiplano-dwellers as an example of the magic of development initiatives. Peace Corps official and chronicler Brent Ashabranner recalls that Vaughn "often spoke about the Peace Corps helping to 'bring the Andean Indians into the twentieth century,'" and quotes Vaughn's speech to staffers about his triumphant experiences with those Indians:

I've been a Latin lover since 1938, and I've seen a lot of strange things. But I've never seen anything like what I saw in Bolivia a few days ago. I had been stationed in Bolivia a couple of times and left there last in mid-1958. The last six months I was in Bolivia with Warren Wiggins, I reached the point where I was reluctant to go up on the high plains near Lake Titicaca to hunt and fish because of the menacing hostile attitude of the Indians. They were all armed, they seemed resentful, didn't speak Spanish and didn't change. That was seven or eight years ago.

I visited five villages in that very same area in 1965. In all five I was carried into town on the backs of the Indians who wanted to show me that they were in the human race. They had all built a new school, the first school in a thousand years. They all had a clinic for child deliveries, the first clinic in a thousand years. They all had potable water piped in, and they had done it themselves. They had made more physical progress in a couple of years than they had made in the previous thousand. But more important was the attitude, the openness, the willingness to look you in the eye and tell you about who they were and what they had done, and the pride and self-respect of citizenship. This was done by the Peace Corps. What the Spaniards and the Incas and the Western miners and the diplomats and AID people couldn't do in a thousand years, the Peace Corps had helped do in about three years.[15]

Through its description of rural Bolivians' transformation from petulance to hero worship, Vaughn's story depicts the ideal endpoint of the modernization doctrines that the Peace Corps sought to embody. Modernization theory allows him to characterize the premodern indigenous Bolivians as simultaneously violent and stagnant, hostile and passive, prehistoric and inhuman. In order to demonstrate their entry into the human race, they carry Vaughn on their backs, their physical closeness to the boxer turned development hero making palatable their new role as laborers in the global capitalist system. The triumph of development is signaled by the Aymaras' complete submission (something neither the Incas nor the Spaniards were able to compel), and simultaneously by their "pride and self-respect of citizenship"; the Peace Corps' vision of brotherhood has been able to subdue them more thoroughly than previous empires ever could. They also show Vaughn their "physical progress" in the form of "a clinic for child deliveries," their ability to regulate women's bodies and the reproduction of their communities proving their modernity and masculinity (and thus their humanity).

Attempting to realize fantasies like Vaughn's, the Peace Corps embodied and enacted the more seductive side of anticommunist modernization doctrines in Bolivia, using Rostow and Shriver's model of desire-production through the promise of homosocial intimacy to induce Bolivians to want to help themselves out of poverty.[16] These doctrines relied on a vision of a passive indigenous peasantry enmeshed in a culture of poverty, as early Peace Corps evaluator James Frits demonstrates in an early report, arguing that in Bolivia "most people expect the government to do everything for them. They have almost no tradition of solving their own problems."[17] Volunteer Stuart Goldschen, upon reaching the Altiplano in 1965, echoed Frits's idea that the most important thing he could teach Bolivians would be a "modern" individualistic way of thinking and living: "Maybe I could impart a taste of modern living that would incite a few to make an effort to better their lot. But how? I could see as I visited these villages that it was going to be a hell of a job."[18] Volunteers' stories indicate their sense that they were encountering blank slates in Bolivia; their accounts chronicle their attempts to assist in both the eradication of indigenous culture and the anticommunist project that the Kennedy administration had linked so closely to the modernization mission.

Frits's 1963 report also reveals the importance of Peace Corps development work in effecting a population and power transfer away from the Altiplano, a center of worker, indigenous, and student radical political activity. The report contrasts the "grim political mining town" of Achacachi with the "relaxed ways" of the lowlands, and highlights Peace Corps activity in temperate Cochabamba, where volunteers had created a for-profit hot-springs resort.[19] Frits's attempt to disparage the "political" climate of the Altiplano in favor of the relaxed yet entrepreneurial spirit found in the "pioneering" settlers of the eastern lowlands signals the Peace Corps' key role in the Cold War modernization schemes devised by the United States and the ruling MNR party. By assisting in the population and power transfer away from the Altiplano, the Peace Corps aided MNR attempts to depoliticize and disempower the Altiplano mining communities and to preempt their alliances with the rural indigenous population.

Throughout the 1960s, the Bolivia Peace Corps continued to emphasize the importance of uniting the nation regionally, attempting to heal geographical divisions while nurturing the split between the "Indians" and the miners. In a 1965 *Peace Corps Volunteer* issue devoted to Bolivia, deputy country director Richard Griscom wrote an article titled "BOLIVIA: Impetus Is to East in Land Beset by Geography." Griscom contrasts the Altiplano, "a cold forbidding plateau" that is "traditionally the more important of the two regions" where "Bolivia's Aymara Indians eke out a living on their farms in much the same way that they have for hundreds of years," with the "lesser known" lowlands, "which now are assuming an ever greater importance in the country's development." Griscom explains that "settlers from the Altiplano, technicians, and money are pouring into this region," marking the change as both inevitable and imperative. "Aware of the importance of homesteads in a developing region," Griscom writes, "the government has in the past five years supported and encouraged the movement of colonizers from the Altiplano to the Oriente. Land is provided to the colonizers on very liberal credit terms, roads are constructed to transport their products to market, and technical assistance is provided in the form of agricultural extension agents. Peace Corps Volunteers are involved in two of the principal colonization areas . . . their role is mainly one of education: teaching the colonizers better health, homemaking, and agricultural techniques—always with an eye to developing lasting community organization and leadership."[20]

In the same issue, volunteers Denis Regan and Mickey Melragon reiterate this emphasis on "pouring" resources into the fertile east. Explaining the Peace Corps' efforts to help resettle thousands of Bolivians, they argue that linking the "barren Altiplano" and the lowlands "has long been Bolivia's desire." Like Griscom, Regan and Melragon narrate the transfer of population, resources, and national productive capacities from the "political" Altiplano as organic and inevitable, writing that "people are escaping the overcrowded plateau and have wandered along the roads, slashing out hillside plots to grow bananas, yucca, corn, and rice. As the roads advance, new towns spring up." They explain that the Peace Corps is working with the Development Corporation of Bolivia "to give resettlement assistance, direction, and [cocoa and coffee] seedlings in order to offer migrants more than subsistence agriculture."[21]

Unlike his superiors and fellow volunteers, Chad Bardone, who worked at settling new colonists in the Alto Beni lowlands and encouraging them to grow cash crops, identified specific problems with this "ambitious colonization project," meant to prepare Bolivia for democracy by compelling its citizens to recolonize its eastern frontiers. Although in a 1964 letter home he recapitulates the Peace Corps' heroic development imaginary—he writes that "community development promises to be one of the most frustrating things a North American can do. It is also one of the most necessary if countries like Bolivia are eventually going to be mature enough to handle the democratic system of government"—he also recognizes the obstacles to instilling a pioneering spirit in Bolivians:

> The area in which I work is an ambitious colonization project financed by BID [the Inter-American Development Bank] and administered by CBF [the Development Corporation of Bolivia]. The overall plan is to bring Bolivians down from the Altiplano to the Alto Beni, where, hopefully, they can build a better life . . . The colonists are now planting cocoa which will be their "cash crop" and it is hoped that they can begin to pay BID back within 4 years . . . Since the key to fulfilling this goal is a successful cocoa operation, you would think that the area would have been carefully examined for producing cocoa in quantity. This was not the case. The area was picked from aerial photographs. The soil conditions here are lousy for cocoa (almost a direct quote from the British agricultural man in this area). About 25% of the lots have a drainage problem and others are on very steep hills. Most of the soil is heavy and clayish, the opposite to that recommended for cocoa.[22]

Bardone's observations indicate that despite the myriad domestic and foreign development workers and planners converging on the Alto Beni site, the organizations blatantly disregarded the specific conditions under which their dreams of development would be realized and hastily planted "cash crops." As Silvia Rivera Cusicanqui observes about the Beni colonization enterprise, the colonists and development workers who supervised them were "shielded from scrutiny by the false equation: green = fertile."[23] However, even as he recognizes the folly of disregarding the specific conditions of the area, Bardone accepts the universalism and inevitability of the modernization mission, evincing anticipatory if wistful zeal about the destruction of native cultures.[24] He writes in a subsequent letter that the millenarian Guaraní community in which he spent only a few days are "very poor, from a material standpoint, but very rich in their religious life." Yet he injects a bit of melancholy into his premature account of their impending demise:

> They have a belief in a promised land of milk and honey that they will someday encounter. Each year a group of men are sent on an expedition to find the promised land. Because of this hope, these Indians have led a nomadic life for some years. They set up their villages, plant mandioca, sugar cane, bananas, corn and rice. When the hunting and fishing become too scarce to sustain the village, they move on. In the years to come they will have more and more contact with the world. It will be sad for the older people who cannot accept a more modern world, but the young people will benefit. I'm just glad that I was able to spend a few days with them as they are now. An experience worth remembering.[25]

In his observations, Bardone constructs a narrative of indigenous Bolivians' perpetual frustration whose only remedy is the forcible imposition of "a more modern world."[26] In recounting the men's futile search for the promised land, he reiterates the developmentalist argument that the men's immersion in the "hopes" and "beliefs" of "traditional society"—in this case a society that sends them on fruitless quests—denies them the masculinity and stability they can only achieve through the transition to modernity.

Although Bardone's prediction about the demise of the Guaraní people and their traditions was premature, his idea that they would disappear into modernity must have seemed plausible, given the number of development organizations and projects converging on the Bolivian lowlands in the 1960s. Another volunteer, Camille Falkett, details the extent of this saturation by development networks, which she discovered after being transferred from an Altiplano community to the lowland town of Charagua. Falkett's letter to a friend from her new post catalogs the overlapping, intertwined development missions spread over the lowlands:

> Well, I am now in Charagua and although I love the people here I don't think it was necessary to send another PCV to this town. The problem is that the local rep down here thinks that Charagua is in the same straits it was 15 mos. ago when the 1st PCV's arrived here. I think that I told you there is a PCV nurse stationed with me—well, there is a lot of work to be done in the public health field but without

this background there is practically nothing for a volunteer to do. That means for someone like myself. Since the 1st PCV's came, Latin American nuns have established a colegio—one of them also gives home economics and first aid classes to the campesinos and works in the town dispensary. A Bolivian doctor arrived 2 months ago and has greatly lightened the burden of the local sanitario. The Jesuits are very active in the CD area and need no help from me—I think they actually resent our moving into this field. There is a home economist in the normal school who will begin traveling by horseback to nearby Indian villages to work with the women. She knows 10× more than I do—I don't know if I can be of any help to her or not—we shall see. The military is stationed nearby and they are planning to give literacy classes in the near future—the local school teachers are in on the program, too . . . Besides the soldiers, there are 35 teachers living in Charagua and teaching *in* town, plus about 20 more who live here but work in rural schools![27]

Here Falkett conveys the ubiquity of development networks, military, religious, and international alike, even as Peace Corps representatives see no change in local conditions. Other volunteers emphasized their frustration with the Peace Corps mission in Bolivia: in 1967, volunteers David and Stephanie Pascale resigned "because we have found ourselves in a situation of continuous frustration, boredom, and feel that we are wasting our time and talents," and several other volunteers resigned that year for similar reasons.[28] Carol Weser, a health volunteer in the Cochabamba valley, worked more harmoniously with local people, but notes the cross-purposes at which the U.S. and other international development missions were working, recalling that "the UN had set up a milk pasteurization plan, which was just a fantastic thing for the area, but then the U.S. government wanted us to give out powdered milk, to support the farmers at home."[29]

Less industrious Peace Corps volunteers were sometimes helped along by other development workers, as in Coroico in 1965, when a Cuban American Franciscan priest, Padre Dionicio, convinced the residents to divide into work committees to improve the town's water system. The Peace Corps volunteer told anthropologists studying the project (who also contributed to the overwhelming development infrastructure in the area), "I didn't have anything to do with this idea of civic action. I'm sure glad it happened, but it was all just a big surprise to me," and the researchers confirmed that the volunteer "was not being unduly modest. He was handicapped by limited Spanish and it was not very clear how he was to work in the community, a question that Civic Action answered for him. On Padre Dionicio's part, he clearly hoped that the Peace Corps Volunteer would be able to get help from United States aid agencies working in Bolivia."[30] But when Padre Dionicio left the town for a vacation, USAID sent in engineers who not only insisted that the community contribute an impossible monetary sum and 50 percent of the labor required for the project, but also refused to count the six weeks of labor the community had already performed. The project promptly fell apart.[31]

In contrast to the agricultural colonization projects in the East, the numerically fewer volunteers in the rural indigenous communities and mining areas of the Altiplano were charged almost entirely with health and education programs. The Peace Corps population control programs that drew outrage in the late 1960s began on the Altiplano, and volunteers there more generally attempted social engineering projects that sought to regulate the behavior of highland individuals and families. The Peace Corps' "modeling" of both male leadership and family life was done mainly in USAID's National Community Development Program (NCDP), instituted in 1964 to train local counterparts, village-level workers (trabajadores de desarrollo de la comunidad, or TDCs) to work with Peace Corps volunteers. The NCDP employed over four hundred TDCs who were "selected from young men who speak the local language and live in rural areas and have at least a sixth grade education" and trained in "a variety of basic skills" and "the theory and practice of the principles of community development."[32] Although Peace Corps volunteers attempted to work with both men and women, only men were selected as TDCs.

Bolivia Peace Corps director Gerold Baumann explained his high hopes for the modernizing work of the NCDP in a 1970 article in *Community Development Journal*, choosing for his epigraph the proverb, "Bolivia is a beggar on a throne of gold." In the article, Baumann reiterates that the NCDP's purpose is "the integration of the alienated *campesino* into the mainstream of the social and economic process of development," then suggests that the village-level worker's task is also one of seduction, writing that "his is the job of stimulating, organizing, and teaching the people to discharge from within themselves and their community the powers for action." Boasting that Peace Corps volunteers had been "intimately involved" with the NCDP since 1964, Baumann explains that in Bolivia "the typical jealousies and mutual fears of an inbred peasant society exist abundantly," and thus "constant prodding is needed to get village tasks done." With this prodding, however, Baumann concludes that "this programme might yet get that beggar off his throne of gold and make him a truly free and economically viable man with dignity and pride in his own country."

Echoing the by-then-ubiquitous development imagery of seduction and masculine challenge, Baumann characterizes the Peace Corps and their village-level counterparts as "constantly prodding" Bolivian villagers in order to "stimulate" them to "discharge" modern capitalist and nationalistic desires. But if the new "economically viable man" will have to rise from his "throne of gold" in order to reinvest the gold in capitalist and nationalist enterprises, the economically viable woman's role is more circumscribed. Baumann mentions that in addition to the (implicitly male) counterparts of village-level workers, the Peace Corps deploys "home economics women who give courses in hygiene; cooking; sewing, child care." He is particularly excited about the twenty-two-couple "model *campesino*" program, explaining that "model *campesino* couples are a unique attempt" to provide Bolivians with a model of properly gendered economic behavior: "i.e. sheep = agriculture through the male, home economics-homemaking-arts and crafts through the female . . . Some emulation has taken place in many areas all over Bolivia."[33]

Connie Jaquith, a member of one of the twenty-two couples chosen for the "model *campesino*" program touted by Baumann, recalls the strange process of transforming herself and her husband into exemplary peasant couples, remembering that their task was difficult but ultimately successful. This success was relatively rare; Jaquith recalls that only six of the "model campesino" couples stayed in Bolivia for the full two years of their service. But she and her then-husband Larry prevailed, constructing a house in their Altiplano town and slowly establishing trust with the local people:

> Things were really slow in the beginning, as I say we did not have a community center . . . maybe we had enough money to buy the *calamina*, the tin for the roof, so we had to apply for special funds to help us. We didn't have access to money, I mean you couldn't get money,

you couldn't have your parents wire you money, they didn't permit any of that. But you know when we left, [Peace Corps staff in Bolivia] Gino and Pete felt it was just one of the best ways to proceed and it just kind of, I don't know it created, it was like, they believed we had come here to live. You know, if we were going to build a house and put all that effort into it, by gosh they're gonna stay with us and live. So I think the trust level increased and you get people coming by and saying, what's that grass growing down at the bottom of the hill . . . I guess we did OK. We couldn't just quit, we had to figure it out, so if I'm proud of anything, I'm proud of our resilience and liberal arts graduates can figure it out, make an adobe house . . . In that way, you know, Peace Corps was right.[34]

In Jaquith's recollection, she and her husband constructed for rural Bolivians an appealing dream, associating themselves with the promise of a modern community that is always in the future, always just out of reach of the ever-"developing" world. In her retelling, she addresses the curious temporality of the development mission: in order to gain the community's trust and usher them into the future, she first had to create an illusion of her permanent closeness to the people:

Some of those experiences were fascinating, especially when the children would come around, you know, and they'd just look at us and smile . . . You know, those are precious memories, that kind of getting to know each other in a very very primitive way, nothing sophisticated . . . all really basic stuff. And like, what will you do when you don't live here anymore. And it all had to do with whether or not our presence in the village would bring harm to them.

People would come into our potato fields . . . we'd look out and women would be sitting among our potatoes . . . they would say, the *viracococha* blesses our potatoes. They just thought that there was something about who we were and how we could connect to the land that was different from who they were.[35]

Here Jaquith tenderly recalls the fragile relationship she was building with the Bolivians, as well as their idea that "there was something about who [the volunteers] were" that is "different from who they were." Her note of incredulity—"they just thought"—invokes the logic of anti-conquest, obscuring the fact that the volunteers actually possessed resources that the indigenous rural communities did not. This memory suggests the enchanting quality Peace Corps volunteers were meant to possess; their constant effacement of their own access to resources allowed them to present their "success" as the result of a mysterious ingenuity bordering on the magical. But Jaquith's fascination with the Altiplano community and their worldview suggests that the enchantment here went both ways: her captivation belies her ostensible dismissal of their views, allowing her to attribute a certain seriousness to their central question, of "whether or not our presence in the village would bring harm to them." This question of the potential harm of development was becoming increasingly central to the Bolivian popular consciousness at the time of Jaquith's stay on the Altiplano.

Falkett, who worked on the Altiplano before being transferred to the lowlands, had a more difficult time modeling proper *campesino* behavior. In a letter to a friend, Falkett explains that she is assigned to a small village on the northern Altiplano, and that she and the other women in her group "will have to learn Aymara since we are supposed to work mainly with the women."[36] "We shall try to organize the *entire* community behind us," she writes in a subsequent letter, soon after arriving at the village. "But this might conceivably never be achieved. Some of the leaders are really sharp and desire to progress. Most of the young people (men) are behind us. The older villagers and the women are as traditional as groups can be." Though she attributes the women's conservatism to the Aymara culture, her answer to a friend's follow-up question indicates that the reasons for their alleged backwardness may also lie in the structure of the USAID program (in fact, the program trained no women for the "counterpart"/TDC positions): "I do not have a female counterpart—Bob & I both share Augustin. Aymaran women are *very* traditional & reluctant to accept change. They are strictly home bodies & will never assume any leadership in a community development process for many years to come."[37]

Despite the contradictions she experienced as a woman assigned to work with other women who were not the true targets of development discourse and programs, Falkett initially felt optimistic about changing her Altiplano community, giving herself "at least six months" to both acquire "a deep understanding of the culture" and instill in the people a desire to change their own communities: "The main task is to get these people to organize themselves to *help themselves*. We could construct many edifices but if the people didn't request them and contribute as much labor and material as was possible—these would become hollow shells which would never be used. The work will be hard. It will require great patience, and a deep understanding of the culture. It may take at least 6 months to simply instill in the people a sense of community and self-reliance."[38] The development mission, as Falkett explains here, not only attempted to instill the desire in every community to organize and "help themselves," but also required the subjects of development to contribute "as much labor and material as was possible," without compensation, to these nebulous self-help projects.

Despite her certainty that the women would not become authentic subjects of development, Falkett worked hard to design various projects for them, leading "a 4-H club in our community, instructions on how to make soap, cooking classes for the women, experimental gardens, the procuring of films (in Aymara) on health and agriculture, and the slow collection of a village library." A few months later, however, Falkett wrote of her attempt to gauge interest in a literacy class, "I have been able to organize some of the women (finally) in Colquencha for a weekly class. Most of them don't read or write and when I proposed a literacy course—they jumped at the idea."[39] However, Falkett never set up the literacy classes; she was transferred to Charagua, where she began to doubt her utility as an agent of change. "What did I say in my letter?" she wrote to her friend from her Charagua post. "I don't remember writing that 15 mos. *had* made a difference. If you still have the letter, please quote it."[40]

Another Altiplano volunteer, John Dwan, evinces similar skepticism in retrospect, writing comically in 2010 of his attempts to incite and manage Bolivians' development and their ability to escape and subvert the modernization mission:

> In my first village, an Aymara Indian village of about three hundred people, my major achievement was to get an employee of the local American Mary knoll priest to allow me to build a latrine for him and his family. There was a Bolivian Army squad of about 13 boys in town and they helped me dig the hole. But, each morning, they wouldn't get into the hole until I did and threw out all the frogs. *Zapos* (frogs) cause disease and they (the soldiers) weren't getting in the hole with them! We finished the latrine and it was an example of

Peace Corps achievement . . . except that it was never used. It was too nice and the owner used it to store quinoa and potatoes. The natives were not used to "*haciendo sus necessidades*," what we call going to the toilet, in such restraining quarters. The women went out every morning and squatted in the fields and chatted. Hey, social time! The men peed wherever and went into the pigs' corrals, where there was one, for their bms. There was no program. We early volunteers were on our own.

I also worked with a Bolivian engineer . . . on a water system for the village . . . which consisted of building a catchment basin on the hill side and running a pipe line to a faucet in the village square. That was why the Bolivian soldiers were there. We got it done, and it worked, but there never was enough water. I revisited the village about 10 years ago and the plaque giving the Peace Corps credit for the system was there, but it didn't work. And, most of the local campesinos had moved to the city.

My partner in this village was a fantastic psychiatric nurse . . . and together, we ran a clinic. We had a bunch of outdated medicines and our major client was the major *brujo*—(witch doctor) who drank too much and came by every morning for aspirin. But, a kid, about 14, got gored by a bull about a mile from Fran's and my place. We were asked to help. We trudged out there and Fran boiled a hypodermic needle over a llama dung fire, put way out dated penicillin in the syringe and then stuck it in the kid's butt. I then took over because the penicillin was so old that it wouldn't pass through the needle. I had to hold the syringe with one hand and push as hard as I could with the other to get the penicillin into the kid's butt. We did this every day for about a month and the kid lived, but walked with limp.[41]

Dwan's recollections both reaffirm the adventurous spirit of many of the early volunteers and demonstrate the frustrating and often farcical nature of their attempts to control the social dynamics and corral the bodies (and bodily productions) of the people with whom he worked. His experience indicates that many of the objects of development rejected the "restraining quarters" offered them by volunteers, instead incorporating modern conveniences into their lives eclectically and continuing to use the systems they had devised for structuring both their sociality and their waste. His testimony indicates that volunteers charged with saving local people from their allegedly stagnant, backward lives were not really trained for the job. Instead, as in the story of the bad penicillin, they injected them over and over with the outdated, universalizing development prescriptions that rarely worked the way they were supposed to, but nonetheless left their mark.

"The Lippes' Loop Capital of the Altiplano": Population Control Projects in Bolivia

Whether assisting in the mass transfer of "colonizers" from the Altiplano to the lowlands, or "modeling" correct *campesino* life, development work in Bolivia consisted of population control and management. Because of the ways development entailed viewing and managing people as populations, as well as destroying "traditional" lifeways, the agency's birth control activities in Bolivia came to stand in for the larger modernization and cultural eradication agenda of the Peace Corps. Peace Corps population control efforts in Bolivia, though not as widespread as the Peace Corps' family planning programs in other countries like India, were concentrated on the Altiplano, an area already affected by the population and power transfers recommended in the Bohan plan and carried out in the 1960s. These efforts were also carried out within the population control framework whose golden age was the "development decade," a moment when a global consensus emerged among elite policy-makers that population control was an urgent and worthy goal. Influenced by modernization theory, population control advocates framed their project not in terms of women's rights but in terms of mass population regulation in the service of capitalist development.[42]

Bolivia was a frequent target of this developmentalist population rhetoric, which decisively influenced U.S. policy there. Kennedy adviser Arthur Schlesinger Jr. took a trip to Bolivia in 1961, returning in early March to write the president a "memo on dilemmas of modernization in the hemisphere" whose first point was, "Because population has been growing faster than output in recent years, Latin America has begun to lose ground in the struggle for development."[43] Kennedy, previously ambivalent about publicly endorsing population control, was convinced, and on March 22 delivered a special message to Congress on foreign aid, in which he inaugurated the sixties as the "development decade" and warned that "the magnitude of the problems is staggering. In Latin

America, for example, population growth is already threatening to out-pace economic growth . . . and the problems are no less serious or de-manding in other developing areas of the world."[44] Later the same year, Kennedy privately suggested to the Ford Foundation that it "concentrate all its resources on the population problem around the world."[45]

Like Schlesinger and Kennedy, Johnson understood the fight to stem global population as an integral part of the modernization project, as when he urged in a July 1965 speech, "Let us in all our lands—including this land—face forthrightly the multiplying problems of our multiply-ing populations and seek the answers to this most profound challenge to the future of the world. Let us act on the fact that less than five dollars invested in population control is worth a hundred dollars invested in economic growth."[46] The Peace Corps, too, explicitly linked population control to development. Harris Wofford writes that "after word spread of Volunteers distributing contraceptives, the Planned Parenthood move-ment wanted to give Shriver a special award for pioneering in the use of federal money for such a purpose. He declined the honor, but agreed with the staff consensus that this was important and appropriate work for any Volunteer willing to do it."[47] The Peace Corps made its popula-tion control goals more explicit in 1966, when it issued a joint statement with the United States Information Agency and USAID stating that all three agencies were giving "high priority to programs designed to limit rates of population growth."[48]

Large-scale population control policies in 1960s Bolivia were not yet off the ground when the scandal broke, but the Peace Corps seems to have been working haphazardly on these efforts throughout the decade. A June 1967 U.S. embassy "Report on Population Problems in Bolivia" warned of the technological and political obstacles to a large-scale pop-ulation control program, but boasted that Peace Corps volunteers had "collaborated effectively" with Methodist missionary doctors, who had fitted women with one thousand IUDs in both major cities and Yungas and Altiplano communities.[49] In accordance with the 1966 joint state-ment, the development organizations seemed to be cautiously proceed-ing with a larger program: in July 1967, Peace Corps director Baumann assured Lima-based USAID official J. Fine that the "Peace Corps is very much with it in reference to birth control and all its implications," and in August cautioned Peace Corps associate director Gary Peterson to "please go slow on the birth-control thing at first. You need to get 'in' with some of the people before going full stream ahead."[50] In December 1968, however, after escalating birth control scandals had brought national notoriety to the agency, Baumann wrote an official memo to all Bolivia volunteers saying, "In accordance with standard PC policy, no artificial birth control devices shall be distributed by PCVs under any circumstances. Peace Corps does not supply such devices nor is any PCV allowed to obtain them for distribution."[51]

Though Baumann's statements indicate that the Peace Corps tentatively began a birth control program and subsequently attempted a hasty cover-up, many volunteers stayed away from birth control during their service. Jaquith recalls failing in her attempts to discuss birth control in her Altiplano community: "We had absolutely no success in birth control. They would not listen, did not want to hear, did not, period. I mean we just couldn't go there and do that."[52] But others were more successful. In April 1966, Collana volunteer Janet Pitts Brome wrote in her journal, "The mothers asked me how they could stop having babies. They said they were embarrassed to talk to a doctor about it. I'll see what can be done." In July of the same year, Brome wrote, "Tomorrow we have a meeting on birth control. The local *sanitario* will speak in Aymara. Next month Dr. Thompson from the hospital in La Paz comes to insert Lippes' Loops. Any woman who has been to one of these meetings WITH her husband is eligible." That December, Brome reported, "People are blaming women who got IUDs. One group of men wanted to get the local *sanitario* to get a list of the women with the loop so they could punish them," suggesting that perhaps early horror at Peace Corps population control efforts was directed primarily at indigenous women. But Brome's account also provides a clue as to how modernization discourses produced Third World and indigenous female desire; in it, a few women's requests for birth control are transformed into justifications for containment and control, validating development workers' competitive efforts to regulate unruly populations. In April, Brome proudly noted that "the IUD program has been successful. Collana is the Lippes' loop capital of the Altiplano."[53]

The story of the plastic-molded IUD in the years of its emergence illuminates the way modernization discourses shaped attempts to control the bodies of women in the Third World. The plastic IUD, introduced in 1958 at Mount Sinai Hospital in New York, quickly became the method of choice for the population control movement in the 1960s. Throughout the early 1960s, studies of IUDs showed high rates of infection and bleeding, but USAID and private entities like the Ford Foundation continued to fund their mass implantation. Population experts like Planned Parenthood president Alan Guttmacher, while aware of these findings, made no recommendations as to follow-up examinations, arguing, "We dare not lose sight of our goal—to apply this method to large populations." At a population control conference in 1964, Guttmacher reassured drug companies that IUDs would not cut into the market for oral contraceptives: "As I see it, the IUDs have special application to underdeveloped areas where two things are lacking: one, money and the other sustained motivation. No contraceptive could be cheaper, and also, once the damn thing is in the patient cannot change her mind. In fact, we can hope she will forget it's there and perhaps in several months wonder why she has not conceived."[54] Guttmacher's assertion that Third World women lack sustained motivation denotes modernization theory's gender split: development workers must cultivate the passivity of underdeveloped women in order for the men in the population to become modern. Part of the nation's transition to modernity entails its eschewal of alleged matriarchy and the assertion by the male subject of his dynamic capitalist character, made easier by a woman who might lack the "sustained motivation" to assert control over her own body.

Carl Pope, a Peace Corps volunteer in India assigned to family planning, recalls somewhat regretfully his program's attempts to manipulate women—and how women resisted these attempts. He writes in his memoir, *Sahib*, of learning that "seventy women had received the loop" and being "excited by the numbers; it was not going to be all that difficult . . . the government offers six rupees to every woman who has a loop inserted and one rupee to the person who persuaded her to do it. Men who undergo sterilization get twenty-five rupees. All of the women that day were very poor; they had come for the money. Their number left [Pope's wife] Judy and me hopeful that family planning was catching on in Barhi."[55] Pope's optimism was soon dashed when he found out that the village midwife had removed for one rupee apiece 32 of the 160 loops they had inserted in two days; the midwife and author of the scheme had also collected a rupee for each woman as "the motivator."[56]

Pope, discovering months later that the midwife was continuing her scheme, began to devise a counter-scheme to prevent "repeaters": tattooing women who came in to get the IUDs. He tested the trap by injecting himself with ink, thinking "perhaps this would be my major contribution to family planning," but after giving himself blood poisoning he thought the better of the scheme, feeling "justly punished" for his attempts to "prevent [the repeaters] from practicing petty fraud on a government that certainly practiced grand larceny on them." He reported that "Dr. Malik solved the problem of repeaters by the simple expedient of remembering their faces. Apparently no one else had ever bothered to try, and I had been convinced that it was impossible. Numbers had been getting to me again, numbers and the sameness that poverty imposed on the women."[57]

Pope's insight that "numbers" were getting to him reveals the concrete ways that population control discourse, and the theories of modernization and "cultural poverty" that undergirded it, dehumanized women. Instead of seeing the women into whom he inserted IUDs as human beings with faces he might remember, Pope began to see them as "repeaters" who might cheat a system that was forcing them to trade their reproductive freedom for their own survival. The Peace Corps volunteers and staffers interested in population control in Bolivia also concerned themselves with numbers. Though not undertaken on a scale anywhere near that of India's program, Peace Corps population control projects in Bolivia were guided by a developmentalist framework that imagined population control as a mechanism through which to improve and regulate the "human capital" necessary for global economic integration. Like Pope, these frameworks failed even to register the humanity of the indigenous women whose bodies they attempted to regulate. Even nonconsensual insertions seem to have happened in Bolivia: in a 2005 interview, Bolivian doctor Walter Fortún, who advised U.S. development agencies on population control programming, recalled discovering a 1963 case in which a Peace Corps volunteer nurse in Coroico implanted an IUD without the woman's knowledge.[58]

Bolivians' discovery of Peace Corps population control programs, and their exposure and denunciation in the film *Yawar Mallku*, occurred in the increasingly militant political climate of the late 1960s. Even as U.S. "technicians and administrators" were "virtually running" Bolivia, anti-imperialist sentiment, combined with renewed indigenous nationalism, was growing. "If you're a gringo in Bolivia now, they'll push you off the pavement," a mining engineer told the *New York Times* in 1966. "The Indians have really taken over, and believe me, the only way to treat an Indian is to treat him rough."[59] In 1971, responding to massive popular sentiment condemning the foreign development establishment, Bolivia expelled the Peace Corps.

Historians so far have only partially understood the motivations behind the Peace Corps' expulsion. James Siekmeier argues persuasively that the Bolivian government used the Peace Corps as a "sacrificial llama," expelling the volunteers to appease the Bolivian left and indigenous communities without substantively renegotiating its relationship with the United States.[60] But leftist and indigenous communities singled out the Peace Corps not because of its insignificance, but rather because of the agency's particular symbolic power as the embodiment of the heroic development discourse espoused by the U.S. and Bolivian governments, a discourse that necessitated the control of the Bolivian population. Bolivian media across the political spectrum came to a similar understanding of the Peace Corps by the end of the sixties, helped along by cultural works like Sanjinés's film as well as popular protest.

The Bolivian media, with the notable exception of the communist press, began the 1960s optimistic about the Peace Corps. The centrist and conservative La Paz daily newspapers *El Diario*, *Presencia*, and *Ultima Hora* devoted substantial coverage to all kinds of development projects, and especially to the Peace Corps, producing a volume of fawning coverage equal to that in U.S. newspapers. The Peace Corps' founding was a front-page story, and *Ultima Hora* paid particular attention to celebrity Peace Corps secretaries Nancy Gore and Sally Bowles, gushing that "the daughters of a subsecretary of state and a senator stand out in today's group of more than a thousand people who have voluntarily offered to submit themselves to the strenuous life of 'the Peace Corps' proposed by President JFK."[61] *Ultima Hora* reported on Peace Corps training throughout the agency's early years, writing several pieces in the vein of a June 1961 front-page story that the agency "has created a severe and careful selection system [in which] five thousand candidates were submitted to rigorous exams [demonstrating] their character, temperament, and health."[62] *El Diario* chimed in, reporting on Kennedy's new "'Good Gringo' policy" and writing with anticipation of the "volunteers who expressed the desire to work for our country."[63]

The newspapers devoted at least two pages daily to development enterprises undertaken and completed by USAID, the Peace Corps, missionary groups, the Bolivian military, and various other municipal and national development committees and organizations, running ponderous full-page stories with titles like "The Peasant of Cochabamba Searches for His Own Development" as well as many editorials considering the meaning and pace of development in Bolivia.[64] One such editorial, published in a January 1967 *El Diario*, is titled "To Make Men," and extols "the praiseworthy work the Peace Corps is doing," commenting that "what counts when it comes to progress is the man and not the dollars or the factories." The editorial goes on to recommend that in Bolivia, "we concentrate all our resources in improving our human capital" in order to "benefit 100 percent from the universal cooperation" and technical assistance provided by the Peace Corps.[65]

The Catholic newspaper *Presencia*, while asserting that "all [Bolivia's institutions] are connected intimately with development," praised military modernization in particular, imagining development as a singular and almost divine goal:

> Even the church, whose more immediate objectives are spiritual, recently held a continent-wide meeting to discuss the ways it could contribute to development. There was no dissent, because they know well that development work is incumbent on us all.
>
> It is good that the military has recognized this. When it embarks on development projects, no one will be able to say that it has strayed from its original goals, since development is an objective for which everyone must work.[66]

These commonplace calls for ceaseless if nebulous national striving demonstrate how Bolivia was saturated in the 1960s not only by development workers, but also by development imperatives. Through the reach of the church, the military, and other institutions "intimately connected" with development, *Presencia*'s editors dreamed that every Bolivian might see himself (and at least potentially, herself) as underdeveloped and, through ceaseless labor, strive to develop himself and his nation.

Ultima Hora also devoted several pages daily to development work, paying particular attention to penetrating the eastern lowlands. In a 1967 editorial they emphasized the need "to 'penetrate' the Beni region by rail—the old thesis that has sadly been abandoned." Associating the penetration of the Beni with both inevitable "geopolitical laws" and Bolivia's salvation, the editors proclaimed, "We should accelerate these projects. We should not leave them for future generations, like previous governments who lacked eyes to see the future. We need to anticipate geopolitical laws. We need to save Bolivia, uniting all the provinces by highways and trains."[67] The *Prensa Libre* of Cochabamba advanced an equally grandiose vision about the lowland colonization projects, lamenting in an editorial titled "Preferred Populations" the "complete underdevelopment" and "shameful neglect in which the populations of these lush regions find themselves." The editors argued for "the transcendent importance of linking the interminable plains of the Beni with the valleys and lowlands of the Altiplano."[68] Emphasizing the "underdevelopment" and "neglect" suffered by particular lowland populations, the Cochabamba editors advised that the colonization of the Beni will bring about a marvelous, modern reality for the "chosen" Benianos and the settlers who elect to join them.

Along with the need to transform and transfer its population in the service of modernization imperatives, the mainstream press initially accepted uncritically the discourse of population control for modernization. In 1967 *El Diario* published a long news story with the headline "Uncontrollable fertility and the capacity to destroy the environment are serious threats to humanity," writing that the U.S.-based "Population Reference Bureau is intensifying its campaigns in Latin America."[69] *Ultima Hora* reported on a seminar in La Paz in May 1967, where Argentine doctor Ernesto Hines presented on "Family Planning as a Global Imperative." According to the article, Hines "explained the role of the doctor in the social and economic development of nations, pointing out that one of his primary tasks is family planning"; "expressed that every household should have the number of children they can feed, educate, clothe, and make into useful citizens for the society"; and "finally recommended the construction of family planning centers in Bolivia."[70] Even *Presencia* accepted the basic arguments advanced by the new population control experts, but argued that Bolivia was a special case, opining in 1967 that "Bolivia is the only country in Latin America without a population explosion."[71]

After the summer of 1968, when the breaking of the Peace Corps sterilization scandal coincided with new World Bank president Robert McNamara's proclamation that development aid would depend on population control policies, *Presencia's* exceptionalist argument against limiting Bolivia's population became widespread.[72] Explaining that Bolivia was underpopulated rather than overpopulated, editors and politicians alike imagined the country as a special case, in need of population augmentation rather than new limits. In December 1968, after the Catholic union Acción Sindical Boliviana reported that "the Peace Corps has initiated a birth control campaign in the countryside and the mines," the Bolivian Senate recommended further investigation into the Peace Corps' birth control activities, passing a resolution to "re-establish our sovereignty" by "exhaustively" investigating whether the Peace Corps had "carried out illegal actions, spreading their propaganda in order to avoid birth in Bolivia."[73] Like the population control establishment, these nationalist counterarguments disregarded the potential harm to women's bodies and autonomy, seeing population control as a problem of "national sovereignty."

Militant leftist challenges to population control, while more substantive than the conservative ones, drew on similar nationalist developmentalist premises to argue that U.S.-backed government policies were designed to keep Bolivia underdeveloped. Marxist intellectual Amado Canelas, in his 1963 critique of U.S. development practices in Bolivia, describes the Alto Beni colonization as "erroneous and damaging to true national development," explaining that the true path to modernity in Bolivia lay in state-guided industrialization rather than the attempts to shift populations from the Altiplano to Alto Beni:

> The just solution for the alleged rural overpopulation in the Altiplano and in the valleys is not to promote a massive migration to remote, untouched, inhospitable territory but, on the contrary, to mobilize a politics of massive concentration of working people on the land, that is to say cooperativization, so that adequate investment in key areas will secure a massive increase in production and the elevation of agricultural activity, and also the promotion of an accelerated process of industrialization not only in urban centers but also in the country . . .
> For example, the most basic economic calculations would demonstrate the undeniable advantages to constructing a state-owned, modern sugar

processing plant in the Alto Beni rather than squandering millions of dollars on the resettlement of one or two thousand, who could be re-settled in better conditions around the sugar-processing plant, in indus-trial and agricultural jobs. In sum, the policy of colonization reveals that this regime proposes, at least subconsciously, to construct a utopic reactionary peasant nation in the second half of the twentieth century, and not to build a booming, modern, industrial/agrarian nation. It is clear that the *yanqui* hand can be found behind this line that is absurdly antinational, exploiting the ignorance of economic laws that charac-terizes its obsequious followers on the Altiplano.[74]

Characterizing himself and the Marxist left—many of whom were also advocating the sugar-processing plant construction—as the true national-ists and developmentalists, Canelas charged that U.S.-backed population control in Bolivia would perpetuate rather than curtail underdevelop-ment. In doing so, he augmented the accusations of other Marxist intel-lectuals, who also used dependency theory to show that the U.S.-backed development schemes were not leading to authentic development.[75] Canelas, like the capitalist modernization theorists, advocates a "mas-sive increase in production" and adherence to "economic laws" to trans-form Bolivia into a "booming, modern nation." This formulation, like many of those of the Bolivian communist left in the sixties, disregards the desires and cultural practices of indigenous rural communities. Canelas does not understand the large-scale resettlement of rural populations as intrinsically violent and disruptive (in its disregard for existing agri-cultural and cultural practices, and in its attempts to manage popula-tions who perhaps would rather not be managed). Rather, he sees it as wasteful in this instance because the Alto Beni colonization does not contribute to a viable statist project of economic growth, moderniza-tion, and, presumably, the eventual investment of the resulting wealth in social programs.

Using mainly this Marxist developmentalist framework, student protestors and other leftists staged regular protests throughout the mid-to-late sixties, destroying Peace Corps and other U.S. government prop-erty. The most well-known example of militant anti–Peace Corps activity before 1968 was the January 1964 kidnapping of volunteer Robert Fer-gerstrom along with two United States Information Agency officials and an adviser to USAID in exchange for the release from prison of labor leaders Ireneo Pimentel and Federico Escobar.[76] In January 1967, students in Cochabamba attacked the Peace Corps office along with the U.S. consulate, throwing stones and looting. Leftist student leaders explained that the attack was in response to the national government's "sellout" (*entreguista*) move to allow private universities into the city, arguing that the private institutions would undercut existing democratic public ones. They almost completely destroyed the Peace Corps offices, taking documents out into the streets and burning them.[77] While reports do not mention how the students specifically linked the Peace Corps to the university privatization efforts, the sellout charge suggests that they saw the privatization as part of a U.S.-backed effort to weaken democratic and democratizing public services in favor of individualism and private enterprise.

When the rumors of forced sterilizations by Peace Corps volunteers surfaced in the summer of 1968, leftist accusations of the duplicity of U.S. development workers gained appeal within the government and the larger society. By October 1968, students were connecting McNamara's equation of population control and development to the agenda of the U.S. foreign aid establishment, convincing even the U.S.-supported Barrientos regime of their cause. A U.S. embassy account reported that a "student demonstration against McNamara statement on birth control" that began in front of the embassy in La Paz then "later moved to USAID building, then Congress, and Presidential Palace." Initially, the demonstration was "broken up by police who arrested one Catholic priest and nine students," the document reports, but "shortly thereafter Barrientos announced arrests were mistake and ordered their release. In subsequent press statement he deplored student demonstration but said their concern over McNamara statement justified."[78]

This ambivalent government reaction demonstrates the power of the population control accusations, even as Barrientos attempted to maintain order and good relations with the United States. But the protests only intensified: students attacked and significantly damaged Peace Corps offices in Santa Cruz three separate times in the summer of 1968, along with the United States Information Agency offices, various consulates, the USAID office, the Bolivian–American Center, and the home of the U.S. ambassador in La Paz. This anti-U.S. sentiment escalated, with periodic bombings in Peace Corps offices beginning in 1969 and continuing in 1970.[79] The students and urban workers attacking USAID and Peace Corps buildings explicitly used dependency theory–influenced arguments about U.S. attempts to hinder true Bolivian development—a sign from a May 1969 student protest read, "Uncle Sam, if you lend me one for every three you steal, when will I progress?"[80]—but they also regularly contextualized their protests by referring to the population control activities that Jorge Sanjinés made iconic in *Yawar Mallku*.

Yawar Mallku and the Rebirth of Indigenous Nationalism in Bolivia

In late 1968, Sanjinés and the Ukamau film collective traveled to the community of Kaata, a village accessible only on foot, with the script for their second feature film. The community leader, Marcelino Yanahuaya, had met them at a screening of their first movie, *Ukamau*, and encouraged them to film in his village, but upon their arrival in Kaata, the Bolivian middle-class filmmakers encountered hostility and suspicion. They offered the villagers high wages and free medical care, but nobody showed up for the filming, and Yanahuaya, though he seemed sympathetic, did not explain the community's absence. After a few frustrating days, the group discovered that an official from a neighboring town was spreading rumors that they were dangerous communists out to rob and kill the townspeople. Sanjinés recalls that "the initial apathy had turned into open hostility, especially on the part of the women, who were more taken in by the official's self-serving intrigues." The film crew persuaded the Quechua priest, the *yatiri*, to perform a ceremonial reading of the coca leaves to determine their fate. As Sanjinés later recalls, the reading helped the crew understand the differences between their worldview and that of their subjects and to develop relationships that would profoundly influence their filmmaking style:

> Basically, what had happened was that we had judged the community by the same standards we would have used to analyze people and groups within bourgeois society. We had thought that by mobilizing one man who was powerful and influential, we could mobilize the rest of the group, whom we assumed to be vertically dependent on their leader. We had not understood, until that moment, that the indigenous people gave priority to collective over individual interests. We

had failed to understand that for them, as for their ancestors, what was not good for all of them could not be good for a single one. That night, after six hours of enormous tension . . . the *yatiri* examined the coca leaves and declared emphatically that our presence was inspired by good, not evil. Our group was accepted and we soon felt the old barriers to communication disappearing in embraces and genuine signs of cordiality . . . In light of this and other experiences, we began to question all the films we had made and were planning to make. We began to understand the ways in which our cinematic style was and is impregnated by the concepts of life and reality inherent to our own social class . . .

Some time later, when we were discussing how to create a vital and authentic revolutionary cinema, free of fictions and melodramatic characters, with the people as the protagonists in acts of creative participation, so that we might achieve films that would be passed from town to town, we decided that there in Kaata, at that unique moment, we should have thrown away the prepared script and shot a movie about that experience instead.[81]

Sanjinés conveys here his retrospective sense of *Yawar Mallku*'s political limitations: while the film dramatizes for Western audiences the modernization project's threat to indigenous ways of being and knowing, he and his crew retain bourgeois stylistic conventions, structuring their film through narratives of individual tragedy and transformation rather than collective action. The film thus enacts a devastating indictment of foreign and domestic modernizing forces, but still fails to break with the discourse of development at the level of style and narrative structure. This is particularly true of the film's gender politics: while ostensibly rejecting development discourses and practices, the film reiterates modernization theory's imperative to transform populations from feminized passive indigeneity to masculine nationalist subjecthood. The film's "impregnation" by the gendered ideologies of modernization and modernity is evident in its portrayal of Quechua women, who, like those in Kaata who Sanjinés asserts were "more taken in" by self-serving officials, represent the tradition and passivity that revolutionary indigenous nationalists must reject. By dramatizing the struggle between U.S. modernizing forces and indigenous nationalism as a contest for control over indigenous women's bodies, *Yawar Mallku* demonstrates the centrality of gender and sexual politics to both modernization discourses and anti-imperialist cultural nationalist ideologies.

Yawar Mallku tracks its indigenous subject as he moves from passivity to active subjectivity, finally attaining revolutionary consciousness and returning to lead his people. This narrative frame marks the film's participation in the genre of radical–developmentalist texts Saldaña-Portillo identifies in her work, designating its story as one of individual transformation from passive alienation to active, masculine revolutionary modernity. However, unlike the revolutionary memoirs on which Saldaña-Portillo focuses, *Yawar Mallku* explicitly condemns modernization and development, even as its narrative structure dramatizes a personal masculine transformation and the attainment of control over women's bodies. The film emphasizes the particular bind this trajectory poses for indigenous women, primarily through the character of Paulina, a young Quechua woman whose subject position must be evacuated to make way for the male characters' development and reabsorption.

The film begins as if it intends to tell Paulina's story, opening on a scene of domestic chaos and violence. Her husband, Ignacio, laments his childlessness and blames her, shouting, "My babies. Paulina, you are cursed, you lost them . . . I told you not to go there, not to trust . . . now I will die alone!" Paulina responds first meekly—"I'm not bad luck. It's not my fault"—then angrily, calling him a drunk. The next morning, her face visibly bruised, she silently accepts his apology and they go together to a sacred mountain to bury the dolls representing their children who have died. The film here attributes to Paulina both a spiritual and intellectual/emotional weakness (she is both intrinsically cursed and too trusting of the foreigners), but also positions itself as an exploration of the way imperialist and domestic violence reinforce each other, converging on the bodies of indigenous women. By starting the film with this scene and ending it with revolution, Sanjinés attempts to bring viewers explicitly to the conclusion that an indigenous nationalist vision is the most appropriate response to both imperialist and domestic violence.

Subsequent scenes retain their investment in Paulina's perspective. After the local police shoot Ignacio, the camera follows her as she rides into the city with his wounded body, tracking the urban landscape through her increasingly fearful, alienated perspective. But despite casting her as the early protagonist, the film soon makes clear that its most important story is not Paulina's. Sixto, Ignacio's assimilated brother to whom Paulina brings her wounded husband, articulates his (and the film's) stance toward women in his first scene, a scuffle depicted as a routine brush with racism. "Indian? Do you know me? Did you see me being born?" he asks his antagonist. "I'm not an Indian, goddammit."[82]

Sixto not only rejects his indigenous blood here, signaling the internalized racism reinforced by the MNR's assimilationist modernization doctrines, but also figures it as carried and transmitted entirely by mothers. The film's portrayal of women as vessels for cultural preservation, carriers of indigenous identity and tradition rather than subjects who can create knowledge or history, is equally evident when Paulina speaks: she tells her story not as an individual but in the collective voice, alternately speaking on behalf of her family and her whole community. "We had three children," she recalls. "We were happy. People liked us. My children were fine. They helped us, until an epidemic came. And they died. Time passed. Ignacio was chosen as head of the community. We all celebrated. Who would have suspected what would threaten us next?"

The threat appears first in flashback, when two of the Progress Corps volunteers accost Paulina on the path into town and demand to buy the eggs in the basket she is carrying to market. Paulina offers to sell them a few, but the female volunteer demands all the eggs in the basket. The male volunteer repeatedly offers her "a good price," but Paulina refuses, repeating that they are for her community. The scene none-too-subtly allegorizes the secret task the volunteers perform inside their shining white health center, the forced sterilization of Bolivian women in the service of cultural eradication, modernization, and global capital. In a final attempt to get all the eggs "for the center" by interpellating Paulina into the modern order, the male volunteer hails her in slow Spanish—"You are Paulina. Paulina Yanahuaya." He then offers her the opportunity to exchange her eggs for differentiated individual subjectivity, dramatizing what Elizabeth Povinelli deems "the dialectic of autology and genealogy," the choice between indigeneity and individual identity.[83] "You know us, right?" the volunteer continues. "Why don't you sell us your eggs? We want them for our center. Sell them to us, Paulina." But Paulina is not tempted for a moment, ignoring the lures of individuality and capital accumulation and saving the eggs for her community.

After the first few flashbacks, the film leaves Paulina's perspective behind and splits into its two principal narratives, interlacing Ignacio's earlier attempts to determine why the women in the community are not having children with the story of the narrative present, in which Sixto embarks on a search for blood to save his wounded brother. Because Sixto has rejected his own indigenous blood, the correctly indigenous Ignacio rejects it, too, and of course the "cursed" Paulina is not a match either. Desperate and broke, Sixto embarks on a quest to beg for money or blood from whiter, wealthier friends and doctors. The flashback structure reiterates the trajectory of development in its move from the rural–communal past to an urban narrative present, mirroring and mocking the journey to modernization in its depictions of Ignacio's horror and Sixto's despair, which increase as each travels alone along the prescribed course from superstitious rural subjection to assimilated urban citizenship.

By allowing the narrative to slip away from Paulina, the film dramatizes the gendered personal transformation that modernization discourse prescribes, the spiritual shift away from a feminized communal identity to a masculine subject position which must take place before a nation is able to insert itself fully into the global economy. The indigenous women's failure at ensuring cultural survival paves the way for this shift from indigenous passivity to masculine agency, providing both the central tragedy of the film and the impetus for the men's heroic drive to revolution. The *yatiri*'s prayers "that fertility makes our women blossom" go unanswered because, like the women of Kaata, the village women are "more taken in": corralled, swindled, manhandled, folded into the "self-serving intrigues" of global capital. Although Paulina refuses to sell them "all the eggs," the foreigners obtain them anyway and transform her against her will. She ceases to function for the good of her community, so the men must take over as both modern revolutionaries and preservers of indigenous life; the women's failure allows the men to both destroy the old nation and give birth to a new one.

The men's usurpation of the female subject position allows a utopian melding of modern and indigenous knowledge. Ignacio, though he has seen the sterilizations through the window of the health center, must confirm his suspicions with the community, just as Sanjinés knew the effects of his film crew's presence would be benign but submitted to the coca leaves anyway. In the film's climactic scene, the *yatiri*, surrounded by men, reads the coca leaves. "Mother Coca, give us the answer," he says, and the good mother speaks in Paulina's stead, confirming the truth of Ignacio's deductions: "the leaf of the foreigners shows up beside death." In both narratives, a lone male adventurer arrives at empirical conclusions and submits them to the collective will, ultimately receiving permission to lead the community in expelling the foreign elements. The last scene begins when Sixto, in indigenous clothing, returns to lead his people, having given birth to himself as a newly revolutionary actor, no longer in need of a mother to tell him who he is. Ignacio's death has restored Sixto, transfusing him once again with indigenous blood. Paulina, a small and shadowy presence, begins alongside him but soon walks entirely out of the frame, leaving the close-up to Sixto and reiterating the numerous evacuations the film performs. The aforementioned final frame shows guns in the air, imagining and inciting indigenous nationalist revolution.

Yawar Mallku, filmed in late 1968 and released in 1969, anticipated and shaped a new phase of indigenous cultural nationalism in Bolivia that would officially begin with the Katarista movement's Tiwanaku Manifesto in 1973. The Katarista movement developed in largely indigenous peasant unions in the late 1960s, as they faced increasing state repression. Much as they had in the 1940s, students, artists, miners, and urban workers united with the indigenous peasants.[84] Rivera Cusicanqui argues that Katarismo "succeeded to a large extent in crystallizing demands for political self-determination by the popular movement, as well as its rejection of left-wing elites' usual methods of political action."[85] The Tiwanaku Manifesto was centrally concerned with questions of development, challenging the assimilationist modernization policies of the 1952 revolution while imagining its own independent development program:

> We peasants want economic development, but it must spring from our own values. We do not want to give up our noble inherited integrity in favor of a pseudo development. We fear the false "developmentalism" imported from abroad because it is not genuine and does not respect the depth of our values. We want an end to state paternalism and we no longer wish to be considered second-class citizens. We are foreigners in our own country.
>
> We do not suggest that this situation can be overcome by paternalist government intervention or by well-meaning people.[86]

In its attempt to fight the cultural eradication imposed in the name of development, the movement rejects the "paternalist government" and "well-meaning people" who would force them to give up their indigenous traditions and "noble inherited integrity." But while it affirms the importance of culture and the "depth of [indigenous] values," the Tiwanaku Manifesto remains somewhat trapped in the rhetoric and trajectory of development and nationalism, rejecting the "pseudo development" imposed from abroad but searching still for the authentic transformation to modernity that true development will bring. This faith in the possibility of a developmentalist transformation appears when they rewrite Bolivia's indigenous history:

> Bolivia is entering a new stage in its political life, one characteristic of which is the awakening of peasant awareness . . .
>
> The peasantry has always been a passive force because that was always what was expected of them. The peasantry is what politicians have always wanted it to be: simply a support for their ambitions. The peasantry will be dynamic only when it is allowed to act as an autonomous and original force.[87]

Erasing Bolivia's long history of indigenous militancy, the Kataristas characterize the Bolivian "peasantry" as "a passive force" whose awareness is finally "awakening." This erasure allows them to imagine themselves traversing the familiar modernization trajectory from sleepy passivity to wakeful, dynamic modernity even as they envision their transformation into "an autonomous and original force," independent of the strictures of "imported" development. Thus, even this most radical of movement documents is constructed within the terms of the development imaginary, reinforcing the implicitly gendered transformation that Saldaña-Portillo identifies as a central part of the development fantasy.[88]

Making Things Come Out Right: Population Control and Its Aftermath

The Katarista movement thus embodied the dream depicted in *Yawar Mallku*, uniting indigenous peasants and radical workers alike in a militant attempt to reclaim indigenous values. As a key text prefiguring and shaping the movement, *Yawar Mallku* demonstrates how radical interracial and cross-class constituencies could coalesce around the cultural nationalist project of reclaiming women's bodies from the population control establishment. The indigenous nationalist movement succeeded in forging an alternative to the corrupt authoritarian state, reaching back into an "authentic" indigenous tradition and forward into a national future, precisely through the "awakening" of patriarchal values, the control over their women's wombs that would ensure the dynamic reproduction and proliferation of indigenous society.[89]

This control was perhaps most evident in the way that *Yawar Mallku* made birth control access difficult for Bolivian women. Sanjinés writes that in Bolivia, "as an immediate result of the film's distribution, the North Americans suspended their mass distribution of contraceptives, recalled all the members of the organization who had been working in the three sterilization centers, and received several staff members' resignations."[90] Sanjinés's equation of the consensual distribution of birth control with genocidal population control programs makes sense, given the population establishment and the Peace Corps' rhetoric and policies that frame Third World contraception similarly. But his conflation obscures the specific acts of violence against indigenous women from which the film draws its symbolic power, foreclosing questions of what might be owed them by the state, the development establishment, and the movement, as well as what they might want to do with their bodies.

Elizabeth Povinelli's work on liberal society and "the intimate event" begins to explore the implications of such erasures. Povinelli argues that indigenous potential subjects are "presented [by the dominant culture] with a mirror that is actually a double bind: either love through liberal ideals of self-sovereignty and de-culture yourself, or love according to the fantasy of the unchanging dictates of your tradition and dehumanize yourself." Paulina faces this precise situation as the development workers name her and attempt to convince her to sell them "all the eggs" at a "good price."[91] But despite her consistent attention to love, intimacy, and family, Povinelli does not frame this double bind as a particularly feminist problem. In fact, the example she offers, of a man whose grandmother forbids his drinking by asserting their genealogical connectedness, presents a relatively easy dilemma compared to the binds indigenous women face around reproductive freedom. In contrast to the man whose grandmother commanded him not to weaken his body lest the communal body weaken, women are required to give over their bodies—and weaken them—for the task of social reproduction.

In order to elaborate this potential problem with cultural nationalist communal visions, I want to return briefly to a moment in *Yawar Mallku* in which Paulina's subjectivity unsettles the male characters' all-encompassing revolutionary desire. In a flashback, the *yatiri* reads Paulina's fortune in the coca leaves and tells her it "seems to come out right," despite "an impediment" to having more children. When the *yatiri* tells her that her future "seems to come out right," she reacts vocally and affirmatively, confirming his reading in Quechua. Yet when he declares that he will see if there are children in her future, the camera closes in, narrowing its gaze to her face: impassive and expressionless as it is at no other moment in the film, leaving her feelings open to interpretation, to representation, by not only the *yatiri* and the onlookers but the viewers as well. And when the *yatiri* declares that there is "an impediment" to her having more children, she remains impassive, the camera tracking her gaze toward her husband, Ignacio, who reacts with anger, storming out of the room. The dynamics of this scene, in which the question of whether things will come out right for Paulina is staged as a separate question from whether she will have children, importantly prefigure the complicated, contradictory ways in which movement, popular, and now government discourses in Bolivia have come to conceptualize the relationship between indigenous women's bodily autonomy and fertility regulation. Paulina's loss of the ability to speak or react for herself at the moment that attention turns toward her womb indicates the larger way in which the ability to talk about women's rights in Bolivia is always a separate question from birth control and reproductive freedom.

An early example of this discourse occurs in mining-community activist Domitila Barrios de Chungara's testimony *Let Me Speak!* Toward the end of her account, Barrios de Chungara describes her frustration when, at the 1974 International Women's Day conference in Mexico City, U.S. and European women wanted to make prostitution and birth control central agenda items. "For us they were real problems, but not the main ones," she explains, before recounting both the population control rhetoric with which the elite women attempted to make their case and her own nationalist response. Barrios de Chungara makes an argument focused on resources and land rather than race or rights:

For example, when they spoke of birth control, they said that we shouldn't have so many children living in poverty, because we didn't even have enough to feed them. And they wanted to see birth control as something which would solve all the problems of humanity and malnutrition.

But, in reality, birth control, as those women presented it, can't be applied in my country. There are so few Bolivians by now that if we limited birth even more, Bolivia would end up without people. And then the wealth of our country would remain as a gift for those who want to control us completely, no?

All that could be different, because Bolivia's a country with lots of natural resources. But our government prefers to see things their way, to justify the low level of life of the Bolivian people and the very low wages it pays the workers. And that's why they resort to indiscriminate birth control.[92]

Recognizing the racism and elitism of population control discourse, Barrios de Chungara counters dominant modernization arguments with familiar resource-centered and territory-based nationalist discourses. However, as her use of the collective voice shows—"if we limited birth even more"—it remains the work of women to hand over their bodies to populate the country in order that their children might live to extract and fight for its natural resources. Explaining her own vision of the future, Barrios de Chungara speaks of the socialist society to come:

Women have the opportunity to do productive work, because there are new jobs so that the people can better themselves collectively. Women no longer have to suffer so much because of their condition as women, like we do when we ruin our bodies with so much work, we ruin our nerves with so much worry about our children's future and about the health of our husbands . . . we know that in a socialist regime, all that changes, because there have to be equal opportunities for everyone, jobs for women and day-care centers where their kids will be well taken care of while they work.[93]

Here the "new jobs" Barrios de Chungara imagines would not allow women to evade the work of reproduction or child care, but instead would allow them to preserve their bodies and nerves for their husbands' and children's well-being as much as their own. Uncomfortable with the individualistic and often imperialist feminism evinced by the women at Mexico City but also unable to work out the particulars of how women would be free and what their labor would look like under socialism, she contents herself with the idea that socialism's promise of "equal opportunities for everyone" will translate into gender equality.

The nationalist labor–leftism articulated by Barrios de Chungara has also shaped Evo Morales's MAS (Movimiento al Socialismo, or Movement for Socialism) government, as it pursues what Escobar calls an "alternative modernization project," a project that rejects neoliberal capitalism but continues to view industrialization and economic growth as both desirable and inevitable.[94] Escobar contrasts this leftist statist project with the "postliberal, postdevelopmentalist alternative to modernity" formulated by "intellectuals and activists working with organized peasant, indigenous, and poor urban communities," whose central elements are "first, territory—the defense of the territory as site of production and the place of culture; second, autonomy—that is, the right over a measure of autonomy and self-determination over the decisions that affect them, for instance, around the control and use of natural resources."[95] Identifying the ways in which this poststatist, pluricultural vision of decentralized power and autonomous cultural production (always vulnerable to neoliberal commodification) is at cross-purposes with MAS's attempts to fend off neoliberal forces through state centralization of resources, Escobar argues that "a key question" for the MAS government "is whether they can maintain their redistributive and anti-neoliberal policies while opening up more decidedly to the autonomous views and demands of social movements."[96] He suggests that one way MAS has attempted to bridge this divide is by adopting a pluricultural ideal, grounding their politics in the nationalist and land-based practices, traditions, and knowledge of particular indigenous communities. Yet Escobar cautions that MAS's strategy runs the risk of celebrating and perpetuating gender and sexual oppression in the name of "tradition." "The dangers of essentializing differences are real," he writes. "These dangers are perhaps felt most acutely by feminists from, or working with, ethnic groups and movements."[97]

The separation of women's bodies and reproductive selves from their subjectivity as workers, people, and community-members means that in conversations around reproduction, women's bodies do not belong to them; someone must always speak for and about them. But attempts to speak on behalf of indigenous women are understandably fraught: as Gayatri Spivak has shown us, such attempts are always compromised, and they are complicated even more in the Bolivian context by the specter of the traitorous intermediary, the representative who sells out the community.[98] Bolivia's former minister of health Nila Heredia, a Marxist doctor who was on the front lines of the anti-imperialist insurgent groups in the early 1970s, demonstrates how women who are trying to represent the interests of indigenous women must emphasize loyalty to men and the family/community (and separate out questions of fertility and reproduction from women's rights more generally), because they are always in danger of being accused of betrayal. When I asked her about feminism in a 2009 interview, she said:

> Feminists operate in a framework of citizenship rather than one of basic needs that acknowledges that some women need to have kids because it's your workforce. For those who don't have money or state protections, what can they do? They need to have children, practically to survive. What's more, it's their future, it's the way we can reproduce our society. The notion of women's rights is Western, here those rights come into conflict with the rights of the community. If a woman has all the rights to her body, to marry, to have twenty kids or not have kids at all, where is the right of the community in all that? But I'm also not in favor of patriarchal rule. It's a very difficult issue.[99]

In Heredia's formulation, indigenous women are always caught in this net of either neoliberal or patriarchal control. She argues that indigenous women's desire for birth control demonstrates how they have been used by NGOs and USAID, tricked into sacrificing the good of the community in the name of women's individual rights, but also notes that many of these same indigenous women use birth control secretly because their husbands oppose it. Like Paulina defending her eggs from the Progress Corps volunteers in *Yawar Mallku*, the indigenous women for whom Heredia speaks must themselves always act as intermediaries for their reproductive lives, proving over and over that they are using their bodies for the good of their communities. And Heredia herself—*mestiza* and trained in Western medicine, and so especially vulnerable to such accusations—must be especially careful to reject the position of traitorous intermediary.

Because of this vulnerability to charges of betrayal stemming from colonial and developmentalist interventions, Bolivians interested in trying to promote indigenous women's bodily autonomy are always stymied by the revived cultural nationalist emphasis on gender complementarity, *chacha warmi* in Aymara, the idea that women and men, husbands and wives, should be complementary, part of an unbroken whole like the complementary elements found in the natural world. We can see this in the movement of the camera in the fortune-telling scene in *Yawar Mallku*; as it tracks seamlessly from Paulina to Ignacio, the camera demarcates an unbreakable tie and yet also establishes the taboo against masculine/feminine sameness, creating a hierarchy between the two genders. Paulina looks at Ignacio, who passes judgment that her infertility is bad for her family and community and suppresses the memory of the *yatiri*'s earlier prediction of things looking good for Paulina. The tension the *yatiri* has suggested, between seeing women as subjects who can potentially act for the good of their communities and seeing their bodies as vessels to be appropriated for their community's survival, is resolved by the logic of gender complementarity; the film elides the question of women's potentially traitorous subjectivity by subsuming their bodies and actions within those of heroic revolutionary men.

Felipa Huanca Yupanqui, La Paz director of the MAS-affiliated women's political organization Las Bartolina Sisas, explained gender complementarity this way in a 2010 interview: like Heredia, she disavows feminism, asserting, "There's no feminism in our culture. For me it's a very Western concept, very individualistic. But we as Aymara women are complementary. Here men and women have to work together, the man works and the woman complements him." Despite her public role as a political leader who fights tirelessly to correct the problem of women's uncompensated labor, Huanca remains true to the vision of complementarity that precludes any denaturalizing of women's places as wives and mothers. Indicating the Bartolinas' drive to translate women's demands into policy, she explains, "We women need to make people respect us [in the political sphere], we're doing all this work and the men do nothing in response, that's the fight happening now, and now we have to put our demands into practice. So, [for example,] it's important to fight for the nutrition of children, so that our children are nourished, so that even if we have a lot of children they are well nourished." Speaking about birth control, she cautioned against medicines that hurt women's bodies, but also said, "A family planning orientation is important, men and women have to plan together. And we must acknowledge the rights to one's body, women's rights."[100] Formulating indigenous women's demands around the privatization and naturalization of reproductive responsibilities (e.g., the nutrition of children) while making those demands contingent on men's work and action, Huanca subsumes women under family and male authority, allowing them only to "complement" men's work. The acknowledgment of the rights to one's body do not mean much here, given that women must acknowledge as primary their responsibility to bear children for their communities.

This desire to bestow rights on women while also not trusting that their bodies will correctly and without coercion serve the nation can be traced to population control discourse and the responses shaped by *Yawar Mallku*, as suggested by Sanjinés's proud claim that the film curtailed the distribution of birth control in Bolivia. As a result of the application and aftermath of population control discourse, neither the modernization regime nor the cultural nationalist response to it has been able to accommodate indigenous women's bodily autonomy, much less their visions of family or community. Birth control has become the purview of NGOs in the country and thus has become even more associated in the Bolivian popular imagination with Western imperialism.

Despite their theoretical denunciations of feminism, women's bodily autonomy, and foreign NGOs that promote these things, both Heredia and Huanca acknowledge and advocate the distribution of birth control to women, even without the consent or knowledge of their husbands. What they seem to object to is the discourse surrounding it, which they worry implies an unacceptable break between women and their partners and communities: women are allowed to plan their families, as long as birth control remains an open secret and they continue to honor a communitarian discourse that frames it as shameful.[101] This discourse of complementarity frames birth control, at least its public distribution, as an impediment not only to pregnancy but also to the relationship of the male and female couple, which in the cultural nationalist reclaiming of indigenous traditions forms the basis for all other relationships.

Despite women's difficulty negotiating charges of traitorousness, Bolivia has a dynamic and thriving feminist activist scene; in La Paz, this scene is largely made up of irreverent collectives, known for their graffiti and performance as well as popular education, support groups, and radio shows. One of the founders of Mujeres Creando, the (now-divided) epicenter of the movement, Julieta Paredes, attempts a different kind of mediation of communitarian values and women's equality, positing a feminism that imagines women capable of community building and revolution making:

> The conceptions of women's bodies generally, and particularly of indigenous women's bodies, are not very different between gringos and indigenous men. One group, the gringos, want to exterminate us, while the indigenous men want to make us breed to strengthen the indigenous community. As communitarian feminists we denounce this patriarchal logic that submits our bodies to their conception of the world and life . . .
>
> We demand the right to decide, free and voluntary motherhood, the legalization of abortion, and bodily autonomy in our communities.[102]

Paredes's vehement disavowal of both complementarity and imperialist developmentalism shapes her communitarian feminist vision. But while her demand for "bodily autonomy in our communities" seems clear enough, its realization always turns out to be a struggle. Paredes and other Bolivian communitarian feminists, as public intellectuals and artists, face resistance: sometimes they must turn to NGOs for funding, which makes them vulnerable to charges of traitorousness; other times the anti-patriarchal slogans of their graffiti—"I can't be the love of your life because I am the love of my own life"—emerge already-co-opted by Western individualist notions of self-love. But because of these feminists' public thinking, these questions—of how to square bodily autonomy and community; of how to combat the territorializing discourse of cultural nationalism while imagining collective futures—are never far from the surface of Bolivian political and intellectual life. These feminists' challenges to the idea of complementarity, and the complicated legacy of developmentalist imperatives it echoes, keep alive the *yatiri*'s promise to Paulina that things might "come out right" for Bolivia's indigenous women after all.

Conclusion

HEROIC DEVELOPMENT IN
AN AGE OF DECLINE

THE MAIN CONTENTION OF THIS BOOK is that the Peace Corps embodied and disseminated a particularly heroic and compelling iteration of modernization theory in the 1960s, due largely to the promise of masculinity and brotherhood it embodied. This gendered modernization project allowed the United States to maintain global hegemony in the face of widespread decolonization struggles by placing modernity, rather than independence or economic justice, at the endpoint of those struggles. The widespread equation of modernity with masculinity also allowed U.S. social scientists and politicians to articulate and resolve anxieties about newly managerial-class, suburb-dwelling white men "going soft." To assuage those anxieties about modernity while preventing them from straying into the dangerous territory of romanticizing racialized poverty, the modernization establishment offered these men homosocial frontier adventures, opportunities for self-realization through real or vicarious development work in the Third World that helped them preserve the comforts that accompanied their affluence even while offering a temporary respite from them. In short, I have argued that the "development decade" was yet another historical period when the anxieties of powerful men, and their attempts to resolve those anxieties, ended up reordering the world.

As I argue in this book's later chapters, this reordering happened not only in the realms of official diplomacy and international development ventures, but also in the worlds of oppositional culture and politics. Undergirded by the financial and military support of the Cold War, development ideology guided the struggles of revolutionary movements abroad and at home, encouraging activists to imagine social change as requiring personal transformation to masculinity, realized through the exertion of control over nature and populations, rather than mass collective action or dialogic decision-making. My point has not been that sexism was unique to the era, but rather that in 1960s movements, authentic masculinity and brotherhood came to stand in for a more precisely articulated vision of social transformation. The dialectical relationship between decolonial nationalism—men united by their "ache to come into the world as men," in James Baldwin's memorable phrasing—and development's vision of transformation to full masculinity, meant that when left movements turned their eyes to the newly problematized "global poor" and to those struggling against imperialism, the heroic ideal of development work embodied by the Peace Corps had effectively gotten there first, providing a script for how one might find personal fulfillment and heroism in connection across difference.[1] This is not to dismiss the incredible creativity of movement leaders or discount the variety of their actions, but rather to emphasize the tremendous power of the international development establishment to produce reality: I argue here that development fantasies were decisive factors in curtailing the transformative politics to which so many aspired. Even activists' attempts to imagine alternative modernities existed within the terms of international development, making it difficult to envision futures that did not entail this strange mix of economic growth and masculine self-realization. Antimodern subcultures were also wrapped up in the logic of modernization: it was possible to "drop out" of this seemingly inexorable trajectory, but less possible to fight it.

Since the 1960s, the Peace Corps' symbolic importance to the United States has declined precipitously. Volunteers draw less news coverage, and that which they do garner tends to be much more critical than the fawning stories of the early years.[2] Numbers of volunteers in the field, too, have dwindled, despite the increasingly grandiose expansion plans proposed by the last three presidents: Bill Clinton signed a bill increasing the number of volunteers to ten thousand by the year 2000; George W. Bush pledged in 2002 to expand the number to fifteen thousand, matching the high point of 1966; and Barack Obama promised during his 2008 campaign to double the Peace Corps' size by 2011. All these attempts have failed, however, with the number of volunteers in the field every year hovering between six and seven thousand.[3] These ambitious yet thwarted plans suggest that while the neoliberal economic order—the move to privatization and trade liberalization that has dramatically increased global inequality since the 1980s—and expensive military occupations have curtailed investments in the Peace Corps, it still carries redemptive potential as a kind of symbolic compensation for U.S. blunders and crimes abroad.

As the Peace Corps has faded from the public eye, the vision of heroic development it represents has lingered. Despite the near-universal scholarly consensus that the model advanced by modernization theorists and enacted by innumerable development agencies has failed to "develop" poor countries, and despite the forty years–on ascendance of the postmodern orientation that was supposed to have disrupted narratives of rational progress, development theories and projects continue to frame popular discussions of global poverty. With the election of Barack Obama, famous for his youthful stint with the Developing Communities Project in Chicago, the United States chose its first development-worker president.[4] From the beginning of his presidency, Obama combined the developmental rhetoric of personal responsibility with a more recent faith in the free market to empower the downtrodden at home and all over the world. In a 2010 speech to the United Nations about African development, he explained that "to unleash transformational change, we're putting a new emphasis on the most powerful force the world has ever known for eradicating poverty and creating opportunity . . . The force I'm speaking about is broad-based economic growth."[5] In the summer of 2013, Obama reiterated this corporate development agenda, organizing a roundtable in Tanzania with African leaders as well as the heads of General Electric, Microsoft, Coca-Cola, and Symbion Power Corp. In a speech at a Tanzanian power plant, the president proclaimed that "we have got enormous opportunity to unleash the next era of African growth. I see Africa as the world's next major economic success story and the United States wants to be a partner in that success."[6]

Obama's seemingly unshakeable faith in eradicating poverty through capitalism suggests that rather than being supplanted by the ethos of neoliberal privatization and the exigencies of the War on Terror, the development imperative provides a logic for these new systems. His defense of the market as a mechanism that will (this time, despite all evidence to the contrary) "unleash the next era of African growth," stamping out poverty forever, indicates the extent to which, as Claire Fox has recently argued, "developmentalist theories circulating in the [Western] hemisphere during the Cold War . . . created the conditions for contemporary neoliberalism to flourish."[7] The development era's relentless drive for economic growth, spurred by highly visible heroic development workers who promised to transform people into fully realized masculine capitalist subjects if only they were worthy and ingenious enough, laid the ideological and infrastructural groundwork for the neoliberal installation of market logic everywhere. Meanwhile, the international development work that was once primarily (though never exclusively) the work of states has been privatized, becoming the purview of countless nongovernmental organizations.

This privatization of development work has been accompanied by its feminization; the Peace Corps, for example, is now 63 percent women. This shift reflects not only the comparatively lower prestige of the development worker, but also the rise of women's empowerment as a central concern in international development. "Women in development," a term that gained currency in the early 1970s, has become a nearly ubiquitous formulation, mirroring the feminization of wage labor that has taken place under neoliberalism, and the targeting of women and the financialization of development interventions have become inextricably linked. In her revelatory study *Microfinance and Its Discontents*, Lamia Karim tracks how microlending organizations purport to heroically empower women while often, in practice, increasing their vulnerability by lending them money they have difficulty repaying, aware that they lack the mobility to skip out on loans.[8] The figure of the heroic moneylender, represented most publicly by Nobel Prize winner Muhammad Yunus of the Grameen Bank, has become accessible to all through microlending websites, most prominently the Christian site Kiva.org. Despite partnering with loan organizations that lend money at predatory interest rates, Kiva markets itself as a charity organization, allowing ordinary people from the global North to evaluate the business plans (and photographs) of the largely female entrepreneurial poor of the global South and lend money directly to those they deem most deserving. Kiva's success indicates ordinary people's continued desire to participate in heroic development work (in this case, without leaving their couches, and with a near-guarantee of repayment), as well as their investment in bringing desiring subjects into the capitalist order.

Thus, even with the ever-increasing visibility of "women in development," the desire for male development heroes has persisted. Perhaps the archetypal example of the heroic development worker in the age of women's empowerment, inflected by what Eunice Sahle has recently called "securitization of development," is Greg Mortenson, the now-discredited adventurer turned philanthropist. Mortenson wrote the best-selling memoir *Three Cups of Tea*, about his alleged experiences building schools for girls in Pakistan and Afghanistan.[9] Despite the project's investment in girls' empowerment, the book makes clear that Mortenson's interactions with local men are key to his success. From a Pakistani man who "fell in love with his personality" to another who implores his community to "protect and embrace these two American brothers in our midst," and asserts that "our land is in poverty because we are without education" to the terrorists Mortenson invents in order to recount his triumphant tale of winning them over, the book is primarily a manual of counterinsurgency through male bonding, with girls' education as prop and pretense.[10] *New York Times* columnist Nicholas Kristof echoed the book's depictions of hero-worship and intimacy, gushing in 2008 that Mortenson had "become a legend in the region, his picture sometimes dangling like a talisman from rearview mirrors."[11] The U.S. military also recognized that Mortenson's work was primarily homosocial: before he came under scrutiny and admitted to lying about much of his story and accepting money for schools that were not operational, Mortenson worked closely with military leaders, inspiring and guiding the strategy of the late-2000s troop surges in Iraq and Afghanistan by emphasizing culturally competent interactions (tea-drinking) with male leaders.[12]

The speed with which Mortenson's stories were discredited (as compared to the writings of a Cold War hero like Tom Dooley, who took a similarly creative approach) indicates that the heroic development myths crafted in the Kennedy era have lost some of their luster. The nation-building counterinsurgency doctrines guided by Mortenson's apocryphal stories were also deemed failures after only a few short years, and the U.S. military abandoned them for a more covert program of targeted assassinations.[13] The example of failed developmentalist counterinsurgency, a strategy quickly replaced by drone strikes, suggests that the decline of these heroic narratives—or at least of popular willingness to believe in development schemes—does not automatically auger a more humane future. Here I join James Ferguson in cautioning that things can always get worse; as Ferguson argues, the ideological damage of forcefully inculcated then frustrated "expectations of modernity," combined with the withdrawal of infrastructure and material investment, has created in various former hubs of development work and investment a state of abjection—a feeling of being "cast out and down" from a status and a community to which they had been promised entry.[14] Violent attempts to desecrate the symbols of modernity have emerged from these states of abjection, as well as creative intellectual movements and new (and revived) everyday coping strategies.[15]

If global responses and coping strategies have varied, the U.S. liberal reaction to the dislocations of neoliberalism has generally taken the form of nostalgia for the development era. Popular memory of the Peace Corps and of Shriver's heroic persona in particular has fueled this nostalgia, leading liberal commentators to wonder, "Who will Obama's Shriver be?"[16] Jeffrey Sachs, the unrepentant economic "shock therapist" who oversaw the neoliberal restructuring of economies from Bolivia to Poland, drastically cutting public services and creating massive inequality, has lately attempted to use Kennedy nostalgia to reinvigorate development economics, arguing that while Kennedy's "challenge was to face the Cold War and the new realities of nuclear weapons," the goal of "our generation" must be "the challenge of sustainable development."[17] Despite Sachs's responsibility for crafting the free-trade policies that have decimated the environment and impoverished millions, his credentials as a "development economist" mean that media outlets, even alternative leftist ones, defer to his expertise on global poverty.[18]

Even those on the North American left who criticize Sachs and his ilk persist in a similar nostalgia for the development era. Naomi Klein, in her best-selling history of neoliberal capitalism *The Shock Doctrine*, vividly depicts the devastation wrought by Sachs and other "shock therapists" but almost entirely effaces the violence of the Cold War scene: professing longing throughout the book for an era she alternately calls "Keynesian" and "developmentalist," she calls development in South America "staggeringly successful."[19] Other popular leftist representations in the United States have perpetuated this nostalgia, ignoring or dismissing the levels of racist and imperialist violence that characterized the development era and the particular violence and imperative to cultural eradication inherent in modernization programs.[20] The academy, too, has participated in this nostalgia, specifically calling for a restoration of the "big ideas" and institution-boosting function of Cold War social scientists; literary scholar Mark McGurl has even called for the restoration of Talcott Parsons's "once towering disciplinary and institutional presence."[21]

While these nostalgic longings are understandable, given the funding that accompanied the Cold War state, and the university in particular, in the age of development, it is worth trying to resist them. The extent to which the violence of modernization and the convergence of liberalism and radicalism fifty years ago matter today is the extent that, as Ferguson asserts in the context of 1990s Zambia, "decline, though often hellish to live through, is 'good to think.'"[22] My hope is that this book will not only show that nostalgia for the development era, however appealing in desperate times, is misguided, but also encourage us to think creatively and carefully about what a world less driven by the development imaginary could look like. In Laura Briggs's words, U.S. leftist intellectuals have for too long been "chasing the tail of a vanishing liberalism, without the imagination of something different."[23] My contention is that critical conversations about development, ones that consciously examine the conflation of economic growth with personal and collective fulfillment, are a necessary step in imagining "something different." Such conversations are even more necessary as we reach (and surpass) environmental crisis points; as fossil-fuel extraction and burning lead to ever-more extreme weather (as well as political) crises; and as the United States bemoans "developing" nations' insatiable desires to "be like us," conveniently forgetting its own Cold War role in forcing capitalist development on, and inculcating modernizing desires in, many of those nations.[24]

If we do want to begin conversations interrogating the principles behind "progress" and development, we might, as Briggs similarly suggests, look to places like Bolivia, where development networks have been so dense and development discourse so pervasive, and where activists and intellectuals are now attempting to move beyond the pursuit of economic growth and Western individualism. Drawing on indigenous traditions, these communities are attempting to imagine other ways of measuring and achieving the good life.[25] This process entails mobilizing discourses of shared and sacred communal resources to challenge both neoliberal privatizing projects, like the successful struggle in 2000 against Bechtel's attempt to privatize the water of Cochabamba, and the ongoing struggle against state-centered development projects, like the TIPNIS highway that would go through the sacred land of the Chimané, Yuracaré, and Mojeno–Trinitario peoples.[26] These attempts have not been able to shake development's legacy entirely: as I discuss in chapter 6, even these reinventions of indigenous values are shaped by attempts to reassert male collective control over territory and women's bodies. But they are also being produced in dialogue and conflict with feminist intellectuals and activists, and they continue to constitute a particularly important site of possibility for a post-development imaginary.[27]

What the Bolivian experience suggests is that if the left in the United States must be nostalgic, we might be nostalgic not for development, but for the liberatory energies that were both crushed and redirected into nationalist, heteropatriarchal, capitalist projects: the visions of decolonization, racial justice, and gender equality, and even the communitarian yearnings of the beats and the counterculture.[28] My hope is that tracking the particular ways development achieved its ideological supremacy through the heroic fantasy of the Peace Corps, and the ways it continues to pervade dominant imaginings of social change, will help amplify the sense of possibility in future movements for justice and equality, wherever and whenever they emerge.

ACKNOWLEDGMENTS

This book has many origin stories. The one I remember best involves conversations with Heidi Hausman, Jessica Casas, Isbelia Casas, Bob Michael, and the late Helen Soos. Nancy Romer, Janet Santos, and Olisa Laufer also had a lot to do with the beginnings of this book, as did Paul Buhle and Shoshana Rihn, who inspired me to turn my preoccupation with the 1960s into a long-term research program. Judith Smith, Rachel Rubin, Lois Rudnick, Shirley Tang, Rajini Srikanth, Joyce Morrissey, Aaron Lecklider, Reiko Maeda, Justin Maher, Drew Hannon, Liza Burbank Gilb, and others too numerous to name provided me with a wonderfully supportive and exciting intellectual community at UMass Boston. Thanks to Nina Silber for being a sharp-eyed, generous, and good-natured adviser, to Bruce Schulman for encouraging me to pursue this project and helping me refine it, and to Jeffrey Rubin and Elora Chowdhury for their contributions and thoughtful questions.

Thanks to Karen Dubinsky, Catherine Krull, and the other organizers of the New World Coming conference for opportunities to think globally about the sixties and present this work early on. Sheyda Jahanbani and Quinn Slobodian pointed me to important sources at key moments; Frank Costigliola and Ruth Feldstein offered encouraging words in the project's early phases; and Erica Nelson and Cecilia Azevedo generously sent me their work. Fernando Purcell, Hannah Gurman, and Raúl Necochea organized panels where I presented parts of this book; Michael LaRosa, Jessica Chapman, Vania Smith-Oka, and Alexander Bloom offered generous and thoughtful commentary. Judith Smith, Elora Chowdhury, and Aaron Lecklider deserve extra thanks for their detailed comments on parts of the book. Thanks also to the Cornell

Foreign Relations Reading Group, particularly Fredrik Logevall, Fritz Bartel, Taomo Zhou, Jason Kelly, Seth Ackerman, and Daniel Bessner, for their critical feedback on chapter drafts. John Weiss and Heather Furnas generously shared sources. Anne Blaschke and Virginia Myhaver have been wonderful colleagues, critics, and travel companions. Thanks to George Lipsitz, Richard Morrison, and Erin Warholm for agreeing to publish this book and helping it through earlier, messier stages.

Countless archivists in the United States and Bolivia helped me locate materials, but Allen Fisher and Regina Greenwell at the Lyndon B. Johnson Library deserve special thanks for their thoughtful attention to my requests before, during, and after my visit. Stephen Plotkin and others at the John F. Kennedy Library provided invaluable assistance. Nancy Romer, Jim Siekmeier, Thomas Field, and Tasha Kimball generously shared resources and contacts in Bolivia, and Luis Oporto helped me locate sources and interview subjects in La Paz. Thanks to Silvia Rivera Cusicanqui for her dazzling insights, her fearlessness, and her friendship, and to everyone in El Colectivo Ch'ixi for their creativity and intellectual community, especially Marco Arnez, Ruth Bautista, Beatriz Chambilla, Violeta Montellano, Mario Murillo, Álvaro Pinaya, Hernán Pruden, Gabriel Ramos, and most of all the intrepid and talented Mercedes Bernabé, who chased interview subjects onto buses with me, accompanied me on numerous archival adventures, and meticulously transcribed my interview testimony. I am grateful to the many returned Peace Corps volunteers who shared their stories with me, especially Judy Alexander, Aubrey Brown, Laura Damon, Kay Dixon, John Dwan, Freida Fairburn, Faith Fogle, Kay Frishman, Sybil Gilchrist, Alice Hageman, Connie Jaquith, Alice O'Grady, Carol Snee, Joe Stork, Susan Strane, and Carol Weser. Many thanks go to Bolivian activists Nila Heredia, Felipa Huanca Yupanqui, Julieta Paredes, Edgar Ramirez, Carlos Soria Galvarro, and Gonzalo Suruco for sharing their ideas and memories.

Finally, thanks to my family: to Rich Geidel and Nancy Braus for being wonderful, feminist parents, and to Jane and Laura Geidel for their love and support. Thanks also to those who shared their homes with me during research and conference trips: Mercedes Bernabé and Marcela and Enrique Reynaga; Silvia Rivera and Nicolas and Lucia Urzagasti; Kaija, Peter, Nate, and Henry Braus; Justin Maher and Tom Hardej; Anna Rue and Charlie McNulty. Thanks also to Herta Geidel;

Jane and the late Jay Braus; Pat Braus; Paul Braus; and Ed, Dan, and Jay Lopez for their love, support, and brainstorming help. Thanks to Joey Birchmore for many great meals, and to Ben and Allie Birchmore for being super. Thanks to Naila, Munir, Lara, and Mary Jirmanus for being my family in Boston, and to the rest of my activist community there for helping me think about solidarity. Finally, I will never be able to give thanks enough to my best friend and coconspirator, Patricia Stuelke, who had faith in this project from the beginning and worked tirelessly and brilliantly to help me get it right. Much of what's good in this book was her idea, while of course I take full responsibility for all shortcomings.

NOTES

Introduction

1. Shrestha, *In the Name of Development*, 55.
2. Ibid., 56.
3. Ibid., 45.
4. Ibid., 82–83.
5. Ibid., 58. Even historians who sympathize with the postwar development establishment's mission agree that the story of these modernization efforts is largely one of "unfulfilled dreams, unintended consequences, bitter rivalries, and tragedies on a global scale." Staples, *Birth of Development*, 1–2. (A notable exception is Erez Manela, whose recent work touts smallpox eradication as an underappreciated success of the modernization regime. Manela, "Pox on Your Narrative.") As Shrestha notes, this acknowledgment of the repeated failures of international development rarely leads political leaders or international organizations to question the discourse of development itself, as evidenced by the UN's continued efforts to pursue the Millennium Development Goals despite its failure to reach them. See Liz Ford, "Reducing Child Deaths: The Millennium Development Goal That Is Slipping Away," *The Guardian*, July 7, 2014, http://www.theguardian.com/global-development/2014/jul/07/child-deaths -mortality-millennium-development-goals. For recent statistics on global inequality see, for example, "Working for the Few," http://www.oxfam.org/en/policy/ working-for-the-few-economic-inequality.
6. Of course, these "traditional" cultures, untouched by colonialism or other forms of modernity, first needed to be invented; see Escobar, *Encountering Development*, 47–54.
7. Wofford, *Of Kennedys and Kings*, 243.
8. Shrestha, *In the Name of Development*, 43.
9. In characterizing these promises and fantasies as homosocial, I draw on Eve Sedgwick's contention that carefully policed and triangulated male desire

operates in modern Western culture to consolidate men's imperial and patriarchal power. See chapter 1 for a further discussion of the term. Here I also follow Frank Costigliola, who has argued that understanding triangulated homosocial desires provides crucial insights into the making of U.S. Cold War policy (and thus the Cold War itself). See Sedgwick, *Between Men*; Costigliola, "Unceasing Pressure for Penetration," and *Roosevelt's Lost Alliances*.

10. Intellectual/organizational histories of modernization theory include Ekbladh, *Great American Mission*; Gilman, *Mandarins of the Future*; and Engerman et al., *Staging Growth*. Important histories of Cold War development that focus on planners and other protagonists include Latham's *Modernization as Ideology* and *Right Kind of Revolution*; Cullather's *Hungry World*; Simpson's *Economists with Guns*; and Field's *From Development to Dictatorship*. Of the two book-length scholarly histories of the 1960s Peace Corps, Hoffman's organizational history *All You Need Is Love* argues that the Peace Corps' ethos shaped the global 1960s, but gives very little attention to the particulars of that ethos, arguing that "idealism" is a better term than "ideology" to explain the Peace Corps' worldview. Fischer's *Making Them Like Us* considers Peace Corps volunteers in relation to modernization theory while making fewer connections to the greater "global sixties." Both writers' insights guide my attempt to track the figure of the heroic development worker. Goldstein's recent book *Poverty in Common*, with its careful discussion of the slippage between self-help and self-determination in 1960s movement cultures, is one exception to this bracketing of development policy from discussions of movement politics. This book has also been able to make use of excellent discussions of the early Peace Corps' modernizing and gendered ideologies in book chapters by Michael Latham, Sheyda Jahanbani, Larry Grubbs, and Robert Dean; see Latham, *Modernization as Ideology*, 109–49; Jahanbani, "One Global War on Poverty"; Grubbs, *Secular Missionaries*, 159–80; Dean, *Imperial Brotherhood*, 169–99.

11. Thomas Piketty's *Capital in the Twenty-First Century*, recently embraced by the political liberal–left in the United States, makes an argument that assumes economic growth to be the primary indicator of social good—for him, societies tend toward instability when the "unproductive" accumulation of wealth (from inheritance, investment, etc., as opposed to the more legitimately gained profits of "productive" capitalists) outpaces GDP. For nostalgia, see the significant faction of the Occupy Wall Street movement interested in bringing back the New Deal, as well as the ubiquity of Naomi Klein's *Shock Doctrine*, which unequivocally celebrates the Keynesian/development era, on Occupy and other left-oriented reading lists. For other examples of Cold War/Eisenhower and Kennedy–era nostalgia, see Michael Moore, dir., *Capitalism: A Love Story*; and Jeffrey Sachs, *Price of Civilization* and *To Move the World*. For academic nostalgia for Cold War

social science see Rodgers, *Age of Fracture*. For nostalgia specifically for Shriver, see John Nichols, "How Sargent Shriver Helped John F. Kennedy Become a Liberal," *The Nation* blog, January 20, 2011, http://www.thenation.com/blog/15 7887/how-sargent-shriver-helped-john-kennedy-become-liberal; Claire Potter, "Why Won't Obama Talk about the Poor?" *Tenured Radical* blog, February 2, 2014, http://chronicle.com/blognetwork/tenuredradical/2014/02/8271/.

12. Upon hearing about my research, many people, particularly those who live or grew up outside the United States, asked me whether I would address the issue of Peace Corps cooperation with the Central Intelligence Agency. While the State Department and the CIA occasionally pressured volunteers to collect information (or used information they unwittingly collected) on leftists in Latin America—at least in Chile in the 1960s and early 1970s, and in Bolivia more recently—my sense is that such cases were rare. It is my contention throughout this book that the Peace Corps' symbolic value in the 1960s, specifically its ability to represent the euphoric future promised by the international development establishment, was far more important in Cold War geopolitics than the pieces of information volunteers might have supplied. See Langley, *America and the Americas*, 243; NACLA, *Latin America and Empire Report*, July–August 1974, 7; Jean Freedman-Rudovsky and Brian Ross, "Exclusive: Peace Corps, Fulbright Scholar Asked to 'Spy' on Cubans, Venezuelans" *ABC News*, February 8, 2008, http://abcnews.go.com/Blotter/story?id=4262036.

13. Ashabranner, *Moment in History*, 23–24; Redmon, *Come as You Are*, 30; Patricia Sullivan, "Warren W. Wiggins," *Washington Post*, April 15, 2007. According to Elizabeth Cobbs Hoffman, lawyer and Kennedy adviser William Josephson co-wrote "A Towering Task" with Wiggins, but Wiggins seems to have received all the credit: only his name survives on the Peace Corps library's draft of the document, and Josephson was absent from the staff meeting at which it was discussed. Hoffman, *All You Need Is Love*, 42–43.

14. Wiggins, "Towering Task," i. Taking seriously Kennedy's imperative to construct "a sound and expanding *economy*" and the centrality of that particular phrase to the Peace Corps' founding, this book understands the Cold War modernization project as driven by capitalist expansionist drives as much as (and in close concert with) the ideological imperatives and anxieties more often highlighted in histories of Cold War modernization. This argument about the capitalist intentions of Cold War development in the Third World echoes the work of many other scholars. Kim's *Ends of Empire*, for example, has similarly characterized the Cold War as primarily about establishing new mechanisms for Third World domination and resource-extraction: Kim argues that the Cold War can be better understood as "one particular phase in the much more established Western trade wars in the globalization of capitalism and the competition for

markets and resources both natural and human." This claim, that the Cold War was impelled by U.S. economic interests, is associated with historians of the revisionist new left tradition and has recently been further supported by the work of Curt Cardwell who, in his meticulous study of the role of the "dollar gap" in the crafting of key Cold War document NSC-68, demonstrates that the lack of access to cheap raw materials that might prevent Japan and Europe from buying U.S. goods was "far more potentially destructive of the American way of life, at least as defined by those in charge of making U.S. foreign policy in the Truman administration, as any threat posed by communism or the Soviet Union." Modernization theorists Walt Rostow and Max Millikan also identify the dollar gap as a key reason for Third World modernization in their 1957 international development proposal. Kim, *Ends of Empire*, 24; Cardwell, *NSC 68*, 3; Millikan and Rostow, *Proposal*, 82–85.

15. "How many of you who are going to be doctors, are willing to spend your days in Ghana? Technicians or engineers, how many of you are willing to work in the Foreign Service and spend your lives traveling around the world? On your willingness to do that, not merely to serve one year or two years in the service, but on your willingness to contribute part of your life to this country, I think will depend the answer whether a free society can compete." "Remarks of Senator John F. Kennedy," http://www.peacecorps.gov/about/history/speech/.

16. Wiggins, "Towering Task," 9.

17. Ibid., 18.

18. Ibid., 14.

19. Ibid., 13–14.

20. Ibid., 15.

21. Wexler, *Tender Violence*; Kramer, *Blood of Government*.

22. Lardizabal, *Pioneer American Teachers and Philippine Education*, 133.

23. Fee, *Woman's Impression of the Philippines*, 1–2.

24. Foucault, *History of Sexuality*.

25. For example, Amy Kaplan demonstrates how white, middle-class men in the United States "saw imperial warfare as an opportunity for the American man to rescue himself from the threatening forces of industrialization and feminization at home," while Gail Bederman argues similarly that the same men reinvented masculinity at home through their adventures abroad, abandoning an increasingly unprofitable ideal of self-abnegating manliness in favor of a masculinity reliant on the prevailing discourse of civilization, a pseudo-Darwinist, millennialist theory of racial competition and salvation. Analyzing women's roles in the U.S. civilizing mission, Laura Wexler contends that white women photographers documenting imperial missions in the Philippines and elsewhere "often used the 'innocent eye' attributed to them by white domestic sentiment

to construct images of war as peace, images that were, in turn, a constitutive element of United States imperialism during the era's annexation and consolidation of the colonies"; in her readings of Frances Benjamin Johnston's photographs of Commodore George Dewey's ship, depicting the sailors dancing, eating, and playing with kittens, Wexler contends that these photos allowed the U.S. public to imagine Dewey's mission in the Philippines as liberatory and pedagogical rather than violent and oppressive. Though Laura Briggs is less concerned with turn-of-the-century shifts in gender and sexual identities, her study of U.S. colonial attempts to regulate Puerto Rican women's sexuality and reproduction, and her argument that those regulation attempts—as well as cultural nationalist responses—crucially shaped Puerto Rican identity, also inspires this book. See Bederman, *Manliness and Civilization*; Kaplan, *Anarchy of Empire in the Making of U.S. Culture*, 92–93; Wexler, *Tender Violence*, 6; Briggs, *Reproducing Empire*.

26. Robert Dean, for example, in his excellent account of 1960s foreign policy-makers' masculinity, emphasizes the continuity between the patrician-warrior ideals of the late nineteenth-century U.S. elite and those that dominated the Cold War political imaginary. In contrast, here I build on the insights of Van Gosse, who discusses the late 1950s "collapse and reinvention of traditional boyhood and manhood" in the United States connected to an imaginative solidarity with Fidel Castro, and with Maria Josefina Saldaña-Portillo's insights about development as a fantasy of masculine subjection. See Dean, *Imperial Brotherhood*; Van Gosse, *Where the Boys Are*, 1; Saldaña-Portillo, *Revolutionary Imagination*.

27. Wiggins, "Towering Task," 16.

28. Escobar, *Encountering Development*. See also Rahnema and Bawtree, *Postdevelopment Reader*; J. Ferguson, *Anti-politics Machine*; Rist, *History of Development*. Most historians have rejected these scholars' Foucauldian framework—often comparing it with the conservative abandonment of state-based projects and dismissing both "extremes"—in favor of ostensibly more neutral or ambivalent assessments of Cold War modernization. However, their often-excellent excavations of both the contradictions within development discourse and the violent consequences of development interventions support rather than undermine Escobar's reading of development as a "historically produced discourse" that made it "impossible to conceptualize social reality in other terms," and a dream "that progressively turned into a nightmare" (4–6). For explicit rejections of Escobar's frame see Engerman et al., *Staging Growth*, 17; Cooper and Packard, *International Development and the Social Sciences*, 3–4.

29. Saldaña-Portillo, *Revolutionary Imagination*, 22. This book builds on *Revolutionary Imagination* and Catherine V. Scott's *Gender and Development* in considering the masculine imperatives of the early postwar development regime; the question of "women in development" only became a major focus of the

development establishment after the 1970 publication of Boserup's book *Woman's Role in Economic Development*. For a critical account of the shift to "women in development," see Kabeer, *Reversed Realities*.

30. Saldaña-Portillo, *Revolutionary Imagination*, 275.

31. This book, particularly its discussions of modernization theorists' participation in Peace Corps planning, provides a challenge to recent work by Daniel Immerwahr, which attempts to draw a sharp distinction between theories of modernization and practices of community development. This book argues that in both theory and practice, the Peace Corps provided the iconic, legible narrative that justified larger-scale modernization projects; thus throughout the book I follow the Peace Corps planners and volunteers in using "modernization" and "development" interchangeably. See Immerwahr, *Thinking Small*.

32. For a good overview of this work, see Cooper, "Development, Modernization, and the Social Sciences."

33. Chakrabarty, *Provincializing Europe*; M. Weber, "Science as a Vocation."

34. We can see this vision of magical—if ultimately violent and untenable—modernity in the great 1960s novel, García Márquez's *One Hundred Years of Solitude*.

35. Lichtenstein, *State of the Union*; Buhle, *Feminism and Its Discontents*; Breines, *Young, White, and Miserable*; Feldstein, *Motherhood in Black and White*; R. Ferguson, *Aberrations in Black*; Melamed, *Represent and Destroy*, 54.

36. Formulated by Franz Boas and his students to counter prevailing anthropological notions, ideas about cultural difference emerged in the early twentieth century as a radical challenge to scientific racism. However, they were quickly adopted by American social scientists in the 1930s and 1940s to diagnose African American and Latin American poverty as "pathological." See Luis-Brown, *Waves of Decolonization*; O'Connor, *Poverty Knowledge*.

37. Hoffman, *All You Need Is Love*, 8.

38. Excellent and provocative histories that place 1960s U.S. social movements in transnational contexts without substantively considering development include Gosse, *Where the Boys Are*; Gaines, *American Africans in Ghana*; and C. Young, *Soul Power*.

39. See Dudziak, *Cold War Civil Rights*; Borstelmann, *Cold War and the Color Line*.

40. In making this argument I build on arguments by Erica Edwards, Ruth Feldstein, Roderick Ferguson, and Robert Carr, who in turn build on Michele Wallace's 1978 work to contend that developmental social science theories attributing racialized poverty to insufficiently patriarchal black families and communities influenced both civil rights and black revolutionary movement thought.

Edwards, *Charisma and the Fictions of Black Leadership*; Feldstein, *Motherhood in Black and White*; R. Ferguson, *Aberrations in Black*; Carr, *Black Nationalism in the New World*; Wallace, *Black Macho and the Myth of the Superwoman*.

41. For accounts of the conflicts within and the splintering of the white new left see Breines, *Community and Organization in the New Left*; Barber, *Hard Rain Fell*; Evans, *Personal Politics*.

42. Escobar, "Latin America at a Crossroads."

43. Thomas Field has recently argued for Bolivia as an under-theorized key location of Kennedy-era military modernization, and I argue similarly that Bolivia's strategic and symbolic importance during the 1960s makes it a critical Cold War battleground site. Field, *From Development to Dictatorship*.

44. Chakrabarty, *Provincializing Europe*, 16.

45. As part of my attempt to understand the reach of development, I interviewed many Bolivians who might have had contact with Peace Corps volunteers in the 1960s. However, due to the sheer number of development workers in Bolivia in that period (see chapter 6 for a fuller account of this phenomenon), most people could not remember whether they had encountered any Peace Corps volunteers at all, as opposed to USAID workers, missionaries, or members of other development organizations. One notable exception: a prominent Bolivian academic definitively recalls a Peace Corps volunteer introducing her to marijuana. Recent work by Latin American historians on the Peace Corps has begun to fill in these gaps by concentrating on interactions between U.S. volunteers and local people. See Purcell, "Connecting Realities"; and Azevedo, *Em Nome da América*.

46. Julius Amin is another writer who encountered Peace Corps volunteers as a child, in his case as his teachers in 1960s Cameroon. Amin has gone on to write careful, ambivalent histories of the agency's work in 1960s Africa, identifying widespread failures of training, particularly in community development, but praising volunteers' "ambition, courage, and friendliness" and arguing that "their presence created an urgency about opening new schools." Amin, *Peace Corps in Cameroon*, 124.

47. Edward Said calls this analytic attention to different, opposing perspectives—and particularly to empire and resistance—"contrapuntal reading." Said, *Culture and Imperialism*, 66–67.

48. Goldstein, *Poverty in Common*, 107.

49. Recent works detailing some of the more violent Cold War interventions rationalized by modernization and/or carried out by development organizations include Latham, *Modernization as Ideology*, esp. chap. 5; Field, *From Development to Dictatorship*; Simpson, *Economists with Guns*; Weld, *Paper Cadavers*, esp. chap. 4; and Franco, *Cruel Modernity*.

1. Fantasies of Brotherhood

1. For an account of Paz's labor policies, spurred by Alliance for Progress money, see Field, *From Development to Dictatorship*; for a firsthand account of the effects of these policies on mining communities, see Barrios de Chungara, *Let Me Speak!*

2. "Bolivian Reformer," *New York Times*, October 26, 1963.

3. "The High, Hard Land (The Hemisphere: BOLIVIA)," *Time*, November 1, 1963. See chapter 6 for an account of the 1952 Bolivian revolution.

4. "Cálida Acogida Brindó Kennedy Al Presidente Victor Paz Estenssoro," *El Diario* (La Paz), October 23, 1963.

5. Saldaña-Portillo, *Revolutionary Imagination*.

6. Saldaña-Portillo designates the shift in the central object of transformation from earlier theories of development to postwar, U.S.-derived modernization theory as one "from territory to interiority." Ibid., 27.

7. Sedgwick, *Between Men*, 3, 201.

8. Dean, *Imperial Brotherhood*; Ibson, "Masculinity under Fire" and *Picturing Men*.

9. Thomsen, *Living Poor*, vii.

10. Gilbert Rist argues that by the 1955 Bandung conference, participating nations' leaders had already decided to attempt to follow a universal development path that entailed the destruction of local ways of life. Rist, *History of Development*, 87; Prashad, in *Darker Nations*, also notes the centrality and universality of development to the imperatives that emerged from Bandung.

11. "The Atlantic Charter," August 14, 1941, http://www.nato.int/cps/en/SID-2788FECD-8FACF71E/natolive/official_texts_16912.htm.

12. "Charter of the United Nations: Purposes and Principles," http://www.un.org/en/documents/charter/chapter1.shtml.

13. M. Young, *Vietnam Wars*, 14.

14. "Final Communiqué of the Asian–African Conference," http://www.issafrica.org/uploads/BANDUNG55.PDF.

15. Borgwardt, *New Deal for the World*, 30.

16. Kennan, "Policy Planning Study 23," 513.

17. See Gilman, *Mandarins of the Future*, 198.

18. Saldaña-Portillo, *Revolutionary Imagination*, 19.

19. Ibid.; and Escobar, *Encountering Development*, esp. 32–34.

20. Adamson, "Eisenhower Administration," 56–60. Odd Arne Westad reminds us that "in the period from 1956–60—in spite of the fear of Soviet advances—only slightly less than 90 percent of all official aid to the Third World came from advanced capitalist countries." Westad, *Global Cold War*, 32.

21. May, *Homeward Bound*, 10–13.

22. Tobin, "Defense, Dollars, and Doctrine," 68.

23. Popular social science books lamenting masculine atrophy in the face of 1950s affluence, conformity, suburbanization, and domesticity include Riesman's *Lonely Crowd*; Whyte's *Organization Man*; Packard's *Status Seekers*; Seeley's *Crestwood Heights*; and Goodman's *Growing Up Absurd*. Sloan Wilson's novel *The Man in the Gray Flannel Suit* (1955, with a 1956 film) is one of the better-known fictional translations of these experts' anxieties and concerns.

24. Breines, *Young, White, and Miserable*, 25–46. Breines, Mari Jo Buhle, Barbara Ehrenreich, Ruth Feldstein, and others have traced this particular set of Cold War anxieties about women's power and converging genders back to Philip Wylie's 1942 best seller *Generation of Vipers*, and have argued that its dominance as an ethos structures popular cultural texts like the 1955 film *Rebel without a Cause* (dir. Nicholas Ray). Buhle, *Feminism and Its Discontents*; Ehrenreich, *Hearts of Men*; Feldstein, *Motherhood in Black and White*.

25. Parsons, "Kinship System of the Contemporary United States," 33.

26. As early as 1944, George Kennan articulated fears of gender convergence and American "matriarchy" in the context of the U.S. rivalry with the Soviets he would soon foment. See Costigliola, "Unceasing Pressure for Penetration," 1323.

27. Schlesinger, *Politics of Hope*, 237–38.

28. D'Emilio and Freedman, *Intimate Matters*, esp. 275–300.

29. Savran, *Taking It Like a Man*, 43. Savran identifies the beat writers of the 1950s as the vanguard of this shift in ideology, citing as the most iconic example William Burroughs's murder of his wife, Joan Vollmer, and Burroughs's later conclusion that killing his wife had liberated him from a feminine presence that had possessed him and suppressed his individuality and creativity.

30. John F. Kennedy, quoted in "The Issue of Purpose," *Time*, November 16, 1959.

31. "'Face-to-Face, Nixon-Kennedy' Vice President Richard M. Nixon and Senator John F. Kennedy, Fourth Joint Television–Radio Broadcast (October 21, 1960 ABC, New York, N.Y)," http://www.jfklibrary.org/Research/Research-Aids/JFK-Speeches/4th-Nixon-Kennedy-Debate_19601021.aspx.

32. Hayden, *Port Huron Statement*; Moynihan, *Negro Family*. While these pivotal 1960s documents diagnose different social problems (white male alienation and black poverty, respectively), both prescribe male bonding to solve those problems.

33. Stossel, *Sarge*, 41.

34. Ibid., 42.

35. Quoted in Shorter, *Kennedy Family and the History of Mental Retardation*, 54. Eunice had decided to work with delinquent girls in order to better understand what had happened to her sister Rosemary, whom Joseph Kennedy had decided to lobotomize as a young teenager because of her sexual precociousness. See Kessler, *Sins of the Father*, 222–38.

36. Peter Grothe, "Love and Quiet Charisma," *San Francisco Sunday Examiner and Chronicle*, March 27, 1966.

37. President John F. Kennedy, "Special Message to Congress on Urgent National Needs, May 25 1961," http://www.presidency.ucsb.edu/ws/index.php ?pid=8151.

38. R. Sargent Shriver, "Transcript of Background Press and Radio News Briefing, Monday March 6, 1961, 3:02 p.m.," Files of Jack Vaughn, Box 12, Folder 7, National Archives, College Park, Md.

39. R. Sargent Shriver, "Commencement Address, De Paul University," June 7, 1961, Peace Corps files, National Archives, College Park, Md.

40. See Kaplan, *Anarchy of Empire in the Making of U.S. Culture*.

41. Adamson, "Eisenhower Administration," 61.

42. See Larrain, *Theories of Development*. Saldaña-Portillo builds on Larrain's work to argue that this focus on the transformation of individual subjectivity as a catalyzing force for modernization constituted a second phase of postwar development discourse. If Roosevelt, Truman, and the World Bank theorized economic development as an urgent imperative, Rostow and his contemporaries newly emphasized "subjectivity as the terrain of development," imagining that development will spring from "free subjects making responsible choices at pivotal historical conjunctures." Saldaña-Portillo, *Revolutionary Imagination*, 28–30.

43. See Adas, *Dominance by Design*, 219–80; Escobar, *Encountering Development*; Latham, *Modernization as Ideology*; Gilman, *Mandarins of the Future*; Ekbladh, *Great American Mission*; and Gilbert Rist, *History of Development*.

44. Lerner, *Passing of Traditional Society*, 47–48.

45. Rostow, *Stages of Economic Growth*, 26.

46. Milne, *America's Rasputin*, 38.

47. Gilman, *Mandarins of the Future*, 13.

48. Ibid.

49. For an account of Parsons's influence on other social scientists, see Westad, *Global Cold War*, 33–34.

50. Parsons, *Structure of Social Action*, 553.

51. Ibid., 556.

52. Ibid.

53. Julian Go identifies this elision of empire as part of a larger trend in postwar sociology, arguing that "Parsons's structural-functionalism and associated

studies of 'modernization' were applied to non-European countries but famously abstracted societal developments from its global field," and that "these trends were general to American sociology, as indexed by the decline in *AJS* articles using the terms 'imperialism,' 'empire,' 'colonial,' or 'colonialism.'" He argues that older, empire-bolstering sociological methods persisted, "however in silent form," and were applied to explain domestic as well as international cultural difference. Go, "Sociology's Imperial Unconscious," 102–3.

54. Saldaña-Portillo, *Revolutionary Imagination*, 41–44; Rostow, *Stages of Economic Growth*, 26–27.

55. "Directors' Staff Meeting, February 18, 1966," Files of Jack Vaughn, Box 19, Folder 7, National Archives, College Park, Md.

56. Ibid.

57. Quoted in Gilman, *Mandarins of the Future*, 201.

58. J. Clement Lapp, "The Peace Corps and Community Development," November 30, 1961, Peace Corps Director Files, National Archives, College Park, Md.

59. Eve Sedgwick describes a slightly different but similarly close connection between homosocial desire and imperial penetration, arguing that under European imperialism "a partly Gothic-derived paranoid racist thematics of male penetration and undermining by subject peoples became a prominent feature of national ideology in western Europe. Its culmination is an image of male rape." Sedgwick, *Between Men*, 182.

60. Shriver, *Point of the Lance*, 56.

61. Ibid.

62. Ibid, 35.

63. Shriver initially claimed Gumucio had said, "The Peace Corps will be the point of the lance (punta de lanza) by which our relations will improve on a day-to-day basis. We need do'ers to help do what needs to be done, persons who will be in constant touch with the people." Press conference, November 18, 1961, Box 28, Folder 12, John F. Kennedy Library, Boston.

64. Shriver, *Point of the Lance*, 1.

65. Hoffman, *All You Need Is Love*, 47.

66. Redmon, *Come as You Are*, 147.

67. Ibid., 35.

68. Diana MacArthur, "Memo for the Director re: Pirating," August 15, 1966, Files of Jack Vaughn, Box 18, Folder 2, National Archives, College Park, Md. The memo reads, in part, "it may be time to re-issue a statement on piracy such as the attached dated January 18, 1963," and describes the outrage of the Kaiser Foundation.

69. Stossel, *Sarge*, 12.

70. Bill Moyers, "Memo to Sargent Shriver," August 7, 1963, Moyers Box 41, Folder: Memos—to and from the Director, 1 of 2, John F. Kennedy Library, Boston.

71. Sargent Shriver, "Interview with Michael L. Gillette," Oral Histories, Lyndon B. Johnson Library, Austin.

72. Redmon, *Come as You Are*, 51.

73. Ibid., 52–53.

74. Nathaniel Davis to Shriver, August 20, 1963, Shriver Papers, Box 12, Folder 6; memo to Paul Geren and William Haddad from Shriver, October 5, 1961, Shriver Papers, Box 12, Folder 8, John F. Kennedy Library, Boston.

75. Memo to Warren Wiggins from Deirdre Henderson, August 3, 1961, Shriver Papers, Box 12, Folder 8. Staffer Gordon Boyce reports having "discouraged" four conscientious objectors interested in applying for staff positions. Memo to Shriver from Gordon Boyce, "Re: Candidates for Director of Private Agency Relations," November 13, 1961, Shriver Papers, Box 12, Folder 7, John F. Kennedy Library, Boston.

76. Memo from Bill Haddad to Shriver, August 15, 1961, Shriver Papers, Box 12, Folder 7, John F. Kennedy Library, Boston.

77. Shriver to Donald Petrie, June 20, 1964, Shriver Papers, Box 16, Folder 3, John F. Kennedy Library, Boston.

78. Shriver, "Memorandum to the President," December 7, 1961, Shriver Papers, Box 12, Folder 11, John F. Kennedy Library, Boston.

79. Redmon, *Come as You Are*, 152.

80. Ibid., 34.

81. "A Challenge to Youth," *New York Times*, March 14, 1961.

82. "People on the Way Up: Peace Corpsman," *Saturday Evening Post*, April 21, 1962.

83. Even during volunteers' terms of service, the corporate world was eager to partner with them. Nigeria volunteer science teacher Jim King wrote to his mother in 1966 that her letters on his behalf had speedily yielded "2 Bulletin board sets from General Motors, a beautiful hardback book on glass manufacturing, 5 charts on blood, heart, etc., from American Heart, lots of loot on chemistry from Dow Chemical, some car jazz from Ford, a bushel of pictures and charts from USS Steel [*sic*], pictures + books from AMA, a chart of microscope from Bausch + Lomb and a beautiful American Heritage book, which I'm keeping, from Eastern Connecticut Power," as well as "big bundles of teaching aids" from Pfizer. Jones, *Letters from Nigeria*, 142, 164.

84. Beschloss, *Taking Charge*, 162–63.

85. Redmon, *Come as You Are*, 396.

86. See LaFeber, *Panama Canal*, 108–13.

87. Letter from Jack Vaughn to Sargent Shriver, April 20, 1964, Shriver Papers, Box 14, Folder 1, John F. Kennedy Library, Boston.

88. Redmon, *Come as You Are*, 396.

89. Sedgwick, *Between Men*, 38.

90. Knapp and Knapp, *Red, White, and Blue Paradise*, 70. For another account of villagers protecting volunteers during the flag riots, see Litwack, "Trabajamos Juntos."

2. Integration and Its Limits

1. James Reston, "Lansing, Mich.: What Ever Happened to the Beat Generation?" *New York Times*, March 20, 1964.

2. The Mothers of Invention, "Who Needs the Peace Corps?" *We're Only in It for the Money* (Verve, 1968).

3. Peter Braestrup, "Goal Seems Near for Peace Corps," *New York Times*, September 24, 1961.

4. "Peace Corps in Action" *Life*, Spanish ed., October 16, 1961; Herblock, "Goodness, Are You the Beat and Angry Young Men I've Heard So Much About?" *Washington Post*, March 12, 1961.

5. "The Peace Corps' First Year," *New York Times*, June 25, 1962; Shriver, "Peace Corps," *Saturday Review*, May 19, 1962.

6. Julius Horwitz, "The Peace Corpsman Returns to Darkest America," *New York Times*, October 24, 1965.

7. Marjorie Hunter, "Shriver Leaves behind Thriving Peace Corps," *New York Times*, January 23, 1966.

8. See Harold Taylor, "The New Young Are Now Heard: A Generation Is Emerging Which Asks of Its Elders, 'What Do You Know? What Can You Do?" *New York Times*, January 29, 1961; "Son of Goldwater Confirms Interest in the Peace Corps," *New York Times*, May 5, 1962.

9. Savran, *Taking It Like a Man*, 41–103.

10. See Breines, *Young, White, and Miserable*; Douglas, *Where the Girls Are*; Ehrenreich, *Hearts of Men*; Lhamon, *Deliberate Speed*.

11. Mailer, "White Negro," 306.

12. Baldwin, "Black Boy Looks at the White Boy," in *Nobody Knows My Name*, 216–41; Wallace, *Black Macho and the Myth of the Superwoman*.

13. Among those who explicitly cite *On the Road* as inspirations for travel and activist/countercultural prominence are Tom Hayden and Janis Joplin. See Hayden, *Reunion*, 42; Hogan, *Many Minds, One Heart*, 102; Dalton, *Piece of My Heart*, 162.

14. Kerouac, *On the Road*, 180.

15. Ibid., 2, 7–8.

16. Savran and Saldaña-Portillo both note that Sal and Dean's journey to Mexico at the end of the novel represents an act of patriotism more than one of rebellion or subterfuge; in order to experience the essence of the American frontier myth, they must go somewhere as-yet (as far as they know) unconquered and enact the conquest yet again. Indeed, Mexico represents the climax of Sal and Dean's adventure, the place where they can finally, if briefly, become the conquering heroes they have been attempting to impersonate throughout their travels. Saldaña-Portillo describes *On the Road* as a journey to fulfill the fantasies of consent upon which the United States was founded, arguing that Sal and Dean reenact the North American origin story, which relies on myths of consent and mutually beneficial transactions as opposed to the paternalistic and coercive rhetoric unabashedly used by European colonizers to justify the subjugation of Native peoples. Savran, *Taking It Like a Man*, 41–103; Saldaña-Portillo, "On the Road with Che and Jack."

17. Kerouac, *On the Road*, 297.

18. "Several times I went to San Francisco with my gun and when a queer approached me in a bar john I took out the gun and said 'Eh? Eh?'"; "the car was what Dean called a 'fag Plymouth.'" Ibid., 73, 207. See Savran, *Taking It Like a Man*, 51–71, for a discussion of the beats' displaced/ambivalent homosexuality.

19. See Parsons, "Kinship System of the Contemporary United States"; and my discussion of his relationship to modernization discourse in chapter 1.

20. For example, Sal sighs "like an old negro cotton-picker," and on the next page claims that a group of Okies "thought I was Mexican, and in a way, of course, I am." Ibid., 97–98. For a discussion of this identification more broadly in beat writing, see Savran, *Taking It Like a Man*.

21. Kerouac, *On the Road*, 289.

22. Rice, *Bold Experiment*, 142.

23. Dean, "Masculinity as Ideology," 58.

24. Nancy Romer, telephone interview with author, March 24, 2006; Bob Powers, "AIDS Quilt Panel Remembers Peace Corps Volunteers," http://www.lgbrpcv.org/articles/quilt.htm; Zimmerman, *Innocents Abroad*, 142.

25. Schlesinger, *Vital Center*, 46.

26. Ibid.

27. O'Connor, *Poverty Knowledge*, 115.

28. Gilman, *Mandarins of the Future*, 172.

29. Lerner, *Passing of Traditional Society*, 411.

30. Ibid., 412.

31. Ibid., 49–50.

32. Lacan, "The Mirror Stage as Formative of the Function of the I." For a concise explanation of the mirror stage, see Gallop, *Reading Lacan*, 74–92.

33. Lerner, *Passing of Traditional Society*, 72.

34. Ibid., 177.

35. Margery Michelmore, a Nigeria volunteer, dropped a postcard referring to "primitive conditions" in the country, which caused anti–Peace Corps riots throughout Lagos.

36. In fact, the United States tied its aid on the Volta River project to the continued Peace Corps presence in the country. See Gaines, *American Africans in Ghana*, 165.

37. *Edward P. Morgan and the News*, ABC, March 16, 1962.

38. C. Klein, *Cold War Orientalism*.

39. Speech of Senator John F. Kennedy, Cow Palace, San Francisco, Calif., November 2, 1960.

40. Dean, *Imperial Brotherhood*, 173.

41. Fischer, *Making Them Like Us*, 32–33.

42. Burdick and Lederer, *Ugly American*, 277.

43. Nashel, *Edward Lansdale's Cold War*, 33; Thomas, *Very Best Men*, 57.

44. Shalom, "Counter-Insurgency in the Philippines."

45. Nashel, *Edward Lansdale's Cold War*, 1.

46. Ibid., 81–84.

47. Fisher, *Dr. America*, 81.

48. Tom Scanlon, a volunteer who served in Chile from 1961 to 1963, recalls that Dooley, "a brash humanitarian," was "a prototype of the Peace Corps volunteer." Recalling Dooley's inspiring presence at his 1960 Notre Dame graduation, Scanlon attributes his decision to join the Peace Corps to Dooley's example, writing that "the Soviet Union was winning impoverished people prepared to make the Faustian bargain of trading their human freedom for material progress. Dooley had a profound understanding of this and acted accordingly." Scanlon, *Waiting for the Snow*, 2.

49. Burdick and Lederer, *Ugly American*, 110.

50. Von Eschen, *Satchmo Blows Up the World*.

51. Burdick and Lederer, *Ugly American*, 112.

52. Mary Louise Pratt uses the term "anti-conquest" to describe representations in travel writing through which bourgeois adventurers consolidate the imperial project by claiming innocence and vulnerability to native peoples. Pratt, *Imperial Eyes*, 7.

53. Burdick and Lederer, *Ugly American*, 174, 180.

54. Ibid., 159, 155–71.

55. Ibid., 199, 201, 204.

56. Ibid., 206, 205, 220.

57. Ibid., 224, 149–50, 234–35.

58. Cowan, *Making of an Un-American*, 105.

59. Rostow, *Stages of Economic Growth*, 20.

60. Peter Easton, "The Crucial Ingredients of Volunteer Impact on Counterparts," *Peace Corps Volunteer*, January 1967.

61. Fanon, *Wretched of the Earth*, 37.

62. Easton, "Crucial Ingredients of Volunteer Impact on Counterparts."

63. Mead Over, "The Counterpart: Binationalism at the Volunteer Level," *Peace Corps Volunteer*, August 1969.

64. B. P. R Vithal, "New Fences and New Frontiers: Problems and Prospects of Peace Corps Service as Seen by an Indian Official," *Peace Corps Volunteer*, June 1967.

65. Richard B. Stolley, "The Re-entry Crisis," *Life*, March 19, 1965.

66. Ibid.

67. Thomsen, *Living Poor*, viii.

68. Ibid., 104, 106.

69. Ibid., 165.

70. Ibid., 193, 247.

71. Ibid., 226, 124.

72. Ibid., 261–62.

73. Ibid., 313–14.

74. Cowan, *Making of an Un-American*, 32–33.

75. Ibid., 79.

76. Ibid., 105, 213–14, 198.

77. Jones, *Letters from Nigeria*, 20, 40, 52.

78. Levitt, *African Season*, 62–63.

79. E. Smith, *Where to, Black Man?* 44–45 (ellipses are Smith's).

80. Elizabeth Roseberry, "Report from Mattru, Jong," Returned Peace Corps Volunteer Country Files, John F. Kennedy Library, Boston.

81. E. Smith, *Where to, Black Man?* 52.

3. Breaking the Bonds

1. Willard Van Dyke, dir., *So That Men Are Free*.

2. Ibid.

3. Stein, *Deconstructing Development Discourse in Peru*, 21.

4. See Babb, *Development of Sexual Inequality in Vicos*, for an account of women's exclusion from productive work at Vicos; Babb argues that women lost significant social status as a result of the project.

5. Van Dyke, dir., *So That Men Are Free*.

6. Stein, *Deconstructing Development Discourse in Peru*, 27.

7. "Report Measures PCV Impact," *Peace Corps Volunteer*, January 1966.

8. Dobyns, Doughty, and Holmberg, *Peace Corps Program Impact*, 68–69.

9. "Vicos: A Hard Lesson," *Peace Corps Volunteer*, January 1966.

10. "Sex Makes an Impact," *Peace Corps Volunteer*, January 1966; Dobyns, Doughty, and Holmberg, *Peace Corps Program Impact*, 260–64.

11. Warren W. Wiggins, "Who Are We," address at Voorhees Chapel, Douglass College, New Brunswick, N.J., October 13, 1964, 9–10, Sargent Shriver Papers, Box 23, Folder 5, John F. Kennedy Library, Boston.

12. Ibid.

13. The Peace Corps was quite reluctant to hire women in higher-level staff positions, despite urging from the likes of Eleanor Roosevelt. See Larry Dennis to Sargent Shriver, July 20, 1961; Sargent Shriver to Eleanor Roosevelt, March 20, 1961; unsigned memo, March 20, 1961; Sargent Shriver to Roger Kent, August 29, 1962; Eleanor Roosevelt to Sargent Shriver, October 2, 1961; résumé of Cobey Black, undated, all in Sargent Shriver Papers, John F. Kennedy Library, Boston.

14. Friedan, *Feminine Mystique*, 120.

15. Ibid., 385.

16. Louchheim, "November 17, 1961, National Council of Negro Women," 181–82.

17. Kaplan, *Anarchy of Empire in the Making of U.S. Culture*; Wexler, *Tender Violence*.

18. Louchheim, "November 17, 1961, National Council of Negro Women," 185.

19. Wingenbach, *Peace Corps*, 65.

20. Melosh's *Engendering Culture* traces the dissemination of similar frontier myths in New Deal culture.

21. "Project Gains Backing of Most Undergraduates—Women Eager: Students Backing Peace Corps Plan," *New York Times*, March 6, 1961.

22. "Peace Corps Woman Injured," *New York Times*, July 19, 1962.

23. "Peace Corps Girls to Teach in Arabic," *New York Times*, February 26, 1967; "Co-ed Volunteers for Peace Corps from Wheel Chair," *New York Times*, April 11, 1965; "5 Peace Corps Girls Tardy in Liberia after Sahara Trek," *New York Times*, March 8, 1964.

24. Lloyd Garrison, "Nigerian Marries Peace Corps Girl," *New York Times*, December 27, 1964. For statistics on volunteer marriage to "host nationals" see "The Married Corps" *Peace Corps Volunteer*, December 1964.

25. "Peace Corps Teacher Weds Sherpa in Nepal," *New York Times*, May 23, 1966.

26. "Diary of a Hitchhike across the Sahara: Peace Corps Girls' Own Story of a Rollicking Adventure," *Life*, April 17, 1964.

27. "Sahara Hitchhike," *Life*, April 8, 1964.

28. "And Away They Go!" *Time*, September 8, 1961.

29. Anonymous e-mail survey, received October 13, 2009.

30. Laura Damon, interview with author, Chautauqua, N.Y., January 9, 2010.

31. Susan Strane, interview with author, Cambridge, Mass., September 30, 2010.

32. Breines, *Young, White, and Miserable*, 11, 23.

33. Anonymous e-mail survey, received October 17, 2009.

34. P. Cowan, *Making of an Un-American*, 78.

35. R. Cowan, *Growing Up Yanqui*, 32.

36. P. Cowan, *Making of an Un-American*, 78.

37. In addition to the works discussed in the remainder of this chapter, see Cosgrove, *Ann Gordon of the Peace Corps*; de Leeuw, *Behold This Dream*; James, *Kathy Martin: Peace Corps Nurse*; Knebel, *Zinzin Road*; Levin, *Safari Smith*; Payes, *Peace Corps Nurse*; David Rodgers, *Peace Corps Girls*; Sullivan, *Peace Corps Nurse*; and Wiley, *Assignment*.

38. Friedan, *Feminine Mystique*, 38.

39. James, *Kathy Martin: African Adventure*, 16.

40. Kaplan, *Anarchy of Empire in the Making of U.S. Culture*; McAlister, *Epic Encounters*.

41. James, *Kathy Martin: African Adventure*, 28.

42. Spencer, *Breaking the Bonds*.

43. Ibid., 3.

44. Ibid., 33.

45. Ibid., 67.

46. Ibid., 72–73. A similar incident occurred within the Nigeria I group after the Margery Michelmore postcard incident; the Nigerian students initially told volunteers to sit at a separate table in the dining hall, but they staged a hunger strike until the students apologized to them. Interview with Aubrey Brown, Boston, June 16, 2010.

47. Pratt, *Imperial Eyes*, 38.

48. Spencer, *Breaking the Bonds*, 145.

49. Kahler, *Enslaved in Ebony*, 108.

50. Chavre, *Peace Corps Bride*, 6.

51. Ibid., 116.

52. "African Tells How to Seduce," *Jet*, October 9, 1969.

53. Evans, *Personal Politics*, 81.

54. Emma Brockes, "Travel Is Nasty," *The Guardian*, June 9, 2003.

55. Pratt, *Imperial Eyes*, 217.

56. Theroux, *Girls at Play*, 9.

57. Ibid., 9–10.

58. Ibid., 59.

59. Ibid., 58.

60. James, *Kathy Martin: Peace Corps Nurse*, 35.

61. Theroux, *Girls at Play*, 59–60, 68, 70.

62. Ibid., 71, 186, 190.

63. Ibid., 190.

64. Laurence Lafore, "Terror and Cruelty, Dressed in Wit and Irony," *New York Times*, September 28, 1969.

65. Jack Maher, "They Didn't Do Right by Judy," *Billboard*, May 4, 1963.

66. "Theater: Poor Judy," *Time*, April 26, 1963.

67. For a typical laudatory review, see Bosley Crowther, "Screen: 'The Ugly American' Opens: Marlon Brando Stars as the U.S. Diplomat," *New York Times*, April 12, 1963. The film also garnered two Golden Globe nominations.

68. Sondheim, Rodgers, and Charnin, "Don't Laugh."

69. Hayden and King, "Sex and Caste." For accounts of SNCC and SDS meetings, see Barber, *Hard Rain Fell*; and Frost, *Interracial Movement of the Poor*.

70. Sally Yudelman, "Finding Jobs for Women," *Peace Corps Volunteer*, October 1968.

71. Carolyn Burgin, Nano Byrnes Podolsky, Paula Limburg, Joan Noonan Andrea Velozo, and Katie Whitaker, "Project Report, Azuero Women's Program," 1968, Returned Peace Corps Volunteer Collection, Box 9, Folder 5, John F. Kennedy Library, Boston.

72. Ibid.

73. Ibid.

74. Castro, *Provocaciones*, 106.

75. "What PCVs Think of Their Service: A Summary of 4,260 Termination Conference Questionnaires," *Peace Corps Volunteer*, November 1967. More than a quarter of health workers reported satisfaction with their work, compared with 86 percent of agricultural volunteers.

76. Gwynne Douglass, "That Girl in the Fourth Row," *Peace Corps Volunteer*, March 1965.

77. Alice O'Grady, interview with M. B. Smith, summer 1963, Returned Peace Corps Volunteer Collection, Box 65. See also Zimmerman, *Innocents Abroad*, 147–48.

78. Gaudino, *Uncomfortable Learning*, 28.

79. Ibid., 139–40.

80. "Jack Vaughn Takes to the Road," *Peace Corps Volunteer*, May 1966.

81. "Director's Staff Meeting," November 29, 1961, Sargent Shriver Papers, 5, John F. Kennedy Library, Boston.

82. Ibid., 2–3.

83. "The Pleasures and Pain of the Single Life," *Time*, September 15, 1967.

84. Larry Hayes, "Big Sis or Plain Jane?" *Peace Corps Volunteer*, December 1967. See also F. Kingston Berlew, "Special Report: Are We Getting 'Bland' Volunteers?" *Peace Corps Volunteer*, January 1964; "Volunteer as Social Enemy Number One" *Peace Corps Volunteer*, January 1967.

85. Schwarz, *What You Can Do for Your Country*, 60.

86. Kay Dixon, telephone interview with author, April 18, 2006.

87. "Director's Staff Meeting," November 29, 1961, Sargent Shriver Papers, 5, John F. Kennedy Library, Boston.

88. Frieda Fairburn, interview with author, Chautauqua, N.Y., January 10, 2010.

89. Schubert, "She's White but She's Black Too," 131.

90. Ibid., 127.

91. Carol Clover explores a similar dynamic when she describes the "double axes of gender and city/country" in *Deliverance* and other films, a parallel that constructs "the city as metaphoric rapist of the country." Clover, *Men, Women, and Chainsaws*, 129.

92. Schubert, "She's White but She's Black Too," 129–30.

93. Ibid., 133.

94. A reference to Vicos turns up in one of the Peace Corps girl novels, Jack Denton Scott's 1969 action/adventure novel *Elephant Grass*, in dialogue spoken by sophisticated volunteer Marthe: "Anyway, here's another letter. Right from the *New York Times*, says my uncle. A team of Cornell University anthropologists sponsored by our government spent two years in the Peruvian Andes studying the activities of fifty Peace Corps volunteers. 'They reported that some of the girls tried to get along on sheer sex appeal, posing a problem for the male volunteers and Peruvian men.' She smiled fetchingly and uncrossed her legs." Scott, *Elephant Grass*, 173.

95. M. Young, *Vietnam Wars*, 141.

96. Weiss, *American Taboo*.

97. Povinelli, *Economies of Abandonment*, esp. 1–46.

98. Breines, *Young, White, and Miserable*, ix.

99. This turn away from movement activism is somewhat borne out by large-scale studies of volunteers: though John W. Cotton reports that college

students who decide to serve in the Peace Corps are slightly more likely to be involved in protest and other activism than average college students, he also cites studies that show that over the course of their service in the 1960s, volunteers became less interested in others and more driven by "the desire to satisfy personal needs or develop oneself." Cotton, "Par for the Corps," 390.

100. Alice O'Grady, interview with author, Chautauqua, N.Y., January 10, 2010.

101. Ibid.

102. Anonymous e-mail survey, received October 16, 2009.

103. Echols, *Daring to Be Bad*, 279.

104. Dixon, interview with author.

105. Anonymous e-mail survey, received October 31, 2009.

106. While I am arguing here that the discourses of modernization and development inhibit structural social critique, particularly of the feminist variety, I am not arguing that second-wave feminism was free of developmentalist thinking. For a revelatory account of how the development agendas (and money) of USAID and the Ford and Rockefeller Foundations shaped the feminist journal *Signs* in the 1970s, see Coogan-Gehr, *Geopolitics of the Cold War and Narratives of Inclusion*.

107. Gaudino, *Uncomfortable Learning*, 216–17.

108. O'Grady, interview with author.

109. Connie Jaquith, telephone interview with author, July 24, 2009.

4. Bringing the Peace Corps Home

1. Young and Rubicam Inc., "Leave the Country," 1968 Peace Corps public service announcement, http://collection.peacecorps.gov/cdm/singleitem/collection/p9009coll16/id/12.

2. Young and Rubicam Inc., "I Didn't Join the Peace Corps for the Greatest Reasons." 1968 Peace Corps public service announcement, http://collection.peacecorps.gov/cdm/ref/collection/p9009coll16/id/17.

3. Dudziak, *Cold War Civil Rights*, 252.

4. Gilman, *Mandarins of the Future*, 18; Edwards, *Charisma and the Fictions of Black Leadership*.

5. For a discussion of the suppression of prewar black radicalism during the Cold War see Gilmore, *Defying Dixie*. Accounts of gender inequality in the transition to Black Power include Fleming, "Black Women and Black Power," and Griffin, "Ironies of the Saint." Recent scholars who have attempted to complicate this frame include Green, "Challenging the Civil Rights Narrative."

6. Lewis and D'Orso, *Walking with the Wind*, 167.

7. Kennedy, "Special Message to Congress on Urgent National Needs." Eric Foner also points out this juxtaposition. See Foner, "Bound for Glory," *New York Times*, March 19, 2006.

8. Wofford, *Of Kennedys and Kings*, 124.

9. Johnson's background working on New Deal projects in Texas influenced his ideas about development (see chapter 5), and the New Deal's social and economic engineering projects influenced many other modernization theorists and development workers. In his recent book *The Great American Mission*, David Ekbladh argues that the success of New Deal projects exercised tremendous symbolic power over the United States' global modernization efforts. However, this chapter elaborates the argument begun in chapter 2 that the focus on nonwhite poverty in postwar social science discourses, both at home and abroad, meant that development workers and popular cultural accounts told significantly different stories about the "underdeveloped" populations they encountered than New Deal administrators had told about the whites who were their main focus.

10. Shriver, *Point of the Lance*, 17.

11. Zimmerman, "Beyond Double Consciousness," 1008.

12. Wofford, *Of Kennedys and Kings*, 93, 98.

13. Ibid., 164–65.

14. Scheper-Hughes, "Way of an Anthropologist Companheira," 101.

15. R. Cowan, *Growing Up Yanqui*, 31.

16. O'Connor, *Poverty Knowledge*, 115.

17. Lewis's language of cultural poverty echoed progressive-era discourses of immigrant assimilation and racial uplift. Framing racial uplift ideology as a revision of Victorian theories of white supremacy that would allow middle-class African Americans a chance at assimilation through the correct performance of bourgeois cultural values, Kevin Gaines argues persuasively that "uplift's representation of class through evolutionary cultural differences based on patriarchal family norms and bourgeois values informed a liberal social science discourse after World War II that explained poverty and ghettoization as pathologies of family disorganization rather than as the result of systemic factors such as exclusion from the labor market and housing discrimination." Although sociologist E. Franklin Frazier famously criticized the black bourgeoisie and racial uplift ideology, he echoed the underlying tenets of uplift in his 1939 work *The Negro Family in America*, arguing that black "motherhood has been free on the whole from institutional and communal control and the woman has played the dominant role." He contended that this dominance constituted family "disorganization" that could be remedied by "assimilation and acculturation" as black men were given better industrial jobs. David Luis-Brown offers a related, transnational

genealogy of the focus on "culture" in the work of anthropologists like Franz Boas, Zora Neale Hurston, and Manuel Gamio in the early twentieth century. He writes that this shift from "racial to cultural discourses" effected by these politically committed anthropologists "at times, pushed forward the possibilities of the political agency of the darker races" and even constituted "a new wave of decolonization." At the same time, he recognizes that "the ethnographic discourse that the Boasian shift from race to culture ushered in could be quite conservative—even reactionary—in its political implications." See Gaines, *Uplifting the Race*, 11; Frazier, *Negro Family in the United States*, 106–7; Luis-Brown, *Waves of Decolonization*, 160.

18. O'Connor, *Poverty Knowledge*, 113–17.

19. Harrington, *Other America*, 10.

20. Ibid., 14.

21. Gay Talese, "Peace Corps Trainees Learn Work in City Slums," *New York Times*, October 11, 1962. For other articles on training in slums and on Indian reservations see "Peace Corps 'Dream' Now Called Practical," *Los Angeles Times*, March 25, 1962; "Peace Corps Recruits Train in D.C. Slums," *Washington Post*, September 6, 1966; "Peace Corps Group Ends Slum Training," *Washington Post*, August 1, 1967.

22. William Beecher, "Kennedy Aides Ponder a Peace Corps to Toil within United States: Volunteers Would Minister to Slum Dwellers, Migrants, Indians, Mental Patients," *Wall Street Journal*, November 15, 1962. See also "The Home Front Peace Corps," *Chicago Daily Tribune*, March 10, 1961; "Slum Children a New Challenge to Peace Corps Group," *Washington Post*, September 8, 1963.

23. O'Connor, *Poverty Knowledge*, 117–23.

24. Beschloss, *Taking Charge*, 204.

25. Wofford, *Of Kennedys and Kings*, 295.

26. Sargent Shriver, interview with Michael L. Gillette, October 23, 1983, Oral Histories, Lyndon B. Johnson Library, Austin.

27. In a 1980 interview, Shriver explicitly differentiates the "cultural poverty" afflicting nonwhite communities from the kind of poverty white men suffered from during the Great Depression: "[The forestry camp program] was much more applicable when Roosevelt did it in the thirties than it was when Johnson came along in the sixties. First, because the entire productive process of the United States had changed significantly. But secondly, because people who went in the CCC camps were people like Lyndon Johnson or me. If you go back and look at the pictures of the CCC camp people, they were all young, middle-class men. And most of them were white. We had then in the sixties, and we have today, a totally different clientele that's unemployed now as compared to those who were unemployed then." See Sargent Shriver, interview with

Michael L. Gillette, August 20, 1980, Oral Histories, Lyndon B. Johnson Library, Austin.

28. Moynihan, *Negro Family*, 29.

29. Ibid., 42–43.

30. O'Connor, *Poverty Knowledge*, 204.

31. Patterson, *Freedom Is Not Enough*, 44.

32. Ibid., 59–60.

33. See Self, *All in the Family*, for a thorough discussion of Moynihan and Shriver's "breadwinner liberalism."

34. Rainwater and Yancey, *Moynihan Report and the Politics of Controversy*, 14.

35. "President Lyndon B. Johnson's Commencement Address at Howard University: 'To Fulfill These Rights,' June 4, 1965," http://www.lbjlib.utexas.edu/johnson/archives.hom/speeches.hom/650604.asp.

36. See Parsons, "Kinship System of the Contemporary United States"; Rostow, *Stages of Economic Growth*; and my discussion of both in chapter 1.

37. Joseph, *Waiting 'Til the Midnight Hour*, 122; King quoted in Lowdnes et al., *Race and American Political Development*, 265.

38. Horne, *Fire This Time*, 3.

39. Schulman, *Lyndon B. Johnson and American Liberalism*, 113.

40. Bauman, *Race and the War on Poverty*, 42. King conflated poverty with weakness; two years later, speaking against the Vietnam War, he would make a similar argument about the Vietnamese nationalists, using dominant developmentalist conceptions of Third World passivity to write of "voiceless" peasants and their "broken cries," even as those peasants waged a revolutionary struggle in which they would defeat the most powerful army in the world. Martin Luther King Jr. "Declaration of Independence from the War in Vietnam," *Ramparts*, May 1967.

41. Martin Luther King Jr., "Next Stop: The North," *Saturday Review*, April 3, 1965, 34.

42. Rist, *History of Development*, 124.

43. Slate, *Colored Cosmopolitanism*, 204–5.

44. "Text of Martin Luther King Jr.'s 'I Have a Dream' Speech," *San Diego Union-Tribune*, August 28, 2013, http://www.utsandiego.com/news/2013/Aug/28/martin-luther-king-i-have-a-dream/3/?#article-copy.

45. Hogan, *Many Minds, One Heart*, 20. Belinda Robnett argues that the nonhierarchical structure of SNCC before 1965 allowed for many people, especially women, to act as "bridge leaders," informal leaders who facilitated connections between the movement and particular communities. Robnett, *How Long? How Long?* 12–35.

46. Raiford, *Imprisoned in a Luminous Glare*.

47. Hogan, *Many Minds, One Heart*, 244.

48. Frost, *Interracial Movement of the Poor*, 34. Clayborne Carson argues that SDS encouraged SNCC to shift its focus to economic issues after 1964. Carson, *In Struggle*, 177.

49. Edwards, *Charisma and the Fictions of Black Leadership*, 168–69.

50. King, "Where Do We Go from Here?" 246.

51. Cleaver, *Soul on Ice*, 84.

52. Donna Jean Murch reports that in the "loose study group" of UC Berkeley and San Francisco State University students that, in dialogue with street rallies, became the early Bay Area Black Power movement, E. Franklin Frazier's *Black Bourgeoisie* was a key text. Though Murch documents how the study group vigorously debated the question of the survival of African traditions, it is less clear that they debated the virtues (or the existence) of black matriarchy or the characterizations of black families as "disorganized." Murch, *Living for the City*, 84–87.

53. See Wallace, *Black Macho and the Myth of the Superwoman*. More recently Roderick Ferguson has made an argument similar to Wallace's, tracing the strict heteronormativity imposed on black communities by social scientists. See R. Ferguson, *Aberrations in Black*.

54. Seale, *Seize the Time*, 35.

55. Ibid., 99–102.

56. Crowe, *Prophets of Rage*, 174–75.

57. Baraka, *Autobiography of Leroi Jones*, 213.

58. Ibid., 214.

59. "Poverty: Six-Star Sargent," *Time*, March 18, 1966.

60. Accounting for the influence of modernization theory on the civil rights movement as it radicalized allows us to reconcile competing views held by scholars of the War on Poverty's relationship to black liberation struggles. One view, recently advanced by William Clayson in his study of the War on Poverty and the movement in Texas, stresses the importance of both "the great hope the War on Poverty initially held out to activists" and "the sense of resentment that emerged when results failed to measure up to expectations" as well as "the extent to which OEO programs subsidized civil rights activism." Clayson and others argue that the War on Poverty provided space and resources to activists, both bolstering and radicalizing the movement when conservative administrators dashed activists' hopes. See Clayson, *Freedom Is Not Enough*, 4. The second group of scholars inverts this argument, echoing Harold Cruse's 1967 claim that "anti-poverty administration is like a lightning rod that draws off the potential energy of the poor—energy that could be galvanized into meaningful political and economic resistance against capitalistic poverty." See Cruse, *Crisis of the*

Negro Intellectual, 93. Contending that the poverty programs tempered the movement's radicalism, recent scholars like Harold S. Jolly (who neatly draws a parallel between U.S. foreign and domestic "puppets") argue that "the War on Poverty threatened to undermine the Black Power movement by co-opting its precious resources and [to] create a puppet regime of middle-class African Americans who would maintain law and order, thus protecting their interests at the expense of African American interests." See Jolly, *Black Liberation in the Midwest*, 142. More recently, Devin Fergus has made a similar if more ambivalently valenced argument, arguing that the history of Black Power is one of "liberalism's capacity to reform revolution," particularly in the 1970s as more and more Black Power activists entered electoral politics and focused their energies on providing public services that might have moved the United States toward social democracy. Fergus, *Liberalism, Black Power, and the Making of American Politics*, 11.

61. Saldaña-Portillo, *Revolutionary Imagination*, 264.

62. Ibid., 270.

63. Ibid., 266.

64. Seale, *Seize the Time*, 3.

65. Carr, *Black Nationalism in the New World*, 192.

66. Seale, *Seize the Time*, 4.

67. Baraka, *Autobiography of Leroi Jones*, 194.

68. Ibid., 200–201.

69. Seale, *Seize the Time*, 235.

70. Ibid., 237–40. This reading of the Panther leadership's break with the mass base of their movement echoes Joshua Bloom and Waldo Martin's conclusions in their political history of the party. They argue that particularly in the early 1970s, concessions from the government and pressure from white liberal donors impelled the national party leadership to moderate its stances, attempt to work within the power structure, and clamp down on the revolutionary impulses of local chapters in favor of a service-based, social democratic program. (Cornel West makes a slightly more extreme version of this argument in 1984, contending that "the revolt of the black masses precipitated a deep crisis . . . among the 'new' black petite bourgeoisie," indicating that "beneath the rhetoric of Black Power, black control, and black self-determination was a budding 'new' black middle class hungry for power and starving for status.") It also draws on Frances Fox Piven and Richard A. Cloward's 1977 insights that Black Power leaders' attempts to suppress and channel "spontaneous" riots and protests allowed leaders to take advantage of the concessions the liberal establishment offered, while simultaneously diminishing the pressure on the government to extend those concessions more broadly to the poor and working-class base of the movement. Bloom and Martin, *Black against Empire*, esp. 339–89; West,

"Paradox of the Afro-American Rebellion," 52; Piven and Cloward, *Poor People's Movements*, 181–263.

71. Baraka, *Autobiography of Leroi Jones*, 260, 266, 273, 274.

72. Moody, *Coming of Age in Mississippi*, 405.

73. "Stokely Carmichael (1941–1998), Speech at University of California, Berkeley, October 29, 1966," http://americanradioworks.publicradio.org/features/sayitplain/scarmichael.html.

74. Ibid.

75. Von Eschen, *Race against Empire*, 160.

76. McClintock, *Imperial Leather*, 41.

77. Zimmerman, "Beyond Double Consciousness," 107.

78. "Black Graduates See the Peace Corps as a Costly Interlude," *Peace Corps Volunteer*, July–August 1968.

79. Juanita Ann Covington, "My Experiences in Ethiopia," *The Crisis*, March 1964.

80. Smith, *Where to, Black Man?* 19.

81. Ibid., 52–53.

82. Wallace, *Invisibility Blues*, 19.

83. E. Smith, *Where to, Black Man?* 74.

84. "Needed: Abroad or at Home?" *Peace Corps Volunteer*, July–August 1968.

85. Ibid.

86. Ibid.

87. For a discussion of reproductive futurism see Edelman, *No Future*. This ethos in black nationalism is described incisively in Toni Cade Bambara's collection *The Black Woman*.

88. Wallace, *Black Macho and the Myth of the Superwoman*, 81

89. Moynihan, *Negro Family*, 197.

90. Baraka, *Autobiography of Leroi Jones*, 216.

91. See Roberts, *Killing the Black Body*. For more on population control and development, see chapter 6.

92. Bambara, *"The Pill,"* in *Black Woman*, 205, 206.

93. Ibid., 211.

94. Bambara, "On the Issue of Roles," in *Black Woman*, 124.

95. Wu, *Radicals on the Road*, 147.

96. Ibid., 148.

97. Ibid., 152.

5. Ambiguous Liberation

1. Warren Wiggins, "From Applied Altruism to Nation Building," Stanford University, Stanford, Calif., October 11, 1965, 1, Papers of Jack Hood Vaughn, Box 12, Folder 7, National Archives, College Park, Md.

2. Ibid., 3.

3. Ibid.

4. Ibid., 5.

5. Oglesby, *Ravens in the Storm*, 90.

6. Kopkind refers to an SDS pamphlet by Paul Booth and Lee Webb. See Breines, *Community and Organization in the New Left*, 76.

7. Andrew Kopkind, "The Peace Corps' Daring New Look," *New Republic*, February 5, 1966. Around the same time, Kopkind wrote, "in ways which journalists themselves perceive dimly or not at all, they are bought or compromised, or manipulated into confirming the official lies." Quoted in McMillian, *Smoking Typewriters*, 84.

8. Kopkind's observation also suggests that the Peace Corps shared a vision of heroic masculinity with the new left, which in the absence of a unifying ideology also relied on notions of rugged adventure and images of seductive male heroes. Van Gosse argues similarly that the new left "drew more from liberalism than from the [old left]; . . . [it] was grounded in a deep if inchoate sympathy with long-oppressed peoples; who were themselves part of the [new left] . . . at the core of this interaction were volcanic tensions over gender roles among middle-class white people." Gosse, *Where the Boys Are*, 255.

9. Wiggins, "From Applied Altruism to Nation Building."

10. Shriver to Johnson, "Weekly Report of Peace Corps Activities," April 27, 1965, National Security Files, Agency File, Box 42, Folder 1, Lyndon B. Johnson Library, Austin.

11. Ibid., May 4, 1965.

12. Schwarz, *What You Can Do for Your Country*, 82.

13. Ibid.

14. Ibid.

15. Szulc, *Dominican Diary*, 75.

16. Kopkind, "Peace Corps' Daring New Look"; P. Cowan, *Making of an Un-American*, 78.

17. Speech of Senator John F. Kennedy, Cow Palace, San Francisco, Calif., November 2, 1960.

18. Speech of Senator John F. Kennedy, Conference on Vietnam Luncheon in the Hotel Willard, Washington, D.C., June 1, 1956.

19. Latham, *Modernization as Ideology*, 154.

20. M. Young, *Vietnam Wars*, 141.

21. Ibid. Johnson was neither the first nor the last U.S. policy-maker to imagine U.S. military intervention as seduction and/or rape. Histories of these discourses and practices include A. Smith, *Conquest*; Enloe, *Bananas, Beaches, and Bases*; Jeffords, *Hard Bodies*; C. Weber, *Faking It*.

22. Halberstam, *Best and the Brightest*, 470.

23. On rape committed by U.S. soldiers in Vietnam, see Turse, *Kill Anything That Moves*.

24. Address of President Lyndon Baines Johnson, John Hopkins University, Baltimore, Md., April 7, 1965.

25. Butterfield, *U.S. Development Aid*, 94.

26. "Personal Notes of a Meeting with President Johnson," 511.

27. William S. Gaud to McGeorge Bundy, "Ex-Peace Corps Personnel for Vietnam," May 12, 1964, National Security Files, Peace Corps File, Box 42, Lyndon B. Johnson Library, Austin.

28. USAID Washington, "Recruitment for Vietnam," March 20, 1964, National Security Files, Peace Corps File, Box 42, Lyndon B. Johnson Library, Austin.

29. Memo from David K. Bell to Sargent Shriver, April 20, 1964, National Security Files, Peace Corps File, Box 42, Lyndon B. Johnson Library, Austin; Latham, *Modernization as Ideology*, 195.

30. "Associate Directors Meeting," November 16, 1965, Office Files of the Regional Director, Box 13, Folder 5, Peace Corps Papers, National Archives, College Park, Md.

31. "Associate Directors Meeting," January 19, 1966, Peace Corps Papers, Box 13, Folder 5, National Archives, College Park, Md.

32. Luce and Sommer, *Viet Nam*, 231–32.

33. Terry, *Bloods*, 87.

34. Ibid., 90.

35. "Peace Corps Planner Expects Draft-Free Status for Enlistees" *New York Times*, February 13, 1961.

36. "Exemptions Are Sought," *New York Times*, October 21, 1965. See also Mark R. Killingsworth, "Topics: Civilian Service Instead of the Draft," *New York Times*, February 15, 1969; Fred P. Graham, "Law: Again the Tough Issue of the C.O.," *New York Times*, April 6, 1969; "Hesburgh Urges College for All Who Serve Nation for a Year," *New York Times*, June 1, 1969; James Reston Jr., "Vietnamize at Home," *New York Times*, August 10, 1971.

37. Peace Corps Office of Public Information, "The Peace Corps and the Draft," November 14, 1966, 2, Office Files of the Director, Box 19, Folder 1, National Archives, College Park, Md.

38. "Peace Corps Volunteer Deemed as Vital to U.S. as Serviceman," *New York Times*, December 9, 1966.

39. Paul Theroux, "When the Peace Corps Was Young," *New York Times*, February 25, 1986; Scheper-Hughes, "Way of an Anthropologist Companheira," 102.

40. Faith Fogle, interview with author, Providence, August 2009.

41. Connie Jaquith, telephone interview with author, July 24, 2009.

42. Susan Strane, interview with author, Cambridge, Mass., August 31, 2010.

43. Office of the White House Press Secretary, "Remarks of the President on Occasion of Fifth Anniversary of the Peace Corps and Swearing-in Ceremony of Jack Hood Vaughn as Director of the Peace Corps in the East Room, as Actually Delivered," March 1, 1966, Shriver Papers, Box 15, Folder 10, John F. Kennedy Library, Boston.

44. Young and Rubicam Inc., "Make Your Own Peace," 1968 Peace Corps Public Service Announcement, http://collection.peacecorps.gov/cdm/ref/collection/p9009coll16/id/18.

45. "The Peace Corps: Yankee, Don't Go Home!" *Time*, January 28, 1966.

46. Greene, *Quiet American*.

47. Peter Grothe, "Love and Quiet Charisma," *San Francisco Sunday Examiner*, March 27, 1966, Vaughn Files, Box 12, National Archives, College Park, Md.

48. Kopkind, "Peace Corps' Daring New Look," 19; Jack Vaughn, "A Poet and Peasant Overture," *Peace Corps Volunteer*, March 1965.

49. Jack Vaughn, "Now We Are Seven," *Saturday Review*, January 6, 1968.

50. See Langland, *Speaking of Flowers*, 127.

51. Jones, *Letters from Nigeria*, 124.

52. Ibid., 73

53. Theroux, "Cowardice," 41.

54. Gaudino, *Uncomfortable Learning*, 223.

55. Surveys of returned Peace Corps volunteers from the mid-to-late 1960s suggest that this increased focus on "desires to satisfy personal needs or develop oneself" at the close of service was common. See Cotton, "Par for the Corps," 390.

56. Gilbert, *Love and Struggle*, 87.

57. United States Congress, *Civilian Casualty, Social Welfare, and Refugee Problems in South Vietnam*, 315.

58. "Are We Losing the 'Other War'?" *New York Times*, September 15, 1967, 44.

59. Schwarz, *What You Can Do for Your Country*, 111.

60. "Dissent: Peace Corps on the Line," *Peace Corps Volunteer*, March–April 1970.

61. Wofford, *Of Kennedys and Kings*, 301.

62. "Workshop Reports," *Peace Corps Volunteer*, April 1965.

63. "Rusk: Peace Takes Effort," *Peace Corps Volunteer*, April 1965.

64. Wofford, *Of Kennedys and Kings*, 307.

65. Ibid.

66. Ibid., 309.

67. Brown, interview with author.

68. Ibid.

69. Joe Stork, interview with author, Washington, D.C., June 17, 2010.

70. Evans, *Journeys That Opened Up the World*, 183.

71. "We, the Undersigned, Oppose the War in Vietnam," *Ramparts*, September 1967, 61.

72. "On Preparing to Debate Vietnam," *Committee of Returned Volunteers Newsletter*, September 1967, 11.

73. Wofford, *Of Kennedys and Kings*, 437.

74. Rita Sklar and Joe Sklar, "Abolish the Peace Corpse," *Movement*, January 1970.

75. Che Guevara, "Message to the Tricontinental," Havana, April 16, 1967.

76. Sklar and Sklar, "Abolish the Peace Corpse."

77. Brown, interview with author.

78. Ibid.

79. One member of the Weather Underground, Diana Oughton, had been radicalized in her two-year stint as a volunteer teacher in Guatemala with the American Friends Service Committee (she never worked for the Peace Corps or joined the CRV, though many 1960s memoirs and histories as well as a 1975 TV movie erroneously characterize her as a Peace Corps girl) and would soon after die in the infamous West Village townhouse bomb-building accident that forced the group underground; Hageman recalls that Oughton was the only Weather delegate who spoke fluent Spanish. Alice Hageman, interview with author, Boston, June 16, 2010; Powers, *Diana*. For characterizations of Oughton as a Peace Corps girl, see Sale, *SDS*; Berger, *Outlaws of America*; Rudd, *Underground*; Hayden, *Reunion*; and the publicity for the 1975 made-for-television movie starring Sissy Spacek titled *Katherine* (dir. Jeremy Kagan).

80. J. W. Fulbright, "The Great Society Is a Sick Society: Says Senator Fulbright," *New York Times*, August 20, 1967.

81. Andy Berman, "Smash the Politics of Guilt! A Brief Reply to Lynn Weikart," *CRV Newsletter*, October 1970.

82. "The People's Peace Treaty," *CRV Newsletter*, December 1970.

83. See Malarney, *Culture, Ritual, and Revolution in Vietnam*.

84. "CRV: 'Abolish Peace Corps," *NACLA Newsletter*, November 1969.

85. Evans, *Journeys That Opened Up the World*, 183.

86. James Herod, "The Counter-Inaugural Demonstration," *CRV Newsletter*, February 1969.

87. While there is certainly some truth to this characterization of movement activists (perhaps particularly in the CRV) as divorced from the working

class, the story is somewhat more complicated, and the popular memory of white working-class support for the war is a distortion; in fact, Americans with less education opposed the war at significantly higher rates than did those with more education. See Lewis, *Hardhats, Hippies, and Hawks*.

88. Brown, interview with author.

89. Ibid.

90. "Women Act!" *CRV Newsletter*, August 1970. While the president was male and the group attempting to restore collective decision-making was female, the demands of the new collective were not explicitly feminist.

91. Stork, interview with author.

92. Qureshi, *Nixon, Kissinger, and Allende*, 160; Diana Jean Schemo, "FBI Watched an American Who Was Killed in Chile Coup," *New York Times*, July 1, 2000; Marc Cooper, "Letter from Santiago," *The Nation*, June 3, 2002. Teruggi's disappearance is fictionalized in the 1982 Costa-Gavras film *Missing*.

93. Nguyen, *Gift of Freedom*, 45.

94. Max Elbaum, Van Gosse, and others caution that the reduction of the new left to SDS badly distorts the breadth of new left activism, particularly erasing the more expansive, diverse, and radical new left that emerges in the late 1960s. I agree with these scholars that the new left cannot be reduced to SDS or the white students; however, I am chiefly interested here in tracing the organizational style and trajectory of SDS in the early-to-mid 1960s, partly because of their many connections and resonances with that of the Peace Corps and the CRV. See Gosse, *Rethinking the New Left*; Elbaum, *Revolution in the Air*.

95. The Peace Corps and SDS also share the presence of United Auto Workers at their founding: John Barnard argues that Walter Reuther came up with and promoted "the germ of the Peace Corps" in the 1950s, in the form of a UN-sponsored technical assistance program. SDS, for its part, drafted *The Port Huron Statement* at a UAW summer camp. Barnard, *American Vanguard*, 344, 420.

96. Goodman, *Growing Up Absurd*, 6.

97. Ibid., 21–22, 42.

98. Among others, Wini Breines argues that Goodman's ideas were pivotal to the new left. She cites a 1965 SDS pamphlet reading "SDS was formed by radical intellectuals, influenced by C. Wright Mills, Paul Goodman, and Camus." Breines, *Community and Organization*, 83.

99. Hayden, *Port Huron Statement*, 47.

100. Ibid., 49–50.

101. Ibid., 51–52.

102. Hayden, *Reunion*, 132. Hayden has continued to admire the Peace Corps: in a 2010 speech he called on Barack Obama to expand the agency,

recalling the heroic "hijos de Kennedy" who "refused to leave their barrios" in the Dominican Republic in 1965, and proclaiming, "The Peace Corps remains a shining example of what US foreign policy might be, and the 200,000 or more Peace Corps graduates in this country are a great and permanent force for service and internationalism." Tom Hayden "The Peace Corps at Fifty," *Huffington Post*, http://www.huffingtonpost.com/tom-hayden/the-peace-corps-at-fifty_b_7601 20.html.

103. Oglesby, *Ravens in the Storm*, 92.

104. Ibid.

105. Rossinow, *Politics of Authenticity*, 17.

106. Frost, *Interracial Movement of the Poor*, 153.

107. Oglesby, *Ravens in the Storm*, 233–34.

108. D. Berger, *Outlaws of America*; Varon, *Bringing the War Home*. I am not suggesting that the movement disappeared with the schism in its leadership. Wini Breines's important 1982 assessment of the new left emphasizes "the resistance of the *movement*, the thousands of people who sat down at the Pentagon or fought the police in the streets of Oakland, to the *leadership*, the organizers, the organization," and what she calls the prefigurative politics of the movement—an existential emphasis on self-realization through action that resisted attempts at hierarchical structure or even coordination. However, the focus on self-expression and brotherhood Breines emphasizes, as much as SDS leaders' more direct experiments with development, seems compatible with the Peace Corps' own vision. Breines, *Community and Organization*, 37.

109. In identifying countercultural currents, I do not mean to draw a neat separation between the counterculture and the "political" new left, which Marilyn Young reminds us "overlapped in terms of personnel, practices, anticapitalist yearnings, and occasional tactics; they were mutually enforcing." Breines concurs, arguing that "in the period until 1968 there was great continuity between the hippie and political wings of the movement." Young, "Ho, Ho, Ho Chi Minh," 226; Breines, *Community and Organization*, 20.

110. For the archetypal example of this juxtaposition of "phony hippies" and authentic development workers, see my discussion of Frank Zappa's "Who Needs the Peace Corps?" in chapter 2.

111. Accounts of development are largely absent from the critical evaluations of the 1960s radicalism and its demise, even as more triumphalist accounts of the decade's liberalism trace clear links between the development ethos and movement cultures. One early exception is Frederic Jameson's 1984 essay "Periodizing the 60s," which argues for the importance of development to the 1960s "First World" movements. In the essay, he argues that the particular form of the global social upheaval of the decade—the foco-revolutionary, cultural nationalist,

and otherwise identity-based movements—was both analogous to and dependent on the Green Revolution and other aspects of the modernization regime, tactics that achieved "a far more thoroughgoing form of penetration and colonization than the older colonial armies." Jameson identifies some of the confluences I have been tracing in this chapter, particularly the way discourses of individual liberation became thoroughly bound up in the modernization project, coming to mean liberation from one's own community, land, and labor, as well as from colonialism. However, in making his sweeping connection between this "ambiguous liberation" that happened at the moment of decolonization and the liberatory dreams of what he calls the "superstructural" movements in the United States, Jameson adheres to an orthodox Marxist model that makes it difficult for him to account for development's lasting impact on social and cultural life. For Jameson, this particular transitional and "liberatory" phase of capitalism makes it temporarily impossible to articulate class grievances, so that movement demands remain at the level of politics and culture rather than economics; he predicts that class will, and must, reassert itself in the neoliberal period. See Jameson, "Periodizing the 60s," 207. Perhaps even more in line with this book's analysis, its sense of the development regime's role in the new left's interest in and disillusionment with both liberal and Marxist teleological structures, is Thomas Pynchon's great countercultural novel *The Crying of Lot 49*, in which questing heroine Oedipa Maas wanders around a Berkeley campus that looks like a Third World university, "the sort that bring governments down"; tangles with conservative fringe groups that are against "industrial anything"; and sits through horrifically violent Jacobean revenge plays. Pynchon, *Crying*, 71, 51.

6. The Peace Corps, Population Control, and Cultural Nationalist Resistance in 1960s Bolivia

1. Gumucio-Dagron, "Yawar Mallku."

2. *La Prensa*, March 1970.

3. "El Esteril Ayuda del Cuerpo de Paz," *El Nacional*, May 26, 1971.

4. Richard West, "Why Latin Americans Say 'Go Home, Yanqui,'" *New York Times*, May 29, 1966.

5. Rivera Cusicanqui, *Oprimidos pero no vencidos*, 53. For a detailed discussion of the rural uprisings, organizing, and agitation leading up to the revolution, see Gotkowitz, *Revolution for Our Rights*.

6. Firsthand accounts of the urban portion of the 1952 revolution can be found in Murillo, *La bala no mata sino el destino*.

7. Rivera Cusicanqui, *Oprimidos pero no vencidos*, 60.

8. Grindle and Domingo, *Proclaiming Revolution*, 4–5; Zunes, "United States and Bolivia."

9. H. Klein, *Bolivia*, 238.

10. For a thorough discussion of military modernization in 1960s Bolivia, see Field, *From Development to Dictatorship*.

11. Samuel D. Eaton to Douglas P. Henderson, October 15, 1963, Douglas Henderson Papers, Box 1, Folder 1, John F. Kennedy Library, Boston.

12. Dunkerley, *Rebellion in the Veins*, 149.

13. Westad, *Global Cold War*, 178.

14. Hedrick Smith, "Peace Corps Aims at Latin Nations: New Policy Shifts Emphasis from Africa and Asia," *New York Times*, December 3, 1962; Charles Costello and John Guy Smith, "Overseas Evaluation: Bolivia," February 2, 1968, Records of the Peace Corps, Box 1, Folder 1, National Archives, College Park, Md.

15. Ashabranner, *Moment in History*, 164.

16. With respect to the veracity of Vaughn's story, Ashabranner writes diplomatically, "I have no doubt that Vaughn saw all those things in the five Bolivian villages that he visited after becoming assistant secretary of state," but also that "Vaughn wanted to see success. He did not want to see failure." Ibid., 165.

17. James Frits, "The Peace Corps in Bolivia," Returned Peace Corps Volunteer Collection, Box 36, Folder 7, John F. Kennedy Library, Boston.

18. Stuart Goldschen, diary, Box 36, Folder 7, John F. Kennedy Library, Boston.

19. Frits, "Peace Corps in Bolivia," 8–9.

20. Richard Griscom, "BOLIVIA: Impetus Is to East in Land Beset by Geography," *Peace Corps Volunteer*, February 1965.

21. Denis Regan and Mickey Melragon, "Alto Beni: A New Life," *Peace Corps Volunteer*, February 1965.

22. Chad Bardone, letter to friends, December 29, 1964, Peace Corps Files, Folder 50, National Anthropological Archives, Suitland, Md.

23. Rivera Cusicanqui, "Que el pasado sea futuro," 112. My translation.

24. Renato Rosaldo has referred to this feeling as "imperialist nostalgia." Rosaldo, *Culture and Truth*, 68–90.

25. Chad Bardone, letter to friends, June 25, 1965, Box 10, Folder 30, Peace Corps Volunteer Papers, National Anthropological Archives, Suitland, Md.

26. For more information about the beliefs of the millennialist Guaraní people Bardone encountered, see Clastres, *La Tierra sin mal*.

27. Camille Falkett to Maude Swingle, May 13, 1965, Maude Swingle Papers, Schlesinger Library, Cambridge, Mass.

28. Gino Baumann to Allen W. Rothenberg, August 8, 1967, Bauman Papers, Box 1, Folder 2 (Chronology Files, June–October 1967), Lyndon B. Johnson Library, Austin; also Baumann to Rothenberg, October 4, 1967.

29. Carol Weser, telephone interview with author, August 24, 2010.

30. McEwen, *Changing Rural Society*, 203.

31. Ibid., 204.

32. Baumann, "National Community Development Programme," 194–95.

33. Ibid.

34. Jaquith, telephone interview with author.

35. Ibid.

36. Camille Falkett to Maude Swingle, August 8, 1965, Maude Swingle Papers, Schlesinger Library, Cambridge, Mass.

37. Falkett to Swingle, October 13, 1965, ibid.

38. Falkett to Swingle, August 8, 1965, ibid.

39. Falkett to Swingle, December 6, 1965, February 4, 1966, ibid.

40. Falkett to Swingle, June 10, 1965, ibid.

41. John Dwan, e-mail correspondence with author, August 26, 2010.

42. See Connolly, *Fatal Misconception*, 194.

43. Schlesinger, *Thousand Days*, 188.

44. John F. Kennedy, "Special Message to the Congress on Foreign Aid: March 22, 1961," http://www.presidency.ucsb.edu/ws/index.php?pid=8545.

45. Connolly, *Fatal Misconception*, 199.

46. Ibid., 212.

47. Wofford, *Of Kennedys and Kings*, 279.

48. Ravenholt, "A.I.D. Population and Family Planning Program," 562.

49. Nelson, "Birth Rights," 45–47.

50. Baumann, letter to Dr. J. Fine, July 20, 1967, and Baumann, letter to Gary Peterson, August 29, 1967, in Baumann Papers, Box 1, Folder 2, Lyndon B. Johnson Library, Austin.

51. Baumann, "Memo," December 17, 1968, Baumann Papers, Box 2, Folder 1, Lyndon B. Johnson Library, Austin.

52. Jaquith, telephone interview with author.

53. Janet Pitts Brome, "Bolivia Journal, 1965–7," RPCV Collection, Box 2, Folder 12, John F. Kennedy Library, Boston.

54. Connolly, *Fatal Misconception*, 205.

55. Pope, *Sahib*, 20

56. Ibid., 21.

57. Ibid., 118. Both Nick Cullather and James Scott write persuasively of development discourse's reduction of complex lived realities to "populations" and numerical values; see Cullather, *Hungry World*; and Scott, *Seeing Like a State*.

58. Nelson, "Birth Rights," 39–40.

59. West, "Why Latin Americans Say 'Go Home, Yanqui.'"

60. Siekmeier, "Sacrificial Llama?"

61. "Las hijas de unsubsecretario de estado y un senador se destacan hoy en el grupo de mas de mil personas que se han ofrecido voluntariamente para someterse a la ardua vida del 'cuerpo de paz' propesta por el presidente JFK," *Ultima Hora*, March 3, 1961.

62. "Voluntarios Para La Paz," *Ultima Hora*, June 23, 1961.

63. "La politica del 'gringo bueno,'" *El Diario*, March 10, 1961; "Arribará hoy el 1er grupo de voluntarios del CDP," *El Diario*, June 30, 1962; "Voluntarios del CDP expresaron su decision de trabajar por nuestro pais," *El Diario*, July 2, 1962.

64. "El Campesino de Cochabamba busca su propia desarrollo," *El Diario*, September 14, 1967.

65. Alberto Ayala, "Formar hombres," *El Diario*, January 22, 1967.

66. "Fuerzas Armadas y desarrollo," *Presencia*, December 6, 1966.

67. "Desarrollo del oriente Boliviano," *Ultima Hora*, December 16, 1967.

68. "Poblaciones preferidas," *Prensa Libre*, August 12, 1966.

69. "La fertilidad incontrolada y capacidad de destruir el medio ambiente son una seria amenaza para la especie humana," *El Diario*, January 8, 1967.

70. "La planificacion familiar es una necesidad mundial," *Ultima Hora*, May 26, 1967.

71. "Despoblamiento de Bolivia," *Presencia*, July 20, 1968, in Nelson, "Birth Rights."

72. McNamara said in the speech, "The World Bank is concerned above all with economic development, and the rapid growth of population is one of the greatest barriers to the economic growth and social well-being of our member states." McNamara, "Address to Board of Governors," 66.

73. "Senado recomienda investigación de denuncia contra Cuerpo de Paz," *Presencia*, December 11, 1968.

74. Canelas, *Radiografía de la alianza para el atraso*, 182–83.

75. Dependency theory, formulated by Latin American economists and sociologists in the 1960s, responded to the persistence of poverty and exploitation in the postwar Third World despite the preponderance of modernization networks and promises. Such theorists argued that the rhetoric of universal modernization masked a neocolonial exploitative global order, positing that the "developed" core relied on the persistent undevelopment of the periphery.

76. Thomas Field vividly details this kidnapping, including Vice President Juan Lechín successfully negotiating the return of the U.S. captives without the labor leaders' release, over the vociferous objections of the more militant

factions of the group (mainly the women in the militant Housewives' Committee), as well as Fergerstrom and USIA officer Thomas Martin's subsequent sympathy with the kidnappers and outrage that the mining leaders had not been released in return for their own freedom. Field, *From Development to Dictatorship*, 98–130.

77. "Violencia universitaria: Pedreas y saqueos a dos dependencias del EEUU en Cochabamba," *El Diario*, February 19, 1967.

78. Joint embassy/USIA message to Secretary of State, October 1968, quoted in Nelson, "Birth Rights," 60.

79. Cables, U.S. embassy to Bolivian Foreign Ministry, May 31, 1968 (Doc # 350); June 25, 1968 (Doc #379); August 9, 1968 (Doc #438); August 20, 1968 (Doc #450); August 23, 1968 (Doc #449); October 27, 1969 (Doc #309); August 23, 1970 (Doc #289), Archivo de Relaciones Exteriores, La Paz.

80. "Pacifica manifestacion universitaria recorrio how las calles de la ciudad: Al concluir grupos reducidos intentaron atacar el centro Boliviano–Americano y Embajada Argentina," *Ultima Hora*, May 2, 1969.

81. Sanjinés, "Revolutionary Cinema," 45–47.

82. Jorge Sanjinés, dir. *Yawar Mallku (Blood of the Condor)*. My translations.

83. Povinelli, *Empire of Love*.

84. Rivera Cusicanqui, *Oprimidos pero no vencidos*, 117.

85. Ibid., 145.

86. "Tiwanaku Manifesto," 1973, in ibid., 169–77.

87. Ibid.

88. See Saldaña-Portillo, *Revolutionary Imagination*, esp. 63–106.

89. Here I borrow from Anne McClintock's explanation of postcolonial cultural nationalist temporality. McClintock, *Imperial Leather*, 296–396.

90. Burton, Cinema and Social Change, 40.

91. Povinelli, *Empire of Love*, 228–33.

92. Barrios de Chungara, *Let Me Speak!* 199–200.

93. Ibid., 198.

94. Escobar, "Latin America at a Crossroads," 5. Evo Morales is Bolivia's first indigenous president; his political power and philosophy, and that of his MAS government, grew out of the indigenous mobilizations of the early 2000s; some of the MAS members who have surrounded and advised him, particularly in the early years of his presidency, were active in the Katarista movement.

95. Ibid., 44, 10–11.

96. Ibid., 41.

97. Ibid.

98. Spivak, *Critique of Postcolonial Reason*.

99. Nila Heredia, interview with author, December 10, 2009, La Paz.

100. Felipa Huanca Yupanqui, interview with author, February 23, 2010, La Paz.

101. For a similar formulation of the discourse around abortion in Bolivia, see Kimball, "An Open Secret."

102. Julieta Paredes, e-mail correspondence with author, December 17, 2009. Maria Galindo, fellow founder of Mujeres Creando, echoes this sentiment: "Although no one wants to recognize that in our society, just as military service has been obligatory for men, women have been obligated to have babies, live for them, and forget about themselves. Motherhood as abnegation and prison is now abolished to make way for free motherhood, meaning a woman will be a mother when she wants and decides to and will have the number of children she wants to." Galindo, *¡A Despatriarcar!* 202.

Conclusion

1. Baldwin, "Princes and Powers," in *Nobody Knows My Name*, 29.

2. For critical *New York Times* coverage see Sheryl Gay Stolberg, "Trail of Medical Missteps in Peace Corps Death," *New York Times*, July 25, 2014; Michael Rosson, "Peace Corps Volunteers in Their Own Words," *New York Times*, July 25, 2014; Stolberg, "Peace Corps Volunteers Speak Out on Rape," *New York Times*, May 10, 2011.

3. Meisler, *When the World Calls*, 178–217.

4. Obama, *Dreams from My Father*, 150.

5. Barack Obama, "Remarks by the President at the Millennium Goals Development Summit in New York, New York," September 22, 2010, http://www.whitehouse.gov/the-press-office/2010/09/22/remarks-president-millennium-development-goals-summit-new-york-new-york.

6. Gabriella Schwarz and Jessica Yellin, "Obama in Tanzania, Sees Africa as Next Global Economic Success," *CNN*, July 1, 2013, http://www.cnn.com/2013/07/01/world/africa/tanzania-obama/.

7. Fox, *Making Art Panamerican*, 215.

8. Karim, *Microfinance and Its Discontents*, xxv.

9. Sahle, *World Orders*.

10. Mortenson, *Three Cups of Tea*, 206, 257. Michelle Murphy has recently argued that "the girl" has become a prominently recognizable "figure of transnational rescue and investment," an "iconic vessel of human capital" who legitimates military interventions as well as transnational corporations "philanthrocapitalist" efforts in the name of a future in which she yields higher-than-expected returns. Murphy, "The Girl." Mortenson's account reinforces this commonsense characterization of girls as high-yield investments, arguing in an

oft-quoted passage that "if you really want to change a culture, to empower women, improve basic hygiene and health care and fight high rates of infant mortality, the answer is to educate girls" (209).

11. Nicholas Kristof, "It Takes a School, Not Missiles," *New York Times*, July 13, 2008.

12. Elisabeth Bumiller, "Unlikely Tutor Giving Military Afghan Advice," *New York Times*, July 17, 2010; Julie Bosman and Stephanie Strom, "'Three Cups of Tea' Author Defends Book," *New York Times*, April 17, 2001; "Greg Mortenson, 'Three Cups of Tea' Author, to Repay Charity," *Reuters*, April 5, 2012.

13. See Chandrasekaran, *Little America*; Andrew J. Bacevich, "War on Terror: Round 3," *Los Angeles Times*, February 19, 2012.

14. J. Ferguson, *Expectations of Modernity*, 237–38. Silvia Rivera Cusicanqui writes of a similar sense of abjection among miners in Bolivia after the implementation of austerity measures in the 1980s: "A century of cultural attacks on the miner–Andean and artisan behaviors of self-sufficiency, removal from capitalist rationality, and ritualization of labor relations finally achieved worker discipline . . . but just at the culmination of this process of cultural change, suddenly all the safeguards secured in decades of integration disappear . . . the sudden disappearance of labor gains, that had cost decades of struggle, could do nothing less then leave in their thousands of victims the bitter taste of deceit and a legitimate thirst for revenge or compensation." Rivera Cusicanqui, *Violencias (re)encubiertas en Bolivia*, 108.

15. One of the recent violent rejections of the new militarized, privatized Western modernity has been, amid the chaos and desperation of the brutally unequal petrostate of Nigeria, the formation of Boko Haram (whose name loosely translates as "Western Education Is Forbidden") and their attacks on schoolgirls. See Watts, *Silent Violence*, xli–xcv.

16. John Nichols, "How Sargent Shriver Helped John Kennedy Become a Liberal," *The Nation*, January 20, 2014; Claire Potter, "Why Won't Obama Talk about the Poor?" *Tenured Radical*, February 2, 2014, http://chronicle.com/blog network/tenuredradical/2014/02/8271/.

17. Sachs, *To Move the World*, 160–62.

18. See "50 Years after March on Washington, Tens of Thousands Say Struggle for MLK's 'Dream' Continues," *Democracy Now*, August 26, 2013; "'Don't Punish the Poor': Economist Jeffrey Sachs Slams Obama–GOP Budget Deal," April 11, 2011; Jeffrey Sachs, "Occupy Wall Street and the Demand for Economic Justice," *Huffington Post*, October 13, 2011, http://www.huffington post.com/jeffrey-sachs/occupy-wall-street-and-th_b_1007609.html.

19. N. Klein, *Shock Doctrine*, 67.

20. Michael Moore's 2009 film *Capitalism: A Love Story* follows Klein in its nostalgic orientation, critiquing the rise of neoliberal capitalism by expressing a profound nostalgia for the postwar (Jim Crow, Vietnam, prefeminist) era with lines like "Mom could work if she wanted, but she didn't have to."

21. Mark McGurl, "Ordinary Doom," 333. Daniel Rodgers's *Age of Fracture* also participates in this longing for "big ideas."

22. J. Ferguson, *Expectations of Modernity*, 257.

23. Briggs, "Activisms and Epistemologies," 91.

24. The now-familiar formulation emphasizes developing countries' desire to pollute. See Emma McBryde, "China May Slow but India Still Loves Coal," *The Observer*, September 19, 2014; Ben Wolfgang, "Obama Pleas to China, India to Forgo Use of Coal Falls of Deaf Ears," *Washington Times*, July 3, 2014; Peter Galuzska, "With China and India Ravenous for Energy, Coal's Future Seems Assured," *New York Times*, November 12, 2012.

25. See Escobar, "Latin America at a Crossroads."

26. See Gutiérrez Aguilar, *Los ritmos del Pachakuti*; Otramérica, "TIPNIS: Amazonia en resistencia contra el Estado colonial en Bolivia" (2013 report).

27. See for example Emily Achtenberg, "Women at the Forefront of the Tipnis Struggle," *NACLA*, August 17, 2012, http://nacla.org/blog/2012/8/17/women-forefront-bolivia%E2%80%99s-tipnis-conflict.

28. For accounts of how development ideology has guided Western feminism, particularly as it found a home in the academy, see Kabeer, *Reversed Realities*; Mohanty, *Feminism without Borders*; and Coogan-Gehr, *Geopolitics of the Cold War*.

BIBLIOGRAPHY

Adamson, Michael R. "'The Most Important Single Aspect of Our Foreign Policy?': The Eisenhower Administration, Foreign Aid, and the Third World." In *The Eisenhower Administration, the Third World, and the Globalization of the Cold War*, edited by Kathryn C. Statler and Andrew L. Johns, 47–72. Oxford, U.K.: Rowman and Littlefield, 2006.

Adas, Michael. *Dominance by Design: Technological Imperatives and America's Civilizing Mission*. Cambridge, Mass.: Belknap Press, 2009.

Amin, Julius A. *The Peace Corps in Cameroon*. Kent, Ohio: Kent State University Press, 1992.

Ashabranner, Brent K. *A Moment in History: The First Ten Years of the Peace Corps*. Garden City, N.Y.: Doubleday, 1971.

Azevedo, Cecilia. *Em nome da América: Os Corpos da Paz no Brasil*. Sao Paulo: Alameda, 2008.

Babb, Florence. *The Development of Sexual Inequality in Vicos, Peru*. Buffalo: Council on International Studies, SUNY Buffalo, 1976.

Baldwin, James. *Nobody Knows My Name: More Notes of a Native Son*. New York: Vintage, 1992 [1961].

Bambara, Toni Cade. *The Black Woman: An Anthology*. New York: Washington Square Press, 1970.

Baraka, Amiri. *The Autobiography of LeRoi Jones*. Chicago: Lawrence Hill Books, 1997 [1984].

Barber, David. *A Hard Rain Fell: SDS and Why It Failed*. Oxford: University of Mississippi Press, 2008.

Barnard, John. *American Vanguard: The United Autoworkers during the Reuther Years, 1935–1970*. Detroit: Wayne State University Press, 2004.

Barrios de Chungara, Domitila. *Let Me Speak! Testimony of Domitila, a Woman of the Bolivian Mines*. New York: Monthly Review Press, 1978.

Bauman, Robert. *Race and the War on Poverty: From Watts to East L.A.* Norman: University of Oklahoma Press, 2008.

Baumann, Gerold. "The National Community Development Programme in Bolivia and the Utilization of Peace Corps Volunteers." *Community Development Journal* 5, no. 4 (1970): 191–96.

Bederman, Gail. *Manliness and Civilization: A Cultural History of Gender and Race in the United States, 1880–1917.* Chicago: University of Chicago Press, 1996.

Berger, Dan. *Outlaws of America: The Weather Underground and the Politics of Solidarity.* New York: AK Press, 2005.

Berger, Mark T. *Under Northern Eyes: Latin American Studies and U.S. Hegemony in the Americas, 1898–1990.* Bloomington: Indiana University Press, 1995.

Beschloss, Michael, ed. *Taking Charge: The Johnson White House Tapes, 1963–64.* New York: Simon and Schuster, 1997.

Bloom, Joshua, and Waldo Martin. *Black against Empire: The History and Politics of the Black Panther Party.* Berkeley: University of California Press, 2013.

Borgwardt, Elizabeth. *A New Deal for the World: America's Vision for Human Rights.* Cambridge, Mass.: Harvard University Press, 2005.

Borstelmann, Thomas. *The Cold War and the Color Line: American Race Relations in the Global Arena.* Cambridge, Mass.: Harvard University Press, 2001.

Boserup, Ester. *Woman's Role in Economic Development.* New York: Earthscan, 2007 [1970].

Breines, Wini. *Community and Organization in the New Left.* New Brunswick, N.J.: Rutgers University Press, 1989 [1982].

———. *Young, White, and Miserable.* Chicago: University of Chicago Press, 1992.

Briggs, Laura. "Activisms and Epistemologies: Problems for Transnationalisms." *Social Text* 26, no. 4 (1998): 79–95.

———. *Reproducing Empire: Race, Sex, Science, and U.S. Imperialism in Puerto Rico.* Berkeley: University of California Press, 2002.

Buhle, Mari Jo. *Feminism and Its Discontents: A Century of Struggle with Psychoanalysis.* Cambridge, Mass.: Harvard University Press, 1998.

Burdick, Eugene, and William J. Lederer. *The Ugly American.* New York: Norton, 1999 [1958].

Burton, Julianne, ed. *Cinema and Social Change in Latin America: Conversations with Filmmakers.* Austin: University of Texas Press, 1986.

Butterfield, Samuel Hale. *U.S. Development Aid—an Historic First: Achievements and Failures in the Twentieth Century.* Westport, Conn.: Greenwood, 2004.

Canelas, Amado. *Radiografía de la alianza para el atraso.* La Paz: Altiplano, 1963.

Cardwell, Curt. *NSC 68 and the Political Economy of the Early Cold War.* Cambridge, U.K.: Cambridge University Press, 2011.

Carr, Robert. *Black Nationalism in the New World: Reading African American and West Indian Experience.* Durham, N.C.: Duke University Press, 2002.

Carson, Clayborne. *In Struggle: SNCC and the Awakening of Black America.* Cambridge, Mass.: Harvard University Press, 1995.

Castro, Rafaela G. *Provocaciones: Letters from the Prettiest Girl in Arvin.* San Jose, Calif.: Chusma House, 2003.

Chakrabarty, Dipesh. *Provincializing Europe: Postcolonial Thought and Historical Difference.* Princeton, N.J.: Princeton University Press, 2000.

Chandrasekaran, Rajiv. *Little America: The War within the War for Afghanistan.* New York: Vintage, 2012.

Chavre, Renee. *Peace Corps Bride.* El Cajón, Calif.: Pompeii Press, 1969.

Christiansen, Samatha, and Zachary A. Scarlett, eds. *The Third World in the Global 1960s.* New York: Berghahn Books, 2013.

Clastres, Helene. *La Tierra sin mal: El profetismo tupí-guaraní.* Buenos Aires: Del Sol, 1975.

Clayson, William S. *Freedom Is Not Enough: The War on Poverty and the Civil Rights Movement in Texas.* Austin: University of Texas Press, 2010.

Cleaver, Eldridge. *Soul on Ice.* New York: Delta, 1999.

Clover, Carol. *Men, Women, and Chainsaws: Gender in the Modern Horror Film.* Princeton, N.J.: Princeton University Press, 1993.

Connolly, Matthew. *Fatal Misconception: The Struggle to Control World Population.* Cambridge, Mass.: Belknap Press, 2008.

Coogan-Gehr, Kelly. *The Geopolitics of the Cold War and Narratives of Inclusion: Excavating a Feminist Archive.* New York: Macmillan, 2011.

Cooper, Frederick. "Development, Modernization, and the Social Sciences in the Era of Decolonization: The Examples of British and French West Africa." *Revue d'Histoire des Sciences Humaines* 1, no. 10 (2004): 9–38.

Cooper, Frederick, and Randall Packard, eds. *International Development and the Social Sciences: Essays on the History and Politics of Knowledge.* Berkeley: University of California Press, 1997.

Cosgrove, Rachel. *Ann Gordon of the Peace Corps.* New York: Avalon Books, 1965.

Costigliola, Frank. *Roosevelt's Lost Alliances: How Personal Politics Helped Start the Cold War.* Princeton, N.J.: Princeton University Press, 2012.

———. "'Unceasing Pressure for Penetration': Gender, Pathology, and Emotion in George Kennan's Formation of the Cold War." *Journal of American History* 83, no. 4 (1997): 1309–39.

Cotton, John. "Par for the Corps: A Review of the Literature on Selection, Training, and Performance of Peace Corps Volunteers." Unpublished MS, University of California, Santa Barbara, 1975.

Cowan, Paul. *The Making of an Un-American: A Dialogue with Experience.* New York: Viking Press, 1970.

Cowan, Rachel. *Growing Up Yanqui*. New York: Viking Press, 1975.

Crosby, Emilye, ed. *Civil Rights History from the Ground Up: Local Struggles, a National Movement*. Athens: University of Georgia Press, 2011.

Crowe, Daniel E. *Prophets of Rage: The Black Freedom Struggle in San Francisco, 1945–69*. New York: Garland, 2000.

Cruse, Harold. *Crisis of the Negro Intellectual*. New York: NYRB Book Classics, 2005 [1967].

Cullather, Nick. *The Hungry World: America's Cold War Battle against Poverty in Asia*. Cambridge, Mass.: Harvard University Press, 2010.

Dalton, David. *Piece of My Heart: A Portrait of Janis Joplin*. New York: Da Capo Press, 1991.

Dean, Robert D. *Imperial Brotherhood: Gender and the Making of the Cold War*. Amherst: University of Massachusetts Press, 2003.

———. "Masculinity as Ideology: John F. Kennedy and the Domestic Politics of Foreign Policy." *Diplomatic History* 22, no. 1 (1998): 29–63.

D'Emilio, John, and Estelle Freedman. *Intimate Matters: A History of Sexuality in the United States*. Chicago: University of Chicago Press, 1997.

De Leeuw, Adele. *Behold This Dream*. New York: McGraw Hill, 1968.

Dobyns, Henry F., Paul L. Doughty, and Allan R. Holmberg. *Peace Corps Program Impact in the Peruvian Andes: Final Report*. Ithaca, N.Y.: Cornell Peru Project, 1966.

Douglas, Susan J. *Where the Girls Are: Growing Up Female with the Mass Media*. New York: Three Rivers Press, 1994.

Dudziak, Mary. *Cold War Civil Rights: Race and the Image of American Democracy*. Princeton, N.J.: Princeton University Press, 2000.

Dunkerley, James. *Rebellion in the Veins: Political Struggle in Bolivia, 1952–1982*. London: Verso, 1984.

Echols, Alice. *Daring to Be Bad: Radical Feminism in America, 1967–1975*. Minneapolis: University of Minnesota Press, 1989.

Edelman, Lee. *No Future: Queer Theory and the Death Drive*. Durham, N.C.: Duke University Press, 2004.

Edwards, Erica. *Charisma and the Fictions of Black Leadership*. Minneapolis: University of Minnesota Press, 2012.

Ehrenreich, Barbara, *The Hearts of Men: American Dreams and the Flight from Commitment*. Garden City, N.Y.: Anchor Press / Doubleday, 1984.

Ekbladh, David. *The Great American Mission: Modernization and the Construction of an American World Order*. Princeton, N.J.: Princeton University Press, 2010.

Elbaum, Max. *Revolution in the Air: Sixties Radicals Turn to Lenin, Mao, and Che*. New York: Verso, 2002.

Engerman, David C., Nils Gilman, Mark Haefele, and Michael E. Latham, eds. *Staging Growth: Modernization, Development, and the Global Cold War*. Amherst: University of Massachusetts Press, 2003.

Enloe, Cynthia. *Bananas, Beaches, and Bases: Making Feminist Sense of International Politics*. Berkeley: University of California Press, 2000.

Escobar, Arturo. *Encountering Development: The Making and Unmaking of the Third World*. Princeton, N.J.: Princeton University Press, 1995.

———. "Latin America at a Crossroads: Alternative Modernizations, Postliberalism, or Postdevelopment?" Revised version of paper presented at University of Oregon, Eugene, January 31–February 2, 2008.

Evans, Sara. *Journeys That Opened Up the World: Women, Student Christian Movements, and Social Justice, 1955–1975*. New Brunswick, N.J.: Rutgers University Press, 2003.

———. *Personal Politics: The Roots of Women's Liberation in the Civil Rights Movement and the New Left*. New York: Vintage, 1980.

Fanon, Frantz. *The Wretched of the Earth*. Translated by Constance Farrington. New York: Grove Press, 1965.

Fee, Mary H. *A Woman's Impression of the Philippines*. Chicago: A. C. McClurg & Co., 1910.

Feldstein, Ruth. *Motherhood in Black and White: Race and Sex in American Liberalism, 1930–1965*. Ithaca, N.Y.: Cornell University Press, 2000.

Fergus, Devin. *Liberalism, Black Power, and the Making of American Politics, 1965–1980*. Athens: University of Georgia Press, 2009.

Ferguson, James. *The Anti-politics Machine: Development, Depoliticization, and Bureaucratic Power in Lesotho*. Minneapolis: University of Minnesota Press, 1994.

———. *Expectations of Modernity: Myths and Meanings of Urban Life on the Zambian Copperbelt*. Berkeley: University of California Press, 1999.

Ferguson, Roderick A. *Aberrations in Black: Toward a Queer of Color Critique*. Minneapolis: University of Minnesota Press, 2004.

Field, Thomas C. *From Development to Dictatorship: Bolivia and the Alliance for Progress in the Kennedy Era*. Ithaca, N.Y.: Cornell University Press, 2014.

Fischer, Fritz. *Making Them Like Us: Peace Corps Volunteers in the 1960s*. Washington, D.C.: Smithsonian University Press, 1998.

Fisher, James T. *Dr. America: The Lives of Thomas A. Dooley*. Amherst: University of Massachusetts Press, 1998.

Fleming, Cynthia Griggs. "Black Women and Black Power: The Case of Ruby Doris Smith Robinson and the Student Nonviolent Coordinating Committee." In *Sisters in the Struggle: African American Women in the Civil Rights and Black Power Movement*, edited by Bettye Collier Thomas and V. P. Franklin, 197–213. New York: New York University Press, 2001.

Foucault, Michel. *The History of Sexuality, Vol. 1: An Introduction*. Translated by Robert Hurley. New York: Vintage, 1990.

Fox, Claire F. *Making Art Panamerican: Cultural Policy and the Cold War*. Minneapolis: University of Minnesota Press, 2013.

Franco, Jean. *Cruel Modernity*. Durham, N.C.: Duke University Press, 2013.

Frazier, E. Franklin. *The Negro Family in the United States*. Chicago: University of Chicago Press, 1939.

Friedan, Betty. *The Feminine Mystique*. New York: Norton, 2001 [1963].

Frost, Jennifer. *An Interracial Movement of the Poor: Community Organizing and the New Left in the 1960s*. New York: New York University Press, 2001.

Gaines, Kevin. *American Africans in Ghana: Black Expatriates and the Civil Rights Era*. Chapel Hill: University of North Carolina Press, 2007.

———. *Uplifting the Race: Black Leadership, Politics, and Culture in the Twentieth Century*. Chapel Hill: University of North Carolina Press, 1996.

Galindo, Maria. *¡A Despatriarcar! Feminismo Urgente*. La Paz: Mujeres Creando-Lavaca, 2013.

Gallop, Jane. *Reading Lacan*. Ithaca, N.Y.: Cornell University Press, 1987.

García Márquez, Gabriel. *One Hundred Years of Solitude*. New York: Harper Perennial Classics, 2006 [1967].

Gaudino, Robert L. *Uncomfortable Learning: Some Americans in India*. Bombay: Popular Prakashan, 1974.

Gilbert, David. *Love and Struggle: My Life in SDS, the Weather Underground, and Beyond*. Oakland, Calif.: PM Press, 2012.

Gilman, Nils. *Mandarins of the Future: Modernization Theory in Cold War America*. Baltimore, Md.: Johns Hopkins University Press, 2003.

Gilmore, Glenda. *Defying Dixie: The Radical Roots of Civil Rights, 1919–1950*. New York: Norton, 2008.

Go, Julian. "Sociology's Imperial Unconscious: The Emergence of American Sociology in the Context of Empire." In *Sociology and Empire*, edited by George Steinmetz, 83–105. Durham, N.C.: Duke University Press, 2013.

Goldstein, Alyosha. *Poverty in Common: The Politics of Community Action during the American Century*. Durham, N.C.: Duke University Press, 2012.

Goodman, Paul. *Growing Up Absurd: Problems of Youth in the Organized Society*. New York: New York Review of Books, 2012 [1956].

Gosse, Van. *Rethinking the New Left: An Interpretative History*. New York: Palgrave Macmillan, 2005.

———. *Where the Boys Are: Cuba, Cold War America, and the Making of a New Left*. New York: Verso, 1996.

Gotkowitz, Laura. *A Revolution for Our Rights: Indigenous Struggles for Land and Justice in Bolivia*. Durham, N.C.: Duke University Press, 2008.

Green, Laurie B. "Challenging the Civil Rights Narrative: Women, Gender, and the Politics of Protection." In *Civil Rights History from the Ground Up: Local Struggles, a National Movement*, edited by Emilye Crosby, 52–80. Athens: University of Georgia Press, 2011.

Greene, Graham. *The Quiet American*. New York: Penguin, 1996 [1955].

Griffin, Farah Jasmine. "'Ironies of the Saint': Malcolm X, Black Women, and the Price of Protection." In *Sisters in the Struggle: African American Women in the Civil Rights and Black Power Movement*, edited by Bettye Collier Thomas and V. P. Franklin, 214–29. New York: New York University Press, 2001.

Grindle, Merilee S., and Pilar Domingo. *Proclaiming Revolution: Bolivia in Comparative Perspective*. Cambridge, Mass.: Harvard University Press, 2003.

Grubbs, Larry. *Secular Missionaries: Americans and African Development in the 1960s*. Amherst: University of Massachusetts Press, 2009.

Gumucio-Dagron, Alfonso. "Yawar Mallku." In *South American Cinema: A Critical Filmography, 1915–1994*, edited by Tim Barnard and Peter Rist, 92–94. Austin: University of Texas Press, 1998.

Gutiérrez Aguilar, Raquel. *Los ritmos del Pachakuti: Movilización y levantamiento indígena-popular en Bolivia*. Buenos Aires: Tinta Limón, 2008.

Halberstam, David. *The Best and the Brightest*. New York: Random House, 2001 [1972].

Harrington, Michael. *The Other America*. New York: Scribner, 1997 [1962].

Hayden, Casey, and Mary King. "Sex and Caste: A Kind of Memo." In *Takin' It to the Streets: A Sixties Reader*, edited by Alexander Bloom and Wini Breines, 47–51. New York: Oxford University Press, 1995.

Hayden, Tom. *The Port Huron Statement: The Visionary Call of the 1960s Revolution*. New York: Thunder's Mouth Press, 2005 [1962].

———. *Reunion: A Memoir*. New York: Random House, 1989.

Hoffman, Elizabeth Cobbs. *All You Need Is Love: The Peace Corps and the Spirit of the 1960s*. Cambridge, Mass.: Harvard University Press, 2000.

Hogan, Wesley. *Many Minds, One Heart: SNCC's Dream for a New America*. Chapel Hill: University of North Carolina Press, 2007.

Horne, Gerald. *The Fire This Time: The Watts Uprising and the 1960s*. Charlottesville: University Press of Virginia, 1995.

Ibson, John. "Masculinity under Fire: LIFE's Presentation of Camaraderie and Homoeroticism before, during, and after the Second World War." In *Looking at LIFE: Framing the American Century in the Pages of LIFE Magazine, 1936–1972*, edited by Erika Doss, 178–99. Washington, D.C.: Smithsonian Institution Press, 2001.

———. *Picturing Men: A Century of Male Relationships in Everyday American Photography*. Washington, D.C.: Smithsonian Institution Press, 2002.

Immerwahr, Daniel. *Thinking Small: The United States and the Lure of Community Development*. Cambridge, Mass.: Harvard University Press, 2015.

Jacobs, Seth. *America's Miracle Man in Vietnam: Ngo Dinh Diem, Religion, Race, and U.S. Intervention in Southeast Asia, 1950–1957*. Durham, N.C.: Duke University Press, 2004.

Jahanbani, Sheyda. "One Global War on Poverty: The Johnson Administration Fights Poverty at Home and Abroad, 1964–68." In *Beyond the Cold War: Lyndon Johnson and the New Global Challenges of the 1960s*, edited by Francis J. Gavin and Mark Atwood Lawrence, 97–117. New York: Oxford University Press, 2014.

James, Josephine. *Kathy Martin: African Adventure*. New York: Golden Press, 1965.

———. *Kathy Martin: Peace Corps Nurse*. New York: Golden Press, 1965.

Jameson, Frederic. "Periodizing the 60s." *Social Text* 9–10 (Spring–Summer 1984): 178–209.

Jeffords, Susan. *Hard Bodies: Hollywood Masculinity in the Reagan Era*. New Brunswick, N.J.: Rutgers University Press, 1993.

Jolly, Kenneth S. *Black Liberation in the Midwest: The Struggle in St. Louis, Missouri, 1964–1970*. New York: Routledge, 2006.

Jones, Eileen M. *Letters from Nigeria: Experiences of a Peace Corps Volunteer before and during the Nigerian Civil War*. Bloomington, Ind.: Booktango, 2013.

Joseph, Peniel. *Waiting 'Til the Midnight Hour: A Narrative History of Black Power in America*. New York: Henry Holt, 2006.

Kabeer, Naila. *Reversed Realities: Gender Hierarchies in Development Thought*. New York: Verso, 1994.

Kahler, Jack. *Enslaved in Ebony: The Strangest Encounter the Peace Corps Has Ever Met*. Van Nuys, Calif.: Triumph News Co., 1968.

Kaplan, Amy. *The Anarchy of Empire in the Making of U.S. Culture*. Cambridge, Mass.: Harvard University Press, 2005.

Karim, Lamia. *Microfinance and Its Discontents: Women in Debt in Bangladesh*. Minneapolis: University of Minnesota Press, 2011.

Kennan, George. "Policy Planning Study 23: Review of Current Trends in U.S. Foreign Policy." *Foreign Relations of the United States* 1 (1948): 509–29.

Kennedy, John F. "Special Message to Congress on Urgent National Needs, May 25, 1961." In *Public Papers of the President: John F. Kennedy*, 403–5. Washington, D.C.: GPO, 1961.

Kerouac, Jack. *On the Road*. New York: Penguin, 2003 [1957].

Kessler, Ronald. *The Sins of the Father: Joseph P. Kennedy and the Dynasty He Founded*. New York: Grand Central Publishing, 1997.

Kim, Jodi. *Ends of Empire: Asian American Critique and the Cold War.* Minneapolis: University of Minnesota Press, 2010.

Kimball, Natalie. "An Open Secret: The Hidden History of Unwanted Pregnancy and Abortion in Highland Bolivia, 1952–2010." Ph.D. diss., University of Pittsburgh, 2013.

King, Martin Luther, Jr. "Where Do We Go from Here?" In *A Testament of Hope: The Essential Writings and Speeches of Martin Luther King Jr.*, edited by James Melvin Washington, 245–52. New York: HarperCollins, 1991.

Klein, Christina. *Cold War Orientalism: Asia in the Middlebrow Imagination, 1945–1961.* Berkeley: University of California Press, 2003.

Klein, Herbert. *Bolivia: The Evolution of a Multi-ethnic Society.* Oxford, U.K.: Oxford University Press, 1992.

Klein, Naomi. *The Shock Doctrine: The Rise of Disaster Capitalism.* New York: Metropolitan Books, 2007.

Knapp, Herbert, and Mary Knapp. *Red, White, and Blue Paradise: The American Canal Zone in Panama.* San Diego, Calif.: Harcourt Brace, 1984.

Knebel, Fletcher. *The Zinzin Road.* New York: Doubleday, 1966.

Kramer, Paul. *Blood of Government: Race, Empire, the United States, and the Philippines.* Chapel Hill: University of North Carolina Press, 2006.

Lacan, Jacques. "The Mirror Stage as Formative of the Function of the I as Revealed in Psychoanalytic Experience." In *Écrits: A Selection*, 1–7. Translated by Alan Sheridan. London: Tavistock, 1977.

LaFeber, Walter. *The Panama Canal: The Crisis in Historical Perspective.* New York: Oxford University Press, 1989.

Langland, Victoria. *Speaking of Flowers: Student Movements and the Making and Remembering of 1968 in Military Brazil.* Durham, N.C.: Duke University Press, 2013.

Langley, Lester D. *America and the Americas: The United States in the Western Hemisphere.* Athens: University of Georgia Press, 1989.

Lardizabal, Amparo Santamaria. *Pioneer American Teachers and Philippine Education.* Quezon City: Phoenix Press, 1991.

Larrain, Jorge. *Theories of Development: Capitalism, Colonialism and Dependency.* Cambridge, U.K.: Polity Press, 1989.

Latham, Michael. *Modernization as Ideology: American Social Science and "Nation Building" in the Cold War Era.* Chapel Hill: University of North Carolina Press, 2000.

———. *The Right Kind of Revolution: Modernization, Development, and U.S. Foreign Policy from the Cold War to the Present.* Ithaca, N.Y.: Cornell University Press, 2010.

Latour, Bruno. *We Have Never Been Modern*. Cambridge, Mass.: Harvard University Press, 1993.

Lerner, Daniel. *The Passing of Traditional Society: Modernizing the Middle East*. New York: Macmillan, 1958.

Levin, Beatrice. *Safari Smith*. New York: Nova Books, 1965.

Levitt, Leonard. *An African Season*. New York: Simon and Schuster, 1966.

Lewis, John, and Michael D'Orso. *Walking with the Wind: A Memoir of the Movement*. New York: Harcourt Houghton Mifflin, 1999.

Lewis, Penny. *Hardhats, Hippies, and Hawks: The Vietnam Antiwar Movement as Myth and Memory*. Ithaca, N.Y.: Cornell University Press, 2013.

Lhamon, W. T. *Deliberate Speed: The Origins of a Cultural Style in the American 1950s*. Cambridge, Mass.: Harvard University Press, 1990.

Lichtenstein, Nelson. *State of the Union: A Century of American Labor*. Princeton, N.J.: Princeton University Press, 2002.

Litwack, Donna. "Trabajamos Juntos." In *Peace Corps in Panama: Fifty Years, Many Voices*, edited by Meredith W. Cornett, 7–10. Oakland, Calif.: Peace Corps Writers, 2013.

Logevall, Fredrik. *Choosing War: The Lost Chance for Peace and the Escalation of War in Vietnam*. Berkeley: University of California Press, 2001.

———. *Embers of War: The Fall of an Empire and the Making of America's Vietnam*. New York: Random House, 2012.

Louchheim, Katie. "November 17, 1961, National Council of Negro Women." In *Women and the Civil Rights Movement, 1954–1965*, edited by Davis W. Houck and David E. Dixon, 179–185. Jackson: University Press of Mississippi, 2009.

Lowndes, Joseph, Julie Novkov, and Dorian Warner, eds. *Race and American Political Development*. New York: Routledge, 2008.

Luce, Don, and John Sommer. *Viet Nam: The Unheard Voices*. Ithaca, N.Y.: Cornell University Press, 1969.

Luis-Brown, David. *Waves of Decolonization: Discourses of Race and Hemispheric Citizenship in Cuba, Mexico, and the United States*. Durham, N.C.: Duke University Press, 2008.

Mailer, Norman. "The White Negro." In *Advertisements for Myself*, 302–22. New York: Signet, 1959.

Malarney, Shaun Kingsley. *Culture, Ritual, and Revolution in Vietnam*. Honolulu: University of Hawaii Press, 2002.

Manela, Erez. "A Pox on Your Narrative: Writing Disease Control into Cold War History." *Diplomatic History* 34, no. 2 (2010): 299–323.

Marcuse, Herbert. *One Dimensional Man*. Boston: Beacon Press, 1991 [1964].

Matusow, Allen J. *The Unraveling of America: A History of Liberalism in the 1960s.* New York: Harper & Row, 1984.

May, Elaine Tyler. *Homeward Bound: American Families in the Cold War.* New York: Basic Books, 1988.

McAlister, Melani. *Epic Encounters: Culture, Media, and U.S. Interests in the Middle East since 1945.* Berkeley: University of California Press, 2005.

McClintock, Anne. *Imperial Leather: Race, Gender, and Sexuality in the Colonial Contest.* New York: Routledge, 1995.

McEwen, William J. *Changing Rural Society: A Study of Communities in Bolivia.* New York: Oxford University Press, 1975.

McGurl, Mark. "Ordinary Doom: Literary Studies in the Waste Land of the Present." *New Literary History* 41, no. 2 (2010): 329–49.

McMillian, John. *Smoking Typewriters: The Sixties Underground Press and the Rise of Alternative Media in America.* Oxford, U.K.: Oxford University Press, 2011.

McNamara, Robert S. "Address to Board of Governors," September 30, 1968. In *Dynamics of Population Policy in Latin America*, edited by Terry L. McCoy. Cambridge, Mass.: Ballinger, 1974.

Meisler, Stanley. *When the World Calls: The Inside Story of the Peace Corps and Its First Fifty Years.* Boston: Beacon Press, 2011.

Melamed, Jodi. *Represent and Destroy: Rationalizing Violence in the New Racial Capitalism.* Minneapolis: University of Minnesota Press, 2011.

———. "The Spirit of Neoliberalism: From Racial Liberalism to Neoliberal Multiculturalism." *Social Text* 89 (Winter 2006).

Melosh, Barbara. *Engendering Culture: Manhood and Womanhood in New Deal Public Art and Theater.* Washington, D.C.: Smithsonian Press, 1991.

Millikan, Max F., and W. W. Rostow. *A Proposal: Key to an Effective Foreign Policy.* New York: Harper and Brothers, 1957.

Mills, C. Wright. *White Collar: The American Middle Classes.* New York: Oxford University Press, 1953.

Milne, David. *America's Rasputin: Walt Rostow and the Vietnam War.* New York: Hill and Wang, 2008.

Mohanty, Chandra Talpade. *Feminism without Borders: Decolonizing Theory, Practicing Solidarity.* Durham, N.C.: Duke University Press, 2003.

Moody, Anne. *Coming of Age in Mississippi.* New York: Delta Trade Paperbacks, 2004 [1968].

Mortenson, Greg. *Three Cups of Tea: One Man's Journey to Fight Terrorism and Build Nations—One School at a Time.* New York: Viking Penguin, 2006.

Moynihan, Daniel Patrick. *The Negro Family: The Case for National Action.* Washington, D.C.: U.S. Department of Labor, Office of Policy Planning and Research, 1965.

Murch, Donna Jean. *Living for the City: Migration, Education, and the Rise of the Black Panther Party in Oakland, California.* Chapel Hill: University of North Carolina Press, 2010.

Murillo, Mario. *La bala no mata sino el destino: Una crónica de la insurrección popular de 1952 en Bolivia.* La Paz: Plural, 2012.

Murphy, Michelle. *"The Girl: Mergers of Feminism and Finance in Neoliberal Times." S&F Online* 11, nos. 1–2 (2012–13): http://sfonline.barnard.edu/gender-justice-and-neoliberal-transformations/the-girl-mergers-of-feminism-and-finance-in-neoliberal-times/.

Nashel, Jonathan. *Edward Lansdale's Cold War.* Amherst: University of Massachusetts Press, 2005.

Nelson, Erica. "Birth Rights: Bolivia's Politics of Race, Region, and Motherhood, 1964–2005." Ph.D. diss., University of Wisconsin, Madison, 2005.

Nguyen, Mimi Thi. *The Gift of Freedom: War, Debt, and Other Refugee Passages.* Durham, N.C.: Duke University Press, 2012.

Obama, Barack. *Dreams from My Father: A Story of Race and Inheritance.* New York: Times Books, 1995.

O'Connor, Alice. *Poverty Knowledge: Social Science, Social Policy, and the Poor in the Twentieth Century.* Princeton, N.J.: Princeton University Press, 2002.

Oglesby, Carl. *Ravens in the Storm: A Personal History of the 1960s Antiwar Movement.* New York: Scribner, 2008.

Packard, Vance. *The Status Seekers.* New York: David McKay, 1959.

Parsons, Talcott. "The Kinship System of the Contemporary United States." *American Anthropologist,* n.s., 45, no. 1 (1943): 22–38.

———. *The Structure of Social Action: A Study in Social Theory with Reference to a Group of Recent European Writers.* New York: General Books, 2010 [1937].

Patterson, James T. *Freedom Is Not Enough: The Moynihan Report and America's Struggle over Black Family Life from LBJ to Obama.* New York: Basic Books, 2010.

Payes, Rachel C. *Peace Corps Nurse.* New York: Valentine Books, 1967.

"Personal Notes of a Meeting with President Johnson." *Foreign Relations of the United States* 2 (April 1, 1965): 511–12.

Piketty, Thomas. *Capital in the Twenty-First Century.* Translated by Arthur Goldhammer. Cambridge, Mass.: Belknap Press, 2014.

Piven, Frances Fox, and Richard A. Cloward. *Poor People's Movements: How They Succeed, Why They Fail.* New York: Vintage, 1979.

Pope, Carl. *Sahib: An American Misadventure in India.* New York: Liveright, 1972.

Povinelli, Elizabeth. *Economies of Abandonment: Social Belonging and Endurance in Late Liberalism.* Durham, N.C.: Duke University Press, 2011.

———. *Empire of Love: Toward a Theory of Intimacy, Genealogy, and Carnality.* Durham, N.C.: Duke University Press, 2006.

Powers, Thomas. *Diana: The Making of a Terrorist.* New York: Houghton Mifflin, 1971.

Prashad, Vijay. *The Darker Nations: A People's History of the Third World.* New York: New Press, 2007.

Pratt, Mary Louise. *Imperial Eyes: Travel Writing and Transculturation.* London: Routledge, 1992.

Purcell, Fernando. "Connecting Realities: Peace Corps Volunteers in South America and the Global War on Poverty during the 1960s." *Historia Crítica* 53 (May–August 2014): 129–54.

Pynchon, Thomas. *The Crying of Lot 49.* New York: Harper Perennial, 2006 [1966].

Qureshi, Lubna. *Nixon, Kissinger, and Allende: U.S. Involvement in the 1973 Coup in Chile.* Plymouth: Lexington Books, 2009.

Rahnema, Majid, and Victoria Bawtree, eds. *A Post-development Reader.* London: Zed Books, 1997.

Raiford, Leigh. *Imprisoned in a Luminous Glare: Photography and the African American Freedom Struggle.* Chapel Hill: University of North Carolina Press, 2013.

Rainwater, Lee, and William L. Yancey. *The Moynihan Report and the Politics of Controversy.* Cambridge, Mass.: MIT Press, 1967.

Ravenholt, R. T. "The A.I.D. Population and Family Planning Program: Goals, Scope, and Progress." *Demography* 5, no. 2 (1968): 561–73.

Redmon, Coates. *Come as You Are: The Peace Corps Story.* San Francisco: Harcourt Brace, 1986.

Rice, Gerard T. *The Bold Experiment.* Notre Dame, Ind.: University of Notre Dame Press, 1985.

Riesman, David. *The Lonely Crowd: A Study of the Changing American Character.* New Haven, Conn.: Yale University Press, 1961 [1950].

Rist, Gilbert. *The History of Development: From Western Origins to Global Faith.* London: Zed Books, 1997.

Rivera Cusicanqui, Silvia. *Oprimidos pero no vencidos: Luchas del campesinado aymara y qhechwa, 1900–1980.* La Paz: La Mirada Salvaje, 2010 [1984].

———. "'Que el pasado sea futuro depende de lo que hagamos en el presente': Enseñanzas de la insurgencia étnica en Bolivia." In *Bolivia en movimiento: Acción colectiva y poder político,* edited by Jesús Espasandín López and Pablo Iglesias Turrión, 101–28. Barcelona: El Viejo Topo, 2007.

———. *Violencias (re)encubiertas en Bolivia.* La Paz: Piedra Rota, 2010.

Roberts, Dorothy. *Killing the Black Body: Race, Reproduction, and the Meaning of Liberty*. New York: Pantheon, 1997.

Robnett, Belinda. *How Long? How Long? African-American Women in the Struggle for Civil Rights*. Oxford, U.K.: Oxford University Press, 1997.

Rodgers, Daniel. *Age of Fracture*. Cambridge, Mass.: Belknap Press, 2012.

Rodgers, David. *The Peace Corps Girls: A Play in Three Acts*. Chicago: Dramatic Publishing Company, 1962.

Rosaldo, Renato. *Culture and Truth: The Remaking of Social Analysis*. Boston: Beacon Press, 1989.

Rossinow, Doug. *The Politics of Authenticity: Liberalism, Christianity, and the New Left in America*. New York: Columbia University Press, 1998.

Rostow, Walt Whitman. *Stages of Economic Growth: A Non-communist Manifesto*. Cambridge, U.K.: Cambridge University Press, 1960.

Rudd, Mark. *Underground: My Life with SDS and the Weathermen*. New York: HarperCollins, 2010.

Sachs, Jeffrey. *The Price of Civilization: Reawakening American Virtue and Prosperity*. New York: Random House, 2011.

———. *To Move the World: JFK's Quest for Peace*. New York: Random House, 2014.

Sahle, Eunice N. *World Orders, Development and Transformation*. New York: Palgrave Macmillan, 2010.

Said, Edward. *Culture and Imperialism*. New York: Vintage, 1993.

Saldaña-Portillo, Maria Josefina. "On the Road with Che and Jack: Melancholia and the Legacy of Colonial Geographies in the Americas." *New Formations* 47 (2002): 87–108.

———. *The Revolutionary Imagination in the Americas and the Age of Development*. Durham, N.C.: Duke University Press, 2003.

Sale, Kirkpatrick. *SDS: The Rise and Development of the Students for a Democratic Society*. New York: Random House, 1973.

Sanjinés, Jorge. "Revolutionary Cinema: The Bolivian Experience." In *Cinema and Social Change in Latin America: Conversations with Filmmakers*, edited by Julianne Burton, 35–48. Austin: University of Texas Press, 1986.

Savran, David. *Taking It Like a Man: White Masculinity, Masochism, and Contemporary American Culture*. Princeton, N.J.: Princeton University Press, 1998.

Scanlon, Tom. *Waiting for the Snow: The Peace Corps Papers of a Charter Volunteer*. Chevy Chase, Md.: Posterity Press, 1996.

Scheper-Hughes, Nancy. "The Way of an Anthropologist Companheira." In *Anthropology and the Peace Corps: Case Studies in Career Preparation*, edited by Brian E. Schwimmer and D. Michael Warren. Ames: Iowa State University Press, 1993.

Schlesinger, Arthur, Jr. *The Politics of Hope*. Boston: Riverside Press, 1962.

———. *A Thousand Days: John F. Kennedy in the White House*. New York: Greenwich House, 1983 [1965].

———. *The Vital Center: The Politics of Freedom*. New Brunswick, N.J.: Transaction, 1998 [1949].

Schubert, Grace. "She's White but She's Black Too." In *Anthropology and the Peace Corps: Case Studies in Career Preparation*, edited by Brian E. Schwimmer and D. Michael Warren. Ames: Iowa State University Press, 1993.

Schulman, Bruce. *Lyndon B. Johnson and American Liberalism: A Brief Biography with Documents*. 2nd ed. Boston: Bedford/St. Martin's Press, 1995.

Schwarz, Karen. *What You Can Do for Your Country: An Oral History of the Peace Corps*. New York: Morrow, 1991.

Scott, Catherine V. *Gender and Development: Rethinking Modernization and Dependency Theory*. Boulder, Colo.: Lynne Rienner, 1995.

Scott, Jack Denton. *Elephant Grass*. London: Barrie and Jenkins, 1969.

Scott, James C. *Seeing Like a State: How Certain Schemes to Improve the Human Condition Have Failed*. New Haven, Conn.: Yale University Press, 1998.

Seale, Bobby. *Seize the Time: The Story of the Black Panther Party and Huey P. Newton*. New York: Vintage, 1970.

Sedgwick, Eve Kosofsky. *Between Men: English Literature and Male Homosocial Desire*. New York: Columbia University Press, 1985.

Seeley, John R. *Crestwood Heights: A Study of the Cultural Suburban Life*. Toronto: University of Toronto Press, 1956.

Self, Robert. *All in the Family: The Realignment of American Democracy since the 1960s*. New York: Hill and Wang, 2012.

Shalom, Stephen R. "Counter-Insurgency in the Philippines." In *The Philippines Reader: A History of Colonialism, Neocolonialism, Dictatorship, and Resistance*, edited by Stephen R. Shalom and Daniel Schermer, 111–24. Boston: South End Press, 1987.

Shorter, Edward. *The Kennedy Family and the History of Mental Retardation*. Philadelphia: Temple University Press, 2000.

Shrestha, Nanda R. *In the Name of Development*. Lanham, Md.: University Press of America, 1997.

Shriver, Sargent. *The Point of the Lance*. New York: Harper & Row, 1964.

Siekmeier, James. "Sacrificial Llama? The Expulsion of the Peace Corps from Bolivia in 1971." *Pacific Historical Review* 69, no. 1 (2000): 65–87.

Simpson, Bradley R. *Economists with Guns: Authoritarian Development and U.S.–Indonesian Relations, 1960–1968*. Stanford, Calif.: Stanford University Press, 2010.

Slate, Nico. *Colored Cosmopolitanism: The Shared Struggle for Freedom in the United States and India*. Cambridge, Mass.: Harvard University Press, 2012.

Smith, Andrea. *Conquest: Sexual Violence and American Indian Genocide*. Boston: South End Press, 2005.

Smith, Ed. *Where to, Black Man?* Chicago: Quadrangle Books, 1967.

Sondheim, Stephen, Mary Rodgers, and Martin Charnin, "Don't Laugh." In *Stephen Sondheim: The Story So Far*. New York: Sony, 2008 [1963].

Spencer, Sharon. *Breaking the Bonds: A Novel about the Peace Corps*. New York: Grosset & Dunlap, 1963.

Spivak, Gayatri Chakravorty. *A Critique of Postcolonial Reason: Toward a History of the Vanishing Present*. Cambridge, Mass.: Harvard University Press, 1999.

Staples, Amy L. S. *The Birth of Development: How the World Bank, Food and Agriculture Organization, and World Health Organization Changed the World, 1945–1965*. Kent, Ohio: Kent State University Press, 2006.

Stein, William W. *Deconstructing Development Discourse in Peru: A Meta-ethnography of the Modernity Project at Vicos*. Lanham, Md.: University Press of America, 2003.

Stossel, Scott. *Sarge: The Life and Times of Sargent Shriver*. Washington, D.C.: Smithsonian Books, 2004.

Sullivan, George. *Peace Corps Nurse*. New York: Nova Books, 1964.

Suri, Jeremi. *Power and Protest: Global Revolution and the Rise of Détente*. Cambridge, Mass.: Harvard University Press, 2003.

Szulc, Tad. *Dominican Diary*. New York: Dell, 1966.

Terry, Wallace. *Bloods: Black Veterans of the Vietnam War: An Oral History*. New York: Ballantine, 2006.

Theroux, Paul. "Cowardice." In *Sunrise with Seamonsters*. Boston: Houghton Mifflin, 1985.

———. *Girls at Play*. New York: Penguin, 1983 [1969].

Thomas, Evan. *The Very Best Men: Four Who Dared: The Early Years of the CIA*. New York: Simon and Schuster, 1996.

Thomsen, Moritz. *Living Poor*. Seattle: University of Washington Press, 1969.

Tobin, James. "Defense, Dollars, and Doctrine." *Yale Review*, March 1958.

Turse, Nick. *Kill Anything That Moves: The Real American War in Vietnam*. New York: Metropolitan Books, 2013.

United States Congress, Senate Committee on the Judiciary, Subcommittee to Investigate Problems Connected with Refugees and Escapees. *Civilian Casualty, Social Welfare, and Refugee Problems in South Vietnam: Hearings, Ninetieth Congress, First Session*. Washington, D.C.: U.S. Government Printing Office, 1968.

Varon, Jeremy. *Bringing the War Home: The Weather Underground, the Red Army Faction, and Revolutionary Violence in the Sixties and Seventies*. Berkeley: University of California Press, 2004.

Von Eschen, Penny. *Race against Empire: Black Americans and Anticolonialism, 1937–1957*. Ithaca, N.Y.: Cornell University Press, 1997.

———. *Satchmo Blows Up the World: Jazz Ambassadors Play the Cold War*. Cambridge, Mass.: Harvard University Press, 2006.

Wallace, Michele. *Black Macho and the Myth of the Superwoman*. New York: Verso, 1999.

———. *Invisibility Blues: From Pop to Theory*. New York: Verso, 1990.

Watts, Michael. *Silent Violence: Food, Famine, and Peasantry in Northern Nigeria*. 2nd ed. Athens: University of Georgia Press, 2013.

Weber, Cynthia. *Faking It: U.S. Hegemony in a "Post-phallic" Era*. Minneapolis: University of Minnesota Press, 1999.

Weber, Max. "Science as a Vocation." In *From Max Weber: Essays in Sociology*, translated and edited by H. H. Gerth and C. Wright Mills, 129–56. New York: Oxford University Press, 1946.

Weiss, Philip. *American Taboo: A Murder in the Peace Corps*. New York: Harper-Collins, 2004.

Weld, Kirsten. *Paper Cadavers: The Archives of Dictatorship in Guatemala*. Durham, N.C.: Duke University Press, 2014.

West, Cornel. "The Paradox of the Afro-American Rebellion." *Social Text* 9–10 (Spring–Summer 1984): 44–58.

Westad, Odd Arne. *The Global Cold War: Third World Interventions and the Making of Our Times*. Cambridge, U.K.: Cambridge University Press, 2005.

Wexler, Laura. *Tender Violence: Domestic Visions in an Age of Empire*. Chapel Hill: University of North Carolina Press, 2000.

Whyte, William H. *The Organization Man*. New York: Simon and Schuster, 1956.

Wiley, Karla. *Assignment: Latin America, the Story of the Peace Corps*. New York: David McKay, 1968.

Wilson, Sloan. *The Man in the Gray Flannel Suit*. New York: Simon and Schuster, 1955.

Wingenbach, Charles. *The Peace Corps: Who, How, and Where*. New York: John Day, 1951.

Wofford, Harris. *Of Kennedys and Kings: Making Sense of the Sixties*. Pittsburgh: University of Pittsburgh Press, 1992.

Wu, Judy Tzu-Chun. *Radicals on the Road: Internationalism, Orientalism, and Feminism during the Vietnam Era*. Ithaca, N.Y.: Cornell University Press, 2013.

Wylie, Philip. *Generation of Vipers*. New York: Farrar and Rinehart, 1942.

Young, Cynthia. *Soul Power: Culture, Radicalism, and the Making of a U.S. Third World Left*. Durham, N.C.: Duke University Press, 2006.

Young, Marilyn. "Ho, Ho, Ho Chi Minh! Ho Chi Minh Is Gonna Win!" In *Why the North Won the Vietnam War*, edited by Marc Jason Gilbert, 219–32. New York: Palgrave, 2002.

———. *The Vietnam Wars, 1945–1990*. New York: Harper Perennial, 1991.

Zimmerman, Jonathan. "Beyond Double Consciousness: Black Peace Corps Volunteers in Africa." *Journal of American History* 82, no. 3 (1995): 999–1028.

———. *Innocents Abroad: American Teachers in the American Century*. Cambridge, Mass.: Harvard University Press, 2006.

Zunes, Stephen. "The United States and Bolivia: The Taming of a Revolution, 1952–1957." *Latin American Perspectives* 28, no. 5 (2001): 33–49.

INDEX

abjection, 26, 40, 47, 236, 282n14
Abraham Lincoln, the Prairie Years (Sandburg), 57
Acción Sindical Boliviana, 212
Act for International Development, 114
Adamson, Michael, 13
Afghanistan, 235–36
African Americans: modernization discourses and, 62–66, 267n60; movement politics and, 104–9, 115–16, 124–37, 142–45, 169–70, 178, 267n60; pathologizing of, 113–35, 141–42, 145–47, 248n40, 264n17; Peace Corps service of, 68–69, 115, 137, 139–43; reproductive control and, 145–47; romantic racism and, 31, 34, 37–45, 50, 55–63, 69, 88–93, 184. *See also* Black Power movement; civil rights movement; poverty; race and racism
African Season, An (Levitt), 66–68
Aguinaldo, Emilio, xii
Aid to Dependent Children, 125
Allende, Salvador, 178
Alliance for Progress, 174, 190–91
All You Need Is Love (Hoffman), xvii

Altiplano, 191, 193–94, 199, 201, 204–15
Amas de Casa program, 97
American Friends Service Committee, 273n79
Amin, Julius, 249n43
anti-conquest, 49, 87, 200, 257n52
Applied Nutrition Program, 99
Armstrong, Louis, 48
Ashabranner, Brent, 191, 277n16
Atlantic Charter, 5–6
authenticity: cultural nationalism and, 215–29; gender and, 37, 41–42, 184; heroic action and, 33–34, 56–62; modernization theory and, 220–21; movement politics and, xviii, 180–81; Peace Corps volunteers and, 63; racial dynamics of, 37–38, 43
Autobiography (Malcolm X), 131
Aymara Indians, 192, 194–96, 201, 206–15, 227

Baker, Ella, 126
Baldwin, James, 38, 232
Bambara, Toni Cade, 145–47
Bandung conference, 5–7, 250n10

Baraka, Amiri, 129–31, 133–35, 144–45

Bardone, Chad, 194–96

Barnard, John, 274n95

Barrientos, Rene, 190

Barrios de Chungara, Domitila, 223–25

BARTS (Black Arts Repertory Theater/School), 129–30

Baumann, Gerold, 198–99, 206

beat generation, 33–45, 55–56, 145, 256n18. *See also* Baraka, Amiri; Burroughs, William; Kerouac, Jack

Bechtel (company), 238

Bederman, Gail, xiii, 246n25

Belafonte, Harry, 168

Berman, Andy, 174

bikas, vii–viii

Billboard, 94

birth control. *See* Bambara, Toni Cade; IUDs; population control

Black, Eugene, 156–57

Black Bourgeoisie (Frazier), 267n52

Black Macho and the Myth of the Superman (Wallace), 143

Black Panther, The (Brown), 148

Black Panther Party, 128–32, 172, 268n70

Black Power movement, xix, 114, 127–35, 137–38, 142–45, 169–70, 178, 267n60

Black Woman, The (collection), 145–46

Blood of the Condor (Sanjinés). *See Yawar Mallku (Blood of the Condor)*

Boas, Franz, 248n36, 264n17

Bohan, Merwin, 190, 204

Boko Haram, 282n15

Bolivia: cultural nationalism and, 184, 215–29; development work in,

189–91; gendering of, 1–4; Peace Corps' expulsion from, xx, 209; Peace Corps formation and, 18–19; population control in, 185, 187–89, 191–93, 198, 204–29; revolution in, 189–90

Booth, Paul, 151, 160, 182–83

Bosch, Juan, 153–54

Bowles, Sally, 209

Braestrup, Peter, 20, 23

Brazil, 98, 115, 164

Breaking the Bonds (Spencer), 85–87, 94

Breines, Wini, 8, 37, 82, 89, 104–5, 274n98, 275n108

Briggs, Laura, 237, 246n25

Brockes, Emma, 90

Brome, Janet Pitts, 206

brotherhood: Peace Corps volunteers and, 4, 17–20, 27, 30–31, 34, 56, 156–57, 181, 232; between sovereign nations, xv, xix, 2, 27–29, 47–48, 52, 104, 157, 181–82, 192, 231. *See also* gender; homosocial intimacy; masculinity

Brown, Aubrey, 169–70, 173, 177

Brown, Earl, 142–43

Brown, Elaine, 147–48

Brown v. Board of Education, 126

Buhle, Mari Jo, 251n24

"Build, Not Burn" (Booth and Oglesby), 151, 160, 182, 184

Bundy, McGeorge, 158

Bunker, Ellsworth, 166

Burdick, Eugene, 45–57, 95

Burroughs, William, 251n29

Bush, George W., 232

Campanella, Joseph, 94–95

Canal Zone, 27–28

Canelas, Amado, 212–13
CAP (Community Action Program), 129, 142
capitalism: development imperative and, 4–15, 71–74, 97–104, 194, 234–35; gender division and, 8–9, 13–20, 41–42, 48, 58–59, 76–78, 121–23, 130, 198–99, 251n24, 251n26; homosocial triangulation and, xiv–xv, 42–43, 50–51; neoliberalism and, 225–26, 232–38, 275n111, 283n20; penetration discourses and, 2–3, 55, 195–96; structural inequality and, 125–26, 130, 132, 135–39, 223–24, 233–34, 263n106; U.S. nationalism and, x–xvii, xvi–xvii, xxi–xxii, 63–65
Capitalism (Moore), 283n20
Cardwell, Curt, 245n14
Carmichael, Stokely, 136–37
Carnegie, Andrew, 171
Carr, Robert, 132, 248n40
Castro, Rafaela, 98
Catholicism, 11–12, 48, 155, 210–14
Chakrabarty, Dipesh, xvi, xx
Chalick, Morris, 167
Charnin, Martin, 95
Chiari, Roberto, 28
Chile, 28, 166, 178
China, 28, 147–48, 156
Churchill, Winston, 5–6
CIA (Central Intelligence Agency), 47, 178, 245n12
Civic Action (program), 190–91, 198
civil rights movement: Black Power movement and, 124–25; development rhetoric and, 124–35, 267n60; gender and, xviii, 104–9, 115–16, 124–35, 141; international

solidarity and, 135–48; Peace Corps volunteers and, 105–6, 168
class: gender's intersections with, 42–43, 180–81; pathology discourses and, viii, 55, 66–68, 113–24, 136–37, 147–48, 213, 264n9, 264n17; racialization and, xii–xiii, 37–38, 45–56, 63–64, 114–35, 265n27. *See also* capitalism; poverty
Clayson, William, 267n60
Cleaver, Eldridge, 128
Clinton, Bill, 232
Clover, Carol, 262n91
Cloward, Richard A., 268n70
Cold War: civil rights movement and, xviii, 105–6, 112–13, 135–48; containment doctrine and, 6–7, 73–74; gender politics of, xv, xvi–xvii, 7–13, 37, 42–43, 45–56, 73–79, 83–94, 96–104, 123, 251n24
Cold War Civil Rights (Dudziak), 112
Colombia, 23, 82, 101, 107
colonialism: anticolonial nationalism and, xi, 145–47, 185–89, 191–93, 198, 204–29; epistemology and, 53–55, 66–68; European, xvi, 91–92, 125–26. *See also* development discourses; gender; modernity; race and racism
Come As You Are (Redmon), 21
Coming of Age in Mississippi (Moody), 135–37
Committee for United Newark, 135
communism: Bolivian modernity and, 212–13; cultural nationalism and, 215–21; decolonization movements and, 46–47, 69–70, 147–48; penetration discourses and, 48–50; Vietnam and, 156–57

community development, 14, 17, 34, 57, 63–64, 96–98, 115–16, 162, 198, 248n31

Congo, 137–38

containment: domestic, 7–8, 10, 37, 83–94, 96–109; international relations and, 6–7, 71–74; movement politics and, 104–9, 114–23

Costigliola, Frank, 243n9

Cotton, John W., 262n99

counterculture, 33–38, 184, 238, 275n109. *See also* beat generation; new left

counterparts, 45–62, 69–73, 201

Covington, Juanita Ann, 139

Cowan, Paul, 52, 62–66, 70, 83

Cowan, Rachel, 63–64, 83

"Cowardice" (Theroux), 165

Crisis, The, 139

Cronkite, Walter, 71–72

Cruse, Harold, 267n60

CRV (Committee of Returned Volunteers), xix, 152–53, 167–80

Crying of Lot 49, The (Pynchon), 275n111

Cuba, 10, 173–74, 178, 183–84

Cullather, Nick, 278n57

cultural nationalism, xviii, xx, 144–47, 184–85, 204–29

culture of poverty, 42, 55, 66–68, 113–24, 136–37, 264n9, 264n17, 265n27. *See also* pathology; poverty; War on Poverty

Dalton, Annmary, 111–12

Damon, Laura, 82

Dean, Robert, 4, 41, 247n26

decolonization: containment policy and, 73–74; filial metaphors and, xiii–xiv, 231, 237–38; Gandhian thought and, 125–26; gendering of, xv, 4–13, 18, 83–94, 102–4; global capitalism and, xiv–xv, 4–15, 71–74, 97–104, 194, 234–35; Marxian analyses of, 15, 69, 233–34; social science and, xiv–xv, 13–20, 27. *See also* Bolivia; capitalism; development discourses; Ghana; India; modernization theory

Deliver Us from Evil (Dooley), 48

Dellinger, Dave, 172

dependency theory, 213, 279n75

Developing Communities Project, 233

Development Corporation of Bolivia, 194

development discourses: Bolivian context and, 188–90; CRV and, 175–85; definitions of, 27; gendering of, xv, xv–xvi, xix, 1–20, 27–30, 42–43, 47–48, 52, 56–62, 73–74, 96–104, 137–38, 156–57, 181–82, 192, 207–8, 215–16, 221, 231–32, 234–35, 247n29; pathology and, viii, 42–56, 58–62, 71–74, 91–92, 111–24, 136–37, 147–48; population control and, 185–89, 191–93, 198, 204–29; racialization and, 56–62, 124–35, 184–85, 237, 267n60; subjecthood and, vii–viii, xiv–xv, xvi, xx–xxi, 24, 42–44, 125–26, 231–32, 234; Vietnam War and, 5, 114, 147–48, 155–67. *See also* Black Power movement; civil rights movement; community development; CRV; feminism; Katarista movement; modernization theory; new left

Dewey, George, 246n25

Dixon, Kay, 101

Dohrn, Bernadine, 183
domestic containment, 7–8, 10–11, 37, 76–77, 104–9, 198. *See also* gender; homosexuality; masculinity; race and racism
Dominican Republic, 150, 153, 159, 274n102
"Don't Laugh" (song), 95–96
Dooley, Tom, 48, 155, 235, 257n48
Douglas, Gwynne, 98
Douglas, Susan, 37
draft: Peace Corps' relation to, 83, 160–62, 166–67
Dudziak, Mary, 112
Dulles, John Foster, 48
Dwan, John, 202–3

Easton, Peter, 53–54
Eaton, Samuel, 191
Echols, Alice, 107
Ecuador, 21, 52, 57–65, 101, 116
education: colonialism and, vii–viii, xi–xii, 52; gendering of, 76–83, 94–104, 281n10; personal transformation and, 127–35; volunteers' assignments and, 65–70
Edwards, Erica, 127, 248n40
Ehrenreich, Barbara, 37, 251n24
Eisenhower, Dwight D., 13, 190
Ekbladh, David, 264n9
Elbaum, Max, 274n94
El Diario, 1–2, 3, 209–11
Elephant Grass (Scott), 262n94
El Sur, 166
enchantment. *See* magic
enclosure system, 16–17
Ends of Empire (Kim), 245n14
Enslaved in Ebony (novel), 88–89
ERAP (SDS's Economic Research and Action Project), 183

Escobar, Arturo, xiv, xviii, 7, 225, 247n28
Escobar, Federico, 214
Ethiopia, 139
Evans, Rowland, 156
Evans, Sara, 182–83

Fairburn, Frieda, 101, 107
Falkett, Camille, 196–97, 201–2
Fanon, Frantz, 53
fantasies: gender ideologies and, 23, 27, 113, 138, 141, 221; modernity's promises and, xvi, 13–27, 39–40, 53–54, 198–99; Peace Corps' homosocial environment and, 4, 12, 23, 26, 31, 56, 163; romantic racism and, 31, 34, 37–45, 50, 55–63, 69, 88–93, 184; Third World spaces and, xv, xvi, 13–20, 27, 38, 46, 49–51, 56–58, 138, 184, 193; women volunteers and, xix, 72–74, 83–104, 111–12. *See also* development discourses; frontier mythology; magic; masculinity; modernity; seduction
FBI (Federal Bureau of Investigation), 41, 178
Fee, Mary, xii–xiii
Feldstein, Ruth, 248n40, 251n24
Feminine Mystique, The (Friedan), 76–77, 84–85, 108–9
femininity: capitalism and, 7–10, 42–43, 83–94, 144–45, 197–99; media attention and, 79–82; new left politics and, 182–85; pathologizing of, 73–74, 124–35, 198, 216–21; Peace Corps girls' imaginary and, xix, 73–94, 100–101; reproductive control and, 185–89, 191–93, 198, 204–29; Third

World's associations with, 15–20, 34–35, 37, 90, 156, 209–11; triangulation formations and, 4, 21–22, 28–30, 40–41, 118–19, 157–58, 243n9. *See also* gender; poverty; race and racism

feminism, xviii, 96, 104–9, 112, 144–47, 188–89, 222–29, 263n106

Fergerstrom, Robert, 213–14, 279n76

Fergus, Devin, 267n60

Ferguson, James, 236, 282n14

Ferguson, Roderick, 248n40, 267n54

Field, Thomas, 249n43, 279n76

Fine, J., 205

flag riots (Panama), 27–28, 30

Fleming, Ian, 57

Fogle, Faith, 161

Ford Foundation, 205, 207, 263n106

Fortún, Walter, 208

Foucault, Michel, xiii

Fox, Claire, 234

France, 5, 11

Frazier, E. Franklin, 117, 264n17, 267n52

freedom riders, 113–14

Freedom Summer, 62–63, 113–16

Friedan, Betty, 76–77, 84–85, 108

Frits, James, 193

"From Applied Altruism to Nation Building" (Wiggins), 149–55, 158, 165

frontier mythology: Bolivian context and, 194–95, 198; masculinity and, xix, 8–10, 14–15, 20–27, 34–45, 56–62, 74–83, 117, 210–11, 247n26; Third World adventure and, xix, 4, 11–13, 18–27, 46–47, 52, 54, 117, 231; women and,

74–83. *See also* development discourses; masculinity

Frost, Jennifer, 182–83

Fulbright, J. William, 174

Gaines, Kevin, 264n17

Galindo, Maria, 281n102

Gamio, Manuel, 264n17

Gandhi, Mahatma, 6, 125–27

García Márquez, Gabriel, 67

Gardner, Deborah, 103

Garrison, Lloyd, 81

gender: cultural nationalism and, 182–85, 215–29; frontier mythology and, xix, 8–10, 14–15, 20–27, 34–45, 56–62, 74–83, 210–11, 247n26; homosocial intimacy and, ix, xv, xix, 2, 4, 21–22, 27–29, 34–45, 47–48, 52, 104, 157, 181–82, 192, 231; material prosperity and, 7–8, 10–11, 18, 26, 231, 246n25, 251n24, 251n26; modernizing discourses and, ix, xv, xv–xvi, xix, 1–4, 7–9, 13–20, 26–27, 60–61, 99–104, 112–13, 137–38, 156, 207–8, 215–16, 221, 231, 234–35, 247n29; movement politics and, 104–9, 127–35, 143–47, 182–85; pathology discourses and, ix, 26–27, 40, 58, 73–74, 113–35, 198, 216–21; Peace Corps girls and, xix, 72–74, 83–104, 111–12; population control and, 185–89, 191–93, 198, 204–29; race's intersections with, 104–9, 140–43, 145–47, 263n5; seduction discourses and, xvi, 2–3, 7, 13–27, 39–40, 49–50, 53–54, 84–95, 198–99; Third World's associations and, 13–20, 30, 41–42, 49–50; whiteness and, xii–xiii, 7.

See also Black Power movement; feminism

Generation of Vipers (Wylie), 251n24

Ghana, 5, 28, 45–46, 68–70, 81, 105, 137–38, 140–41

GI Bill, 7

Gilbert, David, 165–66

Gilman, Nils, 15, 43

Girls at Play (Theroux), 89–94

Go, Julian, 252n53

Goldschen, Stuart, 193

Goldstein, Alyosha, xxi

Goodman, Andrew, 116

Goodman, Paul, 180–81

Gore, Nancy, 209

Grameen Bank, 234

Great American Mission, The (Ekbladh), 264n9

Greene, Graham, 163

Grothe, Peter, 20, 163

Growing Up Absurd (Goodman), 180

Guaraní (people), 195–96

Guardian, 90

Guevara, Che, 172, 191

Gulf of Tonkin incident, 156

Gumucio Reyes, Alfonso, 18–19, 253n63

Guttmacher, Alan, 207

Haddad, William, 22, 24

Hageman, Alice, 170–71, 174, 176

Hanneman, Janet, 55–56

Hardy, Willie, 142–43

Harrington, Michael, 117

Harvest of Shame (documentary), 117

Hayden, Tom, 11, 182–83, 255n13, 274n102

Hayes, Larry, 100–101

Head Start, 136

Henderson, Douglas, 191

Heredia, Nila, 226, 228

Herod, James, 176–77

heroism: authenticity and, 33–34, 56–62; beat generation as antithetical to, 34–45; Bolivian recolonization and, 194–95; development discourses and, 4–13, 56–62, 79–82, 193; Peace Corps volunteers and, viii–ix, xvii, 4–13, 17–18, 27–31, 34–45, 49–50, 159, 169–70, 197–203, 231, 238; racial dynamics of, 56–62; Jack Vaughn's story of, 191–92. *See also* frontier mythology; masculinity; modernity

Hines, Ernesto, 211

Ho Chi Minh, 6, 156

Hoffman, Elizabeth Cobbs, xvii, 20, 244n10

Holland, Jerome "Brud," 22

Holliday, Judy, 94–96

Holloman, Emmanuel, 159–60

Holmberg, Allan, 71–72

homosexuality: beat literature and, 33–34, 39, 41, 51, 256n18; development imagery and, 2, 16, 40, 88, 103, 156, 253n59; masculinity crises and, 4, 41, 76; Peace Corps policies on, 41

homosocial intimacy: beat generation anxieties and, 33–34, 39, 41, 51, 256n18; development's promises and, xv, xix, 2, 27–29, 47–48, 52, 104, 157, 181–82, 192, 231; international relations and, ix, xv, xix, 1–4, 17–18, 48–49, 181–82; Peace Corps and, 4, 17–31, 34, 56, 156–57, 181, 193, 231–32; penetration imagery and, 15–20, 253n59; triangulation and, 4, 21–22, 28–30, 40–41, 118–19, 157–58, 243n9.

See also domestic containment; gender; masculinity

Horman, Paul, 178

Hot Spot (Broadway show), 94–95, 100

Housewives Committee, 279n76

Howard University, 122–24

Huanca Yupanqui, Felipa, 227–28

Hukbalahap insurgency, xiii, 47

Human Rights Watch, 176

humiliation, xv, 2, 16, 19–20, 46, 123

Humphrey, Hubert, 158

Hurston, Zora Neale, 264n17

Hutton, Bobby, 128

Ibson, John, 4

IMF (International Monetary Fund), xiv–xv, 190

Immerwahr, Daniel, 248n31

India, 5, 16, 99–100, 107–8, 125–26, 165, 204, 207–8

International Cooperation Administration, xiii

intimacy. *See* homosocial intimacy

Iraq, 235–36

IUDs, 187–88, 204–15

IVS (International Volunteer Service), 158–59, 166

Jali, R. M., 81

James, William, 164, 171

Jameson, Frederic, 275n111

Jaquith, Connie, 108–9, 161, 199–201, 206

Jet magazine, 88–89

Johnson, George, 168–69

Johnson, Lyndon: Latin America and, 27–29, 191, 205; Peace Corps mission and, 21, 27, 41, 153–54, 264n9, 270n21; Vietnam War and, 14–15, 103, 156–57, 160, 162–63; War on Poverty and, 113, 118–19, 121–24, 128

Johnston, Frances Benjamin, 246n25

Jolly, Harold S., 267n60

Jones, Kirby, 154

Jones, Leroi, 129–35, 144–45

Jones, Margot, 101

Joplin, Janis, 255n13

Josephson, William, 157–58, 245n13

Kaiser Foundation, 20

Kaplan, Amy, xiii, 77, 84, 246n25

Karim, Lamia, 234

Katarista movement, 220–22, 280n94

Kathy Martin, Peace Corps Nurse (James), 84, 91

Katzenbach, Nicholas, 160

Kelly, E. Lowell, 100

Kennan, George, 6–7, 251n26

Kennedy, Eunice, 11–12, 252n35

Kennedy, John F.: Bolivia and, 1–4, 190–91; civil rights movement and, 114–15, 118; frontier masculinity and, 8, 10, 79–82, 193; Peace Corps' mission and, viii–ix, x, x–xi, 11–12, 23, 26, 30, 45–47, 204–5, 245n14, 246n15; photos of, 3; speeches of, x–xi; Vietnam policy and, 155, 157

Kennedy, Joseph, 11–12, 252n35

Kennedy, Robert, 115

Kenyatta, Jomo, 88

Kerouac, Jack, 38, 42, 45–47, 57, 61–62, 69, 134

Khrushchev, Nikita, 8

King, Jim, 65–66, 164–65, 254n83

King, Martin Luther, Jr., 124–28, 135, 266n40

Kinsey, Bill, 103

Kiva.org, 234
Klein, Christina, 46
Klein, Naomi, 236, 244n11
Knapp, Herbert and Mary, 30–31
Kopkind, Andrew, 151–52, 163–64, 270nn7–8
Kristof, Nicholas, 235

labor movements, xvi, xvii, 42–43, 71–74, 86–87, 189–90, 193–94
Lacan, Jacques, 44
Lafore, Laurence, 93
Lansdale, Edward, xiii, 47–48, 155
Laos, 48
La Prensa (newspaper), 187–88
lavender scare, 10
Lawson, James, 126
Lechín, Juan, 279n76
Lederer, William, 47, 50–52, 57
Le Guin, Ursula K., 103–4
Lerner, Daniel, 14, 43–45, 51, 53, 60, 69
Lerner, Max, 35
Let Me Speak! (Barrios de Chungara), 223
Levitt, Leonard, 62, 66–68, 70
Lewis, Oscar, 117, 264n17
Lhamon, W. T., 37
liberalism: Black Power movement and, xix, 31, 124–35, 143–46; civil rights movement and, xix, 113–24; culture of poverty and, xvii, 11, 107–24, 127–35; development and, xvii, 8–20, 24–27, 125–27, 130–39, 143, 222–24, 233–34; feminism and, 107–9; gender and, xviii, 4, 8–9, 13, 42, 73, 84, 107, 109, 117–24, 128–35; heroism and, xviii, 4, 7–9, 13, 27, 34, 84, 103–4, 153–54; neoliberalism and, 225–26, 233–38;

new left politics and, 177, 180–85; Vietnam War and, 148, 151–52; volunteers' ideology and, 153–54, 158, 169–80; whiteness of, 8, 11, 13, 42. *See also* development discourses; gender; modernity; pathology; race and racism; War on Poverty
Liberia, 81, 161
Life magazine, 35, 55–56, 81
Lincoln, Abraham, 171
Lippes' Loops. *See* IUDs
Living Poor (Thomsen), 4, 56–62
Lodge, Henry Cabot, 166
Lonely Crowd, The (Riesman), 8
Louchheim, Katie, 76–77, 79, 82, 97
Luce, Don, 158–59, 166
Luis-Brown, David, 264n17

magic: desire and, 49–50; modernity's associations with, 16–17, 53–54, 71–74, 191, 201; premodern epistemologies and, xvi, 50. *See also* fantasies; seduction
Magsaysay, Ramón, xiii, 47–48
Mailer, Norman, 37–38, 42, 44, 51, 128
Making of an Un-American, The (Cowan), 62–66
Making Them Like Us (Fischer), 244n10
Malcolm X, xvii, 131–33
Mandela, Nelson, 6
Manela, Erez, 243n5
Mankiewicz, Frank, 21–22, 30, 154, 182
Martin, Thomas, 279n76
Marx, Karl, 15, 69, 130, 147, 174, 177, 180, 184, 212–13, 226, 275n11

MAS (Movimiento al Socialismo), 225, 227, 280n94

masculinity: civil rights movement and, xviii, 124–35; cultural nationalism and, 184, 215–21; developing nations and, xv, xix, 2, 27–29, 47–48, 52, 97–98, 104, 157, 181–82, 192, 195–96, 198–99, 231, 234; frontier boldness and, xix, 8–10, 14–15, 20–27, 34–45, 56–62, 74–83, 210–11, 247n26; material prosperity as threat to, 7–8, 12–13, 18, 25, 26, 79, 180–81, 231, 246n25; Peace Corps heroism and, 7–8, 45–56, 197–203, 231; penetration imagery and, 2–3, 16, 20–27, 33–34, 39–40, 45–47, 62–63, 90, 156, 174, 206, 209–11, 253n59; poverty discourses and, 114–35, 143–45, 266n40; race's intersections with, 37–38, 114–23, 127–35, 137–38; rationality and, xvi, 16–17, 115; triangulation and, 4, 21–22, 28–30, 40–41, 118–19, 157–58, 243n9

Mau Mau rebellions, 91–92

May, Elaine Tyler, 8

McAlister, Melani, 84

McCarthyism, 10, 15, 69

McGovern, George, 156

McGurl, Mark, 237

McLucas, Leroy, 133

McNamara, Robert, 119, 155, 168, 212, 214, 279n72

Melamed, Jodi, xvii

Melragon, Mickey, 194

Mexico, 38–41, 117, 173, 223, 225

Michelmore, Margery, 260n46

Microfinance and Its Discontents (Karim), 234

Military–Peasant Pact, 190–91

Millikan, Max, 245n14

Milne, David, 15

minstrelsy, 48–49

mirror stage, 44

MNR (Movimiento Nacionalista Revolucionário), 189–90, 193, 218

modernity: counterparts' roles with respect to, 45–60, 69–70; decolonization and, xii–xiii; education and, 62–68; filial metaphors and, xiii–xiv; gendering of, ix, xv–xvi, xix, 13–20, 30, 60–61, 117, 137–38, 207, 215–16, 221, 231, 234–35; global capitalism and, xiv–xv, xv–xvi, 4–15, 71–74, 97–104, 194, 212–13, 234–35; homosocial intimacy and, ix, xv, xix, 1–4, 27–29, 47–48, 52, 104, 157, 181–82, 192, 231; masculinity and, 114–23, 137–38; personal transformation and, 13–20, 24, 107–9, 116–17, 126, 130–35, 145–47, 192–93; racialization of, xii–xiii, xix, 265n27, 267n60; rationality and, xvi, 233; subjectivity and, vii–viii, xx, 132–35, 142–47, 201–2, 252n42; United States as symbolic of, 57–62

modernization theory: cultural eradication and, 58–60, 188–89, 204–15, 220–21; Peace Corps' founding and, xiv–xv, 14–15, 19–20; personal transformation and, 13–20, 24, 107–9, 116–17, 126, 130–35, 145–47, 192–93, 252n42; structural-functionalism and, 8, 15; temporality of, 18, 20, 200. *See also* Lerner, Daniel; Parsons, Talcott; Rostow, Walt Whitman

Moody, Anne, 135–36
Moore, Michael, 283n20
Morales, Evo, 225, 280n94
Morgan, Edward, 45–46
Mortenson, Greg, 235, 281n10
movement politics. *See* Black Power
  movement; civil rights movement;
  CRV; feminism; Katarista move-
  ment; new left; Vietnam War
Moyers, Bill, 21, 154
Moynihan, Daniel Patrick, 11, 120,
  122–23, 125, 143–44
Mujeres Creando, 229, 281n102
Murch, Donna Jean, 267n52
Murphy, Michelle, 281n10
Murray, Bruce, 166–67

NAACP (National Association for
  the Advancement of Colored
  People), 23, 126
narcissism, 73–74
National Council of Negro Women,
  76
National Liberation Front, 166
NCDP (National Community
  Development Program), 198–99
Negro Family, The (Moynihan), 11,
  120–23, 143–44
Negro Family in America, The
  (Frazier), 264n17
neoliberalism, 225–26, 232–38,
  275n111, 283n20
Nepal, vii–xix, 81
neutrality (of Peace Corps), 153–54,
  164–65, 168–69
Newark uprisings, 134
New Deal, 120, 244n11
New Frontier, 10, 14–15, 23
new left, 152–53, 160, 177, 180–85,
  270nn7–8, 274n94. *See also* CRV;

Dohrn, Bernadine; Hayden, Tom;
  liberalism; Oglesby, Carl; SDS
New Republic, 151
Newton, Huey, 128–29
New York Times, 20–24, 33–35, 79–81,
  93, 117, 154, 160–62, 166, 188–91,
  208–9, 235
NGOs (nongovernmental organiza-
  tions), 226, 228–29, 234
Nguyen, Mimi Thi, 180
Nigeria, 65, 81, 86–88, 101, 164–65,
  172, 254n83, 257n35, 260n46,
  282n15
Nixon, Richard, 8, 10, 176
nonviolence, 124, 126, 174
North Korea, 147–48, 173

Obama, Barack, 232–33, 274n102
Occupy Wall Street, 244n11
O'Connor, Alice, 43, 116–17, 121
OEO (Office of Economic Opportu-
  nity), 115, 118, 122–24
Oglesby, Carl, 151, 160, 182–84
O'Grady, Alice, 105–8
One Hundred Years of Solitude (García
  Márquez), 67
On the Road (Kerouac), 38–41, 45–47,
  61, 255n13, 256n11, 256n16,
  256n18
Operation Rolling Thunder,
  167–68
Oppenheimer, Joel, 133–34
Organization Man, The (Whyte), 8
organization men, 8, 25, 26, 79
Organization of American States, 28
orientalism, 49–50
Oserjeman, Serj, 144
Other America, The (Harrington),
  117
Oughton, Diana, 273n79

Panama, 27–31, 96–98, 163

Paredes, Julieta, 229

Parsons, Talcott, 8–9, 15, 40, 123, 237, 252n53

Pascale, David and Stephanie, 197

Passing of Traditional Society, The (Lerner), 14, 43, 45

pathology: African Americans and, 109, 113–35, 141–42, 145–47, 248n40, 264n17, 265n27; gender imbalances and, 58–59, 63–64, 124–35, 143–45, 216–21, 248n40; penetrability and, 37–42, 46–56, 58; poverty's causes and, viii, 55, 66–68, 113–24, 136–37, 147–48, 213, 264n9, 264n17; Third World's characterization and, 135–47. *See also* African Americans; gender; masculinity; race and racism; whiteness

Paz Estenssoro, Victor, 1–4, 30

Peace Corps: in Bolivia, 191–204; capitalist interests and, xi, 58–60, 198; counterparts of, 45–62, 69–73, 201; creation of, viii–ix, x–xix, 253n63; CRV and, 169–83; draft avoidance and, 83, 160–62, 166–67; gender politics of, 73–104, 111–12, 116, 183–85, 258n4, 259n13; heroism tropes and, viii–ix, xvii, 4–13, 17–18, 27–31, 34–45, 49–50, 231, 238; media coverage of, 23–24, 35, 36, 55–56, 79–82, 160–63, 166, 172, 191, 209–11; modernization theory and, 16–18, 188–89; movement politics and, 104–9, 117, 135–47, 149–53, 165–67; personal contact and, 14, 27–31, 45–56, 154–55, 164, 175, 181–82, 231–32; popular culture representations of,

84–95, 100, 103; racial dynamics in, 31, 34, 55–56, 58, 137–40; recruiting of, 20–27, 35, 41, 74–75, 100–101, 111–13, 115–16, 161, 163, 179, 180; seduction motifs and, 2–3, 7, 17–27, 74–83; Vietnam's development and, 155–67. *See also* frontier mythology; gender; poverty; race and racism

Peace Corps Bride (Chavre), 88–89

Peace Corps girl (in popular fiction), xix, 73–74, 80–94, 104

People's Peace Treaty, 175

"Periodizing the 60s" (Jameson), 275n111

person-to-person contact, 14, 45–56, 154–55, 164, 175, 181–82

Peru, 21–22, 30, 71–74, 94, 101–3, 152, 182–83, 258n4, 262n94

Peterson, Gary, 205–6

Pettine, Raymond, 167

Philippines, xi, xii, xii–xiii, xiv, 47–49, 246n25

"Pill, The" (Bambara), 145–46

Pimentel, Ireneo, 214

Planned Parenthood, 205, 207

"Planting Rice Is Never Fun" (song), 49

Point Four Youth Corps, 155

Point of the Lance (Shriver), 17–19

Pope, Carl, 207–8

population control, xx, 185, 187–89, 191–93, 198, 204–29, 279n72

Port Huron Statement (Hayden), 11, 181

poverty: authenticity discourses and, 37–38; gendering of, ix, 26–27, 40, 42–43, 58; measures of, viii; pathology discourses and, viii, 14,

55, 57, 60, 63–68, 109, 136–37, 143–45, 192–93, 213, 233–34, 264n9, 264n17; population control and, 185–89, 191–93, 198, 204–29, 279n72; racialization of, 35–36; redistributive politics and, xvii, 14, 17, 120, 175, 188, 225; structural diagnoses of, 125–26, 130, 132, 135–39, 188, 223–24, 233–34, 263n106

Poverty in Common (Goldstein), 244n10

Povinelli, Elizabeth, 103–4, 218, 222

Pratt, Mary Louise, 87, 257n52

Prensa Libre, 211

Presencia, 209–10

Pritchard, Ross, 158–59

Priven, Dennis, 103

Progressive Labor Party, 184

psychology: anticommunist wars and, 47–48; gender and, 100–101; Peace Corps' mission and, vii–viii, x, xi, xiii–xiv, 6–7, 17, 41–44, 161; political dissent and, 167; screening processes and, 35, 41, 161; subject formation and, 43–45; Third World's pathology and, 43, 63–64, 135–47, 184

Puerto Rico, 117, 182, 246n25

Pynchon, Thomas, 275n111

Qureshi, Lubna, 178

race and racism: authenticity discourses and, 37–38, 43, 48–50; development parables and, 46–56, 237; gender and, 104–9, 140–43, 145–47, 263n5; modernity discourses and, xii–xiii, 265n27; pathology discourses and, 63–64, 114–35, 265n27; population control and, 145–47, 185–89, 191–93, 198, 204–29; romantic racism and, xix, 31, 34, 37–45, 50, 55–56, 58, 60–62, 69, 88–89, 92–93, 184; structural inequality and, 125–27, 130, 132, 135–37. *See also* African Americans; development discourses; poverty

Ramparts, 170–71

rape, 2, 16, 88, 92, 101–3, 156, 253n59

Redmon, Coates, 21

Regan, Denis, 194

"Report on Population Problems in Bolivia" (report), 205

Reston, James, 33

Returned Peace Corps Volunteers conferences, 167–68

Reuss, Henry, 155, 160

Reuther, Walter, 274n95

Riesman, David, 8, 13

Rist, Gilbert, xxi, 125–26, 250n10

Rivera Cusicanqui, Silvia, 195, 220, 282n14

Robinson, Sugar Ray, 23

Robles, Marcos, 163

Robnett, Belinda, 266n45

Rockefeller Foundation, 263n106

Roosevelt, Eleanor, 259n13

Roosevelt, Franklin Delano, 5

Roosevelt, Theodore, 12

Roseberry, Elizabeth R., 69

Rossinow, Doug, 182

Rostow, Walt Whitman, 2, 7–10, 14–20, 52–53, 123, 155–57, 191–93, 245n14, 252n42

Rusk, Dean, 168–69

Rustin, Bayard, 124–25

Sachs, Jeffrey, 236
Sahib (Pope), 207
Sahle, Eunice, 235
Said, Edward, 249n47
Saigon Student Union, 175
Saldaña-Portillo, Maria Josefina, xv, xvii, 2, 7, 16, 131, 217, 221, 247n26, 250n6, 256n16
Sandburg, Carl, 57
San Francisco Chronicle, 56–57
San Francisco Examiner, 12
Sanjinés, Jorge, xx, 187–89, 215–22, 228–29
Saturday Evening Post, 24
Saturday Review, 35, 125
Savran, David, 10, 26, 37, 251n29, 256n16
Scanlon, Tom, 257n48
Scheper-Hughes, Nancy, 115, 161
Schlesinger, Arthur, Jr., 9–10, 13, 42, 204–5
Schubert, Grace, 101–3
Schurman, Jacob, xii
Scott, Catherine V., 247n29
Scott, Jack Denton, 262n94
Scott, James, 278n57
SDS (Students for a Democratic Society), 62–66, 127, 151, 181–84, 274n94, 275n108
Seale, Bobby, 128–29, 131–35
second-wave feminism, 105, 263n106. *See also* feminism
Sedgwick, Eve, 2–4, 22, 243n9, 253n59
seduction: modernizing projects and, xvi, 13–27, 39–40, 53–54, 198–99; Peace Corps girls and, 74–75, 83–94, 193; penetration discourses and, 2, 19, 88, 103, 156, 253n59; racialized desire and, 37–42, 49–50;

U.S. foreign policy and, 156. *See also* development discourses; fantasies; modernity; rape
Seize the Time (Seale), 131
self-expression (of volunteers), 150–67, 169
sexuality. *See* femininity; homosexuality; homosocial intimacy; masculinity; rape; seduction
Shock Doctrine, The (Klein), 236–37, 244n11
Shrestha, Nanda, vii, viii, ix, xvi, xxi, 243n5
Shriver, R. Sargent: images of, 29; modernization theory and, 17–20, 79–80, 265n27; Peace Corps' creation and, x–xi, 12, 21–22, 24, 35, 45–46, 153–54, 163, 168, 205, 236; personal life of, 11–12; seductiveness of, 28, 253n63; War on Poverty leadership and, xix, 113, 115, 118–20, 128–30
Siekmeier, James, 209
Sierra Leone, 69, 98
Singer, Derek, 21–22, 30
Sklar, Rita and Joe, 172–73
Slate, Nico, 126
"Smash the Politics of Guilt!" (Berman), 174
Smith, Ed, 62, 68–70, 140–41, 143
SNCC (Student Nonviolent Coordinating Committee), 126–27, 135, 172, 266n45
social sciences: modernization theory and, xiv–xv, 14–15, 19–20, 198–99; in U.S. intellectual milieu, 13–20, 63–64, 71–72, 116–17, 130, 248n36, 248n40. *See also* psychology; structural-functionalism

"Some Lessons of History for Africa" (Rostow), 17

Sondheim, Stephen, 95

So That Men Are Free (documentary), 71

Soviet Union, 7, 15, 246n14, 250n20, 251n26, 257n48

Spain, xii

Spencer, Sharon, 85–87, 94

Spivak, Gayatri, 226

Stages of Economic Growth (Rostow), 14–17

Stone, I. F., 170

Stork, Joe, 170, 176

Stossel, Scott, 11

Strane, Susan, 82, 162

strategic hamlet program, 155–56, 162–63

structural-functionalism, 8, 15, 252n53

Structure of Social Action, The (Parsons), 15

subjectivity: colonialism and, 4–6, 58–62; cultural nationalism and, xx, 205–21; development discourses and, vii–viii, xx–xxi, 42–44, 99–104, 231–32; gendering of, xiii, xv, 140–41, 216–23; personal transformation and, 13–20, 24, 107–9, 116–17, 126, 130–35, 145–47, 192–93, 201–2, 231–32, 252n42. *See also* development discourses; gender; modernity

Szulc, Tad, 154

Taft, William Howard, xii–xiii

Tanganyika, 168–70

Tanzania, 137–38

TDCs (trabajadores de desarrollo de la comunidad), 198, 201

Teach for America, xxii

Tepperman, Jean, 183

Teruggi, Frank, 178

Theroux, Paul, 89–94, 161, 165

Third World: counterparts in, 45–62, 69–73, 201; feminizing of, 15–20, 26–27, 30, 35, 37, 41–42, 55, 85–86, 88, 90, 209–11, 215–16, 253n59, 266n40; nonalignment movement and, 5–7, 147–48, 250n10; reproductive control in, 39–40, 112, 145, 185–89, 191–93, 198, 204–29; romantic racism and, 184; solidarity with, 28, 31, 135–48, 169–78; U.S. interests in, x–xi, x–xxii, 4–20, 71–74, 97–104, 114, 147–53, 170–71, 234–35. *See also* development discourses; gender; Peace Corps; race and racism

Thomsen, Moritz, 4, 56–62

Three Cups of Tea (Mortenson), 235

Time magazine, 81–82, 94–95, 100–101, 163

TIPNIS highway, 238

Tiwanaku Manifesto, 220

Tobin, James, 8

Torres, Juan José, 187–88

"Towering Task, A" (Wiggins), x–xix, 74, 245n13

triangulation (of intimacy), 4, 21–22, 30, 40–41, 118–19, 157–58, 243n9

Troutman, Robert, 115

Truman, Harry, 6

Turkey, 82, 162

Twain, Mark, 171

2 . . . 3 . . . Many magazine, 172

Ugly American, The (Burdick and Lederer), 45–56, 95, 155

Ukamau collective, 187–89, 215–21

Ultima Hora, 209–11
underdevelopment. *See* development discourses
United Fruit Company, 28
United Nations, 5–6, 72, 197, 233, 243n5
United States: Black Power movement in, 127–35; Bolivian aid and, 190–91, 205–15; capitalist interests of, x–xi, xii–xiii, xiv–xv, xvi–xvii, xxi–xxii, 4–20, 71–74, 97–104, 234–35; civil rights movement in, 112–14, 135–47; decolonization and, xi–xii, 4–13, 45–56, 71–72, 84–95, 188–89; domestic containment in, 6–7, 71–74, 197–200; exceptionalism of, 26–27, 52, 169–70, 175, 181; frontier mythology and, xix, 8–10, 14–15, 20–27, 34–45, 56–62, 74–83, 210–11, 247n26; gender ideologies in, xv, xxi–xxii, 4, 7–14, 25, 26, 73–74, 79, 84–104; imperialism of, xii–xiii, 27–29, 135–47, 149–67, 170–83, 187–89, 231, 237–38; Peace Corps heroism and, viii–ix, xvii, 4–13, 17–18, 27–31, 34–45, 49–50, 57–62, 231, 238; social sciences in, 13–20, 63–64, 71–72, 116–17, 130, 248n36, 248n40; Vietnam War politics and, 148–53, 168–83
Upward Bound, 136
USAID, 157, 165–66, 191, 198, 201, 205, 207, 210, 213–15, 226, 263n106
USIA (United States Information Agency), 213–14, 279n76

Vaughn, Jack, 23, 27–31, 100, 161, 163–64, 191–93, 277n16
Venceremos Brigade, 173–74, 183
Venezuela, 23, 28
Vicos (Peru), 71–73, 94, 103–4, 152, 183, 258n4, 262n94
Vietnam War: development workers' dissent from, 165–67, 170–77; Johnson's prosecution of, 14–15, 103, 156–59; modernization discourses and, 5, 114, 147–53, 170–71; new left politics and, 183–85; Peace Corps politics and, xix, 83, 149–53, 167–83; psychological warfare and, 48, 50–51
VISTA (Volunteers in Service to America), 182
Vital Center, The (Schlesinger), 42
Vithal, B. P. R., 54–55
Vollmer, Joan, 251n29
Volunteer (publication), 53, 77, 78, 79, 80, 98, 103, 167, 194
volunteers (Peace Corps): African Americans as, 115, 137, 139–40; authenticity of, 63; gendering of, 73–74, 77–83, 96–104; idealism of, viii–ix, ix–x, x–xi, xxi–xxii; masculinity discourses and, 4, 17–20, 23–27, 30–31, 34, 56, 156–57, 181, 202, 232, 254n83; memoirs of, xix, 4, 52–54, 56–70, 98, 100–101, 105, 107–8, 115, 135–36, 140–43, 161, 164, 166, 195–97, 199–203, 206–8; movement politics and, 104–9, 111–13, 168–83, 262n99; political dissent of, 28–31, 62–66, 149–80; romantic racism and, 31, 34, 55–58, 137–40, 184; solidarity movements and, 135–47, 175–83; superiority presumptions of, 53–55, 62–74, 86–87, 175, 200–201; War on Poverty careers and, 116
Von Eschen, Penny, 137

Wallace, Michele, 38, 128, 140, 143–44, 248n40

Wall Street Journal, 118

War on Poverty: Black Power movement and, xix, 114, 127–38, 142–45, 267n60; pathology discourses and, viii, 109, 129–30, 136–37, 143–45, 192–93, 213, 267n60; returned volunteers and, 167–68; Shriver's leadership of, xix, 113, 115, 129–30; volunteers' role with respect to, 111–13. *See also* development discourses; gender; race and racism; social sciences

War on Terror, 233–34

Washington Post, 35

Watts uprisings, 111, 124–25

Weather Underground, 165, 174, 183–84, 273n79

Weber, Max, xvi

Weser, Carol, 197

"We Shall Overcome" (anthem), 168

Wexler, Laura, xiii, 77, 246n25

"What We Want, What We Believe" (Seale and Newton), 129

"White Negro, The" (Mailer), 37–38

whiteness: class dynamics and, 37–38; masculinity and, 140–41, 180–81; modernity discourses and, xiii; poverty and, 138–39, 265n27; romantic racism and, 31, 35–45, 50, 55–62, 69, 88–93, 184;

victimization mentalities and, 10. *See also* race and racism

"Who Are We" (Wiggins), 74

"Who Needs the Peace Corps" (song), 33–34

Whyte, William, 8, 26

Wiggins, Warren: relationship of, to new left and antiwar movement, 149–55, 158, 165, 182–83; role of, in Peace Corps founding, x–xix, 74, 245n13; views of, on women, 74, 79, 81, 100, 108

Williams, Franklin, 21

Wingenbach, Charles, 77

Wofford, Harris, ix, xvi, 115, 168–69, 172, 205

Worker's Brigade, 140–41

World Bank, xiv–xv, 156–57, 212, 279n72

Wu, Judy Tzu-Chun, 147

Wylie, Philip, 251n24

Yanahuaya, Marcelino, 215

Yawar Mallku (Blood of the Condor), xx, 187–89, 208, 215–23, 226–29

Young, Marilyn, 275n108

Youssefou, Niger Omarou, 142

Yunus, Muhammad, 234

Zambia, 237

Zappa, Frank, 33–34

Zimmerman, Jonathan, 115, 138

MOLLY GEIDEL teaches American studies at the University of Manchester, UK.